£4.95

Textual Strategies

Textual Strategies

PERSPECTIVES IN
POST-STRUCTURALIST
CRITICISM

Edited and with an Introduction by

JOSUÉ V. HARARI

Methuen & Co. Ltd

First published in 1979 by
Cornell University Press
124 Roberts Place, Ithaca, NY 14850

First published in the United Kingdom in 1980 by
Methuen & Co. Ltd
11 New Fetter Lane, London EC4P 4EE

© 1979 Cornell University

Printed in the United States of America

British Library Cataloguing in Publication Data

Textual strategies.
 1. Structuralism (Literary analysis)
 I. Harari, Josué V
801'.95   PN98.S7   79-41308

ISBN 0-416-73740-4
ISBN 0-416-73750-1 Pbk

Contents

Preface

The great danger to avoid is the self-isolating nature of critical discourse.

—Jean Starobinski

This anthology attempts to present some of the new critical perspectives which have appeared on the Anglo-American scene in the wake of structuralist criticism. Its aim is to provide a general introduction to post-structuralist theories and practices for students and critics of literature, to help in defining various critical discourses in the concrete. In recent years, the academic obsession with theory has reached such a level that critics need to be reminded that theory is most useful insofar as it serves the criticism of specific works. Most of the essays in this anthology are "exercises" in applying theory to "literary" texts, rather than in abstract theorizing. In a sense, we are presenting an interrogation on the possible points of contact between "literature" and "criticism," attempting to locate the conceptual crossings that make each of these terms always end up by implying the other.

Literary critics must guard against the risk of blindly accepting the illusions created by the last critical fashion. Indeed, listening to the talk of Parisian intellectual circles often brings to mind Rica's unhappy refrain from Montesquieu's *Lettres persanes:* "A woman who quits Paris to go and spend six months in the country comes back as antique as if she had sequestered herself there for thirty years."[1] I have done my best to avoid this problem by including original critical essays that will lead the reader to be aware of significant and lasting changes in the ways we can read literature and understand the nature of "literary" language. I

[1] *Lettres persanes,* letter 99.

have tried as much as possible to stay away from what Richard Macksey calls "the pathologies of literary criticism," in other words, the confusion of critical coordinates, a jargonistic vocabulary, and fashionableness for its own sake. None of the essays included here attempts to use a technical language for the simple pleasure of taking part in a critical fashion or of creating an apparent scientificity. If some of the texts are, in effect, difficult because of the nature of their writing, they are so only because they are posing questions which are as yet seldom raised, or else because they are tentative approaches, types of questioning, that is, which belong to a kind of textual practice that is still being worked out.

This book also responds to a second problem, growing in importance as a result of the great influx of Continental criticism. How is the student of literature to avoid being weighed down by insurmountable methodological problems? How can one warn those who recommend methodology for its own sake that in the long run theoretical abstraction and mere methodological vigilance without textual support can turn against the valuable aims of their advocates? In other words, methodology can kill research instead of stimulating it and can close critical horizons instead of opening them. As Roland Barthes perceptively observed:

> Some speak greedily and urgently about method. It never seems rigorous or formal enough to them. Method becomes Law, but as this Law is deprived of any effect that would be outside of itself (no one can say, in the "human sciences," what a "result" is) it always falls short. . . . As a result, a work that unceasingly declares its will-to-methodology always becomes sterile in the end. Everything takes place inside the method, nothing is left to the "writing,". . . the searcher repeats that his text will be methodological, but this text never arrives. There is nothing more sure to kill research and sweep it off into the leftovers of abandoned works, nothing more sure, than method. At some point one has to turn against method, or at least to treat it without any founding privilege.[2]

In an uncanny way, this remark applies as well to the intellectual atmosphere of some of the more "progressive" Franco-

[2] *Tel Quel,* 47 (1971), 9-10.

American academic circles, in which it is considered essential to be clearly identified with a given methodology. At a time when the lines between "literature" and "criticism" are so ambiguous—one commonly finds oneself reading books of criticism whose subject matter is other books of criticism, themselves critical studies of other books—the idea of a method whose procedures, like a cooking recipe, can be repeated mechanically and which no work can "resist," is a dangerous proposition. It is all the more dangerous because it is so appealing. This kind of operation, the result of a disciple mentality, carries with it the obvious danger of becoming—even in the best of circumstances—a shortcut which replaces more demanding and difficult theoretical knowledge, and in the worst of cases, betrays a lack of familiarity with the object of criticism. To isolate method from text (in the broad sense of the word) is to ignore the fact that all methodological theorizing proceeds from lengthy textual work, with one enriching and complementing the other. Thus, rather than situate this anthology within the realm of methodological dogma and all that it promises to deliver, we prefer to place it in the context of the remark of Starobinski that appears as an epigraph to this prefatory note: "La solitude du discours critique est le grand piège auquel il faut échapper."[3] This temptation can be avoided only by recalling that the locus and the foundation of all theory are in the space between text and the criticism serving as discourse on that text.

This anthology possesses the characteristics of any typical collective work: theoretical ambiguity, methodological pluralism, diversity of approach and procedure, and heterogeneity in the fields of study it presents. The dynamic nature of the poststructuralist thrust is a result precisely of the diversity of its critical predicaments. For that reason, I shall not write the traditional introduction in which one explains the *continuity* from essay to essay in order to justify an "anthological" unity. Each text included here is to a great extent autonomous, and its autonomy should be preserved. It is nonetheless necessary to give

[3]Jean Starobinski, *La Relation critique* (Paris: Gallimard, 1972), p. 52.

some logical pattern for reading, though to do so always creates the risk of favoring a global reading of the whole volume over a variety of individual statements. I have tried to order the essays in the simplest way possible: to move from the general to the particular and from the abstract to the concrete; in other words, from theory to the readings of individual texts, from the defining of certain general concepts—author, text, critic—to textual practices incorporating these newly defined concepts. Out of this order a certain continuity has inevitably come, but it is an arbitrary continuity, even if it is not wholly gratuitous. One must avoid deducing from it the sense of a coherent critical unity. Herein lies the precise meaning of the book's title. If the common denominator of these essays lies in the term *strategies,* there is nonetheless a plurality of strategies at work. These strategies do not add up to a complete overview of post-structuralism (many other profiles are possible), nor are they always congruent to one another. Let us therefore leave these strategies in their uniqueness and not try to erase their borders and the differences between them. The barriers in the domains of criticism are permeable enough for us not to have to impose similarities where they do not exist, only in order to justify the continuity of a collective work. And if at times certain of these strategies converge, it should not be surprising, as the essays refer after all to the same linguistic and philosophical substructures.

Most of the texts are either original essays or appear here for the first time in translation. Paul de Man's essay, which was presented as a paper at a symposium entitled "Texts, Pretexts, Contexts," held at Cornell University, first appeared in *Diacritics,* 3 (Fall 1973) and is published here by permission of *Diacritics.* Roland Barthes's was published originally in French in *Revue d'Esthétique,* 3 (1971) under the title "De l'oeuvre au texte"; my translation appears here with the permission of Christian Bourgois. Gérard Genette's text was published in *MLN,* 87 (May 1972) under the title "Valéry et la poétique du langage." It was first delivered at a Valéry colloquium at the Johns Hopkins University, and the Johns Hopkins University Press has granted me permission to translate and publish a revised version. Jacques Derrida's "Le Supplément de copule" originally appeared in *Marges de la philosophie* (Seuil, 1972); my translation is included here with the permission of Harvard University Press, publishers of the forthcoming English-language edition of the *Marges*. Gilles Deleuze's "The Schizophrenic and Language" is a chapter of *Logique du sens* (1969), entitled "Le Schizophrène et la petite fille"; Editions de Minuit has granted me permission to translate an expanded and revised version. Michel Foucault's essay is a revised version of a talk on the notion of authorship given at SUNY-Buffalo, and my translation appears here with the permission of the author and of the Société Française de Philosophie; a first version of the talk was given at the Société and appeared in its *Bulletin*, 63 (1969). I explain the importance of the differences between the two versions in my Introduction. I am grateful to Deleuze and Foucault for giving me a free hand to edit their texts with an American readership in mind. René Girard's essay was first presented at Stanford University at the conference "The Act of Interpretation: Myth, Symbol, Culture," and appears here in a revised version. Eugene Vance's essay originated as a talk given to the Tudor and Stuart Club, the Johns Hopkins University, and is also revised.

A note on the translations. Given the problems inherent in some post-structuralist styles of writing, I have chosen to find intelligible English renderings, perhaps at the cost of sacrificing some of the rhetorical force of the originals. All quotations and references are given according to original English works or English translations where conveniently available, though some modifications of these translations have been made when a critic's particular use of a text required it. Wherever useful, editorial notes have been included to facilitate the reading of some of the essays.

The list of friends and scholars who have aided me in translating first drafts, second drafts, and nth drafts of some of the French essays is a long one. Special thanks to Maureen O'Meara (Marin), James Creech (Derrida), Sandor Goodhart (Deleuze), Wilda Anderson and Richard Berrong (whose welcome help extended to almost every essay in this anthology), Tom Trezise and John Leavitt for their assistance on the Introduction and the bibliographical material, and Philip Lewis for undertaking the painful task of styling the manuscript and for providing many useful suggestions. My sincere gratitude goes to the many friends who gave their support throughout: Rosalina de la Carrera, Richard Macksey, Hayden White, Carl Rubino, Homer Brown, Roberto González Echevarría, Giuseppe Mazzotta, Michèle Richman, Richard Stamelman, Elizabeth Traube, and, from the School of Criticism and Theory, University of California, Irvine, Ralph Freedman and Murray Krieger. Above all, this volume would not have been completed without the editorial talents of Kay Scheuer and the support and patience of Bernhard Kendler, my editor at Cornell University Press.

JOSUÉ V. HARARI

Baltimore, Maryland

Textual Strategies

JOSUÉ V. HARARI

Critical Factions / Critical Fictions

I

There are distances which are measured only in words.
—Victor Lily

Structuralism has been in fashion in Anglo-American intellectual circles since the late sixties, as is demonstrated by the number of critical anthologies and books which have appeared in the last decade.[1] The critical excitement generated by structuralism reached its peak in America in the mid-seventies: the label became then the product, with the predictable result that any thinker, past or present, who was anyone fit comfortably under the "structuralist umbrella." In talking about literature, one was very careful to use words such as "codes," "arrangements," "systems," and especially "structures" and to avoid words such as "historicity" and "consciousness." All those concerned with critical problems "French style" felt compelled to cite the work of Lévi-Strauss, Lacan, Althusser, Kristeva, and

---

[1] Among anthologies, one might cite, in chronological order: Richard Macksey and Eugenio Donato's *The Structuralist Controversy* (1970, 1972), Jacques Ehrmann's *Structuralism* (1970), Michael Lane's *Introduction to Structuralism* (1972), John K. Simon's *Modern French Criticism: From Proust and Valéry to Structuralism* (1972), Richard and Fernande de George's *The Structuralists from Marx to Lévi-Strauss* (1972), Vernon Gras's *European Literary Theory and Practice: From Existential Phenomenology to Structuralism* (1973), David Robey's *Structuralism: An Introduction* (1973), and Murray Krieger's *Directions for Criticism: Structuralism and Its Alternatives* (1976). The best known theoretical treatments of structuralism are: Jean Piaget's *Structuralism* (1970), Fredric Jameson's *The Prison-House of Language: A Critical Account of Structuralism and Russian Formalism* (1972), Robert Scholes's *Structuralism in Literature: An Introduction* (1974), Jonathan Culler's *Structuralist Poetics* (1975), Philip Pettit's *The Concept of Structuralism: A Critical Analysis* (1975), and the Group Omega's *Keys to the Doors of Structuralism* (Erehwon, 1977).

even more frequently, because of their proximity to the literary domain, that of Saussure, of Todorov, and especially of Barthes the structuralist, the Barthes of *Elements of Semiology* and *On Racine*.

The result of this critical trendiness was not slow to appear, and thinkers who had been responsible through their writings for the diffusion of the structuralist movement were quick to mark their distance both from the concept and from each other, to such an extent that we may rightly question, in the words of Eugenio Donato, "whether the concept of structuralism has any validity and whether such a thing as structuralism ever existed."[2] And yet, there was an intellectual movement comparable to previous "-isms," something that we will call, for want of a more precise term, the structuralist "tendency of thought." That structuralism eventually became a fashion and an ideology is not my concern here. I want simply, in order to establish a context for what follows in this presentation, to recall its major trends.[3] I shall therefore concentrate on two areas: ethnology, using Claude Lévi-Strauss—whose ethnological work has been at the origin of structuralism's success—and literary criticism, using the work of Roland Barthes.

Lévi-Strauss attempts first of all an interpretation of the most pronounced social phenomenon—kinship—which he elaborates on the basis of the Jakobsonian linguistic model, having transposed the latter onto the ethnological plane.[4] The results obtained are convincing. They allow contradictory or seemingly unrelated ethnographic observations to be organized according

[2]"Structuralism: The Aftermath," *Sub-stance,* 7 (1973), 9.

[3]For a more extensive treatment of structuralism, I refer the reader to François Wahl, ed., *Qu'est-ce que le structuralisme?* (Paris: Seuil, 1969), which remains the most advanced general book on the subject. Culler's, Jameson's, and Scholes's books have all become classics (Scholes's being the most introductory of the three) for an understanding of the subject matter. For short and incisive analyses of the movement, as well as of the transformations it brought about in various disciplines, see Eugenio Donato's two articles "Of Structuralism and Literature," *MLN,* 82 (1967), and his already cited "Structuralism: The Aftermath."

[4]Claude Lévi-Strauss, *Structural Anthropology,* I, trans. Jacobson and Schoepf (New York: Basic Books, 1963). Cf. the section on "Language and Kinship," especially the chapter entitled "Structural Analysis in Linguistics and in Anthropology."

to an internal logic. Behind the diversity of kinship ties, Lévi-Strauss discovers an elementary structure which permits the explanation of all such ties known to us. In making use of the linguistic model to explain the deep structure of familial ties, Lévi-Strauss was the first to inscribe social reality within the framework of a general theory of communication. Kinship and marriage rules ensure the "exchange" of women between groups, as economic rules ensure the circulation of goods, and linguistic rules that of messages: "In any society, communication operates on three different levels: communication of women, communication of goods and services, communication of messages. Therefore kinship studies, economics and linguistics approach the same kinds of problems on different strategic levels and really pertain to the same field."[5]

Lévi-Strauss subsequently continued his work in this same direction by trying to uncover the organization—unconscious or hidden—of clanship, customs, rites, and especially myths.[6] He thus revealed very broad homologies: kinship rules that correspond to the system of the myths of a given tribe, the social

---

[5] *Structural Anthopology*, I, p. 296. Cf. on this topic the excellent analysis of Michèle Richman, "Eroticism in the Patriarchal Order," *Diacritics*, 6:1 (1976), 46–53.

[6] The choice and function of myths in Lévi-Strauss's program are important enough to warrant this long quotation, in which the ethnologist defines his enterprise: "In *Les Structures*, we had disentangled a small number of simple principles from the apparently superficial contingency and incoherent diversity of the rules of marriage. Because of those principles a very complex ensemble of usages and customs was drawn together into a meaningful system, though at first they seemed absurd and have been generally so judged....

"The experiment in mythology which we are now undertaking will be even more decisive. Mythology has no evident practical function: unlike the phenomena previously examined, mythology is not in direct contact with a different reality, endowed with an objectivity higher than its own whose orders it transmits to a mind which seems perfectly free to abandon itself to creative spontaneity. If, as a result, we were able to demonstrate that, here too, the arbitrary appearance, the apparently free outsurge and a seemingly unbridled inventiveness presuppose laws which operate at a deeper level, we could posit as ineluctable the conclusion ... that the human mind appears as determined even in its myth; if that is so, then *a fortiori* it must be determined in all its manifestations" ("Overture to The Raw and the Cooked," trans. Joseph McMahon, *Yale French Studies*, 37 [1966], 53–54).

Lévi-Strauss's will-to-codify has not changed, but this time the stakes are higher. If he can prove that even mythic imaginary constructions conform to constraints that can be codified, then, indeed, what can escape codification?

organization of another tribe that corresponds in its underlying structure to culinary customs, and so on.[7] Without pursuing his ethnological work any further in detail, I would like to focus on the philosophical and methodological consequences of his structural approach.

On the philosophical level, history, although not entirely dismissed, falls nevertheless under the tutelage of the *System*. If the notion of "diachrony" replaces that of "history," it is precisely in order to emphasize that temporal variations and transformations obey certain rules and that these rules can be systematized. Thus, temporality and history lose their privilege, to the benefit of closed systems and synchronic organizations. Similarly (cf. note 6), if reason obeys universal laws of operation, man becomes the product of structure. The notion of self or subject—the individual *cogito*—prevalent in the fifties in phenomenology and existentialism, is automatically devalued insofar as human thought functions everywhere according to the same logic. From a Saussurian perspective, we would say that whereas phenomenology and existentialism privileged speech (hence the individual) and claimed that the subject was at the center of the significations it generated, Lévi-Strauss, on the other hand, privileges language (hence the system), in which a subject with no possibility of totalizing the course of his history would inscribe himself.[8] To put it briefly, though schematically, Sartre is to Lévi-Strauss as philosophy is to anthropology, as the subject is to the system, and as history is to structure.

On the methodological level, Lévi-Straussian structuralism asserts itself as a method of scientific knowledge and even lays claim to the rigor of the exact sciences. Therefore, it is opposed to all exclusively phenomenological approaches to knowledge, which pretend to gain immediate access to meaning through a

---

[7]Cf. *The Raw and the Cooked* (1964, tr. 1969), *From Honey to Ashes* (1966, tr. 1973), *L'Origine des manières de table* (1968), and *L'Homme nu* (1971).

[8]Even though the status of the subject, or rather of the subjects—epistemic, transcendental, psychological, logical, subject of desire, subject of the utterance, and so on—is not always clear, it remains nevertheless true that in all the disciplines affected by structuralism, the questioning of the subject as "full subject" is the most obvious philosophical objective. For the most radical questioning of the traditional notion of subject, see the last chapter of Michel Foucault's *The Order of Things* (New York: Vintage, 1973).

descriptive analysis of what we experience or perceive (Lévi-Strauss's *réel* and *vécu*). In opposition to phenomenology, which "postulates a kind of continuity between experience and reality," Lévi-Strauss affirms that "the transition between one order and the other is discontinuous; that to reach reality, one has to first reject experience, if only to reintegrate it into an objective synthesis devoid of any sentimentality."[9] For Lévi-Strauss, intelligibility is therefore not given at the level of perception or of daily experience. It is, rather, the result of a *praxis* based on the construction of models which alone permit access to the hidden meaning of phenomena, a meaning which is formulated in terms of structure.[10] Lévi-Strauss's goal is *not* to change our perception of the concrete, but to reveal the concrete's true nature which, precisely, escapes perception. Hence this well-known passage:

> It is hopeless to expect a structural analysis to change our way of perceiving concrete social relations. It will only explain them better.... But if a distinction is made between the level of observation and symbols to be substituted for it, I fail to see why an algebraic treatment of, let us say symbols for marriage rules, would not teach us, when aptly manipulated, something about the way a given marriage system actually works and bring out properties not immediately apparent to the empirical observer.[11]

The meaning which must be abandoned is that which is immediately experienced at the phenomenological level. The meaning retained is that which subsists at the conclusion of scientific analysis and reveals the essential and invariable properties of phenomena: their underlying structure. The structure that is obtained "has nothing to do with empirical reality but with models which are built up after it."[12] It presents an abstract and

[9]*Tristes Tropiques*, trans. J. and D. Weightman (New York: Atheneum, 1974), p. 58.

[10]For Lévi-Strauss, as for structuralism in general, it is important to emphasize that the structure is not directly observable, since access is gained to it only at the end of a progressive "reduction" which permits one to distinguish the pertinent oppositions (the constitutive units of the system) that alone have signifying value.

[11]"The Meaning and Use of the Notion of Model," in *Structural Anthropology*, II, trans. M. Layton (New York: Basic Books, 1976), p. 80.

[12]*Structural Anthropology*, I, 279.

formal character since it is reduced to the invariable features of phenomena. There is, therefore, a discontinuity, a break between the diversity of the real and the formal abstraction of the structure that signifies it, the movement from one to the other implying a *passage* from diversity to simplicity, from the concrete to the abstract.

It is important to note, in this connection, that Lévi-Straussian structuralism must not be confused with formalism. In contrast to proponents of formalism, Lévi-Strauss refuses to oppose (hence my emphasis on the word *passage*) the concrete to the abstract, and to ascribe to the latter a privileged value: "For the former [formalism], the two domains must be absolutely separate, since form alone is intelligible, and content is only a residual deprived of any significant value. For structuralism, this opposition does not exist. There is not something abstract on one side and something concrete on the other. Form and content are of the same nature, susceptible [to] the same analysis."[13] Unlike formalism, which Lévi-Strauss denounces for misjudging "the complementarity of signifier and signified, which has been recognized since Saussure in all linguistic systems,"[14] his structural analysis places itself resolutely at the level of form *and* of content, that is, *at the level of signification.*

These remarks lead into the central problem of Roland Barthes's critical enterprise, the question of signification. "*Homo significans:* such would be the new man of structural inquiry."[15] The task of literary structuralism is not to discover the meaning of a work, but to reconstitute the rules governing the production of meaning: "[The structuralist mode of thought] seeks less to assign completed meanings to the objects it discovers than to know how meaning is possible, at what cost and by what means."[16] The immediate and most radical consequence of this view is the massive shift that occurs on the critical terrain. In-

[13]"Structure and Form: Reflections on a Work by Vladimir Propp," in *Structural Anthropology*, II, 131.
[14]Ibid., p. 141.
[15]Roland Barthes, *Critical Essays*, trans. Richard Howard (Evanston: Northwestern University Press, 1972), p. 218.
[16]Ibid., p. 218.

terpretation, in traditional literary criticism, was organized around the author, his thought, the influences that had affected him, and so forth. (The signification given to a work always came from the outside; it was necessary only to define the point of view in order to be able to characterize the type of interpretation at work.) Structural analysis, however, bypasses the problems associated with the figure of the author as well as other criteria exterior to the text, and instead focuses its attention on the text, understood as a construct whose mode of functioning must be described. As a result, rather than talking about truth(s), it becomes necessary to speak about a work in terms of the validity and coherence of its language. "In itself," writes Barthes, "a language is not true or false, it is or is not valid: valid, i.e., constitutes a coherent system of signs. The rules of literary language do not concern the conformity of this language to reality (whatever the claims of the realistic schools), but only its submission to the system of signs the author has established (and we must, of course, give the word *system* a very strong sense here)."[17]

Both the strengths and the shortcomings of the structuralist approach in its application to the literary domain are most apparent in the work done on the narrative. In 1966, in the introduction to the special number of *Communications*[18] devoted to the study of the narrative, Barthes summed up the theoretical principles of the structuralist program. A few remarks on the content and history of this essay will help us put in perspective the aims and achievements of "literary structuralism."

At first, structural analysis sought to reconstitute a common language for all narratives, in other words, a model which would

[17]Ibid., p. 258.
[18]"Recherches sémiologiques. L'Analyse structurale du récit," *Communications,* 8 (1966). The structural analysis of narrative begins, generally speaking, with the work of Vladimir Propp (*Morphology of the Folktale*, 1958) and is developed according to more rigorous models with the work of A. J. Greimas (*Sémantique structurale*, 1966), Tzvetan Todorov (*Littérature et signification*, 1966), and Claude Bremond (*Logique du récit*, 1973). These different attitudes toward narrative, which could be characterized as actantial, modal, and sequential, are picked up again and related to each other in Barthes's programmatic essay "An Introduction to the Structural Analysis of Narrative" (originally published in *Communications*, 8, and trans. Lionel Duisit in *New Literary History*, 6 [1975]).

account for their multiplicity. Although Barthes emphasized
from the very beginning of "Introduction to the Structural
Analysis of Narrative" that a grammar of the narrative would
have to rely on linguistics and linguistic categories, clearly he was
never advocating in this structuralist project a wholesale transposition of grammatical structures into narrative structures, that
is, the kind of transposition which would make of narrative
theory an applied linguistics. "The working out of [narrative
theory] may be made much easier if we proceed from a model
that can provide the initial terms and principles. In the current
state of research, it seems reasonable to elect linguistics itself as a
basic model for the structural analysis of narrative."[19] Note first
the mildness of the tone: "it seems reasonable" rather than, for
instance, "it is imperative." Second, linguistics indeed is
suggested as a model but, as Jonathan Culler correctly diagnoses, "it is perhaps less important in determining an analytic
procedure than in offering a set of terms which, because they
are already linked by a theory, can create coherence and give a
certain vigor to the structuralist enterprise."[20] Thus, in spite of
Barthes's numerous assertions that "a narrative is a long sentence," that "[Narrative] Discourse has its units, its rules, its
'grammar'," and that "a discourse is a long 'sentence' (the units
of which are not necessarily sentences), just as a sentence, allowing for certain specification, is a short 'discourse',"[21] the relationship between linguistics and literature *in fact* lies at a much more
abstract level. Linguistics and narrative theory must inevitably
intersect as each one, in its own manner, questions language; but
it is never a matter for Barthes of assimilating one to the other,
or of confusing them.[22] The analogy between them rests on the
practical belief that a number of linguistic concepts can be borrowed to help generate a narrative or a literary model. Here is
how Barthes explains it:

> [Narrative analysis] is compelled to conceive, first a *hypothetical
> model of description* (which American linguists call a "theory"), and

[19]"An Introduction to the Structural Analysis of Narrative," p. 239.
[20]Jonathan Culler, *Structuralist Poetics* (Ithaca: Cornell University Press, 1975),
p. 109.
[21]"An Introduction . . .," pp. 240–241.
[22]Barthes confided in a recent interview: "In linguistics, I have never been
anything but an amateur." *Magazine Littéraire,* 97 (1975), 31.

then to proceed gradually from that model down, towards the species, which at the same time partakes in and deviates from the model. It is only at the level of such conformities or *discrepancies*, and equipped with a single tool of description, that the analyst can turn his attention once more to the plurality of narrative acts. . . .

In order to describe and classify the infinite number of narratives, one needs then a "theory" (*in the pragmatic sense that we are here intending*).[23]

The expression "hypothetical model of description" is the key to the proper understanding of the goals (with their practical limitations) that structural analysis can achieve. The very same key words reappear in Barthes's appraisal, in *Critique et vérité* (1966), of the objectives of the "Nouvelle Critique" of the sixties: "Placed before the impossibility of mastering all of the sentences of a language, the linguist settles for the creation of a *hypothetical model of description* that he can use to explain how the infinite sentences of a language are generated. No matter what corrections one may have to make in it, there is no reason not to try to apply such a method to works of literature."[24] Hence for Barthes, structural analysis provides a "pragmatic" means of describing and explaining narrative acts according to a gradation of deviations from the norm established by the hypothetical model (hypothetical here also means *variable*). Todorov, whose procedure is different, albeit close to that of Barthes, stretches prudence to write: "The literary code, contrary to the linguistic code, has no strictly binding character, and we are obliged to deduce it from each individual text, or at least to *correct* its previous formulation in each new instance."[25] In other words, for Todorov, as for Barthes, the aim is not a fixed, unchanging, a priori model, but a pragmatic model, given the necessity of having to classify a great number of narratives. Classifying always implies at least some formalizing, but this is neither new nor peculiar to narrative theory. Most theoretical criticism, because it has to codify, to reduce to rules, and to take into account a large number of facts, must formalize to a certain extent. In that

[23]"An Introduction . . .," p. 239 (my emphasis).
[24]*Critique et Vérité* (Paris: Seuil, 1966), p. 57.
[25]Tzvetan Todorov, *Poetics of Prose*, trans. Richard Howard (Ithaca: Cornell University Press, 1977), p. 249 (my emphasis).

sense, the often heard accusation that structural analysis is a kind of formalism is indeed correct, but then, what theory is not?

In fact, reading "Introduction to the Structural Analysis of Narrative" approximately ten years after its publication, one is struck by the rather modest claims Barthes makes for structural analysis in the literary domain. I do not believe I would be misrepresenting the case (or at least Barthes's view of it) by saying that structural analysis can be seen to be schematizing *only if one loses sight of its limited objectives,* namely, to cause the possibility of a theory of structure to appear and to make the functioning of narrative discourse apparent. It might be useful to recall here, as they have been vastly overstated, the precise characteristics and aims of structural analysis.

(1) Structural analysis describes and explains a text as a system of narrative transformations. It presents a picture of possible narrative discourses, such that all existing narratives appear as particular instances of a general—although variable— hypothetical model.

(2) A structuralist narrative model is never either exhaustive or definitive. It cannot explain *all* the articulations of narrative discourse.

(3) Structural analysis does not explain the meaning(s) of a text. To study the grammar of narrative is to attempt to specify the possibilities of meaning and not to fulfill them. "What is in question in structural analysis is not the truth of a text, but its plurality."[26]

(4) Literary "science" that is a product of structural analysis remains mostly at the level of description, unless and until it opens up onto a broader problematic that can account for the production of meaning. This is the precise juncture at which we begin to treat the "work" as "text." We shall return to this crucial shift and the manner in which the distance between these two concepts is covered later in our discussion of Barthes's work.

Does there exist, in the end, a philosophy or a method that can be qualified as genuinely structuralist? Or are there only certain structural subjects common to the work of theorists that fit under the convenient unifying structuralist label? The reality of

---

[26]Roland Barthes, "Par où commencer?" *Poétique,* 1 (1970), 9.

the situation is such that various combinations of answers might all be valid, although we would be inclined to choose the second alternative. In our terms, the list of structuralist common denominators would then read: (1) the rejection of the concept of the "full subject" to the benefit of that of structure; (2) the loss of pertinence of the traditional "form/content" division insofar as for all structuralist theorists content derives its reality from its structure; and (3) at the methodological level, a stress on codification and systematization. And yet, even such a general statement is not uniformly true, or rather, it is true to various degrees, depending on the theory under investigation. If one accepted the gradation proposed by Raymond Boudon[27] regarding the objectives of structural analysis (level 1: a theory explaining a small number of facts; level 2: several theories each explaining a small number of facts; level 3: a general theory explaining with a degree of *probability* a great number of facts; level 4: a general theory explaining with *exactitude* a large number of facts), it is clear that although Lévi-Strauss would want to place himself at the fourth level, Barthes and the literary structuralists would place themselves at the third, while others would be satisfied to fit anywhere on the structuralist tree and still benefit from its shade.

The preceding remarks make two principal points. First, there is no unified view of structuralism, and second, structuralism as a movement is most clearly defined on the basis of the transformations it has wrought in the disciplines it has affected. It is perhaps on this basis that one should ask: what is poststructuralism? The question is less ambitious than it might appear; it does not seek a clear or unified answer, but only tentative answers that may perhaps be reduced, in the end, to nothing more than a panorama only slightly different from that offered by structuralism. For this reason, among others, poststructuralism—like structuralism—invites a plural spelling, even if such a spelling is not commonly used. We shall retain the singular notation, but it will become obvious to the reader that

[27]Raymond Boudon, *A quoi sert la notion de "structure"?* (Paris: Gallimard, 1968), pp. 227-228.

we think of it partly in the plural: post-structuralism is also post-structuralisms.

What, then, is post-structuralism? At the heart of the matter is a double problematic, both geographical and philosophical. First, *the problematic of delimitation:* where does structuralism end and post-structuralism begin? What is the relationship of these two movements of thought? Which disciplines are grouped under the structuralist and which under the post-structuralist aegis? Second, *an epistemological problematic,* with all its related questions: what is the difference between structuralism and post-structuralism in the field of knowledge? Is there a simple transformation, a mutation, or a radical break? There are no simple or broad and sweeping answers to these questions. However, a step-by-step approach may lead to partial answers that will shed some light on the subject.

Historically, structuralism was born of linguistics, and all the fields it covers have to do with signs. All the disciplines encompassed by structuralism—linguistics, poetics, ethnology, psychoanalysis and, clearly in the background but still related, philosophy[28]—are grouped under the sciences of the sign, or of sign-systems. Following François Wahl's perceptive analysis,[29] we would say that the most diverse elements of any discipline can be classified under a structuralist heading, provided they adhere to a linguistic system of the type signifier/signified and that they receive their structure from this particular type of system. These linguistic origins become even more obvious when one analyzes in the concrete the work of the structuralist leaders, each in his respective discipline. We have already noted the terminological as well as the conceptual borrowings from Saussurian and Jakobsonian linguistics by Lévi-Strauss in ethnology, and Barthes and Todorov in literature. We could also mention Lacan's well-known formulas: "The unconscious is structured like a language," and "Dreams have the structure of a sentence."[30]

---

[28]Philosophy remains in the background, since in structuralism it tends to be incorporated into other disciplines. Philosophy becomes ethnology with Lévi-Strauss, semiology with Kristeva, psychoanalysis with Lacan, strict epistemology with Foucault, but it is never philosophy in its classical form.

[29]Wahl, ed., *Qu'est-ce que le structuralisme?* pp. 7–12.

[30]Jacques Lacan, *Ecrits* (Paris: Seuil, 1966), pp. 594, 267.

Even Foucault, who has always kept his distance from structuralism, fits into this same linguistic register. The key concept of Foucault's earlier work, the *épistémè,* clearly encompasses a certain semiology. The *épistémè* explains in each instance a form of knowledge modeled on the structure of the sign, so that a change of *épistémè,* which is the appearance of a new mode of signifying, necessarily relates to the type of articulation existing within the sign itself, between what represents and what is represented, between signifier and signified. Thus Foucault, when speaking of mutations occurring in the forms of knowledge, makes the definition of his central concept, the *épistémè,* depend directly on a problematic of representation and hence on the internal structure of the sign.

Perhaps then, retrospectively, it is in and by the sign that the structuralist enterprise is best, or at least most consistently, defined. If structuralism has attempted, philosophically, a radical dismissal of the speaking subject, it has, on the other hand, never put the sign, in its essential structure, into question. The most fundamental difference between the structuralist and poststructuralist enterprises can be seen in the shift from the problematic of the subject to the deconstruction of the concept of representation. I refer here to Jacques Derrida, whose work constitutes a systematic critique of structuralism in the sense in which I have just defined it. For Derrida, linguistics and structuralism rely on idealist presuppositions which are never questioned and which are reflected in their conception of the sign as a closure. Using the tools furnished by structuralism, Derrida's questioning turns them, in a sense, *against* it. It is Derridean discourse, that is, a philosophical discourse—among all contemporary discourses, it is thus philosophical discourse that most clearly dominates post-structuralist thinking—that will confront structuralism in order to prove that the latter has made too restricted a use of the sign. Derridean discourse mobilizes a profound "semiological" knowledge in order to go beyond the central concept of structuralism (the sign) and to upset the epistemological foundation—the impossibility of separating the order of the signified from the order of the signifier in the functioning of the sign—which supported classical structuralism.

And yet, even if the structuralist and post-structuralist enterprises are radically opposed to each other, they exhibit a certain complementarity. The denunciation of the concept of representation is *necessarily* based on the structuralist institution of the sign; it relies on structuralist premises in order, paradoxically, to show that structuralism has not fully pursued the implications of those premises. The post-structuralist attitude is therefore literally unthinkable without structuralism. Just as the Derridean attack on logocentrism in *Of Grammatology* is an extension of Lévi-Strauss's meditations on ethnocentrism in *Tristes Tropiques,* so the Kristevian notions of textual productivity and paragrammatic writing both prolong and surpass earlier formal structuralist accounts of signification, and so the post-structuralist Roland Barthes (cf. his article in this anthology) cannot be understood without the first Roland Barthes, the author of *Mythologies:*

> If I have changed . . . it is a question of displacement, not of rejection. I could now no longer be content with relating forms to ideological contents as I did in *Mythologies.* I don't think this is wrong, but today this kind of relation is established: today, everyone can denounce the petit-bourgeois character of a form. Now it is necessary to take the struggle further, to attempt to split, not signs, not signifiers on one side and signifieds on the other, but the very idea of the sign: an operation one might call a semioclasty. It is Western discourse as such, in its foundations, its elementary forms, that one must today attempt to split.[31]

From "semiology" to "semioclasty" is the trajectory of a "displacement" and not of a "rejection," according to Barthes. In a sense, this is also the trajectory from structuralism to post-structuralism. Without blurring the issues, we could say that whatever came after structuralism and transformed it was also, and at the same time, *before* it (without any exaggeration, one can trace the tradition which questions logocentrism back to

[31] Roland Barthes, interview with Raymond Bellour, in *Le Livre des autres* (Paris: L'Herne, 1971), p. 271. Barthes more than once returns to the fact that it is the structure of the sign which must be attacked. See, for instance, his article "Changer l'objet lui-même," in *Esprit,* 4 (1971).

Nietzsche), *with* it (the example of the two Barthes), and as a *counterpoint* to it (Lévi-Strauss versus Derrida, for instance). It is too simple and too easy to view the post-structuralist thrust as only an extension of structuralist thinking, or as only anti-structuralist, or as altogether non-structuralist (in its aims), for it is all three. In the words of Philip E. Lewis:

> Structuralist methods of analysis and modes of critical thinking continue to be deployed, but with a difference: deployed at the expense of basic concepts and presuppositions that structuralism mobilized in its formative stages. The wind [of post-structuralism] blows against structuralism, using it as a foil in a general reflection on metaphysics, on epistemological and ideological entrapment; yet insofar as the wind blows from structuralism and carries the tools and insights of structuralism with it, it is really a kind of whirlwind, blowing round and round with no clear trajectory and moving energetically from place to place with no fixed center or frame of reference.[32]

A definition of post-structuralism and a full reply to the questions it poses will finally come—as has been the case for all previous movements of thought—only from the results afforded us by post-structuralist theoretical practices. These, then, will be answers, furnished not on the basis of an a priori definition of post-structuralism, but (1) by showing that post-structuralism has wrought transformations in various disciplines, (2) by measuring the scope as well as the limits of these transformations, (3) by showing that in each instance these transformations reveal what one might call a post-structuralist thrust, and (4) by determining the changes—advances and retrenchments—which have occurred in our critical concepts and practices as a result of these transformations. On this basis, one will be able retrospectively to understand better and perhaps to redefine the breadth and the import of post-structuralism. I shall make a first step in that direction by reviewing a few of the problems raised by critics included in this anthology.

[32]Philip E. Lewis, from the text of a lecture delivered at SUNY-Stony Brook.

II

Strategy   [fr. Gr. *strategia*. See STRATAGEM] 1. The science
            and art of employing the armed strength of a bel-
            ligerent to secure the objects of a war. 2. Use of
            stratagem, or artifice . . . .
Stratagem   [fr. Gr. *stratos* army and *agein* to lead] 1a. An ar-
            tifice or trick in war for deceiving and outwitting
            the enemy. 1b. A cleverly contrived trick or scheme
            for gaining an end. 1c. Ability to devise cunning
            plans to gain an end. 2. obs. A violent and bloody
            act. [Slaughter; execution.]
                              —*Webster's International Dictionary*

Derrida is the critic who, in the last several years (beginning
with the publication in 1967 of *L'Ecriture et la différence* and *De la
grammatologie*), has most systematically explored the relations between philosophy and the concept of the sign, with the whole
problematic that it implies. As "The Supplement of Copula"
demonstrates, the question of the sign is *both* a philosophical and
a linguistic question. Hence the necessity of a doubly ambiguous
analysis, that is, of an analysis, on the one hand, of a linguistics
operating within a metaphysics, and on the other, of a
metaphysics inserted into a linguistics. It is on the basis of this
double problematic that Derrida proposes to look for new concepts and new models, for an economy belonging to but *at the
same time* escaping from tradition.[33] Here is his technique in his
own terms:

> Our discourse belongs irreducibly to the system of metaphysical
> oppositions. One can evince the rupture of that adherence only by
> a *certain* organization, a certain *strategic* arrangement which, within
> the field and its own powers, turning against itself its own
> stratagems, produces a *force of dislocation* which spreads itself
> throughout the whole system, splitting it in all directions and *de-
> limiting* it through and through.[34]

[33]One rediscovers the paradoxical character of Derridean strategy in all the
authors whom Derrida studies. It is always a question of exploring two textual
strata, one by which the work adheres to tradition and another by which it
escapes tradition and thus allows a deconstructive strategy.

[34]*L'Ecriture et la différence* (Paris: Seuil, 1967), p. 34.

Deconstruction, as Derrida practices it, is as much a matter of substance as it is a matter of form. Tradition is neither discarded, nor attacked from the outside. Derrida's strategy consists of working within metaphysics,[35] of finding its weak point and of trying to widen the breach thus uncovered. His aim is to show that metaphysics has never had the plenitude it claims to have, and, also, that its entire history involves a dissimulation of this lack of fullness. Time and time again, Derrida denounces the illusion of a full presence or plenitude in Western metaphysics. Just as a dream seemingly satisfies desire by providing a substitute for the object of desire, thus creating the illusion that the fundamental impossibility of the satisfaction of desire can be overcome, so the metaphysics of presence is the substitute which has allowed Western metaphysics to deceive itself into believing it could at once overcome and fulfill its desire for presence.

How does one generate this illusion? How is presence attained *without* really attaining it? We approach here the strange logic of the supplement.

> The concept of the supplement . . . harbors within itself two significations whose cohabitation is as strange as it is necessary. The supplement adds itself, it is a surplus, a plenitude enriching another plenitude, the *fullest measure* of presence. It cumulates and accumulates presence. . . .
>
> But the supplement supplements. It adds only to replace. It intervenes or insinuates itself *in-the-place-of;* if it fills, it is as if one fills a void. If it represents and makes an image, it is by the anterior default of a presence. Compensatory [*suppléant*] and vicarious, the supplement is an adjunct, a subaltern instance which *takes-(the)-place* [*tient-lieu*]. As substitute, it is not simply added to the positivity of a presence, it produces no relief, its place is assigned in the structure by the mark of an emptiness.
>
> This second signification of the supplement cannot be separated from the first. . . . Each of the two significations is [in turn] effaced or becomes discreetly vague in the presence of the other. But their

---

[35]"The step 'outside philosophy' is much more difficult to conceive than is generally imagined by those who think they made it long ago with cavalier ease, and who are in general swallowed up in metaphysics." J. Derrida, "Structure, Sign and Play in the Discourse of the Human Sciences," in Richard Macksey and Eugenio Donato, eds., *The Structuralist Controversy* (Baltimore: Johns Hopkins University Press, 1972), p. 254.

common function is shown in this: whether it adds or substitutes itself, the supplement is *exterior,* outside of the positivity to which it is super-added, alien to that which, in order to be replaced by it, must be other than it.[36]

Let us take an example in order to explain this "supplementary logic": the supplement of a large dictionary.[37] To have a supplement to this dictionary means that we add a volume to previously existing ones. But in addition to being a *surplus* with respect to these other volumes, the supplement also indicates that these volumes were lacking words and that it is to occupy the place the missing words would have had. In other words, the supplement intervenes here as *substitute.*

To recapitulate: the supplement is added to make up for a deficiency, but as such it reveals a lack, for since it is in excess, the supplement can *never* be adequate to the lack ("the supplement is *exterior* . . . alien to that which, in order to be replaced by it, must be other than it.") The plus(es) and minus(es) provided by the supplement are never *quite* equal. Hence the troubling discovery that the structure of the supplement implies that a supplement to the supplement is *always* possible. It is this peculiar quality of the supplement that accounts for the importance of the notion in Derridean deconstruction.

The Derridean demonstration consists of showing that the whole edifice of Western metaphysics rests on the possibility of compensating for a primordial nonpresence by way of the supplement. Once it is proven that the supplement is an integral part of the metaphysical machinery, it becomes easy to show how

[36]Jacques Derrida, *Of Grammatology,* trans. Gayatri C. Spivak (Baltimore: Johns Hopkins University Press, 1976), pp. 144–145. It is interesting that *Webster's International Dictionary* gives, among others, the following two definitions for the verb *to supply* (French: *suppléer*): 3. To make additions to by way of supplement; now, to add (something essential or wanting); as, to *supply* missing words; much left to the imagination to *supply;* 8. To serve instead of; to take the place of; to replace.

[37]Roger Laporte uses this example in his essay "Une Double Stratégie," in *Ecarts* (Paris: Fayard, 1973), pp. 205–264. Intended as an introduction to Derrida's work, Laporte's essay is in fact an extensive and useful analysis of Derrida's deconstructive strategies. Two other perceptive essays on Derrida are M. H. Abrams's "The Deconstructive Angel," in *Critical Inquiry,* 3 (1977), and Edward Said's "The Problem of Textuality: Two Exemplary Positions," also in *Critical Inquiry,* 4 (1978).

in every instance the notion of supplement serves to demystify full presence. Take. for example, masturbation, as in Derrida's case study of Rousseau in *Of Grammatology*. Masturbation is dangerous precisely because it supplements the "natural" relationship; in other words, it is both added to and replaces nature. Each time nature fails us, the supplement is there to entice us, to restore through illusion the absent presence. Thus, the supplement, by definition external and artificial, replaces nature and so becomes an integral part of it, to the point in fact where the artificial and the natural become inseparable, one and the same. Nature, in all its plenitude, then appears in its real form, that of myth *only*, and the pure origin, the metaphysical concept *par excellence*, is altogether undermined, since the supplement is no less originary than that which is natural.

"The Supplement of Copula" is the most decisive demonstration in Derrida's writings of how the notion of supplementarity inscribes itself in the text of philosophy under the guise of the copula *to be*: a peculiar linguistic form which has imposed on all of Western metaphysics the necessity of thinking of being as presence. And if, asks Derrida, we were to show that every philosopher in the history of metaphysics who has attempted to deal with origin and presence was necessarily describing only a supplement of origin and a simulacrum of presence, what would this make of metaphysics? How would philosophy "recast" the ontological operation if it were, as Gayatri Spivak puts it, to "escape the form of mastery represented by the copula is"?[38] This is the question, central both to philosophy and to the Derridean global strategy, that "The Supplement of Copula" attempts to answer.

Let us return for a moment to the point made earlier, namely, that Derridean deconstruction is a matter as much of form as of substance. The difficulty of the Derridean project derives as much from the form it adopts (style of writing, concepts that are anticoncepts) as from the questioning of the metaphysics of the sign. To read Derrida—as it is unnecessary to remind those who do—is to adopt a practice of *contortion*, at the level both of the concept and of the critical trajectory. At the conceptual level, this

[38]G. C. Spivak, Introduction to *Of Grammatology*, p. lxxii.

contortion takes place for two reasons: first, because it is not easy to inhabit old concepts and to refashion words which carry the weight of history without falling back on the traditional significations of these words and concepts; and second, because all Derridean concepts are anticoncepts of the type "neither-nor," or "at once-at once," in other words, all of them—*pharmakon, supplement, hymen, parergon,* and the rest—escape definite classification.[39] The problem is compounded when one asks how long an unclassifiable term can resist institutionalization. Derrida's (anti-) conceptual vocabulary, by the sheer force of its constant use, is itself in danger of becoming another form of accepted signification and thus falling into the very trap it denounces.

But this contortion occurs as well at the level of the critical trajectory. In order to follow a text by Derrida, one must backtrack at each stage of the journey and dismantle the position on which one was relying, while waiting to attain a new position where one stops only long enough to deconstruct the position one has just left, and so on in an interminable self-deconstructing movement. This operation is paradoxical in that the deconstructive movement is at the same time a close reading of texts and a commentary on its own practice of writing; hence it generates a critical text extremely close to and yet very different from the ones it comments on: witness, in "The Supplement of Copula," the text of Derrida's deconstruction of Benveniste's deconstruction of Aristotle (via a partial deconstruction of Kant, Trendelenburg, Brunschvicg, Cassirer, and Heidegger, all of whom had themselves partially deconstructed Aristotle).

Although Derrida's strategy falls under the generally accepted rubric of deconstruction, the concept "deconstruction," as Roger Laporte remarks,[40] is in many ways misleading for the description of Derridean critical practice. Deconstruction[41] implies an

---

[39] Here are two examples: "The *pharmakon* is neither the cure nor the poison, neither good nor evil, neither the inside nor the outside, neither speech nor writing"; "The *supplement* is neither a plus nor a minus, neither an outside nor the complement of an inside, neither an accident nor an essence . . . . Neither/nor is at once *at once* or rather *or rather*." Interview with Derrida in *Diacritics,* 2 (1972), 36.

[40] "Une Double Stratégie," pp. 213–214.

[41] "*Construction:* 2. The manner or method of building; the way in which a thing is made or put together; structure; organization; as, a machine of intricate *construction*" (*Webster's International Dictionary*).

operation involving the dismantling of something into discrete component parts and suggests the ever-present possibility of putting the object back together in its original form. This is clearly not the case with, nor the aim of, Derridean deconstruction, which consists more of the tracing of a path among textual strata in order to stir up and expose forgotten and dormant sediments of meaning which have accumulated and settled into the text's fabric. ("A text always has several epochs and reading must resign itself to this fact."[42]) Thus, deconstruction is really more of a technique of *de-sedimentation* (the word was first used by Derrida in *Of Grammatology* and later abandoned), a technique of de-sedimenting the text in order to allow what was *always already* inscribed in its texture to resurface.

This brings us to one last, important point: the Derridean conception of textuality. The de-sedimentation process just described should help to explain Derrida's view of textuality as a "fabric of grafts" (*tissu de greffes*), of textual energy that is *dissemination,* as opposed to controlled polysemy. We find here Barthes's conception of the text that moves, of the text without a father-author (the Derridean expression is "writing is an orphan"), of the text as everywhere and yet "nowhere *fully* present." This last notion, which itself serves to demystify presence, clearly demonstrates how in Derrida's work, as in that of many other recent thinkers, the concept *text* "represents" in fact the decisive space of our "modernity."

> There is no present text in general, and there is not even a past present text, a text which is past as having been present. The text is not thinkable in an originary or modified form of presence.... Everything begins with reproduction. Always already: repositories of a meaning which was never present, whose signified presence is always reconstituted by deferment, *nachträglich,* belatedly, supplementarily: for *nachträglich* also means *supplementary.* The appeal of the supplement is primal here and breaks open what will be reconstituted by deferment as the present.[43]

No matter how simple it is, no element in the text is fully present to itself; it never refers *only* to itself. "Throughout [the

---

[42]*Of Grammatology*, p. 102.
[43]Jacques Derrida, "Freud and the Scene of Writing," trans. Jeffrey Mehlman, in *Yale French Studies,* 48 (1972), 92.

text] there are only differences and traces of traces."[44] Woven out of these elements that are neither fully present nor absent, the text is thus produced by the perpetual transformation of "another" text. The text "rehearses" its irreducible structure of nonpresence and, by way of its supplementary logic, it self-deconstructs in the very act of constituting itself.

Text is also the terrain on which the Barthesian critical mutation occurs. This mutation is defined as the passage from the notion of the work, as a structure whose functioning one explains, to the theory of the text as productivity of language and production of meaning.

Shortly after publishing his programmatic essay in *Communications,* Barthes began questioning the aims of structural analysis insofar as that analysis, by the very fact that it was dependent on Saussurian linguistics, had built into its premise the notion of closure. In an essay of 1971 whose title speaks for itself ("Changer l'objet lui-même"), Barthes openly redefined and reshaped his critical objective: namely, to call into question the very model according to which meaning is produced, the structure of the sign itself: "the sign itself must be shaken: it is not a question of revealing the (latent) meaning of an utterance, of a tràit, or of a narrative, but of fissuring the very representation of meaning; not to change or purify the symbols but to challenge the symbolic itself."[45]

Thus Barthes and Derrida were the first to confront the problem of the sign and of the closure of meaning through the concept of text understood in its modern sense. To the early Barthes's "a narrative is a large sentence" corresponds the late Barthes's "the text no longer has the sentence for its model,"[46] followed by some of his more programmatic assertions: "First, the text liquidates all metalanguage, whereby it is text: no voice (Science, Cause, Institution) is *behind* what it is saying. Next, the text destroys utterly, *to the point of contradiction,* its own discursive category, its sociolinguistic reference. . . . Lastly, the text can, if it

[44]Jacques Derrida, *Positions* (Paris: Minuit, 1972), p. 38.
[45]*Esprit,* 4 (1971), 614–615.
[46]*The Pleasure of the Text,* trans. Richard Miller (New York: Hill and Wang, 1975), p. 7.

wants, attack the canonical structures of the language itself."[47] Here then is the beginning of Barthes's subversion of the classical notion of the work, and his treatment of the work as "text."

The concept (of the) "text" is a methodological hypothesis that, *as a strategy,* has the advantage of cutting across the traditional distinctions between reading and writing. The problem is not to move from the notion of writing to that of reading, nor from a theory of literature to a theory of reading. The problem consists in changing the level at which the "literary object" is perceived, in other words, in changing the level of perception so that writing and reading are conceived and defined *together.* This was the fundamental purpose of *S/Z:*[48] to uncover "text" (*du texte*) in an otherwise conventional narrative, and to use this notion to radicalize our perception of the literary object. In *S/Z* Barthes tried to accomplish this task by *rewriting* "Sarrasine" in a way that would block the accepted divisions writing/reading, uniting them into a single activity. "No *construction* of the text: everything signifies *ceaselessly and several times,* but without being delegated to a great final ensemble, to an ultimate structure."[49] The result of this strategy is a commentary which, first, altogether transforms the short story "Sarrasine" from a conventional work to a text deploying itself as linguistic and semiotic material, and second, produces a mutation in the way we traditionally conceive of the production of meaning; hence the new concept of the text as productivity, or as Kristeva would have it "productivity *qua* text."[50]

"From Work to Text" attempts to present the articulations of the "theory" of this change of perception by which the literary object (which is clearly no longer an "object") moves from that of a formal, complete, organic whole to that of a "methodological field," a concept whose very premise implies the notions of activity, production, and transformation. It is not a question of bringing disciplines into contact with one another, but rather of

[47]Ibid., pp. 30–31.
[48]*S/Z*, trans. Richard Miller (New York: Hill and Wang, 1974). *S/Z* was written at the same time as "From Work to Text" and illustrates in practice the methodological hypotheses developed in this essay.
[49]Ibid., p. 12 (my emphasis).
[50]Julia Kristeva's "La Productivité dite texte" is the title of one of her articles in *Semiotikè: Recherches pour une sémanalyse* (Paris: Seuil, 1969).

breaking them down in order to produce something new: the field (of the) "text" becomes possible only as a result of a mutation in traditional modes of knowledge: "Interdisciplinary work is not a peaceful operation: it begins *effectively* when the solidarity of the old disciplines breaks down ... to the benefit of a new object and a new language, neither of which is in the domain of those branches of knowledge that one calmly sought to confront .... There now arises a need for a new object, one attained by the displacement or overturning of previous categories. This object is the *Text.*" An indefinite field in permanent metamorphosis, where language is ceaselessly at work, the text offers a new economy in which no one language is privileged over any other. It is the utopian meeting place of subject and language, a *working* space ("... *the text is only experienced in an activity, a production*" where meaning is in permanent flux and where the author is either an effect or a "guest" of the text and not its originator.

An important corollary to Barthes's concept of text(uality) is that the distinction between criticism and literature loses its pertinence. It would be a mistake to read Barthes's essay as providing a theory of the text in the traditional sense which the word "theory" implies. The concept, "text," implies rather that any theory of the text *is itself text.* Criticism is criticism only insofar as it is understood as an experience of language (that is, as text), and hence it loses its specificity as criticism: "[The text's] model being a productive (and no longer a representative) one, it demolishes any criticism which, once produced, would mix with it: to rewrite ... [the text] ... would consist only in disseminating it, in dispersing it within the field of infinite difference."[51] Thus, all types of literary activity, whether "primary" (literature) or "secondary" (criticism), become indistinguishable and are experienced only as forms of production.

III

La science ... une encyclopédie à l'ombre des épées.
                                        —Michel Serres

Foucault stands apart from those who view the text as a "return of language" (Stephen Heath's expression) and from the

[51] *S/Z*, p. 5.

whole methodology accompanying this kind of textual analysis. His project appears radically different: to show that writing is the activation of a multiplicity of forces and that the text is where the struggle among these forces takes place. Foucault denounces textual isolationism, which, in his view, consists either of eliminating all extratextual factors related to the text or of reducing them to a textual function. The very notions of deconstructive criticism and of textual energy as productivity, both of which ascribe to language an autonomy apart from all historical and social frames of reference, amount for Foucault to the further elaboration of the ideology that has engendered the forms of knowledge (and hence the strategies of power) prevalent since the Classical age.

> Today Derrida is the most decisive representative of the [Classical] system in its final brilliance; the reduction of discursive practice to textual traces; the elision of the events that are produced there in order to retain nothing but marks for a reading; the invention of voices behind texts in order not to have to analyze the modes of implication of the subject in discourse; assigning the spoken and the unspoken in the text to an originary place in order not to have to reinstate the discursive practices in the field of transformations where they are effected.
> I do not say that it is a metaphysics, metaphysics itself or its closure, which is hidden in this "textualization" of discursive practices. I shall go much further: I shall say that it is a trifling, historically well-determined pedagogy which very visibly reveals itself.[52]

Beyond contributing to the dissolution of the notion of subject as origin and center of discourse, Foucault, by asking the question "what is an author?" poses as well, in relation to discourse, the question of power. Even though this problematic is not thoroughly outlined, it nevertheless becomes clear by the end of the essay that Foucault is in fact speaking only of power, in particular discursive power, and of the way in which it is exer-

[52]Michel Foucault, *Histoire de la folie* (Paris: Gallimard, 1972), p. 602. Gayatri Spivak, in her introduction to *Of Grammatology* (p. lxi), provides the Derridean point of view on this particular passage of Foucault. Cf. also on this topic Foucault's more general remarks in the description of his Collège de France course "History of Systems of Thought" in his collection of essays *Language, Counter-Memory, Practice,* trans. and ed. Donald F. Bouchard (Ithaca: Cornell University Press, 1977), pp. 199–204.

cised *concretely:* its field of application, its specificity, its techniques, and its tactics.

Foucault's major strategic insight in this essay lies in his displacing the question of power from the economic realm to that
of fiction, and his showing in detail how the figure of the author
imposes on meaning certain forms of repression which participate in the very economy of power. From Foucault's perspective,
it is no longer a matter of envisioning power as the simple reflection of a social structure: "power is not an institution, and it is
not a structure, it is not a certain power with which certain people are endowed; it is the name one gives to a complex, *strategic
situation* in a given society."[53] In this "complex, *strategic situation,*"
discourse is at once the object of the struggle for domination and
the means by which the struggle is waged: hence the centrality of
the question of the author, of the meaning and the functioning
of this notion, in its relation to discourse.

The author, according to Foucault, is neither simply an individual who writes a work, nor a speaking subject, neither an
individual with a particular social status, nor the supervisor of a
discourse. The author is a certain dimension, or more precisely,
a function by which certain discourses in a given society are
characterized. Foucault's hypothesis dramatically reverses the
tables: indeed, if the author is in truth only a certain mode—
among others—of the functioning of discourse, then he is but a
function which is added to or grafted onto discourse, but *one* of
the dimensions of discourse and not, as the traditional conception would have it, the absolute originator of discourse.

After showing why the authorial function can be understood
only from a relativist perspective, Foucault pursues his reflections in the literary realm, asking himself what the function of
the author is in fictional discourse. A meticulous demonstration
enables him to establish that the author is the function that introduces, in the work of fiction, principles of reality, of truth,
of noncontradiction, of causality, and finally, of order. "[The
author] is a certain functional principle by which, in our culture, one limits, excludes, and chooses; in short, by which one
impedes the free circulation, the free manipulation, the free
composition, decomposition, and recomposition of fiction."

[53]Michel Foucault, *La Volonté de savoir* (Paris: Gallimard, 1976), p. 123.

Foucault's essay, as it appears in this anthology, is the second version of an essay which was published, under the same title, in the *Bulletin de la Société Française de Philosophie*.[54] It is worth focusing on the difference between the two versions, which appears in the essays' concluding pages. Whereas the *Bulletin* version concludes with some general considerations on the necessity for future discursive typologies, the version herein ends on a political note. This divergence is crucial to an understanding of Foucault's work in that it reveals the shift from his former fascination with phenomena of language to his more recent politico-historical work. (I refer here to *Discipline and Punish* and *La Volonté de savoir*.) There is indeed a shift, and yet, in many ways, the same problematic—that of discourse—remains at the heart of Foucault's questioning.

But what exactly does discourse mean for Foucault? First, discourse is a vehicle or an instrument of knowledge. Second, the truth of a discourse lies as much in what it says as in the strategies it brings into play. The question thus has to do not only with the meaning of a discourse but with one's intention in using discourse. Third, discourse and power are related in a complex manner. To speak is, above all, to possess the power to speak. Power and discourse are established in and by the same act, any seizure of power being also an appropriation of discourse. Thus, claims Foucault, discourse is like everything else in our society: the object of a struggle for power. Yet there is a difference, for discourse is not only an object of power but, as he has shown in the course of his lengthy work, the decisive stake of power. It is therefore a question, in fact, as we noted earlier, of the two sides of a single problematic: in the words of Bernard-Henri Lévy, "the archeology of knowledge is but the obverse of a geneology of power."[55] If discourse, as discourse of knowledge, is an instrument for the exercise of power, then conversely, the exercise of power constantly creates new forms and new objects of knowledge which themselves engender and consolidate certain modes of power.

It is from this perspective that one should understand the

[54]*Bulletin*, 63 (1969). An excellent translation of this text appears in *Language, Counter-Memory, Practice*, pp. 113–138.
[55]*Le Magazine Littéraire*, 101 (1975), 9.

importance of "What Is an Author?" and especially of its last pages. The authorial function is but an additional instrument for the exercise of a knowledge whose only politics is that of power. The author is "a functional principle by which, in our culture, one limits, excludes, and chooses"; as a principle of order and selection, he is a principle of power, but one which is always presented—and this is the ultimate strategy of power—as being only an instrument of knowledge. The author is put forward, not as a legislator (in the punitive sense) of fiction, but as a theoretical source of knowledge, as an inspirational model for other disciplines. In "The Discourse on Language" Foucault had mapped out the reasons behind the disciplinary measures by which Western societies have traditionally enclosed discourse. "In every society the production of discourse is at once controlled, selected, organized and redistributed according to a certain number of procedures, whose role is to avert its powers and dangers, to cope with chance events, to evade its ponderous, awesome materiality."[56] The author is yet another, more subtle precautionary measure whose function is to control, censure, and police the excesses of the polysemic discourse of fiction. But fiction will go on speaking, will continue to disturb the order of the world. "The question then becomes: How can one reduce the great peril, the great danger with which fiction threatens our world? The answer is: One can reduce it with the author."

In a manner similar to Foucault's, Edward Said deplores the strategy which claims for textuality a privileged stake in the production of meaning. He criticizes the critics devoted to exclusive textual phenomena for their lack of concern about the text's situation in the world.

> Our interpretive worldly-wisdom has been applied, in a sense, to everything except ourselves; we are brilliant at deconstructing the mystifications of a text, at elucidating the blindness of a critical method, but we have seemed unable to apply these techniques to the very life of texts in the world, their materiality, their capacity for the production of misery or liberation, their monumentality as

---

[56]"The Discourse on Language" in *The Archeology of Knowledge*, trans. A. M. Sheridan Smith (New York: Pantheon, 1972), p. 216.

Foucault has spoken of it. As a result we are mesmerized by the text, and convinced that a text is only a text, without realizing how saying that is not only naive, it is worldly-blind.[57]

Said's thesis is that texts turn as much out to the world as they turn inward to textuality, and that to privilege the one over the other is to overlook a text's way of being. "Texts," he writes in his essay, "have ways of existing, both theoretical and practical that even in their more rarefied form are always enmeshed in circumstance, time, place, and society—in short they are in the world, and hence are worldly." Texts are in the world in a *material* sense first of all; they are subjected to the same legal, political, economic, and social constraints as any other cultural product. The understanding of a text consists first of all of placing it in its proper sociopolitical configuration, in having the text confront its historical context, and in calling on a broad anthropological tradition. Hence the questions of placement, situation, and cultural diffusion that Said raises about texts and their relationships to the "world": how a text was produced, how it confirms, justifies, or modifies what came before it, how it reveals what is contemporaneous with it, or what is taking place at the same time in adjacent disciplines; how a text is transmitted or preserved, how institutions accept, modify, or reject it, and in turn, what kind of influence a text can exert on these same institutions which have produced it.

In this same vein, or more precisely as a consequence of his belief in a dialectical relationship between text and culture, Said remarks that to insist upon "the limitlessness of interpretation" (as has been the case with theorists of textuality) is to disregard a text's decisive claim on actuality—its participation in shaping the conditions of production of the interpretive activity which bears upon it. "Texts impose restraints and limits upon their interpretation.... Texts are in the world, but also... one of their functions as texts is to *place* themselves... they *are* themselves by acting, in the world. Moreover, their manner of doing this is to place restraints upon what can be done with (and to) them interpretively." Then, moving one step further, Said discusses the

[57]"Interview with Edward Said," *Diacritics*, 6:3 (1976), 41.

"other side" of the relationship between texts and the culture
that supports and surrounds them: if on the one hand, texts
cannot escape the linguistic, economic, and sociopolitical (as well
as textual) pressures culture exerts on them, on the other hand,
some texts have the power to (re)shape reality by virtue of their
being in the world. Said shows Marx's *Eighteenth Brumaire of Louis
Bonaparte* to be such a text. It is a text that is not only enmeshed
in historical circumstances, but which, by textualizing the events
it describes, provides a different "world historical situation with
circumstances otherwise hidden." Hence Marx's text is an unusual example of an historical text that has acquired such a claim
on actuality that it has become more "real" than history itself.

Said's recent polemical study of the intellectual and political
history of "Orientalism" (that is, the Orient made into a textual
phenomenon) provides an even more dramatic illustration of
the power of texts to shape reality. Here is Said's description of
the process by which a series of texts—Orientalist discourse—
have affected the course of history by the sheer force of their
presence, thus transforming the Oriental from a human and
historical entity into a textual specimen:

> A major part of my study has been the way in which Orientalist
> texts are attempts at textual reconstruction of the Orient, as if the
> "real" or actual Orient ought not by itself to be admitted into
> Western consciousness . . . .
> The focus of interest in Orientalism for me has been the
> partnership between a discursive and archival textuality and
> worldly power, one as an index and refraction of the other. As a
> systematic discourse, Orientalism is written knowledge, but be-
> cause it is in the world and directly about the world, it is *more* than
> knowledge: it is power since, so far as the Oriental is concerned,
> Orientalism is the operative and effective knowledge by which he
> was delivered textually to the West, occupied by the West, milked
> by the West for his resources, humanly quashed by the West.[58]

Toward the end of the essay included here Said extends his
discussion of the "worldliness" of texts to that of criticism
proper. The great failing of modern critics in Said's view is the
uprooting of their critical work from the historical and cultural

[58]Ibid., p. 41.

realities that affect and shape it: "Contemporary criticism achieved its methodological independence by forfeiting an active situation in the world."[59] A predictable consequence of this situation is that criticism is traditionally viewed as an idealized activity, impervious to worldly circumstances. Against this quietistic critical ideology, defined solely in terms of abstract static categories, (aesthetic, psychological, and others), Said advocates an active role for criticism: "rather than being defined by the silent past, commanded by it to speak in the present, criticism, no less than any other text, is the present in the course of its articulation, struggles for definition, attempts at overcoming."

Thus criticism should help shape the process of human history. Criticism is worldly and its task is to challenge dominant value systems—sociopolitical and aesthetic ones—in order to articulate and actualize, to find and expose, differing modes of thought and different aesthetic experiences. For Said, then, the ultimate role and function of criticism is to provide a politics of textual decolonization in the sociopolitical realm, and in the domain of literary production, to contribute new aesthetic values by which (in the words of Wilde as quoted by Said), criticism "treats the work of art as a starting point for a new creation."[60]

The issue of power also arises in the texts of Michel Serres and Louis Marin. Following two different paths, their essays question several of the modalities of domination: how can a discourse derive its power from the legitimacy it claims for itself? Or else, in what way is the rationality of a given system of order—viewed from any angle, whether moral, logical, sociopolitical, or economic—nothing but a rationalization of power?

Michel Serres, who is primarily a philosopher-historian of science (but who does not hesitate, when the subject calls for it, to transcend the traditional divisions between ancient science, philosophy, literature, and modern science[61]) shows how the

[59]Said, "Roads Taken and Not Taken in Contemporary Criticism," *Contemporary Literature,* 17 (1976), 334.

[60]Oscar Wilde, *The Artist as Critic* (New York: Vintage, 1970), p. 347.

[61]See especially Serres's work on Zola and nineteenth-century thermodynamic theories (*Zola: Feux et signaux de brume* [Paris: Grasset, 1976]) and Lucretius and the scientific theories of antiquity (*Fleuves et turbulences: La physique de Lucrèce* [Paris: Minuit, 1977]).

classifications and the divisions that science has established as
natural always lead back to sociopolitical realities of power and
domination. The philosophico-scientific demand for the rational
as a universal phenomenon—"the order of reason," he writes, "is
only a particular exemplar of order in general"—is not an innocent project for science. It brings up an epistemological question
of primary importance. Why has science, from its very beginnings, been linked to war and struggles for mastery? Science is
destined to violence in Serres's analysis because it allies itself, at
its origin, with requirements of order that are determined by
power relationships. Serres explores the subtle epistemology of
these power relationships through an analysis of the fable "The
Wolf and the Lamb." He elaborates at a first level, through the
models of the fable, an ordered structure which reflects relative
strategic positions in the flow of power: *majorant, minorant,
maximus.* From mathematics to metaphysics, from physics to law,
and from La Fontaine's *Fables* to Descartes's *Meditations,* Serres
uncovers the same structure: the search for a maximum which
determines the ultimate winner in the game of power.

In the latter part of his essay, Serres pursues his analysis of
knowledge in the Classical age as a martial game regulated by
game theory. Bacon was the first to have called upon us to become the masters and possessors of nature. Baconian science was
defined by a command-obedience, a master-slave, relationship:
"One commands nature only by obeying it. This is probably a
political ideology—betrayed by the *prosopopeia*—which implies
practices of ruse and subtlety: in short, a whole strategy. Since
nature is stronger than we are, we must bend to its law, and it is
through this subterfuge that we dominate it." But in this Baconian
political ruse—which is also a moral, philosophical, and economic
ruse—there is in truth no last word, no judge, and no decisive
master. The relative can be stronger than the absolute. Enter
Descartes, and the nature of the game changes dramatically.
The instability of the moves is replaced by fixed magisterial relationships. The object of Cartesian strategy is to single out a term
which will escape the relative nature of the relationship in order
to dominate all the relations.

Baconian physics made science into a duel, a combat, a struggle for
domination: it gave it an agonistic model, proposing a form of ruse

for it so that the *weak one* would triumph . . . . But Baconian reason is a weak reason which loses at least the first round, because it first resigns itself to obedience. Descartes rejects this, and, consequently, he suppresses the loss. In the relationship of agonistic forces between ourselves and the exterior world, he seeks the means that will permit us to win at every move. "The reason of the strongest is *always* the best." The best reason *always* permits a winning game.

Knowledge then becomes a victorious hunt, and method a strategy that consists in maximizing one's moves in an absolute fashion. La Fontaine: "The reason of the strongest is *always* the best"; Descartes's universal quantificator: in order to obtain "a *more* certain and *more* evident knowledge than *all* the knowledge I had earlier . . . I [Descartes] shall *always* follow this path"; and finally, Serres: "the foundation of modern science is in this word, *always*. Science is a game, an infinite game, in which we *always* win." The epistemological project of the Classical age resides in this maximization. And it is precisely out of this schema that the fields of knowledge known today as the exact sciences—optics, dioptrics, probability theory, and so on—have evolved. We are thus living today the consequences of the wolfish strategies at play in La Fontaine's *Fables* whereby Classical knowledge and modern science have transformed "force into factual necessity and obedience into an inevitable law . . . . And this is why, since Rousseau, *one no longer hesitates to invoke science in the realm of law, power and politics. It is because science has already pointed the way to the winning strategy.*"

Marin's approach is all the more interesting in that his complex semiological analysis of Pascal's text is conducted in a structuralist vein. However, the specific thrust of his project—deconstructing the operation of representation so as to reveal the ideology that informs it—is indeed a post-structuralist concern. This situation, at the juncture of two critical moments, is characterized in Marin's writing by his attempt to develop a semiotic practice that is aware of its own trappings and thus works at exposing its own ideological grounding.

Marin's objective in the present essay is to question the Classical tradition of thinking and the forms—linguistic, philosophical, and ideological—it takes, while avoiding reinscribing his own critical discourse in the very ideology of knowledge he questions.

He is well aware of the dilemma inherent in any theory which attempts to deconstruct the ideology of representation, namely, that such a theory is itself an ideological representation and thus belongs to the domain being criticized. "It is not by constructing a model of a model, by raising the notion of representation to a higher power, that we break out of its circle. Perhaps our only chance in this game of reflecting representations is to restore, as in a catoptric, certain inverted images and to place them in a clearer perspective.[62] Thus, rather than attempting to escape the realm of representation, we must agree, *up to a point,* to maintain ourselves in it. Within this problematic, Marin's strategy is to attempt a deconstruction of the system of representation through a double operation: by producing simultaneously a theory of representation which belongs to the system of representation *and* a critique of this theory which deconstructs the notion of representation at the very moment of elaborating it. Marin's essay finds its angle of attack in a text that satisfies both these conditions: Pascal's *The Three Discourses on the Condition of the Great.* Marin focuses on the narrative of *The First Discourse,* in which a castaway is thrown by a tempest onto an island whose king has just been lost. Because the castaway resembles the lost king, he is mistaken for him by the inhabitants of the island. After some hesitation, the castaway decides to accept his good fortune but *without* forgetting his true state of being. He acts as a king but continues to think of himself as a castaway, "conceal[ing] the latter thought, and reveal[ing] the other. It was by the former that he [dealt] with the people, and by the latter that he [dealt] with himself."[63]

   This parabolic narrative develops three interrelated questions, which Marin discusses in his essay: (1) a theory of discourse that consists of a description of ordinary language and a criticism of this language; (2) a theory of political discourse that turns out to be exemplary of Classical discourse in general; and (3) a model of the general structure of Classical representation, that shows

---

[62]Louis Marin, *La Critique du discours* (Paris: Minuit, 1975), p. 21. This remark refers of course to Marx's definition of ideology in *The German Ideology.*

[63]Pascal, *Discourses on the Condition of the Great,* in *Blaise Pascal,* ed. Charles W. Eliot (New York: P. F. Collier, 1910), p. 383.

how it is also a model of the production of ideology. A few words on each of these points might be useful here.

(1) The castaway's narrative shows us that the thought by which he deals with himself cancels out the action by which he deals with the others. This thought does not cancel out the action *qua* action, since the castaway acts toward himself as a castaway, but it annuls it in its intrinsic value because he feels that his behavior is that of a usurper. However, since he cannot escape from the constraints of representation (his "look-alike" status), the castaway decides to go along "up to a point" with the people's opinions. Thus he is going to act according to the people's expectations, but at the same time he will adhere to an order that goes beyond the realm of representation. He will behave as if the opinions of the people were true, but will have a *thought in the back of the mind,* a thought which is a strategic force that he uses in order to go beyond the order of representation though without leaving it.

The thought in the back of the mind is the locus of a contradiction: it is a judgment that the castaway makes about himself that cancels out his action, a judgment which contradicts the castaway's political action and yet allows it to remain intact—the castaway continues to act as a king. Proceeding from this paradox, Marin shows how the thought in the back of the mind hollows out ordinary discourse, decentering it from the subject which formulates it, "in order to make [it] into a speech 'totally other' without modifying its form." Thus the thought in the back of the mind provides for a theory of discourse which both explains the mechanics that constitute ordinary language and offers a critique of it: it is possible to speak like the people, but ordinary discourse is not that of truth, for it is only in the operation of the thought in the back of the mind that its true meaning appears.

(2) The thought in the back of the mind is exemplary of the structure of political discourse; thus it becomes in Pascal's discourse a political maxim, in so far as the castaway-become-king is a model of the politically astute man. At first, the narrative bases its commentary on mere chance and a relationship of resemblance (castaway-king) to show that there are no rational, natural, or causal relationships that hold in sociopolitical reality.

But this is not to say that everything in the political realm functions according to a representational relationship based only on resemblance. In fact, if the people in the narrative honor the castaway on account of his resemblance with the lost king, it is only because they transform the representational relationship into a relationship of identity. Thus, by way of a double operation of representation, a (false) relationship of resemblance is "transformed into an ontological identity." The people believe in the castaway as their *true* king according to a political model of the sign in which illusion becomes truth, which means, in political terms, that nobility has a natural right to what it possesses, be it kingship or wealth.

(3) If one were to formalize the general structure of representation, one would obtain two simultaneous operations of repetition and substitution between the thing and the idea through the mediation of the sign, what Foucault calls an operation of "duplicated representation."[64] First substitution: the reality (referent: true king) is reproduced in the form of a sign (Signifier/Signified: look-alike/king); second substitution—which is a repetition, in reverse, of the first operation: the sign substitutes itself for reality (new referent: look-alike *as* king). Thus the fiction signals "the *ideological* operation of representation by which the idea of reality, its reproduced sign, is taken for reality itself." Marin gives us an insightful analysis of how the representational relationship which sustains the astute man's discourse is the model of production of ideology, of an ideology which serves, in turn, as the foundation and philosophical justification of the Classical theory of the sign.

"Power of Signs—Signs of Power"[65] reads the subtitle of another of Marin's articles. It is an eloquent summary not only of Marin's analysis of Pascal's parable, but in a way, of a whole line of thinkers—from Michel Foucault to Michel Serres—who discuss the strategies of discourse in its relationship to power and knowledge and to politics and science.

---

[64]"From the Classical age, the sign is the *representativity* of the representation in so far as it is *representable.*" In *The Order of Things,* p. 65. On the general subject of Classical representation see pp. 63-67.

[65]*"Puss-in-boots:* Power of Signs—Signs of Power," *Diacritics,* 7:2 (1977), 54.

IV

All *a priori* theories of representation, whether religious or philosophical, constitute obstacles in the path of a radical de-mythification.

—René Girard

If the role of Derridean criticism has been to denounce the illusion of a full presence or plenitude of being in Western metaphysics, Deleuze's criticism takes as its task to speak of the "extra-being" as the locus of the production of thought. Deleuze unfolds his analysis in the context of the Stoic philosophy of the incorporeal event and of those texts produced in schizophrenic discourse. On the one hand he pursues the logic of Lewis Carroll in the light of the philosophical writings of the Stoics, and on the other, he displays the catalogue of a series of linguistic experiences as they appear in the work of Antonin Artaud and in the verbal productions of a schizophrenic language student, Louis Wolfson.

Deleuze's interest in these "authors" is in keeping with the general post-structuralist concern with a critique of the closure of the sign. Against Plato and the ensuing Western tradition which sees in meaning the origin, matrix, and principle according to which reality is comprehended, Deleuze posits Carrollian forms of *non-sense* as a privileged approach to an "other" theory of meaning, a theory for which, in Deleuze's terms "meaning is never principle or origin, it is product. It is not something to be discovered, restored, or reused, it is something to be produced by new mechanisms."[66] Deleuze finds these "mechanisms" in the language of incorporeal meaning and it is through this grid that he interprets Carroll's writings. It is not my purpose to retrace the masterly pages of *Logique du sens* on this topic, but rather to characterize succinctly Deleuze's import for the post-structuralist critique of the sign.

A logic of the incorporeal event provides an alternative approach to traditional theories of the sign. Whereas the structure of the sign has been made to depend traditionally on a general

---

[66] *Logique du sens* (Paris: Minuit, 1969), pp. 89–90.

theory of representation, the incorporeal event substitutes for the ternary logic of the sign (signifier, signified, referent) a quaternary logic: expression, designation, signification, and meaning. The sign is no longer the pure and simple connection, whether arbitrary, fixed, individual, or collective, between that which signifies and that which is signified; but it functions according to logical parameters, concepts of time, and a grammar of "the verb," all of which are differently centered.[67] Thus the statement "John is sick," for instance, *expresses* a belief I hold, *designates* John's physical state, *signifies* or affirms a manner of being, and has in addition an intangible *meaning* (a pure expressed): to be sick. It is this Stoic model that Deleuze applies to Carroll's writings in an attempt to explain the organization of Carrollian language. But, more important, in so doing, Deleuze uses the Stoic concept of the *thought-event* to challenge accepted philosophies of signification and to circumvent the constraints of representational thought on the sign.

If the production of meaning is at the center of Carroll's endeavor and thus of his modernity, then Artaud's and Wolfson's "madness" provide Deleuze with a critical, and clinical, insight into the techniques of producing meaning. As Deleuze puts it, the problem of madness is directly related to that of the production of meaning: "The problem is a clinical one: that of the displacement from one mode of organization to another, or of the formation of a progressive and creative disorganization. The problem is also one of criticism, that is, of determining differential levels at which change occurs in the form of non-sense, in the nature of portmanteau words, in the dimension of language as a whole." To this end, Deleuze deals in the latter part of his essay with Wolfson's complex relationship to language, analyzing the linguistic operations by which the schizophrenic attempts to resplice his split self together.

All his life, Wolfson has felt under attack by his mother. Whenever she speaks, her words penetrate him and hurt him

---

[67]Our editorial parenthesis in Deleuze's essay and related footnotes discuss this problem. The best study of this aspect of Deleuze's work is Foucault's "Theatrum Philosophicum" in his *Language, Counter-Memory, Practice,* pp. 165–196, especially pp. 172–176.

profoundly, to the point at which everything that belongs to her linguistic register—the mother's tongue is English—becomes unbearable and destructive to his being. In order to shield himself from the painful splinters of English words, Wolfson develops a "survival kit" consisting of a highly sophisticated arsenal of linguistic strategies. He studies four foreign languages (French, German, Russian, and Hebrew) so as to be able to convert instantaneously—but according to precise rules of decoding and encoding—all English words into foreign words. All of Wolfson's effort goes toward having at his disposal a system of equivalences and rules of transformation which guard him from any possible penetration by the English language. He must prepare for all eventualities, fill in all the gaps, transform everything, leave no English signifier adrift; he must construct a system of conversion and translation which will allow him *always* to cross from the dangerous English side to the safer interlingual space provided by the continuum of the four other languages.

I will not insist on the formal aspect of the schizophrenic transformative rules; Deleuze studies them in his essay and has done so in even greater detail in his introduction to Wolfson's writings.[68] It is important, nevertheless, to point out that Deleuze's merit lies in his having distinguished the two sides of the theoretical question that Wolfson's schizophrenic practice raises. First, what does the Wolfsonian linguistic machine, which takes over its own conditions of production and its signifying structures, explain about the genesis of meaning? And second, how does this machine, which simultaneously converts signifiers and signifieds into something *almost identical* to what they are but articulated on a radically *different mode* of the sign, participate in a critique of the economy of the sign?

Clearly, there will be no "breakthrough" in Wolfson's case, but no matter how unsuccessful his attempt "must" remain, nevertheless his practice of dismembering the sign so as to form an *other* sign, is a most serious attempt at contesting the classical economy of the sign and of meaning. Not only does Wolfson question language's normative conventions, but he openly con-

[68]"Schizologie," preface to Louis Wolfson's *Le Schizo et les langues* (Paris: Gallimard, 1970).

tests the prescriptive codes that govern the functioning of the sign. In so doing he also poses in a most articulate manner the problem of meaning in schizophrenic discourse: a meaning which can be fixed neither in the word nor in the totality of discourse, but which is adumbrated in the process of transforming a codified discourse into a skewed discourse. In Deleuze's hands, the impossible adventure of Wolfson provides a powerful document on the functioning of schizophrenic language within a general economy of meaning.

Where Deleuze chooses psychoanalysis and philosophy for critical coordinates, Girard situates his theory at the point where anthropology joins classical Greek tragedy. And whereas Deleuze circumvents representation by taking the Stoic's route, Girard undercuts it by choosing for his problematic a domain of application that maximizes referentiality. Mimetic phenomena such as victimage and scapegoating are understood as *real and originating* events, thus implying that in his cultural scheme mimesis precedes representation and sign systems.

Girard's theoretical thought is situated at the crossroads of the Derridean and Lévi-Straussian problematics. Whereas structural anthropology proposes solutions of a formal nature in its study of mental states and myths, Girard tends to displace the limits of ethnology by assigning to it the task of dealing with the (traditionally) "philosophical" questions of origin and meaning.

For Girard, relations between men are regulated by a mechanism of imitation and mimetic rivalry. At the outset he posits an a priori mimetic impulse separate from any "desired" object. The movement of the mimetic process is to go from the mimetic impulse (the desire to imitate a "model") to mimetic appropriation (the desire to appropriate the object that the "other," by appropriating it himself, designates as desirable).

> The desiring mimesis precedes the appearance of its object . . . . In the limiting case, mimesis engenders the object, although as seen from the outside, mimesis always appears as a triangular configuration whose three summits are occupied respectively by the two rivals and their common object. The object always moves into the foreground and the mimesis hides behind it, even to the eyes of

the desiring subjects. [But] it is the convergence of the desires which determines the object.[69]

Thus the "desiring mimesis" occurs first, followed by the "designation" of the object which receives the status of coveted object and becomes automatically the point of contention between the two rival protagonists (the model-become-rival and his imitator). From then on, the elements of the system react ceaselessly to one another. The more one of the protagonists desires the object, the more the other desires it. As mimetic fascination gets stronger and stronger, desire breaks away from the object and fixes its attention on the rival protagonist, so that at the height of the crisis, both protagonists lose sight altogether of the object, and the conflict becomes purely and simply a mimetic one (each protagonist serving as the other's model). Mimetic rivalry feeds violence, which in turn increases mimesis, and so on. As the rivalries become more and more symmetrical, they become increasingly violent as well. This situation of reciprocal violence is, to paraphrase Girard, one of constant mirror effects, in which the rival protagonists become each other's *doubles*[70] and lose their individual identities.

Imagine a further escalation of the conflict. Enter a third, fourth, or nth individual, to the point where the whole community becomes polarized: each participant will take a side in the conflict. Ultimately, however, all will "gang up" against one. Thus the reciprocal violence of the *doubles* is transformed into the unanimous violence of all against one. This scapegoating process, the shift from reciprocal to unilateral violence, when mimetic hostility is mobilized against one individual, constitutes for Girard the cultural mechanism by which the human community is founded. It is therefore at the origin of the cultural system that one must place mimetic desire and violence: mimetic violence, crisis, and then reconciliation of the community at the

[69]René Girard, "Système du délire," *Critique,* 306 (1972), 964.

[70]The situation of doubles in Girard's system occurs when two (real) individuals become caught in the circle of reciprocal violence, with each in a situation of *méconnaissance,* thus "misreading" the symmetry of his actions in relationship to the other.

expense of a scapegoat (the surrogate victim) constitute the genesis of social institutions.

Two important remarks need to be made at this point. First, the choice of the victim is arbitrary. Indeed, since all instances of mimetic violence are symmetrical, all victims are identical. Insofar as all the participants are one another's *doubles* in the heat of the conflict, there is no significant reason why one individual rather than another should be designated as the responsible party. Thus in light of the real reasons that originally started the conflict, the choice of the victim must be regarded as arbitrary. Second, one should note that with regard to this conflict, it is not the result—victory or defeat of one or the other protagonist— that matters, but the *difference* (as the negation of reciprocity) which emerges from the struggle among the protagonists. Thus the surrogate victim is crucial in that it represents the entire community at the moment in which it breaks out of a situation of *doubles*, that is, at the point at which it escapes from a generalized and violent state of mimetism.

From a critical perspective, the Girardian genetic cultural model is important because it permits an explicit critique of the formalist tendencies of ethnological structuralism. Whereas Lévi-Strauss posits, at the origin, the notion of a differentiated dual structure (a system of binary oppositions), Girard's model operates from the notion of the *doubles*, that is, from the notion of an undifferentiated structure. In a sense, Girard's critique of Lévi-Strauss consists of showing that since, for ethnological structuralism, differentiation forms the basis of human thought, such an approach cannot explain the problematic of the undifferentiated crisis in its own terms. Indeed, for Lévi-Strauss this crisis means the dissolution of man and the collapse of thought. Girard argues, on the other hand, that on the basis of the problematic of mimetism and of the surrogate victim, one sees how social forms are founded on mimesis, how they collapse in mimetic crises, and how they reappear in new forms through the mechanism of the surrogate victim. It is worth noting that this is an operation that takes place on more than one level: if the surrogate victim is the model of *difference in the process of emergence,* then it is a model from which can be elaborated not only a theory of culture but also a theory of meaning (as meaning is produced in language through differences). Just as the mimetic crisis constitutes the collapse of the community and the death of meaning, the surrogate victim who brings about the redistribution of differences marks the production of meaning as well as the emergence of novel forms of social relations.

Girard retraces this view of a "total cultural crisis" in Shakespeare's tragedies. He is interested in Shakespeare's writings precisely because they operate beyond the parameters of structural analysis, moving away from a careful differential system and toward a dynamic model of mimetic undifferentiation. *A Midsummer Night's Dream* concerns the dangerous consequences of the mimesis of appropriation. The context is that of the festival, with the inversion and mixture of all the natural differences. The mimetic crisis spreads to the point where one can no longer see the difference between seasons or between characters.

> ... The spring, the summer,
> The childing autumn, angry winter, change
> Their wonted liveries, and the mazed world,
> By their increase now knows not which is which.
> [II.i.111-114]

But even more to the point, Girard sees his conception of cultural crisis reflected in a passage from *Troilus and Cressida,* namely, in Ulysses's famous speech on the concept of *degree.*[71] Here, Shakespeare reveals both the process and the results of the collapse of differences.

> ... O, when degree is shaked,
> Which is the ladder to all high designs,
> The enterprise is sick! How could communities,
> Degrees in schools, and brotherhoods in cities,
> Peaceful commerce from dividable shores,

[71]"Degree, from the Latin *gradus,* means a step, a measured distance, the necessary difference thanks to which two cultural objects, people, or institutions can be said to have a *being* of their own, an individual or categorical identity." René Girard, "The Plague in Literature and Myth," *Texas Studies in Literature and Language,* 15 (1974), 838.

> The primogenitive and due of birth,
> Prerogative of age, crowns, sceptres, laurels,
> But by degree, stand in authentic place?
> Take but degree away, untune that string,
> And, hark, what discord follows! Each thing meets
> In mere oppugnancy. . . .
>
> [I.iii.101-111]

The passage clearly reflects Lévi-Straussian thinking when it
says that cultural order is possible only on the basis of differentiated relationships, when it shows that difference and degree organize culture. And yet Shakespeare goes one step beyond Lévi-Strauss, and in Girard's direction, when he sees at the
basis of cultural order ("when degree is shaked") the violent
identity of the *doubles* in crisis. In Girard's version of Shakespeare's play, *A Midsummer Night's Dream* becomes the text of
culture and Shakespeare the master decoder of mimetic relationships.

                                    V

> Everything we do must be a repetition of the past with a
> difference.
>   —William Carlos Williams

   The other papers in this volume reflect interests along more
or less established—and, by now one hopes, recognizable—lines.
They have in common a number of features: in one form or
another they imply a critique of structuralism; they are less given
to generalization and abstraction than the ones previously discussed; they involve a critic discussing in the body of his text the
theoretical premises that govern his essay; and they tend to focus
their attention on more familiar literary figures (Flaubert, Yeats,
and Proust, Olson and Pound, Lautréamont, Valéry, and Mallarmé). I shall comment briefly on each contribution, indicating
how it fits in with the conceptual frameworks already analyzed.
   Donato, de Man, Riddel, and Vance illustrate and extend the
methods and aims of a deconstructive approach. Their readings
favor, on the whole, a Derridean problematic, but not without

giving it alternative orientations by entering into dialogue with other contemporary theorists.

Eugenio Donato's essay "The Museum's Furnace" sustains the most ambitious argument of any advanced in this volume. It presents a reading of *Bouvard and Pécuchet* as the cornerstone of a critique of representation which sets the stage for the passage from a Newtonian to a thermodynamic view of history. At the same time, it confronts methodologically three different problematics, as developed by Derrida, Said, and Serres, reorienting them toward what constitutes an original Flaubertian reading.

Donato's point of departure is an analysis of *Bouvard and Pécuchet* in terms of the metaphor of the *Encyclopedia-Library* which, since the work of Foucault and Hugh Kenner, has been at the center of modern interpretations of fiction. But Donato goes further, by underscoring that such a reading, despite its focus on linguistic and representational considerations, falls short of a radical critique of representation. If, on the one hand, many of the two bachelors' failures can be attributed to their confusion between the concept of encyclopedic knowledge which they adopt and the reality principle, on the other hand, some of their failures have nothing to do with the incapacity of linguistic or symbolic representation to account for reality. For example, as Donato points out, "when wind and rain destroy their fruit crops, or when a storm destroys their wheat crop, there is no way of accounting for the storm within any representational system." Donato's critique of representation thus starts with the question: is there any way to account for natural disaster within a problematic of representation? Can we reach the truth of things within *any* representational system?

On his way to an answer, Donato introduces the concept of the *Museum* (the Museum of Natural History), which he sees as the privileged epistemological operator bridging the gap between reality and its representation. The *Museum* is the concept through which the nineteenth century gives the *adequate* representation of human reality and history. Here, Donato presents a persuasive case against representation by showing the impossibility of reaching, through the *Museum*, "any truth, essence, or origin . . . [for] the museum can only display objects metonymically at least twice removed from that which they are originally supposed to represent or signify."[72] Furthermore, the concept of the *Museum* is doomed to failure because of the anthropocentrism of meaning: "If the *Museum* fails at reaching the nature and essence of the objects it displays, it is because it tries to understand them in relation to the spectator rather than in relation to the objects themselves."

The trajectory of history in which Donato inscribes Flaubert's work moves from classical mechanics to thermodynamics. Whereas the *Museum* and Newtonian physics depend epistemologically on the same schema—a spatial versus a temporal continuum— Flaubert's view of history is presented by Donato as rejecting the old temporality in favor of a temporality similar to that of the new physics. In keeping with the second principle of thermodynamics which states that energy goes irreversibly from a differentiated to an undifferentiated state—a process which abolishes differences, origins and temporality—Donato shows Flaubert's notion of history to depend upon "metaphors of decay, decadence, corruption; in a word, a notion of history based upon any metaphor that can be read as abolishing differences." He makes a powerful case for Flaubert's historical and epistemological nihilism in an essay that no doubt will transform the Flaubertian critical canon.

Paul de Man's "Semiology and Rhetoric" undertakes the analysis of the paradoxical discrepancies present in the figurative and grammatical processes of literary language. After briefly reviewing the "positive" developments in recent French semiological criticism, de Man strikes at the central question in the debate going on in contemporary poetics: literary semiologists use grammatical structures conjointly with rhetorical structures, as if passing from the one to the other where completely unproblematic. But, asks de Man, can these really function in

[72]To be precise, one could say that there is a *triple* metonymic displacement between objects displayed in a museum and their original meaning. They are metonymically selected *twice* (for example, a bone stands for a man—first synecdoche—who in turn stands for Man from that period—second synecdoche), and metonymically ordered *once* (two bones in *contiguous* display cases are supposed to signify the history of mankind from 2000 B.C. to 1000 B.C., for instance).

perfect continuity? Is the reduction of figure to grammar legitimate? And if not, how are we to distinguish the epistemology of
grammar from that of rhetoric?

The example of Edith Bunker (Archie Bunker's wife), inquir-
ing whether Archie wants his bowling shoes laced over or laced
under, with Archie's resulting anger at her collapsing of rhetoric
into grammar, provides the first step in de Man's deconstruction
of two coherent but incompatible readings. In this case, Archie's
answer, "what's the difference," meaning "it's all the same," is
taken literally by Edith who goes on to explain the difference,
indeed, between lacing over and lacing under! Yeats's poem
"Among School Children" serves as a second illustration of the
"rhetorization of grammar," to which a deconstructive reading
that ends up in indetermination is applied. De Man then trans-
fers the schema grammar/rhetoric to the act of reading and
interpretation and applies it to a passage from Proust that describes an experience of reading. Proust's example differs from
the previous two in that it deals with a rhetorical structure that
turns out to be dependent on grammatical patterns instead of a
grammatical structure which also functions rhetorically. What is
involved in a rhetorically conscious reading like that presented
in Proust's reading scene leads de Man to speculate on the nature of deconstruction: "The deconstruction is not something we
have added to the text; it constituted the text in the first place. A
literary text simultaneously asserts and denies the authority of its
own rhetorical mode,"[73] in order to conclude—rejoining Derrida on this point—that it is a necessity "to recognize the existence of the deconstructive moment as constitutive of all literary
language."

After showing that the "grammatization of rhetoric" ends up
also "suspended in the ignorance of its own truth or falsehood,"
de Man goes on to suggest in his final pages that it was literature,
before philosophy, which began the systematic dismantling of

[73]Cf. also de Man's *Blindness and Insight* (New York: Oxford University Press,
1971), p. 136: "working our way toward a definition . . . [we call] 'literary,' in the
full sense of the term, any text that implicitly or explicitly signifies its own
rhetorical mode and prefigures its own misunderstanding as the correlative of its
rhetorical nature; that is, of its 'rhetoricity.'"

the founding categories of metaphysics. Thus he concludes that the same pattern of deconstruction operative in Proust's text can be shown to occur in Nietzsche's critique of metaphysics.

Joseph Riddel's "Decentering the Image" is another essay, in support of the deconstructive stand, to adopt as methodology an analytical rhetoric that combines the language of literature (poetry) and of philosophy. "How to begin to find a shape—to begin to begin again?" With this opening line from William Carlos Williams, Riddel sets himself the task of developing the problematic of an "American" poetry in a line of American poets running from Emerson, who called for "a purely American idiom" to Olson, with his notion of "Projective Verse." Riddel links the question of a pure notion of beginnings that "American" literature poses itself— "a new writing that would repeat, yet be different from, a first writing, considering that the very notion of a first writing can only be represented in writing"—to the Derridean problematic which demystifies the notion of a "natural origin." In the course of his discussion of Olson, Eliot, Fenellosa, and Pound, Riddel uses Fenellosa's essay "The Chinese Written Character as a Medium for Poetry," which he sees as tying together one strain of American poetics, to provide the occasion for an unusual critical "exchange" between Hugh Kenner and Derrida on the status of Pound's ideogrammatic poetry. In branching out from this same question, Riddel argues that Pound's theory of the Image as "graphic play," by providing freedom from the "commanding origin," has made possible the emergence of the long modern poem.

But if on the one hand, it is the decentering of Imagism that puts into question what Riddel calls "the idea of the unified or autotelic text, or the thought of poetic closure," on the other, it is in Olson's attack on logocentrism that Riddel finds new grounds for a theory of poetic language. To this effect, he returns, toward the end of his essay, to an analysis of Olson's concept of "Projective Verse" in the light of Derrida's concept of writing, which results in a dramatic reappraisal of all the privileged figures that form Olson's project for a decentered "poetic line."

In keeping with recent critical methodologies, Eugene Vance brings to the *Song of Roland* an approach that combines modern philosophical notions of language—the philosophical problem, as posed by Derrida, of man's anguish before the sign—with a concept not unfamiliar to a Girardian problematic: the notion of communal commemoration.

A preponderant amount of the criticism of the *Roland,* since its rediscovery in the nineteenth century, has centered on questions of the poem's historical genesis, of its "unity," or of its style (an approach best exemplified by Auerbach). The transition from an oral to a written culture is also an area that has received much attention recently. But Vance sets himself off from all these critical approaches by showing the *Roland* to be "less a tragedy *in* language than a tragedy *of* language." In so doing, Vance demonstrates, through an original and perceptive analysis of the poem, that the historical "crisis" or tragedy that the *Roland* depicts doubles a deeper epistemological crisis that attended the passage from an oral (commemorative) to a written (*sign*ifying) culture; paradoxically, a passage from a fullness of meaning to a loss of it.

The essays by Hertz, Genette, and Riffaterre confront the problem posed by the relationship of form to content in "literary" language. Hertz's "Freud and the Sandman" raises the question of the centrality of literature by analyzing the place of "The Uncanny" in Freud's literary and psychoanalytic canon. Genette's discussion is concerned with a semiological definition of the literary phenomenon known as Cratylism, and Riffaterre's essay sheds a new light on Lautréamont and the production of literary language.

Neil Hertz's essay first addresses the question of the relationship between the figures of psychoanalytic discourse and the forces of desire, showing how the motifs of the uncanny and of repetition that appeared in Freud's writings were *at the same time* being played out in Freud's life. Starting with Freud's retelling of Hoffmann's story "The Sandman," and showing how Freud's narrative technique is very much a function of his emotional identification with the thematic concerns of the story, Hertz proceeds to juxtapose that identification with Freud's relationship to his colleague and follower Victor Tausk, described in Paul Roazen's account (*Brother Animal: The Story of Freud and Tausk*). We shall not go into Roazen's or Hertz's ideas about how the feelings of rivalry between Freud and Tausk were played out with the help, first of Lou Andreas-Salomé, and then of Helene Deutsch, who took—and then had to drop—Tausk as a patient while she herself was in analysis with Freud. Suffice it to say here that as a result of these complex triangular relationships, Tausk committed suicide on the eve of his marriage, at just about the same time that Freud announced to Lou Salomé that he had stumbled on a "remarkable notion"—a notion remarkable indeed since it turned out to be, as we can see in retrospect, his first postulation of the death instinct.

Examining the uncanny superposition of the sequence of triangular relations in "The Sandman" (Coppelius/Coppola—Nathanael—Klara/Olympia) on Roazen's sequence of triangles, Hertz demonstrates convincingly how chronology and thematics intertwined with Freud's theoretical concerns. Can the question of psychoanalysis—the probing of the forces of repetition and desire—be disentangled from the question of figurative language? In trying to do so, Hertz raises the critical question of the "documentary status" of psychoanalysis and that of "literary priority." Or, as Freud once said: "I invented psychoanalysis because it had no literature."

The adventure of the sign that was begun with Barthes, Derrida, and Deleuze continues with Genette. In the *Cratylus* of Plato, two theses on language confront each other. One, held by Hermogenes, would have it that names are a result of agreement and convention. The other, defended by Cratylus, affirms that a natural harmony exists between a person and the name he receives. This debate is the starting point for Genette's essay, which presents us with one version of the history of Cratylism in France. Genette distinguishes a certain number of versions—or degrees—of Cratylism, which he proceeds to analyze. He is concerned with a typology of Cratylism as it is illustrated by a particular group of examples, notably in the works of Mallarmé and Valéry—both of whom took up the idea of converting Cratylism into a theory of poetic language—but also in the writings of Claudel, Sartre, Proust, and Jakobson.

Genette's essay has two aims. On the one hand, he wants to explain Cratylism as a form of semiotic—or presemiotic—theory.

On the other hand, he is quick to remind us, as a balance to his theoretical project, that Cratylism is a thought "that is first and foremost the expression of a desire," and hence, the Cratylian project is also a personal project in which the linguistic *imagination* invents its own poetic world. This pleasure, which is evident in the relationship of every logophiliac to the sign, can be seen in Genette's writing. Poets, as well as critics of language, display a fascination with language's mimetic virtues, the same fascination recognizable in another logophiliac: Louis Wolfson. So similar, and yet so different. . . .

The final essay in this volume, "Generating Lautréamont's Text," is the work of Michael Riffaterre, the pioneer in structural stylistics. It is concerned with the nature and function of stylistics in an overall theory of literary language.

Riffaterre's major impact in the general field of literary studies comes from the fact that he displaces the locus of structuralist critical activity from the text to the space *between* text and reader: it is in the *apprehension* of the verbal process of a text by the reader that the significance and specificity of the text resides. Riffaterre uses readers' reactions as a point of departure for his stylistic analysis. His main contention is that one can grasp the literary phenomenon in its specificity only by describing the verbal combinations that catch the readers' attention. Since the language of the text always functions according to predictable language patterns, it can be assumed that when a stylistic element deviates enough from the pattern to catch the awareness of several readers, this is the result of a *pertinent stylistic device* particular to the text being studied. Although all texts use, stylistically speaking, a ready-made lexicon and an already tested collection of images, clichés, and stereotypes which give the readers "a feeling of *déjà-vu*," nevertheless, each text combines these elements in a unique manner. Each text obeys what Riffaterre calls "rules of textual idiolect," meaning that the style of a text is a prescriptive and limitative subcode, and it is this subcode that imposes itself on the readers' attention. Thus Riffaterre sees the verbal process that constitutes a text as being actualized along the lines predetermined by the system of the text. All the stylistic features present in a text converge toward the significance

selected by the system, and they "all function as structural variants of that obsessive, rapidly overwhelming semantic variant."[74]
In other words:

> The chief characteristic of a poetic text, as opposed to the purely
> cognitive use of language, is that while the text seems to progress
> from image to image, from episode to episode, it is in fact repeat-
> ing the same information. The text progresses syntactically and
> lexically, and it keeps adding meanings, but each step forward is
> actually a repetition of one significance. Each of these steps is only
> a transcodage of that significance from one means of expression to
> another. . . .The significance is found in the structure given by the
> text. Every subsequent transcodage is a variant of this structure.[75]

Riffaterre sets out to demonstrate the value of his stylistic practice in his essay on Lautréamont. Starting with the consistent
nature of readers' reactions to Lautréamont's poetic language,
Riffaterre gives us a powerful demonstration of how far
discourse analysis can go in formalizing phenomena generally
believed to extend beyond the jurisdiction of language. References to reality, mythological traditions, philosophical maxims,
religious themes, as well as all of the predictable literary
arsenal—*topoi,* themes, motifs—become subject, under Riffaterre's insightful guidance, to matrix analyses. In effect, his work
opens up the exciting possibility of a semantic stylistics whereby
the rules of formation of "literary" language can be explained.

VI

> [It is now] possible to understand once and for all that criti-
> cism creates its subject matter.
>
> —Edward Said

   To begin again: I have been talking at great length about
strategy in this introduction, but one talks about strategies
mostly when entering a fight. I have presented the various
critical strategies at play among contemporary theorists. It remains to inscribe these strategies in a more global framework, to

---

[74]"Interpretation and Descriptive Poetry," *New Literary History,* 4 (1973), 238.
[75]"The Self-sufficient Text," *Diacritics,* 3:3 (1973), 44.

put them in the ring of criticism as it were, and to determine how the rounds are to be scored. It is not a matter here of declaring one critic the winner and another the loser—in this game, everyone is eventually a loser—but of defining precisely what is at stake: in this case a definition of a post-modern critical attitude and a perspective on the critical implications it brings forth.

To make this point clearer, I would like to couch it in terms of Leo Spitzer's critical attitude. His is one of confidence in the text. His reading takes the text at face value: it hides nothing and has nothing to add beyond what it declares explicitly. This view of the text results in an interpretive activity which, in Jean Starobinski's words, "is only interested in moving from the explicit to the more explicit.... The critical operation is all-encompassing; it has no remainder. All is visible for the [critic] who knows how to read."[76] Such a critical stance is clearly of historical pertinence; it is a well-documented fact that "author" and "criticism" have developed together along institutionalized lines from the sixteenth century until the present day. Criticism—in the sense we have traditionally come to understand it—has provided its public with what every reader anxiously seeks in a work: a transparent communication, an order to things, an ideology, and a truth. Thus when it attempts to reconstruct and explain a work, criticism becomes a reassuring operation, as in the case of Spitzerian interpretation.

In contrast to this satisfied attitude, today's representative critical view is much more problematic. Witness Derrida, for instance: "A text is a text only if it conceals, from the first glance, from the first comer, the law of its composition and the rule of its game."[77] Such a conception of the text results in a critical attitude most clearly expressed by Girard: "To examine a work of art ... [is] to attempt to discover what the work *omits* as much as—if not more than—what it includes. That is surely the first step in any critical venture."[78] Indeed, to say that a text is constituted by concealment more than by revelation and that critical

[76]*La Relation critique* (Paris: Gallimard, 1972), pp. 52–53.
[77]*La Dissémination* (Paris: Seuil, 1972), p. 71.
[78]*Violence and the Sacred,* trans. Patrick Gregory (Baltimore: Johns Hopkins University Press, 1977), p. 207.

activity is structurally linked to this concealment, has two immediate corollaries, namely: (1) that critical activity does not
receive its legitimacy exclusively from the text being commented
upon, and (2) that critical discourse can no longer aim at completely mastering a text. Although these two corollaries are
phrased in a negative way, they nevertheless result in a profound and, I believe, positive rethinking of the nature of the
critical activity.

   To posit that a text operates in the mode of concealment is to
recognize that there is no autonomy proper to the text, and thus
that criticism is not a simple "adjunct" to the so-called primary
text but is a continuous activity which is intrinsic to and extends
the text. Hence the critic is, as well, a *producer* of text. We recognize here under its more general formulation, the modern critical stand which recasts criticism into a primary operation. "Textual" critics for whom theory itself is experienced as textual toil
and reassumed as an experience of language, and "referential"
critics as well, such as Said for whom criticism is also an original
activity—"an intellectual adventure with a large part of independent creation in [it]"[79]—all agree on this general view, although the forms it takes vary. Far from being condemned to
existence as a secondary activity, criticism remains, even when it
repeats and mimes a text, a productive activity. To borrow Said's
illustration of this point: "In making over the authors he imitated,
Proust set himself the aim of *producing* them from the opening to
the conclusion of a passage."[80] And indeed, reading the essays
in this volume, one is constantly reminded that—whether a
critic is discussing semiological, anthropological or psychoanalytic approaches to literature, modern American poetics, historical
or ideological perspectives, the modes of production of a poem,
an epic text, poetic or scientific language—criticism has reached
a stage of maturity where it is now openly challenging the primacy of literature. Criticism has become an independent operation that is primary in the production of texts. This is the one
point toward which all the contributions in this volume necessar-

---

[79]"Roads Taken and Not Taken in Contemporary Criticism," p. 344.
[80]Ibid., p. 348 (my emphasis).

ily converge, and it is precisely this point which is at stake in the modern battleground of "literature" and "criticism."

Toward the end of *Moses and Monotheism,* Freud remarks that a good deal of the main thesis of *Totem and Taboo* was based on Robertson Smith's totemic theory, which shortly thereafter was discarded by most ethnologists. Freud was then reproached for not changing his opinions—and his hypothesis—in later editions of *Totem and Taboo.* To these objections he responded:

> I would reply that these alleged advances in science are well known to me. Yet I have not been convinced either of their correctness or of Robertson Smith's error. Contradiction is not always refutation; a new theory does not necessarily denote progress. Above all, however, I am not an ethnologist, but a psychoanalyst. It was my good right to select from ethnological data what would serve me for my analytic work. The writings of the highly gifted Robertson Smith provided me with valuable points of contact with the psychological material of analysis and suggestions for the use of it. I cannot say the same of the work of his opponents.[81]

I would like to let this passage stand for what has been—and what has not been—attempted in this introduction. It claims neither a privileged vantage point nor definitive conclusions. It does not attempt to avoid contradictions in order to homogenize the critical overview. At times it does not even attempt to establish what would normally be considered valid links among critics. At other times it attempts to bring together what I consider to be the fundamental points of a given theory. But it represents only one point of view, and one among many others. Readers may object to my selection process, and there is no reason why they should not: in more than one way, it is their objections that will make the content of this volume valuable. Last but not least, this introduction asks certain kinds of questions only: to ask whether structuralism has succeeded in dismissing the speaking subject or whether post-structuralism has succeeded in its critique of representation is not my purpose, which is rather to present and explain the various problematics at play in post-structuralism. I do not stake this claim in order to avoid controversy, but in

[81] *Moses and Monotheism* (New York: Vintage, 1957), p. 169.

order to explain the parameters within which I have written
these pages. And yet I realize that any claim or disclaimer on my
part belongs to, and should be read within, the critical configuration I have outlined: all criticism *is* strategic. To the question:
how should the critic approach knowledge? I know of only one
answer: *strategically*. The power and productivity, the gains and
losses, the advances and retrenchments of criticism are inscribed
in this term: strategy, reminding us of its obsolete—obsolete?—
definition: "A violent and bloody act." In the game of knowledge, method has become a strategy: the "violent and bloody"
agent by which criticism *executes* the work and in so doing,
paradoxically, canonizes it.

Roland Barthes

From Work to Text

Over the past several years, a change has been taking place in our ideas about language and, as a consequence, about the (literary) work, which owes at least its phenomenal existence to language. This change is obviously linked to current developments in, among other fields, linguistics, anthropology, Marxism, and psychoanalysis (the word "link" is used here in a deliberately neutral fashion: it implies no decision about a determination, be it multiple and dialectical). The change affecting the notion of the work does not necessarily come from the internal renewal of each of these disciplines, but proceeds, rather, from their encounter at the level of an object that traditionally depends on none of them. *Interdisciplinary* activity, valued today as an important aspect of research, cannot be accomplished by simple confrontations between various specialized branches of knowledge. Interdisciplinary work is not a peaceful operation: it begins *effectively* when the solidarity of the old disciplines breaks down—a process made more violent, perhaps, by the jolts of fashion—to the benefit of a new object and a new language, neither of which is in the domain of those branches of knowledge that one calmly sought to confront.

It is precisely this uneasiness with classification that allows for the diagnosis of a certain mutation. The mutation that seems to be taking hold of the idea of the work must not, however, be overestimated: it is part of an epistemological shift [*glissement*] rather than of a real break [*coupure*], a break of the kind which, as has often been remarked, supposedly occurred during the last

century, with the appearance of Marxism and Freudianism. No
new break seems to have occurred since, and it can be said that,
in a way, we have been involved in repetition for the past
hundred years. Today history, our history, allows only displacement, variation, going-beyond, and rejection. Just as
Einsteinian science requires the inclusion of the *relativity of reference points* in the object studied, so the combined activity of Marxism, Freudianism, and structuralism requires, in the case of literature, the relativization of the *scriptor*'s, the reader's, and the
observer's (the critic's) relationships. In opposition to the notion
of the *work*—a traditional notion that has long been and still is
thought of in what might be called Newtonian fashion—there
now arises a need for a new object, one obtained by the displacement or overturning of previous categories. This object is
the *Text*. I realize that this word is fashionable and therefore
suspect in certain quarters, but that is precisely why I would like
to review the principal propositions at the intersection of which
the Text is situated today. These propositions are to be understood as enunciations rather than arguments, as mere indications, as it were, approaches that "agree" to remain metaphoric.
Here, then, are those propositions: they deal with method,
genre, the sign, the plural, filiation, reading (in an active sense),
and pleasure.

(1) The Text must not be thought of as a defined object. It
would be useless to attempt a material separation of works and
texts. One must take particular care not to say that works are
classical while texts are avant-garde. Distinguishing them is not a
matter of establishing a crude list in the name of modernity and
declaring certain literary productions to be "in" and others "out"
on the basis of their chronological situation. A very ancient work
can contain "some text," while many products of contemporary
literature are not texts at all. The difference is as follows: the
work is concrete, occupying a portion of book-space (in a library,
for example); the Text, on the other hand, is a methodological
field.

This opposition recalls the distinction proposed by Lacan between "reality" and the "real": the one is displayed, the other
demonstrated. In the same way, the work can be seen in

bookstores, in card catalogues, and on course lists, while the text reveals itself, articulates itself according to or against certain rules. While the work is held in the hand, the text is held in language: it exists only as discourse. The Text is not the decomposition of the work; rather it is the work that is the Text's imaginary tail. In other words, *the Text is experienced only in an activity, a production.* It follows that the Text cannot stop, at the end of a library shelf, for example; the constitutive movement of the Text is a *traversal* [*traversée*]: it can cut across a work, several works.

(2) Similarly, the Text does not come to a stop with (good) literature; it cannot be apprehended as part of a hierarchy or even a simple division of genres. What constitutes the Text is, on the contrary (or precisely), its subversive force with regard to old classifications. How can one classify Georges Bataille? Is this writer a novelist, a poet, an essayist, an economist, a philosopher, a mystic? The answer is so uncertain that manuals of literature generally chose to forget about Bataille; yet Bataille wrote texts—even, perhaps, always one and the same text.

If the Text raises problems of classification, that is because it always implies an experience of limits. Thibaudet used to speak (but in a very restricted sense) about limit-works (such as Chateaubriand's *Life of Rancé,* a work that today indeed seems to be a "text"): the Text is that which goes to the limit of the rules of enunciation (rationality, readability, and so on). The Text tries to situate itself exactly *behind* the limit of *doxa* (is not public opinion—constitutive of our democratic societies and powerfully aided by mass communication—defined by its limits, its energy of exclusion, its *censorship?*). One could literally say that the Text is always *paradoxical.*

(3) Whereas the Text is approached and experienced in relation to the sign, the work closes itself on a signified. Two modes of signification can be attributed to this signified: on the one hand, one can assume that it is obvious, in which case the work becomes the object of a "science of the letter" (philology); on the other hand, one can assume that the signified is secret and ultimate, in which case one must search for it, and the work then depends upon a hermeneutic, an interpretation (Marxist,

psychoanalytic, thematic, for example). In brief, the work itself functions as a general sign and thus represents an institutional category of the civilization of the Sign. The Text, on the contrary, practices the infinite deferral of the signified [*le recul infini du signifié*]: the Text is *dilatory;* its field is that of the signifier. The signifier must not be conceived as "the first stage of meaning," its material vestibule, but rather, on the contrary, as its *aftermath* [*après-coup*]. In the same way, the signifier's *infinitude* does not refer back to some idea of the ineffable (of an unnamable signified) but to the idea of *play.* The engendering of the perpetual signifier within the field of the text should not be identified with an organic process of maturation or a hermeneutic process of deepening, but rather with a serial movement of dislocations, overlappings, and variations. The logic that governs the Text is not comprehensive (seeking to define "what the work means") but metonymic; and the activity of associations, contiguities, and cross-references coincides with a liberation of symbolic energy. The work (in the best of cases) is moderately symbolic (its symbolism runs out, comes to a halt), but the Text is *radically* symbolic. *A work whose integrally symbolic nature one conceives, perceives, and receives is a text.*

In this way the Text is restored to language: like language, it is structured but decentered, without closure (here one might note, in reply to the scornful insinuation of "faddishness" which is often directed against structuralism, that the epistemological privilege presently granted to language proceeds precisely from our discovery in language of a paradoxical idea of structure, a system without end or center).

(4) The Text is plural. This does not mean just that is has several meanings, but rather that it achieves plurality of meaning, an *irreducible* plurality. The Text is not coexistence of meanings but passage, traversal; thus it answers not to an interpretation, liberal though it may be, but to an explosion, a dissemination. The Text's plurality does not depend on the ambiguity of its contents, but rather on what could be called the *stereographic plurality* of the signifiers that weave it (etymologically the text is a cloth; *textus,* from which text derives, means "woven").

The reader of the Text could be compared to an idle subject (a subject having relaxed his "imaginary"[1]): this fairly empty subject strolls along the side of a valley at the bottom of which runs a *wadi* (I use *wadi* here to stress a certain feeling of unfamiliarity). What he sees is multiple and irreducible; it emerges from substances and levels that are heterogeneous and disconnected: lights, colors, vegetation, heat, air, bursts of noise, high-pitched bird calls, children's cries from the other side of the valley, paths, gestures, clothing of close and distant inhabitants. All these *occurrences* are partially identifiable: they proceed from known codes, but their combination is unique, founding the stroll in difference that can be repeated only as difference. This is what happens in the case of the Text: it can be itself only in its difference (which does not mean its "individuality"); its reading is semelfactive (which renders all inductive-deductive sciences of texts illusory—there is no "grammar" of the text) and yet completely woven with quotations, references, and echoes. These are cultural languages (and what language is not?), past or present, that traverse the text from one end to the other in a vast stereophony.

Every text, being itself the intertext of another text, belongs to the intertextual, which must not be confused with a text's origins: to search for the "sources of" and "influence upon" a work is to satisfy the myth of filiation. The quotations from which a text is constructed are anonymous, irrecoverable, and yet *already read:* they are quotations without quotation marks. The work does not upset monistic philosophies, for which plurality is evil. Thus, when it is compared with the work, the text might well take as its motto the words of the man possessed by devils: "My name is legion, for we are many" (Mark 5:9).

The plural or demonic texture that divides text from work can carry with it profound modifications in the activity of reading and precisely in the areas where monologism seems to be the law. Some of the "texts" of the Scriptures that have traditionally been recuperated by theological (historical or anagogical)

---

[1]"Qui aurait détendu en lui tout imaginaire." *Imaginary* is not simply the opposite of real. Used in the Lacanian sense, it is the register, the dimension of all images, conscious or unconscious, perceived or imagined.—Ed.

monism may perhaps lend themselves to a diffraction of meaning, while the Marxist interpretation of the work, until now resolutely monistic, may be able to materialize itself even further by
pluralizing itself (if, of course, Marxist "institutions" allow this).

(5) The work is caught up in a process of filiation. Three
things are postulated here: a *determination* of the work by the
outside world (by race, then by history), a *consecution* of works
among themselves, and an *allocation* of the work to its author.
The author is regarded as the father and the owner of his work;
literary research therefore learns to *respect* the manuscript and
the author's declared intentions, while society posits the legal
nature of the author's relationship with his work (these are the
"author's rights," which are actually quite recent; they were not
legalized in France until the Revolution).

The Text, on the other hand, is read without the father's
signature. The metaphor that describes the Text is also distinct
from that describing the work. The latter refers to the image of
an *organism* that grows by vital expansion, by "development" (a
significantly ambiguous word, both biological and rhetorical).
The Text's metaphor is that of the *network:*[2] if the Text expands,
it is under the effect of a *combinatorial,* a *systematics*[3] (an image
which comes close to modern biology's views on the living being).

Therefore, no vital "respect" is owed to the Text: it can be
broken (this is exactly what the Middle Ages did with two authoritative texts, the Scriptures and Aristotle). The Text can be
read without its father's guarantee: the restitution of the intertext paradoxically abolishes the concept of filiation. It is not that
the author cannot "come back" into the Text, into his text; however, he can only do so as a "guest," so to speak. If the author is a
novelist, he inscribes himself in his text as one of his characters,
as another figure sewn into the rug; his signature is no longer
privileged and paternal, the locus of genuine truth, but rather,
ludic. He becomes a "paper author": his life is no longer the
origin of his fables, but a fable that runs concurrently with his
work. There is a reversal, and it is the work which affects the life,

[2]Barthes uses here the word *réseau.* I have chosen to translate it by "network" (rather than "web," for instance) at the risk of overemphasizing the
mechanical implications of the metaphor.—Ed.

[3]*Systematics* is the science (or method) of classification of living forms.—Ed.

not the life which affects the work: the work of Proust and Genet allows us to read their lives as a text. The word "bio-graphy" reassumes its strong meaning, in accordance with its etymology. At the same time, the enunciation's sincerity, which has been a veritable "cross" of literary morality, becomes a false problem: the *I* that writes the text is never, itself, anything more than a paper *I*.

(6) The work is ordinarily an object of consumption. I intend no demagoguery in referring here to so-called consumer culture, but one must realize that today it is the work's "quality" (this implies, ultimately, an appreciation in terms of "taste") and not the actual process of reading that can establish differences between books. There is no structural difference between "cultured" reading and casual subway reading. The Text (if only because of its frequent "unreadability") decants the work from its consumption and gathers it up as play, task, production, and activity. This means that the Text requires an attempt to abolish (or at least to lessen) the distance between writing and reading, not by intensifying the reader's projection into the work, but by linking the two together in a single signifying process [*pratique significante*].

The distance separating writing from reading is historical: during the era of greatest social division (before the institution of democratic cultures), both reading and writing were class privileges. Rhetoric, the great literary code of those times, taught *writing* (even though speeches and not texts were generally produced). It is significant that the advent of democracy reversed the order: (secondary) school now prides itself on teaching how to *read* (well), and not how to *write*.

In fact, *reading* in the sense of *consuming* is not *playing* with the text. Here "playing" must be understood in all its polysemy. The text itself *plays* (like a door on its hinges, like a device in which there is some "play"); and the reader himself plays twice over: playing the Text as one plays a game, he searches for a practice that will re-produce the Text; but, to keep that practice from being reduced to a passive, inner mimesis (the Text being precisely what resists such a reduction), he also *plays* the Text in the musical sense of the term. The history of music (as practice, not as "art") happens to run quite parallel to the history of the Text.

There was a time when "practicing" music lovers were numerous (at least within the confines of a certain class), when "playing" and "listening" constituted an almost undifferentiated activity. Then two roles appeared in succession: first, that of the *interpreter,* to whom the bourgeois public delegated its playing; second, that of the music lover who listened to music without knowing how to play it. Today, post-serial music has disrupted the role of the "interpreter" by requiring him to be, in a certain sense, the co-author of a score which he completes rather than "interprets."

The Text is largely a score of this new type: it asks the reader for an active collaboration. This is a great innovation, because it compels us to ask "who *executes* the work?" (a question raised by Mallarmé, who wanted the audience to *produce* the book). Today only the critic *executes* the work (in both senses). The reduction of reading to consumption is obviously responsible for the "boredom" that many people feel when confronting the modern ("unreadable") text, or the avant-garde movie or painting: to suffer from boredom means that one cannot produce the text, play it, open it out, *make it go.*

(7) This suggests one final approach to the Text, that of pleasure. I do not know if a hedonistic aesthetic ever existed, but there certainly exists a pleasure associated with the work (at least with certain works). I can enjoy reading and rereading Proust, Flaubert, Balzac, and even—why not?—Alexandre Dumas; but this pleasure, as keen as it may be and even if disengaged from all prejudice, remains partly (unless there has been an exceptional critical effort) a pleasure of consumption. If I can read those authors, I also know that I cannot *rewrite* them (that today, one can no longer write "like that"); that rather depressing knowledge is enough to separate one from the production of those works at the very moment when their remoteness founds one's modernity (for what is "being modern" but the full realization that one cannot begin to write the same works once again?). The Text, on the other hand, is linked to enjoyment [*jouissance*], to pleasure without separation. Order of the signifier, the Text participates in a social utopia of its own: prior to history, the Text achieves, if not the transparency of social relations, at least the transparency of language relations. It is the space in which no one language has a hold over any other, in which all languages circulate freely.

These few propositions, inevitably, do not constitute the articulation of a theory of the Text. This is not just a consequence of the presenter's insufficiencies (besides, I have in many respects only recapitulated what is being developed around me); rather, it proceeds from the fact that a theory of the Text cannot be fully satisfied by a metalinguistic exposition. The destruction of metalanguage, or at least (since it may become necessary to return to it provisionally) the questioning of it, is part of the theory itself. Discourse on the Text should itself be only "text," search, and textual toil, since the Text is that *social* space that leaves no language safe or untouched, that allows no enunciative subject to hold the position of judge, teacher, analyst, confessor, or decoder. The theory of the Text can coincide only with the activity of writing.

JACQUES DERRIDA

The Supplement of Copula:
Philosophy before Linguistics

If one attempted to elaborate a theory of *philosophical* discourse on the basis of the naive opposition between language system [*langue*] and speech act [*parole*], between language and discourse, it would be difficult to circumvent the classical question: is philosophical discourse governed—to what degree and in which ways—by the constraints of language? In other words, if we consider the history of philosophy as a great and powerful discursive chain, does it not dip into a reserve of language, the systematic fund of a lexicology, of a grammar, an ensemble of signs and values? Is it not henceforth limited by the resources and the organization of that reserve?

How are we to define and situate the language of philosophy? Is it a "natural language" or a family of natural languages (Greek, Latin, German, Indo-European, and so on)? Or is it rather a formal code elaborated on the basis of these natural languages? These questions have a long history, dating no doubt from the origin of philosophy itself. One could not re-elaborate them, however, without transforming or displacing the conceptual pairs by which philosophy is constituted. Couples such as natural language/formal language, language system/speech act, insofar as they are productions of philosophical discourse, belong to the field they are supposed to analyze. Although this fact does not deprive them of all authority, it gives them no particular relevance for determining the relationship of philosophical discourse to its constraining limits.

Moreover, these questions, which long remained localized and implicit in philosophical discourse, at a certain moment become dominant and obsessive. This is significant with respect to the "historical" relationship that philosophy has to its own limit and to the singular form of its closure. The manifestation of this singularity is usually cast as follows: whoever alleges that philosophical discourse belongs to the closure of a language must nevertheless proceed within that language and with the oppositions it provides. According to a law which could be formalized, philosophy always reappropriates for itself the discourse that delimits it.

Finally, although the question concerning linguistic constraints has a certain philosophical permanence, the form in which we pose it today is no doubt constituted within a very particular and complex historico-theoretical configuration. This configuration brings together numerous fields of criticism, but, most important, it is inseparable from the development of historical linguistics in the nineteenth century. When he reminded philosophers that they remain walled up inside language, Nietzsche was being more violent and explicit than others, but he was also exploiting a possibility that had been surfacing virtually everywhere for half a century—even if it was most often taken up by philosophical interests. In this situation, Nietzschean discourse was no more able than any other to escape the law of this reappropriation. For example, Nietzsche classifies as liberation (or freedom of thought) the movement by which one breaks away from language and grammar, which previously governed the philosophical order. In this very traditional fashion he comes to define the law of language or the signifier as an "enslavement" from which we must extricate ourselves. At the most critical moment of his enterprise, at the "turning point," he remains a philosopher—*provisionally,* as it were: "Logic is only slavery within the bounds of language. Language has within it, however, an illogical element, the metaphor. Its principal force brings about an identification of the nonidentical; it is thus an operation of the imagination. It is on this that the existence of concepts, forms, etc., rests."[1] This movement is regularly re-

<hr />

[1] *Das Philosophenbuch, Theoretische Studien*, p. 207 of a bilingual edition, trans. A. K. Marietti, under the title *Le Livre du philosophe, études théoriques* (Paris: Aubier-Flammarion, 1969). No English translation of this text is available, hence the reference to the French-German edition.—Ed.

peated, and especially when Nietzsche analyzes the philosophical illusion of "truth" as the subjection to an order of signs whose "arbitrariness" we forget. But by recalling the arbitrariness of the sign, has not philosophy always sought to posit the contingent and superficial exteriority of language to thought, the secondary nature of the sign in relation to the idea? Having a totally different aim, Nietzsche must resort to an analogous argument:

> Only by means of forgetfulness can man ever arrive at imagining that he possesses "truth" in that degree just indicated. If he does not mean to content himself with truth in the shape of tautology, that is, with empty husks, he will always obtain illusions instead of truth. What is a word? The expression of a nerve-stimulus in sounds. But to infer a cause outside us from the nerve-stimulus is already the result of a wrong and unjustifiable application of the proposition of causality. How should we dare, if truth with the genesis of language, if the point of view of certainty with the designations had alone been decisive; how indeed should we dare to say: the stone is hard; as if "hard" was known to us otherwise; and not merely as an entirely subjective stimulus! We divide things according to gender; we designate the tree as masculine, the plant as feminine: what arbitrary metaphors! How far flown beyond the canon of certainty![2]

There follows the example of the "serpent" and an interpretation of metaphor as the very structure or condition of possibility of all language and concepts.

In anticipation of a future elaboration, let us note that the illusion Nietzsche diagnoses bears on the import of "is," whose function is to transform a "subjective excitation" into an objective judgment, into a pretension to truth. Is this a grammatical function? Is it a lexicological function? This is a question that will be determined later on.

The example of the stone or the serpent illustrates a semantic or lexicological arbitrariness. Most often, however, Nietzsche incriminates grammar or syntax, whose structure buttresses the metaphysical edifice in its entirety:

> Our oldest metaphysical ground is the last one of which we will rid ourselves—supposing we could succeed in getting rid of it—this ground that has incorporated itself in language and in the

---

[2]"On Truth and Falsity in their Ultramoral Sense," in *The Complete Works of Friedrich Nietzsche,* ed. Oscar Levy (London: Allen & Unwin, 1911), II, 177.

grammatical categories, and has made itself so indispensable at this point, that it seems we would have to cease thinking if we renounced this metaphysics. Philosophers are properly those who have the most difficulty in freeing themselves from the belief that the fundamental concepts and categories of reason belong by nature to the realm of metaphysical certainties. They always believe in reason as a fragment of the metaphysical world itself; this backward belief always reappears in their work as an all-powerful regression.[3]

Therefore, at a certain moment in his critical campaign against metaphysics, Nietzsche must resort to philosophical schemes (for example the arbitrariness of the sign or the emancipation of thought from a given language). This is not an incoherency for which we need to seek a *logical* solution, but a textual strategy and stratification requiring an analytical *practice.* One could undertake the same analytical practice by following the direction Heidegger took in coming to grips with analogous difficulties. These difficulties are explicitly formulated in the "Letter on Humanism," where he speaks of "the metaphysics which, in the form of Western logic and grammar, early took possession of the interpretation of language. Today we can but begin to surmise what lies hidden in this process. The freeing of language from grammar, and placing it in a more original and essential framework, is reserved for thought and poetry."[4] And elsewhere, recalling that *Sein und Zeit* remained unfinished: "Here, the whole thing is reversed. The section in question was suppressed because the thinking failed to find language adequate to this reversal and did not succeed through the aid of the language of metaphysics."[5]

Rhapsodies

Rather than continue on the open seas, so to speak, with this immense problematic, and given the exigencies and limits of the

[3]*La Volonté de puissance,* 2 vols., trans. G. Bianquis (Paris: Gallimard, 1947). The above is a fragment of 1886 (I, 65) which is not included in either the Kaufmann or the Levy edition of *The Will to Power.* The translation of this fragment is made from the French text of the Bianquis edition.—Ed.

[4]"Letter on Humanism," in *Philosophy in the Twentieth Century,* trans. Edgar Lohner, ed. William Barrett and Henry D. Aiken (New York: Random House, 1962), p. 271.

[5]Ibid., p. 280.

present essay, perhaps it would be better to begin here with the propositions of a modern linguist. In his well-known essay entitled "Categories of Thought and Language,"[6] Emile Benveniste analyzed the constraints by which the Greek language limited the system of Aristotelian categories. His propositions are part of a stratified whole; he does not limit himself to the Aristotelian text that directly articulates his thesis (a fact which will concern us later at the appropriate time). This thesis has already encountered philosophical objections, resulting in a debate whose elaboration will be valuable to us.[7]

But first, here is the thesis: "Now it seems to us—and we shall try to show—that these distinctions are primarily categories of language and that, in fact, Aristotle, reasoning in the absolute, is simply identifying certain fundamental categories of the language in which he thought" (p. 57).

What are the reasons and motives of this thesis? As a starting point Benveniste chooses a certain number of characteristics generally recognized in language at least since Saussure. Heading the list is the proposition that "the reality of language" is "unconscious," a concept which is equally commensurate with any number of Saussure's propositions regarding the fact that "language is not a function of the speaking subject." We shall not linger over this premise, even though it raises more than one difficulty, and for more reasons than just its empirical form. ("In their diversity, these uses [of language] have, however, two characteristics in common. One is that the reality of language, as a general rule, remains unconscious... " [p. 55].) What does "reality of language" mean here? What about "reality" in the expression "reality of language?" Why only "as a general rule?" Is it or is it not an essential predicate of the aforementioned reality that it remains unconscious? The difficulty of the division into conscious and unconscious reaches a point of maximum

---

[6]"Categories of Thought and Language," in *Problems in General Linguistics,* trans. Mary E. Meek (Coral Gables: University of Miami Press, 1971), pp. 55–64. All further references to Benveniste will be in parentheses following the quotes.

[7]Cf. Pierre Aubenque, "Aristote et le langage, note annexe sur les catégories d'Aristote. A propos d'un article de M. Benveniste" in *Annales de la faculté des lettres d'Aix,* 43 (1965), 103–105. Cf. Also J. Vuillemin, *De la logique à la théologie: Cinq études sur Aristote* (Paris: Flammarion, 1967), pp. 75ff.

obscurity in questions of language and language usage. This difficulty is not lessened (on the contrary) when the unconscious risks becoming a weakened consciousness ("the reality of language, as a general rule, remains unconscious; except when language is especially studied for itself, we have no more than a very faint and fleeting awareness of the operations which we accomplish in order to talk" [p. 55]), or when the activity of linguistics in its relation to language is determined as a coming to awareness or an increase in consciousness. In raising these questions our aim is not to insist on the (no doubt) secondary links in Benveniste's demonstration, nor to take exception to his discourse, but only to indicate an example of the aporias that one seems to encounter once one sets out to define the constraints which limit philosophical discourse. It is from this discourse that we must borrow the uncriticized notions that we apply to its delimitation. We could just as easily have focused on the notions of system, form, and content which serve to define the characteristics of language ("Now this language has a configuration in all its parts and as a totality. It is in addition organized as an arrangement of distinct and distinguishing 'signs,' capable themselves of being broken down into inferior units or of being grouped into complex units. This great structure, which includes substructures of several levels, gives its *form* to the content of thought" [p. 55]). Now, the notion of linguistic *system,* even if it is opposed to the notions of logical system or system of categories, and even if one wanted to reduce the latter to the former, would never have been possible outside the history of (or history and) the concepts of metaphysics as theory, *épistémè,* etc. Whatever the displacements, breaks, secondary discontinuities of all sorts (and we must most carefully take account of them all), the filiation linguistics-philosophy has never been absolutely interrupted. Benveniste recognizes it elsewhere,[8] and here he finds himself in the position of having to criticize immediately as a metaphor or "image" one of the great classical oppositions

[8]"Everyone knows that Western linguistics originated in Greek philosophy. This appears from all the evidence. Our linguistic terminology is made up in large part of Greek terms adopted directly or through their Latin translation" (p. 18).

inherited from philosophy. And yet it is this opposition that was central to the passage just quoted: "To speak of the container and the contents is to simplify. The image should not delude us. Strictly speaking, thought is not matter to which language lends form, since at no time could this 'container' be imagined as empty of its 'contents,' nor the 'contents' as independent of their 'container'" (p. 56). Precautions of this type could be taken concerning each concept; and in these few examples we are pointing out the constraints inherent only in the structure of a discourse or a project, not in the initiative of an author.

Here we leave the propaedeutical opening of Benveniste's text and come to the major problem, which is posed in the following terms:

> And so the question becomes the following: while granting absolutely that thought cannot be grasped except as formed and made a reality in language, have we any means to recognize in thought such characteristics as would belong to it alone and owe nothing to linguistic expression? We can describe language by itself. It would be necessary in the same way to apprehend thought directly. If it were possible to define thought by features belonging to it exclusively, it would be seen at once how it accommodates itself to language and what the nature of their relationship is.
>
> It might be convenient to approach the problem by way of "categories," which appear as intermediaries. They present different aspects, depending on whether they are categories of thought or language. This difference might shed light on their respective natures. For example, we immediately perceive that thought can freely specify its categories and invent new ones, while linguistic categories, as attributes of a system which each speaker receives and maintains, are not modifiable according to each person's whim. We also see this other difference: that thought can claim to set up universal categories but that linguistic categories are always categories of a particular language. At first sight, this would confirm the preeminent and independent position of thought with regard to language.
>
> We cannot, however, as so many authors have done, simply pose the question in such general terms. We must enter into a concrete historical situation and study the categories of a specific thought and a specific language. Only on this condition will we avoid arbitrary stands and speculative solutions. Now, we are fortunate to have at our disposal data which one would say were ready for our examination, already worked out and stated objectively within a well-known system: Aristotle's categories. In the examination of

these categories, we may dispense with philosophical technicalities. We will consider them simply as an inventory of properties which a Greek thinker thought could be predicated of a subject and, consequently, as the list of a priori concepts which, according to him, organize experience. It is a document of great value for our purpose. [pp. 56-77]

Defined in this way, this problematic seems to encompass at least three presuppositions, all concerning a certain "historicity" of concepts.

(1) It was necessary to have recourse, if only provisionally, or as a point of departure that could subsequently be criticized, to the difference or opposition between language and thought. ("We can describe language by itself. It would be necessary in the same way to apprehend thought directly. If it were possible to define thought by features belonging to it exclusively, it would be seen at once how it accommodates itself to language and what the nature of their relationship is" [p. 56].) No doubt Benveniste begins with this separation only to reduce it later by restoring to language-structures those characteristics that are supposed to belong exclusively to thought. But during the entire analysis no question is raised about (a) the origin and the possibility of this initial distinction, and (b) what it is that made the presumption of this noncoincidence historically possible. In other words, no question is ever posed about the very inception of the problem. What is it, at least in the structure of language (since everything is already there: "We can describe language by itself"), that opened this split and determined it as the difference between thought and language?

(2) The second paragraph we quoted deals with a possible or pretended opposition of "thought categories" and "language categories." What is never questioned at all, however, is the category of category that is common to both, this *categoriality in general* on the basis of which we can dissociate the categories of language and thought. In the history of philosophy and science (in Aristotle's *Organon* and *Categories*), the concept, the category of category, systematically comes into play at the point where the opposition of language to thought becomes impossible or has only derivative meaning. Without having reduced thought to language in a fashion similar to Benveniste's, Aristotle tried to

direct his analysis back to the point of emergence, which is to say back to the common root of the couple language/thought. This point is the locus of "being." Aristotle's categories are at one and the same time language and thought categories, language categories insofar as they are determined as answers to the question of how being *is expressed* (*legetai*); but also, how we express *being,* how what *is* is said, insofar as it is and such as it is: a question of thought, the word "thought" which Benveniste uses as if its meaning and history were self-evident, or in any case as if it never signified anything outside of its relation to being, to the truth of being such as it is and insofar as it is (expressed). "Thought"—what goes by that name in the West—was never able to emerge or manifest itself except on the basis of a certain configuration of *noein, legein, einai* and the strange sameness of *noein* and *einai* mentioned in the poem of Parmenides. Now, without pursuing this development, we must indicate that when Aristotle posits categories, the category of category (which is the inaugural gesture for the very idea of logic—that is, the science of science—followed by the idea of a particular science, a rational grammar, a linguistic system, etc.), he intends to answer a question that does not allow the distinction between language and thought—at least at the point at which it is asked. The category is one of the ways for "being" to express or signify itself, or in other words, to open language to its outside, to what is insofar as it is or such as it is: to truth. "Being" presents itself in language precisely as that which opens it up to nonlanguage, as that which is beyond what would be only the inside ("subjective," "empirical" in the anachronistic sense of these words) of a language. It is evident—and Benveniste formulates it explicitly—that to reduce thought categories to language categories is to affirm that the pretensions of language to "thought"—to truth, to universality, to ontologicality—are abusive. But as it turns out, the category of category is only a systematic formulation [*mise en forme*] of this pretension to what is outside of language, at once both language and thought because language is questioned at the point where the signification "being" is produced.

Among the various presentations of categories, the most complete list is no doubt the one Benveniste quotes (*Categories,* chap.

IV, 1, b25). But the text of the *Metaphysics* (E 2 1026 a33), which also proposes a list of categories, precedes it with a principial definition. The categories answer the question, "in what sense is being said?", since being is said *pollakôs* (in many ways):

> The science which studies this will be prior to physics, and will be primary philosophy, and universal in this sense, that it is primary. And it will be the province of this science to study Being *qua* Being; what it is, and what the attributes are which belong to it *qua* Being. But since the simple term "being" is used in various senses [*pollakôs legetai*], of which we saw that one was *accidental*, and another *true* (not-being being used in the sense of "false"); and since besides these there are the categories [*ta skhemata tes categorias*], e.g., the "what," quality, quantity, place, time, and any other similar meanings [*ton tropon tauton*] (1026 a30-b2), . . .[9]

Aristotle therefore knows that he is questioning the *ways of saying*[10] being in so far as it is *pollakôs legomenon*. Categories are figures (*skhemata*) by means of which being properly speaking is expressed insofar as it is expressed through several twists, several tropes. The system of categories is the system of the ways in which being is construed. It relates the problematic of the analogy of being—its equivocality and univocality—with the problematic of the metaphor in general. Aristotle links them together explicitly by affirming that the best metaphor is prescribed according to analogies of proportionality. This would suffice to prove that the question of metaphor is no more marginal to metaphysics than metaphorical style and figurative usage are accessory embellishments or secondary aids to philosophical discourse.

One cannot therefore use the word "category" as if it had no history. And it is difficult to oppose language category and

[9]*Metaphysics,* trans. Hugh Tredennick (Cambridge: Harvard University Press, 1933), pp. 297–299.
[10]Cf. Aubenque, p. 104: "It is therefore a fact of language—the equivocality of being—that Aristotle has in mind expressly, and he attempts to order or, as we said, 'to administer it' by a procedure that is itself 'linguistic': distinguishing the multiple significations for the word in question. Nowhere, on the other hand, does Aristotle present the categories as properties of things or as laws of thought. We must therefore give up imputing to Aristotle a supposed 'unconsciousness' of the relationship between his ontology and language."

thought category as if the idea of category in general (and particularly language category, a notion never criticized by Benveniste) were somehow natural. Is it not necessary first to wonder where it comes from? Is it not essential to take into account that this idea was produced on the very terrain where the simple opposition of language and thought was called into question? Knowledge of what a category is—what a language is, a theory of language as system, a science of language in general and so on—would not have been possible without the emergence of a distinct notion of category in general, a notion whose principal effect was precisely to problematize this simple opposition of two supposed entities such as language and thought. When Benveniste reminds us that there is no simple relation of exteriority between "container" and "content," language and thought, and similar pairings, when he directs this proposition against Aristotle , to what extent is he acceding to the fact that his argument remains under Aristotelian influence—at least so long as the function of "being," which is to represent the opening of language and thought onto each other, has not been questioned in a radically new way.

(3) This historical haste stands out in another way. Once the issue is thus formulated, Benveniste moves on to maintain that, for studying the *general* problem, "we are fortunate enough to have at our disposal data which one would say were ready for our examination, . . . a document of great value for our purpose," namely, Aristotle's text on the *Categories.* He seems to suggest that this general problem is in no way specifically Aristotelian, that it is not linked to the history that goes under Aristotle's name and "legacy." It is as if the same problem could have been formulated in the same terms with no reference to Aristotelian discourse. That discourse then becomes nothing more than a lucky find, a rather convenient illustration that we have been fortunate enough to encounter in our libraries. And then, announcing the "document of great value for our purpose" in the accepted style of paraphrase, without batting an eye, the linguist has transposed the terms of this document into an anachronistic and singularly Kantian conceptuality (except for a few approximations to which we must return later): "In the examination of these categories, we may dispense with philosophi-

cal technicalities. We will consider them simply as an inventory of *properties* which a Greek thinker thought could be *predicated of a subject* and, consequently, as the list of *a priori concepts* which, according to him, organize *experience*" (p. 57—my emphasis).

We are still at the preamble. The question is asked but the content of the answer is not yet elaborated. This is what he says:

> Let us recall at first the fundamental text, which gives the most complete list of these properties, ten in all (*Categories*, IV):
>
> Each expression when it is not part of a combination means: the *substance*, or *how much*, or *of what kind*, or *relating to what*, or *where*, or *when*, or *to be in a position*, or *to be in a condition*, or *to do*, or *to undergo*. "Substance," for example, "man," "horse";—"how much," for example, "two cubits," "three cubits";—"of what kind," for example, "white," "educated";—"relating to what," for example, "double," "half," "larger";—"where," for example, "at the Lyceum," "at the market";—"when," for example, "today," "last year";—"to be in a position," for example, "he is lying down," "he is seated";— "to be in a condition," for example, "he is shod," "he is armed";— "to do," for example, "he cuts," "he burns";—"to undergo," for example, "he is cut," "he is burned."
>
> Aristotle thus posits the totality of predications that may be made about a being, and he aims to define the logical status of each one of them. Now it seems to us—and we shall try to show—that these distinctions are primarily categories of language and that, in fact, Aristotle, reasoning in the absolute, is simply identifying certain fundamental categories of the language in which he thought. Even a cursory look at the statement of the categories and the examples that illustrate them, will easily verify this interpretation, which apparently has not been proposed before. Let us consider the ten terms in order. [p. 57]

"This interpretation, which *apparently* has not been proposed before:" indeed, prudence was not a bad idea. Aristotle has been quite often reproached for not knowing the origin of categories, for having assembled them according to an empirical procedure (in a passage that we shall discuss later, Benveniste also says: "Unconsciously he took as a criterion the empirical necessity of a distinct *expression* for each of his predications" [p. 61]), and even reproached for having been content merely to reflect the grammatical structures of the Greek language. But among all those who have accused Aristotle of constituting empirically what Leibniz used to call *eine Musterrolle* (a catalogue of paradigms comparable to a muster roll), it is Kant whom we must mention first. There is a classic text that precisely makes Benveniste's point while providing him with his vocabulary if not his concepts. It is hardly a question of language or grammar here, only an empirical survey of categories—but categories as they *manifest themselves*. And where would they manifest themselves if not in language? The text in question comes from the presentation of the table of categories in Kant's *Analytic of Concepts.*

> In this manner there arise precisely the same number of pure concepts of the understanding which apply *a priori* to objects of intuition in general, as, in the preceding table, there have been found to be logical functions in all possible judgments. For these functions specify the understanding completely, and yield an exhaustive inventory of its powers. These concepts we shall, with Aristotle, call *categories,* for our primary purpose is the same as his, although widely diverging from it in manner of execution.

> ### TABLE OF CATEGORIES

> This then is the list of all original pure concepts of synthesis that the understanding contains within itself *a priori.* Indeed, it is because it contains these concepts that it is called pure understanding; for by them alone can it *understand* anything in the manifold of intuition, that is, think an object of intuition. This division is developed systematically from a common principle, namely, the faculty of judgment (which is the same as the faculty of thought). It has not arisen rhapsodically, as the result of a haphazard search after pure concepts, the complete enumeration of which, as based on induction only, could never be guaranteed. Nor could we, if this were our procedure, discover why just these concepts, and no others, have their seat in the pure understanding. It was an enterprise worthy of an acute thinker like Aristotle to make search for these fundamental concepts. But as he did so on no principle, he merely picked them up as they came his way, and at first procured ten of them, which he called *categories* (predicaments). Afterwards he believed that he had discovered five others, which he added under the name of post-predicaments. But his table still remained defective.[11]

[11]*Critique of Pure Reason,* trans. Norman Kemp Smith (London: Macmillan, 1929), pp. 113-114.

This accusation of empiricism was taken up again by Hegel,[12] Prantl, Hemelin, and others. The chief reason for calling it to mind is not to establish that Benveniste elaborates his problematic on the basis of motifs whose history remains hidden to him. It is rather this: given that, beginning with Aristotle, several attempts have been made to constitute tables of categories which would not be the effect or the empirical reflection of language, should not the linguist direct his demonstration to these endeavors? To proceed otherwise is to act as if nothing had happened since Aristotle, and while this is not unthinkable, it would require demonstration, and the task would not be easy. One would have to prove, for example, that Kantian categories are effects of language. To say the least, the problematic would be complicated and would require us, without prejudicing the results, to perform a complete transformation of the concepts of language and thought used by Benveniste. Is grammar still the argumentative thread of Kant's research when he proposes a system of categories that should be regulated according to the "power of judging," which is the same as the "power of thinking"? Such a possibility can hardly be excluded, but into what historical labyrinth would we then be drawn! What an entanglement of linguistic and philosophical structures would then have to be taken into account! In effect, the relation of Kantian categories to language would be mediated by an entire philosophical stratification (for example, the total legacy of Aristotle, i.e., a great deal) and by a whole set of linguistic displacements whose complexity one can easily imagine. However, the immensity of this task does not diminish its necessity. For that reason, what is important here is not to impugn Benveniste's question—quite the contrary—but rather to try and analyze certain of its presuppositions and perhaps, however minimally, to pursue its elaboration.

Not only did later thinkers point out Aristotle's empiricism (or at least believe they had done so), but also productions of language have long been specifically recognized in his cate-

---

[12] *"Er stellte sie so neben einander"* (he juxtaposed them), *Lectures on the History of Philosophy,* quoted by Hermann Bonitz in *Über die Kategorien des Aristoteles,* 1853 (Darmstadt: Wissenschaftliche Buch-Gesellschaft, 1967), p. 38.

gories. The most precise and systematic attempt in this direction was that of Friedrich Trendelenburg (1846).[13] As Aubenque also remarks,[14] Benveniste has an immediate predecessor (whom at times he seems to paraphrase) in the person of Léon Brunschvicg who, in *Les Ages de l'intelligence* (1939), also accused Aristotle of taking "the universe of discourse" for "the universe of reason." Brunschvicg thought he could unmask "the entirely verbal character of his [Aristotle's] ontology," "and doubtless of any ontology," because "being as such is the type of word that can be nothing more than a word." "He [Aristotle] seeks knowledge of things only through sensible perception . . . and through language, or more precisely through the language he spoke and from which he *unconsciously* [my emphasis] elevates particular characteristics into necessary and universal conditions for thought." Quoting Charles Serrus, Brunschvicg says elsewhere that in doing this Aristotle was only "explaining a certain spontaneous metaphysics of the Greek language." Aubenque again cites a thesis of Louis Rougier: "Bergson said that Aristotle's metaphysics is the spontaneous metaphysics of the human mind: it would be more accurate to say that it is the spontaneous metaphysics of Indo-European languages, and of Greek in particular."[15]

Cassirer, who was never quoted in the debate on Aristotle's metaphysics, is no doubt the most remarkable and the most immediate of Benveniste's predecessors. In "The Influence of Language upon the Development of Scientific Thought," he in turn recalls the attempts of his predecessors, notably Trendelenburg.

> When, in the analyses in his theory of categories, Aristotle follows language and entrusts himself to its direction, we do not, from a modern point of view, have to discuss this procedure. But we would demand that he distinguish carefully between the "universal" and the "particular," that he not turn certain determinations which have their own legitimacy and reasons for existing inside a

[13]Quoted by Vuillemin, p. 75, and Aubenque, p. 103. On Trendelenburg's interpretation and the debate to which it gave rise, see Bonitz, pp. 37ff.
    [14]Aubenque, pp. 87–88.
    [15]"Pseudo-problèmes résolus et soulevés par la logique d'Aristote," in *Actes du Congrès international de philosophie scientifique* (Paris: Hermann, 1936), III, 36.

certain language or group of languages, into characteristics true of language and thought in general. If we are judging as historians, we do in fact understand how and why Aristotle found it impossible to fulfill this condition. There was for him as yet no possibility of comparison and of sure delimitation. He could not think outside of nor against the Greek language, but only in it and with it.[16]

And after a long reference to the works of W. von Humboldt, Cassirer continues:

For Aristotle, it has long been recognized that the particular categories of being he distinguishes are closely related to the categories of language and grammar. Aristotle's theory of categories sets out to describe and determine being to the extent to which it is somehow made explicit and analyzed according to the different forms of the enunciations. But all enunciating requires first of all a *subject* to which it can be connected, a thing about which one expresses a predicate. Therefore the category of being is placed at the head of the theory of categories. Aristotle defines this being [*ousia*] in a sense that is both ontological and linguistic.... The unity of *physis* and *logos* appears thus in Aristotle's system not as accidental but as necessary.[17]

The purpose of this brief review has been simply to suggest that Benveniste's interpretation has been "proposed" more than once and that its "verification" invites at least moderately "long commentaries." Some philosophers are often reproached, and rightly so, for extracting certain "scientific" propositions from their context in order to manipulate them for nonscientific ends. But is the philosophical text any more *immediately* available and open to appropriation than scientific argumentation? Can we extract from such a text any evidential fragment or "document" that we are "fortunate enough to have at our disposal"? It would be wrong to believe in the immediate and ahistorical accessibility of a philosophical argument, just as it would be wrong to believe

[16]"The Influence of Language upon the Development of Scientific Thought," in *Journal of Philosophy*, 39 (1942), 309-327. The above quote is translated from p. 136 of the reworked French version of this same article, which appeared under the title "L'Influence du langage sur le développement de la pensée dans les sciences de la nature" in *Journal de Psychologie normale et pathologique*, 39 (1946), 129-152.—Ed.
[17]Ibid., French version, pp. 137-139.

that we could, without a preliminary and very complex elaboration, subject a metaphysical text to some "scientific" deciphering
grid—be it linguistic, psychoanalytical, or other. One of the first
precautions must concern the origin and metaphysical bearings
of the concepts which often constitute such a "scientific" grid. In
the present instance, for example, none of the concepts used by
Benveniste would have ever seen the light of day—neither linguistics as a science, nor the very notion of language—without
this little "document" on the categories. Philosophy is not only
before linguistics in the way that one can be *faced* with a new
science, outlook, or object; it is also *before* linguistics in the sense
of preceding, providing it with all its concepts, for better or
worse. Sometimes philosophy intervenes in the most critical operations, sometimes in the most dogmatic and least scientific
operations of the linguist. Of course, if the philosopher rushes in
uncritically to wield scientific propositions whose effective production remains hidden from him, and if likewise there is a haste
on the part of the "scientist" in his appropriation of the
philosophical text, the laurels belong to the rhapsodists who dis-
qualify the component parts of a philosophical text whose
functioning they cannot see, by using a scientific alibi about
which they know nothing.

Transferral

Transcription, transposition, projection of language categories into
thought categories: this is how Benveniste defines Aristotle's
unconscious operation, and inversely, the symmetrical decoding
which he takes up.

> The ten categories can now be transcribed in linguistic terms. Each
> of them is given by its designation and followed by its equivalent:
> *ousia* ("substance"), substantive; *poson, poion* ("what, in what
> number"), adjectives derived from pronouns like the Latin *qualis*
> and *quantus; pros ti* ("relating to what"), comparative adjective;
> *pou* ("where"), *poté* ("when"), adverbs of place and time; *keisthai*
> ("to be placed"), middle voice; *ekein* ("to be in a state"), the per-
> fect; *poiein* ("to do"), active voice; *paskhein* ("to undergo"), passive
> voice. [p. 60]

The linguist, then, *transcribes* in terms of language what the philosopher had previously "unconsciously" *transposed* and *projected* from language into conceptual terms:

> We have thus an answer to the question raised in the beginning which led us to this analysis. We asked ourselves what was the nature of the relationship between categories of thought and categories of language. No matter how much validity Aristotle's categories have as categories of thought, they turn out to be transposed from categories of language. It is what one can *say* which delimits and organizes what one can think. Language provides the fundamental configuration of the properties of things as recognized by the mind. This table of predication informs us above all about the class structure of a particular language.
>
> It follows that what Aristotle gave us as a table of general and permanent conditions is only a conceptual projection of a given linguistic state. [p. 61]

This transcription does not amount to a *translation*, that is, to an *intralinguistic* movement guaranteeing the transposition of a signified from one language to another, from one system of signifiers to another. Therefore, the movement of one nonlinguistic categorial structure (that "of thought") to a linguistic categorial structure (that "of language") cannot be called translation. The meaning of "transcription" refers us to what is later named "transposition" or "projection." The linguist's transcription travels in the opposite direction; it channels back into language that which pretended to escape from it through transposition and projection.

But what about this strange transfer? How could it have been produced? By what necessity? Benveniste recognizes the unique correspondence that one hesitates, for obvious reasons, to call *homology;* but he questions neither the status of the operation, nor the conditions for the trap, nor the space or the medium in which projection and then transcription occur—for example, the field of categoriality in general. Doubtless in order to avoid the "philosophical technicalities" excluded at the outset, Benveniste does not ask himself by what aberration it was possible to give names of thought categories to (what were only) names of language categories. (There is double recourse to homonymy

and to synonymy: Aristotle gave the same name to different
things [thought and language] and different names [thought
and language] to what is fundamentally the same thing [lan-
guage]. How can the same name be given to discernible concepts
and things? How can different names be given to identical concepts and things? We should note in passing that this question is
also asked, in explicit terms, by Aristotle. It is found in the *Organon,* to be precise, at the beginning of the text on the *Categories.*
And when the question happens to be concerned with its own
element, namely, language in general, it takes a very singular
form. It supposes, among a great many other things, that some
kind of clarity can be achieved regarding what language and
thought can *be* or *mean*—and already this latter alternative contains and reflects the whole problem.)

In Benveniste's entire analysis, only one sentence seems to
offer an explanation and to be related to the questions just
raised. "Unconsciously he [Aristotle] took as a criterion the
empirical necessity of a distinct *expression* for each of his predications" (p. 61). What does "empirical" mean here? Taken
literally, this explanation would imply that Aristotle—having
predicates or *conceivable* classes of predicates at his disposition
outside language, and faced with the *empirical* necessity of expressing these contents (the word *"expression"* is italicized by
Benveniste)—has confused the distinction between predicates
with the distinction between expressions. He has mistaken the
chain of expressing units for the chain of expressed units. "Unconsciously" and without having wanted to, he has mistaken the
"class of forms" as given by the system of language for the system of the expressed or expressible. (Moreover, assuming this to
be the case, isn't there a structural necessity in the practice of a
language that always generates this "unconsciousness," with the
result that what Benveniste points to in Aristotle is only the
confirmation of this general law of unconsciousness, posed as a
preamble?)

We must stress the adjective "empirical." Although, grammatically, "empirical" in any case qualifies "necessity," the word
"necessity," as it is construed here and by virtue of the terms
it governs in the sentence, shifts the frame of reference of
"empirical" toward the word "expression" or toward "distinct

expression" ("the empirical necessity of a distinct expression").
These two possibilities give rise to two hypotheses.

In the first and more likely hypothesis, it is the *necessity* of
expressing (each of the predicates) that would remain empirical.
"Empirical" would qualify not only the situation within a language in general, and then within a natural language, but also
the link between the structure of a predicate conceived outside
of language and its "expression" within language. Language-
system and language usage would become—in keeping with the
most traditional motif—the contingent exteriority of thought, of
conceivable and signifiable meaning. In addition, it might also
be possible to distinguish between logos (or language in general)
and natural language in order to postulate that the empirical
necessity concerns not the link between thought and language in
general, but rather the link between a somehow universal logos
and a natural language. Although they are not identical, these
two possibilities are related by the strictest analogy. They both
amount to positing language-system [*langue*] as an empirical
shell of meaning in general, of essential or universal thought or
language [*langage*].[18] In the first hypothesis, Benveniste can only
repeat the operation he himself imputes to Aristotle: namely, to
distinguish *speech* and *thought* (in his words) and consider only an
empirical relation between them. There is one difference: Aristotle would maintain the distinction in order to remain within
the disjunction, believing he was dealing with thought when in
fact it was a question of speech; and Benveniste would maintain
the distinction in order to demonstrate that, by substitution, articulations of language have been mistaken for articulations of
thought.

This first reading of "empirical necessity of a distinct expression" finds its confirmation in several statements from the same
text, notably in its conclusions.

> Surely it is not by chance that modern epistemology does not try to
> set up a table of categories. It is more productive to conceive of the

---

[18]To the extent that this essentially metaphysical presupposition *also* remains
at work in Benveniste's text, it is no longer paradoxical that the *philosophical*
objections that his project has already encountered should be fundamentally of
the same type.

mind as a virtuality than as a framework, as a dynamism than as a structure. It is a fact that, to satisfy the requirements of scientific methods, thought everywhere adopts the same procedures in whatever language it chooses to describe experience. In this sense, it becomes independent, not of language, but of particular linguistic structures. Chinese thought may well have invented categories as specific as the *tao,* the *yin,* and the *yang;* it is nonetheless able to assimilate the concepts of dialectical materialism or quantum mechanics without the structure of the Chinese language proving a hindrance. No type of language can by itself alone foster or hamper the activity of the mind. The advance of thought is linked much more closely to the capacities of man, to general conditions of culture, and to the organization of society than to the particular nature of a language. But the possibility of thought is linked to the faculty of speech, for language is a structure informed with signification, and to think is to manipulate the signs of language. [pp. 63–64]

No doubt inseparable from language in general, "the thrust of thought" and "the activity of the mind" would not therefore be essentially linked to a particular language. This is tantamount to granting that there can be "contents" of thought without any essential link with the "forms" of a particular language. In that case neither Aristotle nor any of the philosophers who have since tried to constitute a table of thought categories independent of language categories would in principle have been wrong. Thought is not language—a *particular* language—or so Benveniste seems to admit here. But Aristotle deluded himself *in practice:* he believed in a *table* and above all, unconsciously and empirically, he confused what he ought to have distinguished.

We are still working with the first hypothesis. Is it not strange to qualify as empirical the necessity of an expression, the necessity of enunciating the thinkable in a given language? In the final analysis, empiricity as a quality has never managed to refer to anything more than the variability of perceptible and individual data; and by extension, to every passivity or activity devoid of concept, for example (to quote Leibniz), to "a simple practice without theory."[19]

Now, to the extent that one can concede the existence of pure empiricity in the practice of language, it could be conceivable

[19]*Monadology,* §28.

only with respect to the sensible and singular occurrence of a material (phonic or graphic) signifier. And this supposes that that kind of pure and unrepeatable event, escaping all formal generalization, could ever occur in linguistic or semiotic practice. Above all, how is it possible to affirm the empiricity of the movement which leads to signifying in general and to signifying within a given language (that is to say resorting to an organization of forms, a distribution of classes, etc.)? Finally, on the basis of what system and what historical ground do we receive and understand the signification of empiricity even before positing the empirical character of signification? No analysis of this subject can bypass the Aristotelian impulse. This does not imply that Aristotle is the author or the source of the concept of empiricity, even though his metaphysics is shrouded in one way or another by the opposition of the empirical and the theoretical (the a priori, the scientific, the objective, the systematic, and so on). Even if such a concept is not affixed once and for all to an "origin," we cannot understand the system of its mutations or transformations without taking into account the general code of metaphysics, and in it, the decisive mark of Aristotelianism. As Heidegger had already noted in *Die Zeit des Weltbildes* (1938): "Aristotle was the first to have understood what *empeiria* signified."[20] If one wanted to use the word "empirical" in a sense totally foreign to Aristotle and the history of philosophy, a specific commitment to the work of such a transformation would be necessary. Nothing in Benveniste's text signals or announces this displacement.

But in that case, one might object that we cannot even use a little word as innocent as *empirical*—a word that everybody understands ordinarily—in a demonstration of broader scope and higher import. I would be tempted to answer that—given the stakes of the demonstration and its strategically decisive character—even if one would, at less important moments in the development, introduce certain terms without endless precaution, it would certainly not be this term, since it in fact carries the whole weight of the critical argument.

Second hypothesis: "empirical necessity" would govern not so

[20]Heidegger, *Holzwege* (Frankfurt: V. Klostermann, 1950), p. 74.

much "expression" as, more indirectly, expression to the extent that it is "distinct for each of its predications." In this case, Aristotle did not simply or essentially give in to the so-called empirical necessity to *express* predicates; rather, by giving in, by establishing the list of classes, he proceeded in an empirical manner. Not only the project, but its very inception, the procedures of its realization, were empirical.

In this case the argument would be tenuous. On the one hand it would echo the most traditional philosophical objection. On the other, it would contradict what is most convincing and new in Benveniste's analysis which demonstrates, as J. Vuillemin has quite correctly asserted, (1) that the table of categories is systematic and not rhapsodic, (2) that since it performs a *selection* in the categories of language, it is not a simple copy or empirical reflection of them.[21]

The Transcendental and Language

We have not yet reached the principal locus of the problem, which becomes fully evident when Benveniste proposes to "elaborate on this remark" that "what Aristotle gave us as a table of general and permanent conditions is only a conceptual pro-

---

[21]A long quote from Vuillemin is required at this point:

"[Benveniste's] demonstration possesses a double merit. First of all it points up the organization of the table of categories, something which had always been criticized for its rhapsodic character. The first six categories all refer to nominal forms, the last four to verbal forms. Except in one case, the enumeration proceeds within this division by paired oppositions. The category of substantives seems to constitute an exception to this rule; but it is itself subdivided into proper nouns (primary substances) and common nouns (secondary substances). The adjective *poson* and *poion* go together (*osos/oios, tosos/toios*) just as do the adverbs *pou* and *poté* (*ou/oté, tou/toté*). *Pros ti,* which appears alone, 'expresses only the fundamental property of Greek adjectives which is to provide a comparative.' As for the four verbal forms, if *poiein* and *paskhein* ('to do'/'to undergo') visibly constitute an opposition which corresponds to the opposition of active and passive, then *keisthai* 'to be placed') and *ekhein* ('to be in a state') also form a couple when they are interpreted as language categories: 'There are, indeed, various relationships, both formal and functional, between the Greek perfect and the middle voice, which, as inherited from Indo-European, formed a complex system; for example, an active perfect, *gegona* goes with middle present, *gignomai.*' [Benveniste, p. 60]

"In the second place, one must conclude that, believing he was classifying concepts, Aristotle in reality classified language categories, such that the par-

jection of a given linguistic state." This occurs in the last pages, after he deems the general aim of the essay to have been achieved and the argument well established.

> This table of predications informs us above all about the class structure of a particular language.
>   It follows that what Aristotle gave us as a table of general and permanent conditions is only a conceptual projection of a given linguistic state. This remark can be elaborated further. Beyond the Aristotelian terms, above that categorization, there is the notion of "being" which envelops everything. Without being a predicate itself, "being" is the condition of all predicates. All the varieties of "being-such," of "state," all the possible views of "time," etc., depend on the notion of "being." Now here again, this concept reflects a very specific linguistic quality. [p. 61]

One can see the scope of this kind of postscript. It does a great deal more than "elaborate on" his remark. We are finally reaching the point where we can conceive the possibility of the field of categories, the very inception of the Aristotelian project: to constitute a table containing the figures of predication which give shape to simple being ("properly speaking") which is expressed

------

ticularities of the Greek language have dominated the destiny of Western philosophy.
    "In fact, this second conclusion goes beyond the limits of what the logical argument has demonstrated. Indeed, on the basis of the argument that philosophy borrows from language the concepts and oppositions basic to thought, it is illegitimate to conclude that, not only does language propose its own suggestions to thought, but that it is impossible to think what is not expressed in language. In any case, it is not legitimate to conclude that the table of thought categories reflects the table of language categories. In order to arrive at this point it would have been necessary to show that the table of categories borrowed from language is also, with regard to language, the *complete* list of these categories. In the opposite case, there is selection; and if the philosopher chooses from among linguistic categories, it is precisely because his choice is no longer dictated solely by linguistic considerations. Now, this is exactly what happens, since no one pretends that the structure of the categories of the Greek language is exhausted in Aristotle's table.
    "In fact, his table of categories follows a logical articulation which possesses an ontological dimension at the same time" (Vuillemin, pp. 76–77).
    The two principal arguments (systemacity and selection), to which it is difficult not to subscribe, are nevertheless developed on grounds that seem to us quite problematic. For example, does philosophy "borrow" from language? And what does "to borrow" mean here? Does one borrow "from language the concepts and oppositions basic to thought" in the same way one borrows a tool?—a tool

in many ways. This time we are no longer dealing with a category, or at least not with one category among others[22] in the
system; and it can no longer be a question of "projecting" or of
"transcribing" a particular category in another, or indeed of
proceeding more or less empirically in this task. The elaboration
of the "remark" takes a leap: it suddenly goes beyond the field
delineated by the title and by the initial formulation of the problem. What Benveniste hastily calls the "notion of being" is no
longer simply a category homogeneous with the others: it is the
transcategorial condition of categories. Benveniste acknowledges this: "Beyond the Aristotelian terms, above that categori-
zation, there is the notion of 'being' which envelops everything.
Without being a predicate itself, 'being' is the condition of all
predicates." This reminder must be read within the immense
problematic vein which runs from the *Sophist* (which Benveniste's phrase literally evokes: " . . . and *many* forms, different

---

whose value moreover is recognized by "thought." How are we to understand
the statement that language proposes "its own suggestions to thought"? The formula is restated and treated even more thoroughly elsewhere: "Morphology
and syntax thus reunited do indeed constitute a language, but this philosophical
language diverges as much as is necessary from the suggestions that the Greek
language originally imposes." The general presupposition of this argument seems
to be the inverse—the symmetrical inverse—of the presupposition sustaining
Benveniste's analysis (at least when Benveniste proceeds as a linguist, and not
as a philosopher of the "activity of the mind" and the "advance of thought"):
the contents of thought are essentially, principially, structurally independent
of language in spite of "borrowings" and "suggestions." As has been said, the
"logical" and the "ontological" have no intrinsic link with the "linguistic." The
specular symmetry of the theses presented here, their profound resemblance
in an in(de)terminable opposition, already suffice to invite a re-elaboration of
the problem. This would be a re-elaboration in which one would, for example,
not take for granted at the outset, as if it went without saying—with this feeling
of familiarity, of mastery, of "knowledge"—the access to the "essence" of "thought"
or of the "language-system"; nor their opposition or identity. This is only one
example.

[22]This point being assured, and it is sufficient for what concerns us here, we
cannot go into the complexity of its context. Analysis and references can be
found in P. Aubenque's *Le Problème de l'être chez Aristote* (Paris: Presses Universitaires de France, 1966) notably pp. 171ff. "As we can see, essence itself is
presented here as a predicate, although it is elsewhere defined as that which is
always a subject and never a predicate (*Pr. Anal.*, I, 27, 43 a25; *Phys.*, I, 7, 190
a34; *Met.*, Z, 3, 1028 b36). But essence, which is in fact the subject of every
conceivable attribution, can be attributed secondarily to itself. It is in this sense
that it is a category, i.e., one of the figures of predication, one of the possible
meanings of the copula." Cf. also pp. 190ff.

from one another, embraced from without by one form, and again *one* form connected in a unity through many wholes . . . " [253d][23]) to Aristotle's statement to the effect that being is not a genus, to the assertion in the *Critique of Pure Reason:* ("*Being* is obviously not a real predicate; that is, it is not a concept of something which could be added to the concept of a thing. It is merely the positing of a thing, or of certain determinations, as existing in themselves"[24]) and to questions raised by Heidegger, notably in *Kants These Über das Sein.*[25]

"Being" therefore is not on the table. Nor anywhere else. The linguist or the logician who wants to establish a rule of translation or correspondence between language categories and thought categories will never encounter anything which he could simply call "being."

What Benveniste uncovers through this "elaboration" is the absolutely unique relationship between language and the transcendental. Here we are using the word "transcendental" in its most rigorous sense, in its most firmly established "technicalness," just as it has been defined in the course of the development of the Aristotelian problematic of categories as well as for what stands beyond the categories. Transcendental means transcategorial. Literally: "what *transcends* every genus." (This definition of a word that was most probably coined by Chancellor Philippe [1128] is also commensurate, in spite of certain contextual differences, with the Kantian and Husserlian notions of the transcendental.)

So where does this leave the issue of the transcendental character of "being" with regard to language? This is our question.

In order to acknowledge the fundamental grounding of "being" in a very specific natural language, Benveniste underscores the fact that not all languages make use of the verb "to be." "Greek not only possesses a verb 'to be' (which is by no means a necessity in every language), but it makes very peculiar uses of

[23]*The Collected Dialogues of Plato,* ed. E. Hamilton and H. Cairns (New York: Pantheon, 1961), p. 999.
[24]Kant, p. 504.
[25]In *Existenz und Ordnung. Festschrift für Erik Wolf* (Frankfurt: Klostermann, 1962), pp. 217–245.

this verb" (p. 61). This peculiarity is described in a paragraph that we shall quote in order to focus on certain problematic places.

> It [Greek] gave it [the verb "to be"] a logical function, that of the copula (Aristotle himself had remarked earlier that in that function the verb did not actually signify anything, that it operated simply as a *synthesis*), and consequently, this verb received a larger extension than any other whatever. In addition, "to be" could become, thanks to the article, a nominal notion, treated as a thing; it gave rise to varieties, for example its present participle, which itself had been made a substantive, and in several kinds (*to on; oi ontes; ta onta*); it could serve as a predicate itself, as in the locution *to ti en einai* designating the conceptual essence of a thing, not to mention the astonishing diversity of particular predicates with which it could be construed, by means of case forms and prepositions.... Listing this abundance of uses would be endless; but they really are facts of language, of syntax, and of derivation. Let us emphasize this, because it is in a linguistic situation thus characterized that the whole Greek metaphysics of "being" was able to come into existence and develop—the magnificent images of the poem of Parmenides as well as the dialectic of *The Sophist*. The language did not, of course, give direction to the metaphysical definition of "being"—each Greek thinker has his own—but it made it possible to set up "being" as an objectifiable notion which philosophical thought could handle, analyze, and define just as any other concept. [pp. 61-62]

(1) If "to be," at least as a copula, does not "actually signify anything," since it extends infinitely, then it is no longer linked to the particular form of a word, or a noun (in the Aristotelian sense of the smallest semantic unit [*onoma*], this category including in turn nouns and verbs). In other words, it is no longer linked to the *phonè semantikè*[26] unit possessing a sense content. From this point, is it not an impossible or a contradictory operation to define the *presence* of the copula in one language and its *absence* in another? We shall return to this later.

(2) What assurance does one have that "they really are facts of language, of syntax, and of derivation"? No definition of language has yet been given, nor a definition of the self-immanence

---

[26]On this point, see Derrida, "La Mythologie blanche" in *Marges* (Paris: Minuit, 1972). English translation in *New Literary History*, VI (1974).—Ed.

of the language-system in general. What is the status of this immanence, of the inclusion within language of a structure or an operation which has the effect—a linguistic effect, if one wants to call it that—of opening up language to its outside, of articulating language onto the nonlinguistic? The question arises especially in the case of "being" and everything that depends on it *preeminently* and *by definition*.

(3) How can the word "images" (a historically charged philosophical term of complex derivation) be used to designate the paths, the crossroad, bifurcation, palintrope, sphere, veil, axis, wheel, sun, moon, etc., of Parmenides' "poem"? That text, by positing a certain sameness of "thinking" and "being," has *pointed out* the opening in language to the presence of being, to truth, to what has always *represented intrusion* within language's closure upon itself.

(4) "The language did not, of course, give direction to the metaphysical definition of 'being'—each Greek thinker has his own." How can this statement be reconciled with all the other affirmations that reduce thought categories to language categories? What does "to give direction to" mean in this case? Could it be that the "metaphysical definition of 'being'" is completely free now with regard to language? If linguistic constraint did not weigh on the "metaphysical definition of 'being'" (a very obscure notion indeed), upon what then did it bear? On a formal function without semantic content? In that case, how can this function be exclusively reserved for Greek grammar or lexicology? A moment ago we noted that we would have to confront this problem. Well, if language has given so little "direction to" the "metaphysical definition of 'being'" that "each Greek thinker has his own," what has it governed in philosophy? Where then is the trap for the philosopher who mistook language for thought? And can one say (but what is one then saying?) that "each Greek thinker has his own"? Never would the constraint of language have been so lax. And what are we to say of the inheritors of "Greek metaphysics" who have thought-spoken-written in Latin or German? All of this is far from demonstrating the absence of linguistic constraint upon philosophy, but it surely points up the necessity of re-elaborating the current concept of linguistic constraint. This obscurity and these contradictions are condensed

when Benveniste uses the notions of "predisposition" and "vocation," just as J. Vuillemin spoke of "borrowings" and "suggestions": "All we wish to show here is that the linguistic structure of
Greek predisposed the notion of 'being' to a philosophical vocation" (p. 63).

(5) Finally, since, in point of fact, "without being a predicate
itself, 'being' is the condition of all predicates," then it is no
longer possible to believe that "philosophical thought could
handle, analyze, and define [it] just as any other concept."

To "elaborate on this remark," one should not only enlarge
the domain of the demonstration, but shake up the structure of
the already occupied territory. Without the transcategoriality of
"being" which "envelops everything," the passage between language and thought categories would not have been possible in
either direction, for either Aristotle or Benveniste.

The Remainder by Way of Supplement:
Concerning the Third Person Singular of the
Present Indicative of the Verb "To Be"

These difficulties propagate their own effects. They mark the
counterproof proposed by Benveniste. If Greek metaphysics—
with its pretension to truth and universality—depends on a particular linguistic fact that has gone unnoticed by philosophers,
examination of another language should confirm the argument.

> That this is primarily a matter of language will be better realized if
> the behavior of this same notion in a different language is consid-
> ered. It is best to choose a language of an entirely different type to
> compare with the Greek, because it is precisely in the internal
> organization of their categories that linguistic types differ the
> most. Let us only state that what we are comparing here are facts of
> linguistic expression, not conceptual developments.
>   In the Ewe language (spoken in Togo), which we have chosen
> for this contrast, the notion of "to be," or what we shall designate as
> such, is divided among several verbs. [p. 62]

Let us immediately point out that this analysis (which
strangely enough proposes to concentrate only on "facts of linguistic expression" without considering "conceptual developments") is concerned not with the pure and simple *absence* of the

verb "to be," as one might have expected—"Greek not only possesses the verb 'to be' (which is by no means a necessity in every
language)"—but rather with a distribution, a different division
of its function "among several verbs." Now, even in Indo-
European languages, the "ontological" function is not entrusted
to one single verb or verbal form.[27] Benveniste's analysis of the
Ewe language consists of discovering in a language without "the
verb 'to be'" a multiplicity of analogous and differently distributed functions. What then is the resource for translation that is
at work here? Benveniste himself asks this question; but though
he notes that his own description is "a bit contrived" (p. 63), he
fails to ask how such an artifice is possible and why it is not totally
absurd or inoperative.

> This description of the state of things in Ewe is a bit contrived. It is
> made from the standpoint of *our* language and not, as it should
> have been, within the framework of the language itself. Within the
> morphology or syntax of Ewe, nothing brings these five verbs into
> relationship with one another. It is in connection with our own
> linguistic usages that we discover something common to them. But
> that is precisely the advantage of this "egocentric" comparison: it
> throws light on ourselves; it shows us, among that variety of uses of
> "to be" in Greek, a phenomenon peculiar to the Indo-European
> languages which is not at all a universal situation or a necessary
> condition. Of course the Greek thinkers in their turn acted upon
> the language, enriched the meanings, and created new forms. It is
> indeed from philosophical reflection on "being" that the abstract
> substantive derived from *einai* arose; we see it being created in the
> course of history: at first as *essia* in Dorian Pythagorism and in
> Plato, then as *ousia*, which won out. All we wish to show here is that
> the linguistic structure of Greek predisposed the notion of "being"
> to a philosophical vocation. By comparison, the Ewe language of-
> fers us only a narrow notion and particularized uses. We cannot
> say what place "being" holds in Ewe metaphysics, but, a priori, the
> notion must be articulated in a completely different way. [p. 63]

Is there a "metaphysics" outside of the Indo-European organization of the "being" function? This question is anything but
ethnocentric. Far from suggesting that other languages might be

[27]Benveniste himself notes this on p. 63. Cf. also Heidegger, "On the
Grammar and Etymology of the Word 'Being'" in *An Introduction to Metaphysics,*
trans. Ralph Manheim (New York: Anchor Books, 1961), pp. 42ff.

deprived of excellent philosophical and metaphysical vocations, it avoids projecting our particular forms of "history" and "culture" outside of the West.

One must therefore wonder how the absence of the—unique—verbal function "to be" should be read in any language whatever. Is such an absence possible? How can it be interpreted? It is not the absence of one word in a lexicon, in the first place because the function "to be" is spread among several words in Indo-European languages. Nor for that matter is it the absence of a specific semantic content, of a simple signified, since "being" signifies nothing that is determinable. Therefore it is even less the absence of a thing that could be referred to.

Heidegger asked the same question:

> Let us suppose that this indeterminate meaning of being does not exist and that we also do not understand what this meaning means. What then? Would there merely be a noun and a verb less in our language? No. *There would be no language at all.* No essent *as such* would disclose itself in words, it would no longer be possible to invoke it and speak about it in words. For to speak of an essent as such includes: to understand it in advance as an essent, that is, to understand its being. Assuming that we did not understand being at all, assuming that the word "being" did not even have its vaporous meaning, there would not be a single word.[28]

Even if Heideggerian thought were ethnocentric, it would never be so simplistic as to refuse the name of language (at least in a sense not derived from philosophical tradition) to any non-Western system of signification. These statements must have another aim. If we point out that elsewhere Heidegger distinguishes the meaning of "being" from the word "being" and from the concept of "being," this is the same as saying that for Heidegger the condition for a language's being a language is no longer the presence within it of the word or the concept (*signified*) "being," but rather the presence of another concept that remains to be defined. The very concept of "ethnocentricism" gives us no critical assurance so long as the elaboration of this other possibility remains unfinished.

[28]Ibid., p. 69.

In order to approach this possibility—since we cannot systematically examine the entire Heideggerian text here—let us return to Benveniste. But this time we shall consider another text than the one we have dealt with so far, a study published two years later: "The Linguistic Functions of 'To Be' and 'To Have.'"[29] His point of departure is precisely the absence or, to adopt the word Benveniste uses, the "lack" of the verb "to be," not only in certain non-Indo-European languages, but in certain operations typical of "our" languages.[30]

> The study of sentences with the verb "to be" is obscured by the difficulty, indeed the impossibility, of setting up a satisfactory definition of the nature and functions of the verb "to be." First of all, is "to be" a verb? If it is one, why is it so often missing? And if it is not, how does it happen that it has taken on the status and forms of a verb while remaining what is called a "substantive-verb"? [p. 163]

Benveniste points out what he calls a "contradiction." It seems to be a contradiction between Benveniste's two texts as well, or at least between the assertion that the verb "to be" does not belong to all languages, and the assertion that there is always an *equivalent* for each sentence that uses the verb "to be." It is in this substitutive equivalence that the entire difficulty resides.

> The fact that there is a "nominal sentence" characterized by the absence of the verb and that this is a universal phenomenon seems to contradict the fact, also very widespread, that it has a sentence with the verb "to be" as its equivalent. The data seem to elude analysis, and the whole problem is still so poorly worked out that one finds no firm ground to stand on. The cause for this is probably that one reasons, implicitly at least, as if the verb "to be" were a logical and chronological continuation of a stage of language which did not have such a verb. But this lineal reasoning collides at all points with the contradictions of linguistic reality without, however, satisfying any theoretical necessity. [p. 163]

One can only agree with this last proposition. But does it not invalidate certain affirmations of his text on categories? How is it

---

[29] In *Problems in General Linguistics,* pp. 163–179.

[30] One might study Mallarmé's language from this point of view, and, within his language, the rarefaction of "to be" and "is." Cf. Derrida, "La Double Séance," in *La Dissémination* (Paris: Seuil, 1972).

now conceivable that *all* languages have an equivalent for sentences using the verb "to be"?

(1) The function of "the copula" or "the grammatical mark of equivalence" (p. 163) is absolutely distinct from the "full-fledged" use of the verb "to be." "*The two have coexisted* and will always be able to coexist since they are completely different. But in many languages they have merged" (p. 163). As a result, "when one speaks of the verb 'to be,' it is necessary to state specifically if it is a matter of the grammatical notion or the lexical. Without this distinction, the problem is insoluble and cannot even be stated clearly" (pp. 163–164).

As for the grammatical function of the copula, however, Benveniste demonstrates its universality with a great abundance of examples. It belongs to all languages that are lacking the lexical presence of the verb "to be."

(2) In all languages, a certain supplementary function is available to offset the lexical "absence" of the verb "to be." In fact, this supplementarity serves to fill in for something absent only in the eyes of those like ourselves who make use of a language in which the two functions—grammatical and lexical—have "merged" (at least up to a certain point), leading to all the fundamental "historical" consequences that one can conceive. Is it not the case that what we perceive outside the West as a supplement offsetting this absence or as a vicarious mode is in fact an original possibility that gets added to—and thus manages without that function just as well, indeed can do without any reference to it? Doesn't this happen even within Indo-European languages?

The most general form of this supplement of the copula is the nominal phrase.

> Here the most generally found expression does not require any verb. This is the "nominal sentence" as it appears today in Russian or Hungarian, for example, in which a zero morpheme, the pause, assures the conjunction of the terms and asserts that they are identical, no matter what the modality of this assertion may be: a formal equation ("Rome is the capital of Italy"), class inclusion ("the dog is a mammal"), or class membership ("Pierre is French"), etc.
>
> What matters is to see clearly that there is no connection, either by nature or by necessity, between the verbal notion of "to exist, to really be there" and the function of the "copula." One need not ask

how it happens that the verb "to be" can be lacking or omitted. This is to reason in reverse. The real question should be the opposite; how is it that there is a verb "to be" which gives verbal expression and lexical consistency to a logical relationship in an assertive utterance? [p. 164]

It happens, then, that the lexical absence is "supplemented" only by an absence which is just absence; the grammatical function of "to be" is then assumed by a blank space, by a somehow effaced punctuation mark, by a *pause:* an oral interruption or a halt of the voice (is it then an *oral phenomenon?*), which is marked by no *graphic* sign (in the commonly accepted sense of that word), by no written matter. The absence of "to be," the absence of that singular lexeme, is absence itself. Is not the semantic value of *absence* in general dependent on the lexical-semantic value of "to be"? It is within the horizon of this question that we should perhaps analyze what Benveniste again calls a "supplementary feature," that is, only a "probable" feature which *exists* or *consists* in nothing but a certain suspension.

> As is known, ancient Semitic did not have a verb "to be." It sufficed to juxtapose the nominal terms of the utterance in order to get a nominal sentence with the supplementary feature—probable, although not graphemically represented—of a pause between the terms. The example of Russian and Hungarian and other languages gives this pause the value of an element in the utterance; it is actually the sign of the predication. It is probable that wherever the structure of a language permits the construction of a predicative utterance by the juxtaposition of two nominal forms in a free order, one should grant that a pause separates them. [p. 165]

(3) Another, very common form of this supplement of the copula is the syntactic play of the pronoun, for example, its repetition at the end of a proposition. In certain oriental dialects one finds: *män yaš män,* "I am young" (me young me); *sän yaš sän,* "you are young"; and in Altaic: *ol bay ol,* "he is rich" (him rich him). "This syntactic assigning of the pronoun to the function of a copula is a phenomenon whose general significance must be emphasized" (p. 166).

The process of objectification henceforth leads to the constant privileging of the third person singular. The hidden relation between such a privilege and the law of the supplement of the copula opens up a problem that linguistics and ontology *as such* can designate only from afar, first of all because, as a *science* and a *philosophy*, they are principally subjugated to the authority of that "is" whose possibility must be investigated. Let us illustrate this by a simple comparison. Here we must consult another essay by Benveniste, "The Nominal Sentence."[31]

> Since the memorable article [*Mémoires de la Société Linguistique de Paris* 14] in which A. Meillet defined the situation of the nominal sentence in Indo-European, thus giving it its first linguistic status, several studies relating in particular to the ancient Indo-European languages have contributed to the historical description of this type of utterance. Briefly characterized, the nominal sentence consists of a predicate nominative, without a verb or copula, and it is considered the normal expression in Indo-European where a possible verbal form would have been the *third person of the present indicative of "to be."* These definitions have been widely used, even outside the domain of Indo-European, but without leading to a parallel study of the conditions that made this linguistic situation possible. The theory of this highly peculiar syntactic phenomenon has not by any means kept pace with the gradual realization of how widespread it is.
>
> This type of sentence is not limited to one family or to certain families of languages. Those in which it has been noticed are only the first of a list that can now be considerably lengthened. The nominal sentence is encountered not only in Indo-European, in Semitic, in Finno-Ugric, and in Bantu, but also in the most diverse languages: Sumerian, Egyptian, Caucasian, Altaic, Dravidian, Siberian, Amerindian, etc. . . . To what necessity is the nominal sentence bound for it to be produced in similar ways by so many different languages, and how does it happen—the question will seem strange but the strangeness is in the facts—that the verb of existence, out of all other verbs, has this privilege of being present in an utterance in which it does not appear? As soon as one probes further into the problem, one is forced to envisage the relationships of the verb and noun as a whole, and then the particular nature of the verb "to be." [pp. 131–132—my emphasis]

This insistence of the third person singular present indicative of the verb "to be" must have also marked the history of languages in which "to be" included a lexical presence. Therefore, the copula function would have invisibly governed the interpre-

[31]In *Problems in General Linguistics,* pp. 131–144.

tation of the meaning of "to be" having, as it were, always worked upon it.

Citing Heidegger again:

> We understand the verbal substantive "Sein" ["being"] through the infinitive, which in turn is related to the "is" and its diversity that we have described. The definite and particular verb form "is," the *third person singular of the present indicative,* has here a pre-eminent rank. We understand "being" not in regard to the "thou art," "you are," "I am," or "they would be," though all of these, just as much as "is," represent verbal inflections of "to be." "To be" [*Sein*] is for us the infinitive of "is." And involuntarily, almost as though nothing else were possible, we explain the infinitive "to be" to ourselves through the "is."
>
> Accordingly, "being" has the meaning indicated above, recalling the Greek view of the essence of being [*Wesen des Seins*], hence a determinateness which has not just dropped on us accidentally from somewhere but has dominated our historical being-there [*Dasein*] since antiquity.[32]

Although always uneasy and worked upon from within, the fusion of the grammatical and the lexical functions of "to be" surely has an essential link with the history of metaphysics and everything that is coordinated with it in the West.

It is a great temptation, in fact hardly repressible, to consider the growing predominance of the formal copula function as a process of falling, abstraction, degradation, as evacuation of the semantic plenitude of the lexeme "to be" and of all other lexemes which, like "to be," have been allowed to wane or be replaced. When we investigate this "history" (but the word "history" belongs to this process of meaning) as the history of meaning, when we ask the "question of being" as a question of the "meaning of being" (Heidegger), are we not limiting the destruction of classical ontology to a sphere constituted by the reappropriation of the semantic plenitude of "to be," by the reactivation of lost origins, etc? Are we not making the supplement of the copula into a historical accident, even if it is considered structurally necessary? Are we not expecting to find a kind of original fall, and everything that such a perspective would imply?

Why does the sphere of meaning dominate the questioning of

---

[32] *Introduction to Metaphysics,* p. 77.

both the linguist and the philosopher? What desire impels them both, as such, to proceed analogically toward a supralapsarian state, prior to the supplement of the copula? Their procedure and their sphere remain analogous, as we see in what follows:

The entire range of the inflections of the verb "*sein*" [to be] is determined by three different stems.

The first two stems to be named are Indo-European and also occur in the Greek and Latin words for "being."

1. The oldest, the actual radical word is *es,* Sanskrit *asus,* life, the living, that which from out of itself stands and which moves and rests in itself. . . . It is noteworthy that the "*ist*" [is] has maintained itself in all [Indo-European] languages from the very start (Greek—*estin,* Latin—*est,* German—*ist*).

2. The other Indo-European radical is *bhu, bheu.* To it belong the Greek *phuo,* to emerge, to be powerful, of itself to come to stand and remain standing. Up until now this *bhu* has been interpreted according to the usual superficial view of *physis* and *phyein.* . . .

3. The third stem occurs only in the inflection of the Germanic verb "*sein*": this is *wes;* Sanskrit: *vasami;* Germanic: *wesan,* to dwell, to sojourn. . . . The substantive "*Wesen*" did not originally mean "whatness," quiddity, but enduring as presence, presence [*Anwesen*] and absence [*Ab-wesen*]. The *sens* in the Latin *prae-sens* and *ab-sens* has been lost. . . . From the three stems we derive the three initial concrete meanings: to live, to emerge, to linger or endure. These are established by linguistics which also establishes that these initial meanings are extinct today, that only an "abstract" meaning "to be" has been preserved. . . .

We must ask a whole series of questions. . . .

8. Can the meaning of being, which on the basis of a purely logical, grammatical interpretation strikes us as "abstract" and hence derived, be inherently whole and fundamental?

9. Can this be shown through language if we take a sufficiently basic view of it? . . . "Being" remains barely a sound to us, a *threadbare* appellation. If nothing more is left to us, *we must seek at least* to grasp *this last vestige of a possession.* Therefore we ask "How does it stand with the *word* 'being'?" [my emphasis]

We have answered this question in two ways which have led us into the grammar and the etymology of the word. Let us sum up the results of this twofold discussion of the word "*Das Sein.*"

1. Grammatical investigation of the word form shows that in the infinitive the definite meanings of the word no longer make themselves felt; they are *effaced.* Substantivization completely stabilizes and objectifies this *effacement.* The word becomes a name for something indeterminate. [my emphasis]

2. Etymological investigation of the word's meaning has shown that in respect to meaning what we have long called by the name of "*Das Sein*" is a *compromise and mixture* of three different radical meanings. None of these reaches up independently to determine the meaning of the word. *Mixture and effacement* go hand in hand. [my emphasis][33]

Benveniste writes:

It remains to complete these suggestions by examining the situation of the verb "to be" with respect to the nominal sentence. We must insist upon the necessity for rejecting every implication of a lexical "to be" in the analysis of the nominal sentence, and of reforming the habits of translation imposed by the different structure of modern Western languages. One can start a strict interpretation of the nominal sentence only by freeing oneself from that servitude and by recognizing the verb *esti* in Indo-European as a verb just like the others. It is such, not only in that it bears all the morphological marks of its class and that it serves the same syntactic function but because it must have had a definite lexical meaning before *falling*—at the end of a long historical development—to the rank of "copula." It is no longer possible to attain this meaning directly, but the fact that **bhu-*, "to put forth, to grow," furnished part of the forms of **es* gives an inkling of it. In any case, even in interpreting it as "to exist, to have real substance" (cf. the sense of "truth" attached to the adjectives *sannr* in Old Icelandic, *sons* in Latin, and *satya-* in Sanskrit), one has defined it sufficiently by its function as an intransitive capable of being used either absolutely or accompanied by an appositive adjective; so that *esti* used absolutely or *esti* with the adjective functions like a great number of intransitive verbs in this double position (such as seem, appear, grow, remain, lie, spring, fall, etc.). We must *restore its full force and its authentic function to the verb "to be"* in order to measure the distance between a nominal assertion and an assertion with "to be." [p. 138—my emphasis]

This will perhaps appear (if indeed it appears at all) to be the case from a position [*lieu*] that is less important to name than to elaborate. In any event, the position could not be an ontology, a regional science, or anything else ordered according to a hierarchy. In effect such a hierarchy could regulate the particular sciences according to regional ontologies, and these in turn ac-

[33]Ibid., pp. 58–61.

cording to a fundamental ontology, only by presupposing what (*is*) comes here into question.

What about the *word* in all this? And what about this opposition of the lexical (semantic, etymological) and the grammatical, which so dominates these discourses without being investigated for itself? Where and how was it constituted? Why does *is* still give its form to all these questions? What about the relation between truth, meaning (of being), and the third person singular of the present indicative of the verb "to be"? What is it *to remain* or not *to remain*? What remains in a copula supplement?

If one were still seeking an answer in the form of the word, it would fall neither to philosophy nor to linguistics (as such) to say it.

PAUL DE MAN

Semiology and Rhetoric

To judge from various recent publications, the spirit of the times is not blowing in the direction of formalist and intrinsic criticism. We may no longer be hearing very much about relevance, but we do continue to hear a great deal about reference, about the nonverbal "outside" to which language refers, by which it is conditioned, and upon which it acts. The stress falls not so much on the fictional status of literature—a property now perhaps somewhat too easily taken for granted—but on the interplay between these fictions and categories that are said to partake of reality, such as the self, man, society, "the artist, his culture, and the human community," as one critic puts it. Hence the emphasis on hybrid texts considered to be partly literary and partly referential, on popular fictions deliberately aimed toward social and psychological gratification, on literary autobiography as a key to the understanding of the self, and so on. We speak as if, with the problems of literary form resolved once and forever, and with the techniques of structural analysis refined to near-perfection, we could now move "beyond formalism" toward the questions that really interest us and reap, at last, the fruits of the ascetic concentration on techniques that prepared us for this decisive step. With the internal law and order of literature well policed, we can now confidently devote ourselves to the foreign affairs, the external politics of literature. Not only do we feel able to do so, but we also think we owe it to ourselves to take this step: our moral conscience would not allow us to do otherwise. Behind the assurance that valid interpretation is possible, behind the recent interest in writing and reading as potentially effective public speech acts, stands a highly respectable moral imperative that strives to reconcile the internal, formal, private structures of literary language with their external, referential, and public effects.

I want, for the moment, to consider briefly this tendency in itself, as an undeniable and recurrent historical fact, without regard for its truth or falseness or for its value as desirable or pernicious. It is a fact that this sort of thing happens again and again in literary studies. On the one hand, literature cannot merely be received as a definite unit of referential meaning that can be decoded without leaving a residue. The code is unusually conspicuous, complex, and enigmatic; it attracts an inordinate amount of attention to itself, and this attention has to acquire the rigor of a method. The structural moment of concentration on the code for its own sake cannot be avoided, and literature necessarily breeds its own formalism. Technical innovations in the methodical study of literature only occur when this kind of attention predominates. It can legitimately be said, for example, that, from a technical point of view, very little has happened in American criticism since the innovative works of the New Criticism. There certainly have been numerous excellent books of criticism since, but in none of them have the techniques of description and interpretation evolved beyond the techniques of close reading established in the forties. Formalism, it seems, is an all-absorbing and tyrannical muse; the hope that one can be at the same time technically original and discursively eloquent is not borne out by the history of literary criticism.

On the other hand—and this is the real mystery—no literary formalism, no matter how accurate and enriching in its analytic powers, is ever allowed to come into being without seeming reductive. When form is considered to be the external trappings of literary meaning or content, it seems superficial and expendable. The development of intrinsic, formalist criticism in the twentieth century has changed this model: form is now a solipsistic category of self-reflection, and the referential meaning is said to be extrinsic. The polarities of inside and outside have been reversed, but they are still the same polarities that are at play: internal meaning has become outside reference, and the outer form has become the intrinsic structure. A new version of reductiveness at once follows this reversal: formalism nowadays is mostly described in an imagery of imprisonment and claustrophobia: the "prison house of language," "the impasse of formalist criticism," and the like. Like the grandmother in Proust's novel, ceaselessly driving the young Marcel out into the garden, away from the unhealthy inwardness of his closeted reading, critics cry out for the fresh air of referential meaning. Thus, with the structure of the code so opaque, but with the meaning so anxious to blot out the obstacle of form, it is no wonder that the reconciliation of form and meaning seems so attractive. The attraction of reconciliation is the elective breeding-ground of false models and metaphors; it accounts for the metaphorical model of literature as a kind of box that separates an inside from an outside, with the reader or critic as the person who opens the lid in order to release into the open what was secreted but inaccessible inside. It matters little whether we call the inside of the box the content or the form and the outside the meaning or the appearance. The recurrent debate opposing intrinsic to extrinsic criticism stands under the aegis of an inside/outside metaphor that has never been seriously questioned.

Metaphors are much more tenacious than facts, and I certainly don't expect to dislodge this age-old model in one short expository essay. I merely wish to speculate on a different set of terms, perhaps less simple in their differential relationship than the strictly polar, binary opposition between inside and outside, and therefore less likely to enter into the easy play of chiasmic reversals. I derive these terms (which are as old as the hills) pragmatically from the observation of developments and debates in recent critical methodology.

One of the most controversial among these developments coincides with a new approach to poetics—or, as it is called in Germany, poetology—as a branch of general semiotics. In France, a semiology of literature was the outcome of the long-deferred but all the more explosive encounter of the nimble French literary mind with the category of form. Semiology, as opposed to semantics, is the science or study of signs as signifiers; it does not ask what words mean but how they mean. Unlike American New Criticism, which derived the internalization of form from the practice of highly self-conscious modern writers, French semiology turned to linguistics for its model and adopted Saussure and Jakobson rather than Valéry or Proust for its masters. By an awareness of the arbitrariness of the sign (Saussure) and of literature as an autotelic statement "focused on the way it is expressed" (Jakobson), the entire question of meaning can be bracketed, thus freeing critical discourse from the debilitating burden of paraphrase. The demystifying power of semiology, within the context of French historical and thematic criticism, has been considerable. It demonstrated that the perception of the literary dimensions of language is largely obscured if one submits uncritically to the authority of reference. It also revealed how tenaciously this authority continues to assert itself in a variety of disguises, ranging from the crudest ideology to the most refined forms of aesthetic and ethical judgment. It especially exploded the myth of semantic correspondence between sign and referent, the wishful hope of having it both ways, of being, to paraphrase Marx, a formalist critic in the morning and a communal moralist in the afternoon, of serving both the technique of form and the substance of meaning. The results, in the practice of French criticism, have been as fruitful as they are irreversible. Perhaps for the first time since the late eighteenth century, French critics can come at least somewhat closer to the kind of linguistic awareness that never ceased to be operative in French poets and novelists, that forced all of them, including Sainte-Beuve, to write their main works "contre Sainte-Beuve." The distance was never so considerable in England and the United States, which does not mean, however, that we may be able, in this country, to dispense with a preventative semiological hygiene altogether.

One of the most striking characteristics of literary semiology as it is practiced today, in France and elsewhere, is the use of grammatical (especially syntactical) structures conjointly with rhetorical structures, without apparent awareness of a possible discrepancy between them. In their literary analyses, Barthes, Genette, Todorov, Greimas, and their disciples all simplify and regress from Jakobson in letting grammar and rhetoric function in perfect continuity, and in passing from grammatical to rhetorical structures without difficulty or interruption. Indeed, as the study of grammatical structures is refined in contemporary theories of generative, transformational, and distributive grammar, the study of tropes and of figures (which is how the term rhetoric is used throughout this essay, not in the derived sense of comment, eloquence, or persuasion) becomes a mere extension of grammatical models, a particular subset of syntactical relations. In the recent *Dictionnaire encyclopédique des sciences du langage,* Ducrot and Todorov write: " ... rhetoric has always been satisfied with a paradigmatic view over words (words substituting for each other), without questioning their syntagmatic relationship (the contiguity of words to each other). There ought to be another perspective, complementary to the first, in which metaphor, for example, would not be defined as a substitution but as a particular type of combination. Research inspired by linguistics or, more narrowly, by syntactical studies, has begun to reveal this possibility—but it remains to be explored."[1] Todorov, who calls one of his books a *Grammar of the Decameron,* rightly thinks of his own work and that of his associates as first explorations in the elaboration of a systematic grammar of literary modes, genres, and also literary figures. Perhaps the most perceptive work to come out of this school, Genette's studies of figural modes, can be shown to be assimilations of rhetorical transformations or combinations to syntactical, grammatical patterns. Thus a recent study, now printed in *Figures III* and entitled "Métonymie chez Proust," shows the combined presence, in a wide and astute selection of passages, of paradigmatic, metaphorical figures with syntagmatic, metonymic structures.[2] The combination of both is treated descriptively and nondialectically without suggesting the possibility of logical tensions.

One can ask whether this reduction of figure to grammar is legitimate. The existence of grammatical structures within and beyond the unit of the sentence in literary texts is undeniable, and their description and classification are indispensable. The question remains if and how figures of rhetoric can be included in such a taxonomy. This question is at the core of the debate

[1]From the entry on rhetoric in Ducrot and Todorov, *Dictionnaire encyclopédique des sciences du langage* (Paris: Seuil, 1972), p. 352.
[2]Gérard Genette, *Figures III* (Paris: Seuil, 1972), pp. 41–63.

going on, in a wide variety of apparently unrelated forms, in contemporary poetics; but I do not plan to make clear the connection between this "real" problem and the countless pseudo-problems that agitate literary studies. The historical picture of contemporary criticism is too confused to make the mapping out of such a topography a useful exercise. Not only are these questions mixed in and mixed up within particular groups or local trends, but they are often co-present, without apparent contradiction, within the work of a single author.

Neither is the theory of the question suitable for quick expository treatment. To distinguish the epistemology of grammar from the epistemology of rhetoric is a redoubtable task. On an entirely naive level, we tend to conceive of grammatical systems as tending toward universality and as simply generative, that is, as capable of deriving an infinity of versions from a single model (that may govern transformations as well as derivations) without the intervention of another model that would upset the first. We therefore think of the relationship between grammar and logic, the passage from grammar to propositions, as being relatively unproblematic: no true propositions are conceivable in the absence of grammatical consistency or of controlled deviation from a system of consistency no matter how complex. Grammar and logic stand to each other in a dyadic relationship of unsubverted support. In a logic of acts rather than of statements, as in Austin's theory of speech acts, which has had such a strong influence on recent American work in literary semiology, it is also possible to move between speech acts and grammar without difficulty. The performance of what are called illocutionary acts, such as ordering, questioning, denying, and assuming, within the language is congruent with the grammatical structures of syntax in the corresponding imperative, interrogative, negative, and optative sentences. "The rules for illocutionary acts," writes Richard Ohmann in a recent paper, "determine whether performance of a given act is well-executed, in just the same way as grammatical rules determine whether the product of a locutionary act—a sentence—is well formed. . . . But whereas the rules of grammar concern the relationships among sound, syntax, and meaning, the rules of illocutionary acts concern relationships among people."[3] And since rhetoric is then conceived exclusively as persuasion, as actual action upon others (and not as an intralinguistic figure or trope), the continuity between the illocutionary realm of grammar and the perlocutionary realm of rhetoric is self-evident. It becomes the basis for a new rhetoric that, exactly as is the case for Todorov and Genette, would also be a new grammar.

Without engaging the substance of the question, it can be pointed out, without having to go beyond recent and American examples, and without calling upon the strength of an age-old tradition, that the continuity here assumed between grammar and rhetoric is not borne out by theoretical and philosophical speculation. Kenneth Burke mentions *deflection* (which he compares structurally to Freudian displacement), defined as "any slight bias or even unintended error," as the rhetorical basis of language, and deflection is then conceived as a dialectical subversion of the consistent link between sign and meaning that operates within grammatical patterns;[4] hence Burke's well-known insistence on the distinction between grammar and rhetoric. Charles Sanders Peirce, who, with Nietzsche and Saussure, laid the philosophical foundation for modern semiology, stressed the distinction between grammar and rhetoric in his celebrated and so suggestively unfathomable definition of the sign. He insists, as is well known, on the necessary presence of a third element, called the interpretant, within any relationship that the sign entertains with its object. The sign must be interpreted if we are to understand the idea it is to convey, and this is so because the sign is not the thing but a meaning derived from the thing by a process—here called representation—that is not simply generative, that is, dependent on a univocal origin. The interpretation of the sign is not, for Peirce, a meaning but another sign; it is a reading, not a decodage, and this reading has, in its turn, to be interpreted into another sign, and so on, ad

[3]"Speech, Literature, and the Space in Between," *New Literary History*, 4 (1971), 50.
[4]Kenneth Burke, "Rhetoric—Old and New," *Journal of General Education*, 5 (1951), rpt. in Martin Steinmann, Jr., ed., *New Rhetorics* (New York: Scribner, 1967), p. 75.

infinitum. Peirce calls this process by means of which "one sign gives birth to another" pure rhetoric, as distinguished from pure grammar, which postulates the possibility of unproblematic, dyadic meaning, and pure logic, which postulates the possibility of the universal truth of meanings. Only if the sign engendered meaning in the same way that the object engenders the sign— that is, by representation—would there be no need to distinguish between grammar and rhetoric.[5]

These remarks should indicate at least the existence and the difficulty of the question, a difficulty which puts its concise theoretical exposition beyond my powers. I must retreat therefore into a pragmatic discourse and try to illustrate the tension between grammar and rhetoric in a few specific textual examples. Let me begin by considering what is perhaps the most commonly known instance of an apparent symbiosis between a grammatical and a rhetorical structure, the so-called rhetorical question, in which the figure is conveyed directly by means of a syntactical device. I take the first example from the subliterature of the mass media: asked by his wife whether he wants to have his bowling shoes laced over or laced under, Archie Bunker answers with a question. He asks, "What's the difference?" Being a reader of sublime simplicity, his wife replies by patiently explaining the difference between lacing over and lacing under, whatever this may be, but provokes only ire. "What's the difference?" did not ask for difference but meant instead "I don't give a damn what the difference is." The same grammatical pattern engenders two meanings that are mutually exclusive: the literal meaning asks for the concept (difference) whose existence is denied by the figurative meaning. As long as we are talking about bowling shoes, the consequences are relatively trivial; Archie Bunker, who is a great believer in the authority of origins

---

[5]See Peirce, *Collected Papers,* ed. Charles Hartshorne and Paul Weiss (Cambridge, Mass.: Harvard University Press, 1960), II, 156–157: " . . . if a sunflower, in turning toward the sun, becomes by that very act fully capable, without further condition, of reproducing a sunflower which turns in precisely corresponding ways toward the sun, and of so doing with the same reproductive power, the sunflower would become a Representamen [and not a sign] of the sun." It seems, however, that thought-signs, or words, are in this respect precisely not heliotropic.

(as long, of course, as they are the right origins), muddles along in a world where literal and figurative meanings get in each other's way, though not without discomforts. But if a *de*-Bunker rather than a Bunker, a de-bunker of the *archē* (origin), an "Archie Debunker" such as Nietszche or Jacques Derrida, asks the question "What is the Difference?" we cannot even tell from his grammar whether he "really" wants to know "what" difference is or is merely telling us that we should not even try to find out. Confronted with the question of the difference between grammar and rhetoric, grammar allows us to ask the question, but the sentence by means of which we ask it may deny the very possibility of asking. For what is the use of asking, I ask, when we cannot even authoritatively decide whether a question asks or doesn't ask?

The point is as follows. A perfectly clear syntactical paradigm (the question) engenders a sentence that has at least two meanings, one which asserts and the other which denies its own illocutionary mode. It is not that there are simply two meanings, one literal and the other figural, and that we have to decide which one of these meanings is the right one in this particular situation. The confusion can only be cleared up by the intervention of an extratextual intention, such as Archie Bunker setting his wife straight; but the very anger he displays is indicative of more than impatience: it reveals his despair when confronted with a structure of linguistic meaning that he cannot control and that holds the discouraging prospect of an infinity of similar future confusions, all of them potentially catastrophic in their consequences. Nor is this intervention really a part of the minitext constituted by the figure, which holds our attention only as long as it remains suspended and unresolved. I follow the usage of common speech in calling this semiological enigma "rhetorical." The grammatical model of the question becomes rhetorical not when we have, on the one hand, a literal meaning and, on the other hand, a figural meaning, but when it is impossible to decide by grammatical or other linguistic devices which of the two meanings (that can be entirely contradictory) prevails. Rhetoric radically suspends logic and opens up vertiginous possibilities of referential aberration. And although it would perhaps be somewhat more remote from common usage, I would not hesitate to

equate the rhetorical, figural potentiality of language with literature itself. I could point to a great number of antecedents to this
equation of literature with figure; the most recent reference
would be to Monroe Beardsley's insistence in his contribution to
the essays in honor of William Wimsatt that literary language is
characterized by being "distinctly above the norm in ratio of
implicit (or, I would say rhetorical) to explicit meaning."[6]

Let me pursue the question of the rhetorical question through
one more example. Yeats's "Among School Children" ends with
the famous line: "How can we know the dancer from the
dance?" Although there are some revealing inconsistencies
within the commentaries, the line is usually interpreted as stating, with the increased emphasis of a rhetorical device, the potential unity between form and experience, between creator and
creation. It could be said that it denies the discrepancy between
the sign and the referent from which we started. Many elements
in the imagery and the dramatic development of the poem
strengthen this traditional reading; without having to look any
further than the immediately preceding lines, one finds powerful consecrated images of the continuity from part to whole that
makes synecdoche into the most seductive of metaphors: the
organic beauty of the tree, stated in the parallel syntax of a
similar rhetorical question, or the convergence, in the dance, of
erotic desire with musical form:

> O chestnut tree, great-rooted blossomer,
> Are you the leaf, the blossom or the bole?
> O body swayed to music, O brightening glance,
> How can we know the dancer from the dance?

A more extended reading, always assuming that the final line is
to be read as a rhetorical question, reveals that the thematic and
rhetorical grammar of the poem yields a consistent reading that
extends from the first line to the last and that can account for all
the details in the text. It is equally possible, however, to read the
last line literally rather than figuratively, as asking with some

[6]Frank Brady, John Palmer, and Martin Price, eds., *Literary Theory and Structure: Essays in Honor of William K. Wimsatt* (New Haven: Yale University Press,
1973), p. 37.

urgency the question asked at the beginning of this essay within
the context of contemporary criticism: it is *not* that sign and
referent are so exquisitely fitted to each other that all difference
between them is at times blotted out; but, rather, since the two
essentially different elements, sign and meaning, are so intri-
cately intertwined in the imagined "presence" which the poem
addresses, how can we possibly make the distinctions that would
shelter us from the error of identifying what cannot be identified? The clumsiness of the paraphrase reveals that it is not
necessarily the literal reading which is simpler than the figurative one, as was the case in my first example; here the figural
reading, which assumes the question to be rhetorical, is perhaps
naive, whereas the literal reading leads to greater complications
of theme and statement. For it turns out that the entire scheme
set up by the first reading can be undermined, or reconstructed,
in the terms of the second, in which the final line is read literally
as meaning that, since the dancer and the dance are not the
same, it might be useful, perhaps even desperately necessary—
for the question can be given a ring of urgency: "Please tell me,
how *can* I know the dancer from the dance?"—to tell them
apart. But this will replace the reading of each symbolic detail by
a divergent interpretation. The oneness of trunk, leaf, and blossom, for example, that would have appealed to Goethe, would
find itself replaced by the much less reassuring Tree of Life
from the Mabinogion that appears in the poem "Vacillation," in
which the fiery blossom and the earthly leaf are held together, as
well as apart, by the crucified and castrated god Attis, of whose
body it can hardly be said that it is "not bruised to pleasure soul."
This hint should suffice to suggest that two entirely coherent but
entirely incompatible readings can be made to hinge on one line
whose grammatical structure is devoid of ambiguity but whose
rhetorical mode turns the mood as well as the mode of the entire
poem upside down. Neither can we say, as was already the case
in the first example, that the poem simply has two meanings
which exist side by side. The two readings have to engage each
other in direct confrontation, for the one reading is precisely the
error denounced by the other and has to be undone by it. Nor
can we in any way make a valid decision as to which of the
readings can be given priority over the other; neither can exist in

the other's absence. There can be no dance without a dancer, no sign without a referent. On the other hand, the authority of the meaning engendered by the grammatical structure is fully obscured by the duplicity of a figure that cries out for the differentiation that it conceals.

Yeats's poem is not explicitly "about" rhetorical questions but about images or metaphors, and about the possibility of convergence between experiences of consciousness such as memory or emotions (what the poem calls passion, piety, and affection) and entities accessible to the senses, such as bodies, persons, or icons. We return to the inside/outside model from which we started and which the poem puts into question by means of a syntactical device (the question) made to operate on a grammatical as well as on a rhetorical level. The couple grammar/rhetoric, certainly not a binary opposition since they in no way exclude each other, disrupts and confuses the neat antithesis of the inside/outside pattern. We can transfer this scheme to the act of reading and interpretation. By reading we get, as we say, inside a text that was first something alien to us and which we now make our own by an act of understanding. But this understanding becomes at once the representation of an extratextual meaning; in Austin's terms, the illocutionary speech act becomes a perlocutionary actual act; in Frege's terms, *Bedeutung* becomes *Sinn*. Our recurrent question is whether this transformation is semantically controlled along grammatical or along rhetorical lines. Does the metaphor of reading really unite outer meaning and inner understanding, action and reflection, into one single totality? The assertion is powerfully and suggestively made in a passage from Proust that describes the experience of reading as such a union. It describes the young Marcel hiding in the closed space of his room in order to read. The example differs from the earlier ones in that we are not dealing with a grammatical structure which also functions rhetorically but have instead the representation, the dramatization, in terms of the experience of a subject, of a rhetorical structure—just as, in many other passages, Proust dramatizes tropes by means of landscapes or descriptions of objects. The figure here dramatized is that of metaphor, an inside/outside correspondence as represented by the act of reading. The reading scene is the

culmination of a series of actions taking place in enclosed spaces
and leading up to the "dark coolness" of Marcel's room.

> I had stretched out on my bed, with a book, in my room which
> sheltered, tremblingly, its transparent and fragile coolness against
> the afternoon sun, behind the almost closed blinds through which
> a glimmer of daylight had nevertheless managed to push its yellow
> wings, remaining motionless between the wood and the glass, in a
> corner, poised like a butterfly. It was hardly light enough to read,
> and the sensation of the light's splendor was given me only by the
> noise of Camus . . . hammering dusty crates; resounding in the
> sonorous atmosphere that is peculiar to hot weather, they seemed
> to spark off scarlet stars; and also by the flies executing their little
> concert, the chamber music of summer: evocative not in the man-
> ner of a human tune that, heard perchance during the summer,
> afterwards reminds you of it; it is connected to summer by a more
> necessary link: born from beautiful days, resurrecting only when
> they return, containing some of their essence, it does not only
> awaken their image in our memory; it guarantees their return,
> their actual, persistent, unmediated presence.
>
>   The dark coolness of my room related to the full sunlight of the
> street as the shadow relates to the ray of light, that is to say it was
> just as luminous and it gave my imagination the total spectacle of
> the summer, whereas my senses, if I had been on a walk, could
> only have enjoyed it by fragments; it matched my repose which
> (thanks to the adventures told by my book and stirring my tran-
> quillity) supported, like the quiet of a motionless hand in the mid-
> dle of a running brook, the shock and the motion of a torrent of
> activity.[7]

From the beginning of the passage, inwardness is valorized
positively as something desirable that has to protect itself against
the intrusion of outside forces, but that nevertheless has to borrow, as it were, some of its constitutive properties from the outside. A chain of binary properties is set up and antithetically
differentiated in terms of the inside/outside polarity: properties
of coolness, darkness, repose, silence, imagination, and totality,
associated with inwardness, contrast with the heat, the light, the
activity, the sounds, the senses, and the fragmentation that govern the outside. By the act of reading, these static oppositions
are put in motion, thus allowing for the play of substitutions by

[7] *A la recherche du temps perdu* (Paris: Pléiade, 1954), I, 83. Translation mine.

means of which the claim for totalization can be made. Thus, in a beautifully seductive effect of chiaroscuro, mediated by the metaphor of light as a poised butterfly, the inner room is convincingly said to acquire the amount of light necessary to reading. In the wake of this light, warmth can also enter the room, incarnate in the auditive synaesthesia of the various sounds. According to the narrator, these metaphorical substitutions and reversals render the presence of summer in the room more completely than the actual experience of summer in the outside world could have done. The text achieves this synthesis and comments on it in normative terms, comparable to the manner in which treatises of practical rhetoric recommend the use of one figure in preference to another in a given situation: here it is the substitutive totalization by metaphor which is said to be more effective than the mere contiguity of metonymic association. As opposed to the random contingency of metonymy (*"par hasard"*), the metaphor is linked to its proper meaning by, says Proust, the "necessary link" that leads to perfect synthesis. In the wake of this synthesis, the entire conceptual vocabulary of metaphysics enters the text: a terminology of generation, of transcendental necessity, of totality, of essence, of permanence, and of unmediated presence. The passage acts out and asserts the priority of metaphor over metonymy in terms of the categories of metaphysics and with reference to the act of reading.

The actual test of the truth of the assertion comes in the second paragraph when the absurd ratio set up at the beginning has to be verified by a further substitution. This time, what has to be exchanged are not only the properties of light and dark, warm and cool, fragment and totality (part and whole), but the properties of action and repose. The full seduction of the text can come into being only when the formal totalization of light and dark is completed by the transfer from rest to action that represents the extratextual, referential moment. The text asserts the transfer in the concluding sentence: "The dark coolness of my room. . . supported, like the quiet of a motionless hand in the middle of a running brook, the shock and the motion of a torrent of activity." The verb "to support" here carries the full weight of uniting rest and action (*repos et activité*), fiction and reality, as firmly as the base supports the column. The transfer, as is so often the case in Proust, is carried out by the liquid element of the running brook. The natural, representational connotation of the passage is with coolness, so particularly attractive within the predominant summer-mood of the entire *Recherche*. But coolness, it will be remembered, is one of the characteristic properties of the "inside" world. It cannot therefore by itself transfer us into the opposite world of activity. The movement of the water evokes a freshness which in the binary logic of the passage is associated with the inward, imaginary world of reading and fiction. In order to accede to action, it would be necessary to capture one of the properties belonging to the opposite chain, such as warmth. The mere "cool" action of fiction cannot suffice: it is necessary to reconcile the cool immobility of the hand with the heat of action if the claim made by the sentence is to stand up as true. This transfer is carried out, within the same sentence, when it is said that repose supports "a torrent of activity." The expression "torrent d'activité" is not, or is no longer, a metaphor in French: it is a cliché, a dead or sleeping metaphor that has lost the suggestive, connotative values contained in the word "torrent." It simply means "a great deal of activity," the amount of activity that is likely to agitate one to the point of getting hot. Heat is thus surreptitiously smuggled into the passage from a cold source, closing the ring of antithetical properties and allowing for their exchange and substitution: from the moment tranquillity can be active and warm without losing its coolness and its distinctive quality of repose, the fragmented experience of reality can become whole without losing its quality of being real.

The transfer is made to seem convincing and seductive by the double play of the cliché "torrent of activity." The proximate, contiguous image of the brook awakens, as it were, the sleeping beauty of the dozing metaphor which, in its common use, had become the metonymic association of two words united by sheer habit and no longer by the inner necessity, the "necessary link," of a transcendental signification. "Torrent" functions in a double semantic register: in its reawakened literal meaning it relays the attribute of coolness that is actually part of the running water, whereas in its figural nonmeaning it designates the quantity of activity connotative of the contrary property of warmth.

The rhetorical structure of this sentence is therefore not simply metaphorical. It is at least doubly metonymic, first because the coupling of words in a cliché is governed not by the necessary link that reveals their potential identity but by the contingent habit of proximity; second, because the reawakening of the metaphorical term "torrent" is carried out by a statement that happens to be in the vicinity, but without there being any necessity for this proximity on the level of the referential meaning. The most striking thing is that this doubly metonymic structure is found in a text that also contains highly seductive and successful metaphors (as in the chiaroscuro effect of the beginning, or in the condensation of light in the butterfly image) and that explicitly asserts the superiority of metaphor over metonymy in terms of metaphysical categories.

That these metaphysical categories do not remain unaffected by such a reading would become clear from an inclusive reading of Proust's novel and would become even more explicit in a language-conscious philosopher such as Nietzsche who, as a philosopher, has to be concerned with the epistemological consequences of the kind of rhetorical seductions exemplified by the Proust passage. It can be shown that the systematic critique of the main categories of metaphysics undertaken by Nietzsche in his late work, the critique of the concepts of causality, of the subject, of identity, of referential and revealed truth, and others, occurs along the same pattern of deconstruction that is operative in Proust's text; and it can also be shown that this pattern exactly corresponds to Nietzsche's description, in texts that precede *The Will to Power* by more than fifteen years, of the structure of the main rhetorical tropes. The key to this critique of metaphysics, which is itself a recurrent gesture throughout the history of thought, is the rhetorical model of the trope or, if one prefers to call it that, literature. It turns out that in these innocent-looking didactic exercises we are in fact playing for very sizable stakes.

It is therefore all the more necessary to know what is linguistically involved in a rhetorically conscious reading of the type here undertaken on a brief fragment from a novel and extended by Nietzsche to the entire text of post-Hellenic thought. Our first examples, which dealt with rhetorical questions, were rhetorizations of grammar, figures generated by syntactical paradigms, whereas the Proust example could be better described as a grammatization of rhetoric. The passage from a paradigmatic structure based on substitution, such as metaphor, to a syntagmatic structure based on contingent association, such as metonymy, shows the mechanical, repetitive aspect of grammatical forms to be operative in a passage that seems at first sight to celebrate the self-willed and autonomous inventiveness of a subject. Figures are assumed to be inventions, the products of a highly particularized individual talent, whereas no one can claim credit for the programmed pattern of grammar. Yet our reading of the Proust passage shows that precisely when the highest claims are being made for the unifying power of metaphor, these very images rely in fact on the deceptive use of semi-automatic grammatical patterns. The deconstruction of metaphor and of all rhetorical patterns, such as mimesis, paranomasis, or personification, that use resemblance as a way to disguise differences, takes us back to the impersonal precision of grammar and of a semiology derived from grammatical patterns. Such a deconstruction puts into question a whole series of concepts that underlie the value judgments of our critical discourse: the metaphors of primacy, of genetic history, and, most notably, of the autonomous power to will of the self.

There seems to be a difference, then, between what I called the rhetorization of grammar (as in the rhetorical question) and the grammatization of rhetoric, as in the deconstructive readings of the type sketched in the passage from Proust. The former ends up in indetermination, in a suspended uncertainty that was unable to choose between two modes of reading, whereas the latter seems to reach a truth, albeit by the negative road of exposing an error, a false pretense. After the deconstructive reading of the Proust passage we can no longer believe the assertion made in this passage about the intrinsic, metaphysical superiority of metaphor over metonymy. We seem to end up in a mood of negative assurance that is highly productive of critical discourse. The further text of Proust's novel, for example, responds perfectly to an extended application of this deconstructive pattern: not only can similar gestures be repeated throughout the novel, at all the crucial articulations or all passages where large aesthetic and metaphysical claims are being made (the scenes of involuntary memory, the workshop of Elstir, the septette of Vinteuil, the convergence of author and narrator at the end of the novel), but a vast thematic and semiotic network is revealed, a network that structures the entire narrative and that remains invisible to a reader caught in a naive metaphorical mystification. The whole of literature would respond in similar fashion, although the techniques and the patterns would have to vary considerably, of course, from author to author. But there is absolutely no reason why analyses of the kind here suggested for Proust would not be applicable, with proper modifications of technique, to Milton or to Dante or to Hölderlin. This will in fact be the task of literary criticism in the coming years.

It would seem that we are saying that criticism is the deconstruction of literature, the reduction to the rigors of grammar of rhetorical mystifications. And if we hold up Nietzsche as the philosopher of such a critical deconstruction, then the literary critic would become the philosopher's ally in his struggle with the poets. Criticism and literature would separate around the epistemological axis that distinguishes grammar from rhetoric. It is easy enough to see that this apparent glorification of the critic-philosopher in the name of truth is in fact a glorification of the poet as the primary source of this truth; if truth is the recognition of the systematic character of a certain kind of error, then it would be fully dependent on the prior existence of this error. Philosophers of science like Gaston Bachelard or Wittgenstein are notoriously dependent on the aberrations of the poets. We are back at our unanswered question: does the grammatization of rhetoric end up in negative certainty, or does it, like the rhetorization of grammar, remain suspended in the ignorance of its own truth or falsehood?

Two concluding remarks should suffice to answer the question. First of all, it is not true that Proust's text can simply be reduced to the mystified assertion—the superiority of metaphor over metonymy—that our reading deconstructs. The reading is not "our" reading, since it uses only the linguistic elements provided by the text itself; the distinction between author and reader is one of the false distinctions that the deconstruction makes evident. The deconstruction is not something we have added to the text; it constituted the text in the first place. A literary text simultaneously asserts and denies the authority of its own rhetorical mode; and, by reading the text as we did, we were only trying to come closer to being as rigorous a reader as the author had to be in order to write the sentence in the first place. Poetic writing is the most advanced and refined mode of deconstruction; it may differ from critical or discursive writing in the economy of its articulation, but it is not different in kind.

But if we recognize the existence of the deconstructive moment as constitutive of all literary language, we have surreptitiously reintroduced the categories that this deconstruction was supposed to eliminate and that have merely been displaced. We have, for example, displaced the question of the self from the referent into the figure of the narrator, who then becomes the *signifié* of the passage. It again becomes possible to ask such naive questions as what Proust's, or Marcel's, motives may have been in thus manipulating language: was he fooling himself, or was he represented as fooling himself and fooling us into believing that fiction and action are as easy to unite, by reading, as the passage asserts? The pathos of the entire section, which would have been more noticeable if the quotation had been a little more extended, the narrator's constant vacillation between guilt and well-being, invites such questions. They are absurd questions, of course, since the reconciliation of fact and fiction occurs itself as a mere assertion made in a text, and is thus productive of more text at the moment when it asserts its decision to escape from textual confinement. But even if we free ourselves of all false questions of intent and rightfully reduce the narrator to the status of a mere grammatical pronoun, without which the deconstructive narrative could not come into being, this subject remains endowed with a function that is not grammatical but rhetorical, in that it gives voice, so to speak, to a grammatical syntagm. The term "voice," even when used in a grammatical terminology, as when we speak of the passive or interrogative voice, is, of course, a metaphor inferring by analogy the intent of the subject from the structure of the predicate. In the case of the deconstructive discourse that we call literary, or rhetorical, or poetic, this creates a distinctive complication illustrated by the Proust passage. The deconstructive reading revealed a first paradox: the passage valorizes metaphor as being the "right" literary figure, but then proceeds to constitute itself by means of the epistemologically incompatible figure of metonymy. The deconstructive critical discourse reveals the presence of this delusion and affirms it as the irreversible mode of its truth. It cannot pause there however. For if we then ask the obvious and simple next question, whether the rhetorical mode of the text in question is that of metaphor or metonymy, it is impossible to give an answer. Individual metaphors, such as the chiaroscuro effect or the butterfly, are shown to be subordinate figures in a general clause whose syntax is metonymic; from this point of view, it seems that the rhetoric is superseded by a grammar that deconstructs it. But this metonymic clause has as its subject a voice whose relationship to this clause is again metaphorical. The narrator who tells us about the impossibility of metaphor is himself, or itself, a metaphor, the metaphor of a grammatical syntagm whose meaning is the denial of metaphor stated, by antiphrasis, as its priority. And this subject-metaphor is, in its turn, open to the kind of deconstruction to the second degree, the rhetorical deconstruction of psycholinguistics, in which the more advanced investigations of literature are presently engaged, against considerable resistance.

We end up, therefore, in the case of the rhetorical grammatization of semiology, just as in the grammatical rhetorization of illocutionary phrases, in the same state of suspended ignorance. Any question about the rhetorical mode of a literary text is always a rhetorical question that does not even know whether it is really questioning. The resulting pathos is an anxiety (or bliss, depending on one's momentary mood or individual temperament) of ignorance, not an anxiety of reference—as becomes thematically clear in Proust's novel when reading is dramatized, in the relationship between Marcel and Albertine, not as an emotive reaction to what language does, but as an emotive reaction to the impossibility of knowing what it might be up to. Literature as well as criticism—the difference between them being delusive—is condemned (or privileged) to be forever the most rigorous and, consequently, the most unreliable language in terms of which man names and modifies himself.

MICHEL FOUCAULT

What Is an Author?

The coming into being of the notion of "author" constitutes the privileged moment of *individualization* in the history of ideas, knowledge, literature, philosophy, and the sciences. Even today, when we reconstruct the history of a concept, literary genre, or school of philosophy, such categories seem relatively weak, secondary, and superimposed scansions in comparison with the solid and fundamental unit of the author and the work.

I shall not offer here a sociohistorical analysis of the author's persona. Certainly it would be worth examining how the author became individualized in a culture like ours, what status he has been given, at what moment studies of authenticity and attribution began, in what kind of system of valorization the author was involved, at what point we began to recount the lives of authors rather than of heroes, and how this fundamental category of "the-man-and-his-work criticism" began. For the moment, however, I want to deal solely with the relationship between text and author and with the manner in which the text points to this "figure" that, at least in appearance, is outside it and antecedes it.

Beckett nicely formulates the theme with which I would like to begin: "'What does it matter who is speaking,' someone said, 'what does it matter who is speaking.'" In this indifference appears one of the fundamental ethical principles of contemporary writing [*écriture*]. I say "ethical" because this indifference is not really a trait characterizing the manner in which one speaks and writes, but rather a kind of immanent rule, taken up over and over again, never fully applied, not designating writing as something completed, but dominating it as a practice. Since it is too familiar to require a lengthy analysis, this immanent rule can be adequately illustrated here by tracing two of its major themes.

First of all, we can say that today's writing has freed itself from the dimension of expression. Referring only to itself, but without being restricted to the confines of its interiority, writing is identified with its own unfolded exteriority. This means that it is an interplay of signs arranged less according to its signified content than according to the very nature of the signifier. Writing unfolds like a game [*jeu*] that invariably goes beyond its own rules and transgresses its limits. In writing, the point is not to manifest or exalt the act of writing, nor is it to pin a subject within language; it is rather a question of creating a space into which the writing subject constantly disappears.

The second theme, writing's relationship with death, is even more familiar. This link subverts an old tradition exemplified by the Greek epic, which was intended to perpetuate the immortality of the hero: if he was willing to die young, it was so that his life, consecrated and magnified by death, might pass into immortality; the narrative then redeemed this accepted death. In another way, the motivation, as well as the theme and the pretext of Arabian narratives—such as *The Thousand and One Nights*—was also the eluding of death: one spoke, telling stories into the early morning, in order to forestall death, to postpone the day of reckoning that would silence the narrator. Scheherazade's narrative is an effort, renewed each night, to keep death outside the circle of life.

Our culture has metamorphosed this idea of narrative, or writing, as something designed to ward off death. Writing has become linked to sacrifice, even to the sacrifice of life: it is now a voluntary effacement which does not need to be represented in books, since it is brought about in the writer's very existence. The work, which once had the duty of providing immortality, now possesses the right to kill, to be its author's murderer, as in the cases of Flaubert, Proust, and Kafka. That is not all, however: this relationship between writing and death is also manifested in the effacement of the writing subject's individual characteristics. Using all the contrivances that he sets up between himself and what he writes, the writing subject cancels out the signs of his particular individuality. As a result, the mark of the writer is reduced to nothing more than the singularity of his absence; he must assume the role of the dead man in the game of writing.

None of this is recent; criticism and philosophy took note of the disappearance—or death—of the author some time ago. But the consequences of their discovery of it have not been sufficiently examined, nor has its import been accurately measured. A certain number of notions that are intended to replace the privileged position of the author actually seem to preserve that privilege and suppress the real meaning of his disappearance. I shall examine two of these notions, both of great importance today.

The first is the idea of the work. It is a very familiar thesis that the task of criticism is not to bring out the work's relationships with the author, nor to reconstruct through the text a thought or experience, but rather, to analyze the work through its structure, its architecture, its intrinsic form, and the play of its internal relationships. At this point, however, a problem arises: "What is a work? What is this curious unity which we designate as a work? Of what elements is it composed? Is it not what an author has written?" Difficulties appear immediately. If an individual were not an author, could we say that what he wrote, said, left behind in his papers, or what has been collected of his remarks, could be called a "work"? When Sade was not considered an author, what was the status of his papers? Were they simply rolls of paper onto which he ceaselessly uncoiled his fantasies during his imprisonment?

Even when an individual has been accepted as an author, we must still ask whether everything that he wrote, said, or left behind is part of his work. The problem is both theoretical and technical. When undertaking the publication of Nietzsche's works, for example, where should one stop? Surely everything must be published, but what is "everything"? Everything that Nietzsche himself published, certainly. And what about the rough drafts for his works? Obviously. The plans for his aphorisms? Yes. The deleted passages and the notes at the bottom of the page? Yes. What if, within a workbook filled with aphorisms, one finds a reference, the notation of a meeting or of an address, or a laundry list: is it a work, or not? Why not? And so on, ad infinitum. How can one define a work amid the millions of traces left by someone after his death? A theory of the work does not exist, and the empirical task of those who naively undertake the editing of works often suffers in the absence of such a theory.

We could go even further: does *The Thousand and One Nights* constitute a work? What about Clement of Alexandria's *Miscellanies* or Diogenes Laertius' *Lives*? A multitude of questions arises with regard to this notion of the work. Consequently, it is not enough to declare that we should do without the writer (the author) and study the work in itself. The word "work" and the unity that it designates are probably as problematic as the status of the author's individuality.

Another notion which has hindered us from taking full measure of the author's disappearance, blurring and concealing the moment of this effacement and subtly preserving the author's existence, is the notion of writing [*écriture*]. When rigorously applied, this notion should allow us not only to circumvent references to the author, but also to situate his recent absence. The notion of writing, as currently employed, is concerned with neither the act of writing nor the indication—be it symptom or sign—of a meaning which someone might have wanted to express. We try, with great effort, to imagine the general condition of each text, the condition of both the space in which it is dispersed and the time in which it unfolds.

In current usage, however, the notion of writing seems to transpose the empirical characteristics of the author into a transcendental anonymity. We are content to efface the more visible marks of the author's empiricity by playing off, one against the other, two ways of characterizing writing, namely, the critical and the religious approaches. Giving writing a primal status seems to be a way of retranslating, in transcendental terms, both the theological affirmation of its sacred character and the critical affirmation of its creative character. To admit that writing is, because of the very history that it made possible, subject to the test of oblivion and repression, seems to represent, in transcendental terms, the religious principle of the hidden meaning (which requires interpretation) and the critical principle of implicit significations, silent determinations, and obscured contents (which gives rise to commentary). To imagine writing as absence seems to be a simple repetition, in transcendental terms, of both the religious principle of inalterable and yet never fulfilled tradition, and the aesthetic principle of the work's survival, its perpetuation beyond the author's death, and its enigmatic *excess* in relation to him.

This usage of the notion of writing runs the risk of maintaining the author's privileges under the protection of writing's a priori status: it keeps alive, in the grey light of neutralization, the interplay of those representations that formed a particular image of the author. The author's disappearance, which, since Mallarmé, has been a constantly recurring event, is subject to a series of transcendental barriers. There seems to be an important dividing line between those who believe that they can still locate today's discontinuities [*ruptures*] in the historico-transcendental tradition of the nineteenth century, and those who try to free themselves once and for all from that tradition.[1]

It is not enough, however, to repeat the empty affirmation that the author has disappeared. For the same reason, it is not enough to keep repeating (after Nietzsche) that God and man have died a common death. Instead, we must locate the space left empty by the author's disappearance, follow the distribution of gaps and breaches, and watch for the openings that this disappearance uncovers.

First, we need to clarify briefly the problems arising from the use of the author's name. What is an author's name? How does it function? Far from offering a solution, I shall only indicate some of the difficulties that it presents.

The author's name is a proper name, and therefore it raises the problems common to all proper names. (Here I refer to Searle's analyses, among others.[2]) Obviously, one cannot turn a

---

[1]For a discussion of the notions of discontinuity and historical tradition see Foucault's *Les Mots et les choses* (Paris: Gallimard, 1966), translated as *The Order of Things* (New York: Pantheon, 1971).—Ed.

[2]John Searle, *Speech Acts: An Essay in the Philosophy of Language* (Cambridge: Cambridge University Press, 1969), pp. 162–174.—Ed.

proper name into a pure and simple reference. It has other than indicative functions: more than an indication, a gesture, a finger pointed at someone, it is the equivalent of a description. When one says "Aristotle," one employs a word that is the equivalent of one, or a series of, definite descriptions, such as "the author of the *Analytics*," "the founder of ontology," and so forth. One cannot stop there, however, because a proper name does not have just one signification. When we discover that Rimbaud did not write *La Chasse spirituelle*, we cannot pretend that the meaning of this proper name, or that of the author, has been altered. The proper name and the author's name are situated between the two poles of description and designation: they must have a certain link with what they name, but one that is neither entirely in the mode of designation nor in that of description; it must be a *specific* link. However—and it is here that the particular difficulties of the author's name arise—the links between the proper name and the individual named and between the author's name and what it names are not isomorphic and do not function in the same way. There are several differences.

If, for example, Pierre Dupont does not have blue eyes, or was not born in Paris, or is not a doctor, the name Pierre Dupont will still always refer to the same person; such things do not modify the link of designation. The problems raised by the author's name are much more complex, however. If I discover that Shakespeare was not born in the house that we visit today, this is a modification which, obviously, will not alter the functioning of the author's name. But if we proved that Shakespeare did not write those sonnets which pass for his, that would constitute a significant change and affect the manner in which the author's name functions. If we proved that Shakespeare wrote Bacon's *Organon* by showing that the same author wrote both the works of Bacon and those of Shakespeare, that would be a third type of change which would entirely modify the functioning of the author's name. The author's name is not, therefore, just a proper name like the rest.

Many other facts point out the paradoxical singularity of the author's name. To say that Pierre Dupont does not exist is not at all the same as saying that Homer or Hermes Trismegistus did not exist. In the first case, it means that no one has the name

Pierre Dupont; in the second, it means that several people were mixed together under one name, or that the true author had none of the traits traditionally ascribed to the personae of Homer or Hermes. To say that X's real name is actually Jacques Durand instead of Pierre Dupont is not the same as saying that Stendhal's name was Henri Beyle. One could also question the meaning and functioning of propositions like "Bourbaki is so-and-so, so-and-so, etc." and "Victor Eremita, Climacus, Anticlimacus, Frater Taciturnus, Constantine Constantius, all of these are Kierkegaard."

These differences may result from the fact that an author's name is not simply an element in a discourse (capable of being either subject or object, of being replaced by a pronoun, and the like); it performs a certain role with regard to narrative discourse, assuring a classificatory function. Such a name permits one to group together a certain number of texts, define them, differentiate them from and contrast them to others. In addition, it establishes a relationship among the texts. Hermes Trismegistus did not exist, nor did Hippocrates—in the sense that Balzac existed—but the fact that several texts have been placed under the same name indicates that there has been established among them a relationship of homogeneity, filiation, authentification of some texts by the use of others, reciprocal explication, or concomitant utilization. The author's name serves to characterize a certain mode of being of discourse: the fact that the discourse has an author's name, that one can say "this was written by so-and-so" or "so-and-so is its author," shows that this discourse is not ordinary everyday speech that merely comes and goes, not something that is immediately consumable. On the contrary, it is a speech that must be received in a certain mode and that, in a given culture, must receive a certain status.

It would seem that the author's name, unlike other proper names, does not pass from the interior of a discourse to the real and exterior individual who produced it; instead, the name seems always to be present, marking off the edges of the text, revealing, or at least characterizing, its mode of being. The author's name manifests the appearance of a certain discursive set and indicates the status of this discourse within a society and a culture. It has no legal status, nor is it located in the fiction of the work; rather, it is located in the break that founds a certain discursive construct and its very particular mode of being. As a result, we could say that in a civilization like our own there are a certain number of discourses that are endowed with the "author-function," while others are deprived of it. A private letter may well have a signer—it does not have an author; a contract may well have a guarantor—it does not have an author. An anonymous text posted on a wall probably has a writer—but not an author. The author-function is therefore characteristic of the mode of existence, circulation, and functioning of certain discourses within a society.

Let us analyze this "author-function" as we have just described it. In our culture, how does one characterize a discourse containing the author-function? In what way is this discourse different from other discourses? If we limit our remarks to the author of a book or a text, we can isolate four different characteristics.

First of all, discourses are objects of appropriation. The form of ownership from which they spring is of a rather particular type, one that has been codified for many years. We should note that, historically, this type of ownership has always been subsequent to what one might call penal appropriation. Texts, books, and discourses really began to have authors (other than mythical, "sacralized" and "sacralizing" figures) to the extent that authors became subject to punishment, that is, to the extent that discourses could be transgressive. In our culture (and doubtless in many others), discourse was not originally a product, a thing, a kind of goods; it was essentially an act—an act placed in the bipolar field of the sacred and the profane, the licit and the illicit, the religious and the blasphemous. Historically, it was a gesture fraught with risks before becoming goods caught up in a circuit of ownership.

Once a system of ownership for texts came into being, once strict rules concerning author's rights, author-publisher relations, rights of reproduction, and related matters were enacted—at the end of the eighteenth and the beginning of the nineteenth century—the possibility of transgression attached to the act of writing took on, more and more, the form of an imperative peculiar to literature. It is as if the author, beginning with the moment at which he was placed in the system of property that characterizes our society, compensated for the status that he thus acquired by rediscovering the old bipolar field of discourse, systematically practicing transgression and thereby restoring danger to a writing which was now guaranteed the benefits of ownership.

The author-function does not affect all discourses in a universal and constant way, however. This is its second characteristic. In our civilization, it has not always been the same types of texts which have required attribution to an author. There was a time when the texts that we today call "literary" (narratives, stories, epics, tragedies, comedies) were accepted, put into circulation, and valorized without any question about the identity of their author; their anonymity caused no difficulties since their ancientness, whether real or imagined, was regarded as a sufficient guarantee of their status. On the other hand, those texts that we now would call scientific—those dealing with cosmology and the heavens, medicine and illnesses, natural sciences and geography—were accepted in the Middle Ages, and accepted as "true," only when marked with the name of their author. "Hippocrates said," "Pliny recounts," were not really formulas of an argument based on authority; they were the markers inserted in discourses that were supposed to be received as statements of demonstrated truth.

A reversal occurred in the seventeenth or eighteenth century. Scientific discourses began to be received for themselves, in the anonymity of an established or always redemonstrable truth; their membership in a systematic ensemble, and not the reference to the individual who produced them, stood as their guarantee. The author-function faded away, and the inventor's name served only to christen a theorem, proposition, particular effect, property, body, group of elements, or pathological syndrome. By the same token, literary discourses came to be accepted only when endowed with the author-function. We now ask of each poetic or fictional text: from where does it come, who wrote it, when, under what circumstances, or beginning with what design? The meaning ascribed to it and the status or value accorded it depend upon the manner in which we answer these questions. And if a text should be discovered in a state of anonymity—whether as a consequence of an accident or the author's explicit wish—the game becomes one of rediscovering the author. Since literary anonymity is not tolerable, we can accept it only in the guise of an enigma. As a result, the author-function today plays an important role in our view of literary works. (These are obviously generalizations that would have to be refined insofar as recent critical practice is concerned.)

The third characteristic of this author-function is that it does not develop spontaneously as the attribution of a discourse to an individual. It is, rather, the result of a complex operation which constructs a certain rational being that we call "author." Critics doubtless try to give this intelligible being a realistic status, by discerning, in the individual, a "deep" motive, a "creative" power, or a "design," the milieu in which writing originates. Nevertheless, these aspects of an individual which we designate as making him an author are only a projection, in more or less psychologizing terms, of the operations that we force texts to undergo, the connections that we make, the traits that we establish as pertinent, the continuities that we recognize, or the exclusions that we practice. All these operations vary according to periods and types of discourse. We do not construct a "philosophical author" as we do a "poet," just as, in the eighteenth century, one did not construct a novelist as we do today. Still, we can find through the ages certain constants in the rules of author-construction.

It seems, for example, that the manner in which literary criticism once defined the author—or rather constructed the figure of the author beginning with existing texts and discourses—is directly derived from the manner in which Christian tradition authenticated (or rejected) the texts at its disposal. In order to "rediscover" an author in a work, modern criticism uses methods similar to those that Christian exegesis employed when trying to prove the value of a text by its author's saintliness. In *De viris illustribus,* Saint Jerome explains that homonymy is not sufficient to identify legitimately authors of more than one work: different individuals could have had the same name, or one man could have, illegitimately, borrowed another's patronymic. The name as an individual trademark is not enough when one works within a textual tradition.

How then can one attribute several discourses to one and the same author? How can one use the author-function to determine if one is dealing with one or several individuals? Saint Jerome proposes four criteria: (1) if among several books attributed to an author one is inferior to the others, it must be withdrawn from the list of the author's works (the author is therefore defined as a constant level of value); (2) the same should be done if certain texts contradict the doctrine expounded in the author's other works (the author is thus defined as a field of conceptual or theoretical coherence); (3) one must also exclude works that are written in a different style, containing words and expressions not ordinarily found in the writer's production (the author is here conceived as a stylistic unity); (4) finally, passages quoting statements that were made, or mentioning events that occurred after the author's death must be regarded as interpolated texts (the author is here seen as a historical figure at the crossroads of a certain number of events).

Modern literary criticism, even when—as is now customary—it is not concerned with questions of authentication, still defines the author the same way: the author provides the basis for explaining not only the presence of certain events in a work, but also their transformations, distortions, and diverse modifications (through his biography, the determination of his individual perspective, the analysis of his social position, and the revelation of his basic design). The author is also the principle of a certain unity of writing—all differences having to be resolved, at least in part, by the principles of evolution, maturation, or influence. The author also serves to neutralize the contradictions that may emerge in a series of texts: there must be—at a certain level of his thought or desire, of his consciousness or unconscious—a point where contradictions are resolved, where incompatible elements are at last tied together or organized around a fundamental or originating contradiction. Finally, the author is a particular source of expression that, in more or less completed forms, is manifested equally well, and with similar validity, in works, sketches, letters, fragments, and so on. Clearly, Saint Jerome's four criteria of authenticity (criteria which seem totally insufficient for today's exegetes) do define the four modalities according to which modern criticism brings the author-function into play.

But the author-function is not a pure and simple reconstruction made secondhand from a text given as passive material. The text always contains a certain number of signs referring to the author. These signs, well known to grammarians, are personal pronouns, adverbs of time and place, and verb conjugation. Such elements do not play the same role in discourses provided with the author-function as in those lacking it. In the latter, such "shifters" refer to the real speaker and to the spatio-temporal coordinates of his discourse (although certain modifications can occur, as in the operation of relating discourses in the first person). In the former, however, their role is more complex and variable. Everyone knows that, in a novel narrated in the first person, neither the first person pronoun, nor the present indicative refer exactly either to the writer or to the moment in which he writes, but rather to an alter ego whose distance from the author varies, often changing in the course of the work. It would be just as wrong to equate the author with the real writer as to equate him with the fictitious speaker; the author-function is carried out and operates in the scission itself, in this division and this distance.

One might object that this is a characteristic peculiar to novelistic or poetic discourse, a "game" in which only "quasi-discourses" participate. In fact, however, all discourses endowed with the author-function do possess this plurality of self. The self that speaks in the preface to a treatise on mathematics—and that indicates the circumstances of the treatise's composition—is identical neither in its position nor in its functioning to the self that speaks in the course of a demonstration, and that appears in the form of "I conclude" or "I suppose." In the first case, the "I" refers to an individual without an equivalent who, in a determined place and time, completed a certain task; in the second, the "I" indicates an instance and a level of demonstration which any individual could perform provided that he accept the same system of symbols, play of axioms, and set of previous demonstrations. We could also, in the same treatise, locate a third self, one that speaks to tell the work's meaning, the obstacles encountered, the results obtained, and the remaining problems; this self is situated in the field of already existing or yet-to-appear mathematical discourses. The author-function is not assumed by the first of these selves at the expense of the other two, which would then be nothing more than a fictitious splitting in two of the first one. On the contrary, in these discourses the author-function operates so as to effect the dispersion of these three simultaneous selves.

No doubt analysis could discover still more characteristic traits of the author-function. I will limit myself to these four, however, because they seem both the most visible and the most important. They can be summarized as follows: (1) the author-function is linked to the juridical and institutional system that encompasses, determines, and articulates the universe of discourses; (2) it does not affect all discourses in the same way at all times and in all types of civilization; (3) it is not defined by the spontaneous attribution of a discourse to its producer, but rather by a series of specific and complex operations; (4) it does not refer purely and simply to a real individual, since it can give rise simultaneously to several selves, to several subjects—positions that can be occupied by different classes of individuals.

Up to this point I have unjustifiably limited my subject. Certainly the author-function in painting, music, and other arts should have been discussed, but even supposing that we remain within the world of discourse, as I want to do, I seem to have given the term "author" much too narrow a meaning. I have discussed the author only in the limited sense of a person to whom the production of a text, a book, or a work can be legitimately attributed. It is easy to see that in the sphere of discourse one can be the author of much more than a book—one can be the author of a theory, tradition, or discipline in which other books and authors will in their turn find a place. These authors are in a position which we shall call "transdiscursive." This is a recurring phenomenon—certainly as old as our civilization. Homer, Aristotle, and the Church Fathers, as well as the first mathematicians and the originators of the Hippocratic tradition, all played this role.

Furthermore, in the course of the nineteenth century, there appeared in Europe another, more uncommon, kind of author, whom one should confuse with neither the "great" literary authors, nor the authors of religious texts, nor the founders of science. In a somewhat arbitrary way we shall call those who belong in this last group "founders of discursivity." They are unique in that they are not just the authors of their own works. They have produced something else: the possibilities and the rules for the formation of other texts. In this sense, they are very different, for example, from a novelist, who is, in fact, nothing more than the author of his own text. Freud is not just the author of *The Interpretation of Dreams* or *Jokes and their Relation to the Unconscious;* Marx is not just the author of the *Communist Manifesto* or *Capital:* they both have established an endless possibility of discourse.

Obviously, it is easy to object. One might say that it is not true that the author of a novel is only the author of his own text; in a sense, he also, provided that he acquires some "importance," governs and commands more than that. To take a very simple example, one could say that Ann Radcliffe not only wrote *The Castles of Athlin and Dunbayne* and several other novels, but also made possible the appearance of the Gothic horror novel at the beginning of the nineteenth century; in that respect, her author-function exceeds her own work. But I think there is an answer to this objection. These founders of discursivity (I use Marx and Freud as examples, because I believe them to be both the first and the most important cases) make possible something altogether different from what a novelist makes possible. Ann Radcliffe's texts opened the way for a certain number of resemblances and analogies which have their model or principle in her work. The latter contains characteristic signs, figures, relationships, and structures which could be reused by others. In other words, to say that Ann Radcliffe founded the Gothic horror novel means that in the nineteenth-century Gothic novel one will find, as in Ann Radcliffe's works, the theme of the heroine caught in the trap of her own innocence, the hidden castle, the character of the black, cursed hero devoted to making the world expiate the evil done to him, and all the rest of it.

On the other hand, when I speak of Marx or Freud as founders of discursivity, I mean that they made possible not only a certain number of analogies, but also (and equally important) a certain number of differences. They have created a possibility for something other than their discourse, yet something belong-

ing to what they founded. To say that Freud founded
psychoanalysis does not (simply) mean that we find the concept
of the libido or the technique of dream analysis in the works of
Karl Abraham or Melanie Klein; it means that Freud made possible a certain number of divergences—with respect to his own
texts, concepts, and hypotheses—that all arise from the
psychoanalytical discourse itself.

This would seem to present a new difficulty, however: is the
above not true, after all, of any founder of a science, or of any
author who has introduced some important transformation into
a science? After all, Galileo made possible not only those discourses that repeated the laws that he had formulated, but also
statements very different from what he himself had said. If
Cuvier is the founder of biology or Saussure the founder of
linguistics, it is not because they were imitated, nor because
people have since taken up again the concept of organism or
sign; it is because Cuvier made possible, to a certain extent, a
theory of evolution diametrically opposed to his own fixism; it is
because Saussure made possible a generative grammar radically
different from his structural analyses. Superficially, then, the
initiation of discursive practices appears similar to the founding
of any scientific endeavor.

Still, there is a difference, and a notable one. In the case of a
science, the act that founds it is on an equal footing with its
future transformations; this act becomes in some respects part of
the set of modifications that it makes possible. Of course, this
belonging can take several forms. In the future development of
a science, the founding act may appear as little more than a
particular instance of a more general phenomenon which unveils itself in the process. It can also turn out to be marred by
intuition and empirical bias; one must then reformulate it, making it the object of a certain number of supplementary theoretical operations which establish it more rigorously, etc. Finally, it
can seem to be a hasty generalization which must be limited,
and whose restricted domain of validity must be retraced. In
other words, the founding act of a science can always be reintroduced within the machinery of those transformations that
derive from it.

In contrast, the initiation of a discursive practice is hetero-geneous to its subsequent transformations. To expand a type of discursivity, such as psychoanalysis as founded by Freud, is not to give it a formal generality that it would not have permit-ted at the outset, but rather to open it up to a certain number of possible applications. To limit psychoanalysis as a type of discur-sivity is, in reality, to try to isolate in the founding act an eventu-ally restricted number of propositions or statements to which, alone, one grants a founding value, and in relation to which certain concepts or theories accepted by Freud might be consid-ered as derived, secondary, and accessory. In addition, one does not declare certain propositions in the work of these founders to be false: instead, when trying to seize the act of founding, one sets aside those statements that are not pertinent, either because they are deemed inessential, or because they are considered "prehistoric" and derived from another type of discursivity. In other words, unlike the founding of a science, the initiation of a discursive practice does not participate in its later transforma-tions.

As a result, one defines a proposition's theoretical validity in relation to the work of the founders—while, in the case of Galileo and Newton, it is in relation to what physics or cosmology *is* (in its intrinsic structure and "normativity") that one affirms the validity of any proposition that those men may have put forth. To phrase it very schematically: the work of initiators of discursivity is not situated in the space that science defines; rather, it is the science or the discursivity which refers back to their work as primary coordinates.

In this way we can understand the inevitable necessity, within these fields of discursivity, for a "return to the origin." This return, which is part of the discursive field itself, never stops modifying it. The return is not a historical supplement which would be added to the discursivity, or merely an ornament; on the contrary, it constitutes an effective and necessary task of transforming the discursive practice itself. Re-examination of Galileo's text may well change our knowledge of the history of mechanics, but it will never be able to change mechanics itself. On the other hand, re-examining Freud's texts modifies psychoanalysis itself just as a re-examination of Marx's would modify Marxism.[3]

What I have just outlined regarding the initiation of discursive practices is, of course, very schematic; this is true, in particular, of the opposition that I have tried to draw between discursive initiation and scientific founding. It is not always easy to distinguish between the two; moreover, nothing proves that they are two mutually exclusive procedures. I have attempted the distinction for only one reason: to show that the author-function, which is complex enough when one tries to situate it at the level of a book or a series of texts that carry a given signature, involves still more determining factors when one tries to analyze it in larger units, such as groups of works or entire disciplines.

To conclude, I would like to review the reasons why I attach a certain importance to what I have said.

First, there are theoretical reasons. On the one hand, an analysis in the direction that I have outlined might provide for an approach to a typology of discourse. It seems to me, at least at first glance, that such a typology cannot be constructed solely from the grammatical features, formal structures, and objects of discourse: more likely there exist properties or relationships peculiar to discourse (not reducible to the rules of grammar and logic), and one must use these to distinguish the major categories of discourse. The relationship (or nonrelationship) with an au-

[3]To define these returns more clearly, one must also emphasize that they tend to reinforce the enigmatic link between an author and his works. A text has an inaugurative value precisely because it is the work of a particular author, and our returns are conditioned by this knowledge. As in the case of Galileo, there is no possibility that the rediscovery of an unknown text by Newton or Cantor will modify classical cosmology or set theory as we know them (at best, such an exhumation might modify our historical knowledge of their genesis). On the other hand, the discovery of a text like Freud's "Project for a Scientific Psychology"—insofar as it is a text by Freud—always threatens to modify not the historical knowledge of psychoanalysis, but its theoretical field, even if only by shifting the accentuation or the center of gravity. Through such returns, which are part of their make-up, these discursive practices maintain a relationship with regard to their "fundamental" and indirect author unlike that which an ordinary text entertains with its immediate author.—Ed.

thor, and the different forms this relationship takes, constitute—
in a quite visible manner—one of these discursive properties.

On the other hand, I believe that one could find here an
introduction to the historical analysis of discourse. Perhaps it is
time to study discourses not only in terms of their expressive
value or formal transformations, but according to their modes of
existence. The modes of circulation, valorization, attribution,
and appropriation of discourses vary with each culture and are
modified within each. The manner in which they are articulated
according to social relationships can be more readily understood, I believe, in the activity of the author-function and in its
modifications, than in the themes or concepts that discourses set
in motion.

It would seem that one could also, beginning with analyses
of this type, re-examine the privileges of the subject. I realize
that in undertaking the internal and architectonic analysis of a
work (be it a literary text, philosophical system, or scientific
work), in setting aside biographical and psychological references, one has already called back into question the absolute
character and founding role of the subject. Still, perhaps one
must return to this question, not in order to re-establish the
theme of an originating subject, but to grasp the subject's points
of insertion, modes of functioning, and system of dependencies.
Doing so means overturning the traditional problem, no longer
raising the questions "How can a free subject penetrate the substance of things and give it meaning? How can it activate the
rules of a language from within and thus give rise to the designs
which are properly its own?" Instead, these questions will be
raised: "How, under what conditions and in what forms can
something like a subject appear in the order of discourse? What
place can it occupy in each type of discourse, what functions can
it assume, and by obeying what rules?" In short, it is a matter of
depriving the subject (or its substitute) of its role as originator,
and of analyzing the subject as a variable and complex function
of discourse.

Second, there are reasons dealing with the "ideological" status
of the author. The question then becomes: How can one reduce
the great peril, the great danger with which fiction threatens our
world? The answer is: One can reduce it with the author. The

author allows a limitation of the cancerous and dangerous proliferation of significations within a world where one is thrifty not
only with one's resources and riches, but also with one's discourses and their significations. The author is the principle of
thrift in the proliferation of meaning. As a result, we must entirely reverse the traditional idea of the author. We are accustomed, as we have seen earlier, to saying that the author is the
genial creator of a work in which he deposits, with infinite
wealth and generosity, an inexhaustible world of significations.
We are used to thinking that the author is so different from all
other men, and so transcendent with regard to all languages
that, as soon as he speaks, meaning begins to proliferate, to
proliferate indefinitely.

The truth is quite the contrary: the author is not an indefinite
source of significations which fill a work; the author does not
precede the works, he is a certain functional principle by which,
in our culture, one limits, excludes, and chooses; in short, by
which one impedes the free circulation, the free manipulation,
the free composition, decomposition, and recomposition of fiction. In fact, if we are accustomed to presenting the author as a
genius, as a perpetual surging of invention, it is because, in
reality, we make him function in exactly the opposite fashion.
One can say that the author is an ideological product, since we
represent him as the opposite of his historically real function.
(When a historically given function is represented in a figure
that inverts it, one has an ideological production.) The author is
therefore the ideological figure by which one marks the manner
in which we fear the proliferation of meaning.

In saying this, I seem to call for a form of culture in which
fiction would not be limited by the figure of the author. It would
be pure romanticism, however, to imagine a culture in which the
fictive would operate in an absolutely free state, in which fiction
would be put at the disposal of everyone and would develop
without passing through something like a necessary or constraining figure. Although, since the eighteenth century, the author
has played the role of the regulator of the fictive, a role quite
characteristic of our era of industrial and bourgeois society, of
individualism and private property, still, given the historical
modifications that are taking place, it does not seem necessary

that the author-function remain constant in form, complexity, and even in existence. I think that, as our society changes, at the very moment when it is in the process of changing, the author-function will disappear, and in such a manner that fiction and its polysemic texts will once again function according to another mode, but still with a system of constraint—one which will no longer be the author, but which will have to be determined or, perhaps, experienced.

All discourses, whatever their status, form, value, and whatever the treatment to which they will be subjected, would then develop in the anonymity of a murmur. We would no longer hear the questions that have been rehashed for so long: "Who really spoke? Is it really he and not someone else? With what authenticity or originality? And what part of his deepest self did he express in his discourse?" Instead, there would be other questions, like these: "What are the modes of existence of this discourse? Where has it been used, how can it circulate, and who can appropriate it for himself? What are the places in it where there is room for possible subjects? Who can assume these various subject-functions?" And behind all these questions, we would hear hardly anything but the stirring of an indifference: "What difference does it make who is speaking?"

EDWARD W. SAID

The Text, the World, the Critic

Since he deserted the concert stage during the 1960's, the
Canadian pianist Glenn Gould has confined his work to records,
television, and radio. There is some disagreement among critics
as to whether Gould is always, or only sometimes, a convincing
interpreter of one or another piano piece, but there is scarcely a
doubt that each of his performances now is at least special. A few
years ago, Gould issued a record of his performance of Beethoven's Fifth Symphony in the Liszt piano transcription. Quite
aside from being a surprisingly eccentric choice of piece even for
the arch-eccentric Gould, who had always been associated with
classical music, this particular release had a number of other od-
dities about it. The piece was not only of the nineteenth century,
but of its most discredited aspect, pianistically speaking: the aspect that did not content itself with transforming the concert
experience into a feast for the virtuoso's exhibitionism, but also
raided the literature of other instruments, making of their music
a flamboyant occasion for the pianist's skill. Most transcriptions
tend on the whole to sound thick or muddy, since frequently the
piano is attempting to copy the sound texture of an orchestra or
organ. Liszt's Fifth Symphony was less offensive than most transcriptions, mainly because it was brilliantly reduced for the
piano, but even at its most clear the sound was an unusual one
for Gould to be producing. His sound previously had been the
clearest and most unadorned of all pianists', which was why he
had the uncanny ability to turn Bach's counterpoint into an almost visual experience. The Liszt transcription, in short, was an

entirely different idiom, yet Gould was very successful in it. He
sounded as Lisztian now as he had sounded Bachian in the past.

Nor was this all. Accompanying the main disc was another
one, a longish, informal interview of Gould by a record company
executive. During the interview Gould told his interlocutor that
one reason for his escape from "live" performance was the development of a bad habit in his pianism. On his tours of the
Soviet Union, for example, he would notice that the large halls
in which he was performing caused him perforce to distort the
phrases in a Bach partita—here he demonstrated by playing the
distorted phrases—so that he could more effectively "catch" and
address his listeners in the eighth balcony. He then played the
same phrases to illustrate how much more correctly, and less
seductively, he was performing music now that no actual audience was present.

It may seem slightly heavy-handed to draw out some of the
little ironies from this situation—transcription, interview, and
illustrated performance styles all included. But doing so serves
my main point about Gould and the Fifth Symphony: that any
occasion involving the aesthetic document or experience on the
one hand, and the critic's role and his "worldliness" on the other,
cannot be a simple one. Indeed Gould's strategy is something of
a parody of all the directions we might take in trying to get at
what occurs between the world and the aesthetic object. Here is a
pianist who once represented the ascetic performer in the ser-
vice of the music, transformed now into unashamed virtuoso,
whose principal aesthetic standard is supposed to be little higher
than that of a musical whore. A man who left the recital stage
because it had led him to solicit his audience's attention by alter-
ing his playing, now markets his record as a "first" and then adds
to it, not more music, but the kind of bid for attention and
immediacy offered by a personal interview. And finally all this is
fixed on a mechanically replicable object, which controls the
most obvious signs of immediacy (Gould's voice, the peacocklike
style of the Liszt transcription, the brash informality of an interview packed along with a disembodied performance) beneath, or
inside (or is it outside?) a dumb, anonymous, and disposable disc
of black plastic.

If one thinks about Gould and his record, parallels will

emerge out of the circumstances of written performance. First of all, there is the reproducible material existence of a text. Both a recording and a printed object are subject to similar legal, political, economic, and social constraints, insofar as their sustained production and distribution are concerned; why and how they are distributed are different matters that need not occupy us here. The main thing is that a written text of the sort we care about is originally the result of some immediate contact between author and medium. Thereafter it can be reproduced for the benefit of the world; however much the author demurs at the publicity he receives, once he lets the text go into more than one copy his work is in the world.

Second, a written and a musical performance are both instances on some level at least of style, in the simplest and least honorific sense of that very complex phenomenon. Once again I must arbitrarily exclude all the more interesting complexities that go into making up the very question of style, in order to insist on style as, from the standpoint of producer and receiver, the recognizable, repeatable, preservable sign of an author who reckons with an audience. Even if the audience is as restricted as his self or as wide as the whole world, the author's style is partially a phenomenon of repetition and reception. But what makes style receivable as the signature of its author's manner is a collection of features variously called idiolect, voice, or more firmly, irreducible individuality. The paradox is that something as impersonal as a text, or a record, can nevertheless deliver an imprint or a trace of something as lively, immediate, and transitory as a "voice." Glenn Gould's interview simply makes brutally explicit the frequent need for recognition that a text carries even in its most pristine, enshrined form; a text needs to show how it bears a personality, for which a common analogy is a talking voice addressing someone. Considered as I have been considering it, style neutralizes, if it does not cancel, the worldlessness, the silent, seemingly uncircumstanced existence of a solitary text. It is not only that any text, if it is not immediately destroyed, is a network of often colliding forces, but also that a text in being a text is a being in the world; it addresses anyone who reads, just as Gould addresses everyone who hears throughout the very same record that is supposed to represent both his withdrawal from the world and his "new" silent style of playing without a live audience.

Of course, texts do not speak in the ordinary sense of the word. Yet any simple diametric opposition that is asserted between speech, on the one hand—or that aspect of speech described by Paul Ricoeur as the situation of discourse and the function of reference—and, on the other hand, the text as an *interception* or *suspension* of speech's worldliness is, I think, misleading and grossly simplified. Here is how Ricoeur puts this opposition, which he claims to be setting up only for the sake of analytic clarification:

> In speech the function of reference is linked to the role of the *situation of discourse* within the exchange of language itself: in exchanging speech, the speakers are present to each other, but also to the circumstantial setting of discourse, not only the perceptual surroundings, but also the cultural background known by both speakers. It is in relation to this situation that discourse is fully meaningful: the reference to reality is in the last analysis reference to that reality which can be pointed out "around," so to speak, the instance of discourse itself. Language . . . and in general all the ostensive indicators of language serve to anchor discourse in the circumstantial reality which surrounds the instance of discourse. Thus, in living speech, the *ideal* meaning of what one says bends towards a *real* reference, namely to that "about which" one speaks. . . .
>
> This is no longer the case when a text takes the place of speech. . . . A text. . . is not without reference; it will be precisely the task of reading, as interpretation, to actualize the reference. At least, in this suspension wherein reference is deferred, in the sense that it is postponed, a text is somehow "in the air" outside of the world or without a world; by means of this obliteration of all relation to the world, every text is free to enter into relation with all the other texts which come to take the place of the circumstantial reality shown by living speech.[1]

I cannot see that such an idealization of the difference between speech and writing is useful. Speech and circumstantial

---

[1] "What is a Text? Explanation and Interpretation," in David Rasmussen, *Mythic-Symbolic Language and Philosophical Anthropology: A Constructive Interpretation of the Thought of Paul Ricoeur* (The Hague: Nijhoff, 1971), p. 138. For a more interesting distinction between *oeuvre* and *texte,* see Roland Barthes's essay in this volume.

reality exist, according to Ricoeur, in a state of presence, in reality, in the world; writing, the text, exist in a state of suspension—that is, outside circumstantial reality—until they are "actualized" and made present by the reader-critic. There are so many things wrong with this set of ideas that I scarcely know where to begin my attack. Ricoeur makes it seem as if the text and circumstantial reality, or what I shall call worldliness, play a game of musical chairs with each other, one intercepting and replacing the other according to fairly crude signals. But, we might ask, where does this game take place? Certainly not in reality, but in the interpreter's head, a locale presumably without worldliness or circumstantiality. The critic-interpreter has his position reduced to that of a central stock-exchange on whose floor the transaction occurs by which the text is shown to be meaning X while saying Y. And what becomes of what Ricoeur calls "deferred reference" during the interpretation? Quite simply, on the basis of a model of direct exchange, it comes back, brought back whole and actual by the critic's reading.

I suppose the principal difficulty with Ricoeur's opposition is that he assumes, quite without sufficient argument, that circumstantial reality, worldliness as I shall call it, is symmetrically and exclusively the property of speech or the speech situation, or what the writer would have wanted *to say* had he been able to do so, had he not instead chosen to write. My contention is that worldliness does not come and go, nor is it here and there in the apologetic and soupy way we often say that something is "historical," a euphemism in such cases for the impossibly vague notion that all things take place in history. Moreover a critic may often be, but is not merely, the alchemical translator of texts into circumstantial reality or worldliness; for he too is subject to and a producer of circumstances, and these are felt regardless of whatever objectivity his method possesses. Texts have ways of existing, both theoretical and practical, that even in their most rarefied form are always enmeshed in circumstance, time, place, and society—in short, they are in the world, and hence are worldly.[2] The same is doubtless true of the critic, as reader and

---

[2] I have discussed this in chapter 4 of *Beginnings: Intention and Method* (New York: Basic Books, 1975).

as writer. I shall not be hammering away at these points so much as, in the main part of this essay, trying to note them, to illustrate them as concretely as possible, given the very complex circumstances surrounding and involving all verbal activity.

If my use of Gould's recording of the Beethoven Fifth Symphony served any serious purpose, it provided an instance of a quasi-textual object whose ways of engaging the world are both numerous and complicated, more complicated than the demarcation drawn between text and speech by Ricoeur. These engagements are what I have been calling worldliness. But my principal concern here is not with an aesthetic object in general, but rather with the text in particular. Most critics will subscribe to the notion—a sloppy one, I think—that every literary text, for example, is in some way burdened with its occasion, with the brute empirical realities out of which it emerged. Pressed too far, such a notion earns the justified polemic of a stylistician like Michael Riffaterre, who in an essay entitled "The Self-sufficient Text" calls any reduction of a text to its circumstances a fallacy, biographical, genetic, psychological, or analogic.[3] Most critics would probably go along with Riffaterre in saying, yes, let us make sure that the text does not disappear under the weight of these fallacies, but, and here I speak mainly for myself, they are not entirely satisfied with the idea of a self-sufficient text. Is the alternative to the various fallacies *only* a quite hermetic textual cosmos, a cosmos whose significant dimension of meaning is, as Riffaterre says, a wholly inward one? Is there no way to deal with a text and its worldliness fairly? Is there no means of grappling with the problems of literary language except by cutting those off from the more plainly urgent ones of everyday worldly language?

I have found a way of starting to deal with these questions in an unexpected place, which is why I shall seem to be digressing now from the immediate subject at hand. Several years ago I had the leisure to explore the relatively untapped field of Arabic linguistic speculation. At the time I was very interested, as I still am, in speculation about language in Europe, that is, in that special combination of theoretical imagination and empirical ob-

---

[3]"The Self-sufficient Text," *Diacritics,* 3 (Fall 1973), 40.

servation characterizing romantic philology, the rise of linguistics in the early nineteenth century, and the whole rich phenomenon of what Foucault has called the discovery of language. I was staggered at my discovery that there had existed among Islamic linguists, during the eleventh century in Andalusia, a remarkably sophisticated and unexpectedly prophetic school of philosophic grammarians, whose polemics anticipated in an uncanny way twentieth-century debates between structuralists and generative grammarians, between descriptivists and behaviorists. Nor was this all. I discovered a small group of linguists whose energies were directed against tendencies among rival linguists to turn the question of meaning in language into esoteric and allegorical exercises. I am referring to three eleventh-century linguists and theoretical grammarians, Ibn Hazm, Ibn Ginni, and Ibn Mada al-Qurtobi, all of Cordova, all Zahirites, all antagonists of Batinism. Batinites—as their name implies—believed that meaning in language is concealed within the words; meaning is therefore available only as the result of what we would call an inward-tending exegesis. The Zahirites—their name derives from the word in Arabic for clear and apparent and phenomenal—argued for the surface meaning of words, a meaning anchored to a particular usage, circumstance, historical and religious anomaly.

Both groups trace their origins back to readings of the sacred text, the Koran, and how that unique event—for the Koran, unlike the Bible, is an event—is to be read, understood, transmitted, and taught by later generations of believers. The Cordovan Zahirites attacked the excesses of the Batinites, arguing that the very profession of grammar (in Arabic, *nahu*) was an invitation to spinning out private meanings in an otherwise divinely pronounced text. According to Ibn Mada, it was absurd even to associate grammar with a logic of understanding, since as a science grammar simply assumed, even created reasons and functions for language use that implied a hidden level beneath words, available only to private initiates.[4] Once you resort to such a level, anything more or less becomes permissible in the

---

[4] This is the main, polemical point in his tract *Ar-rad ala l nuhat,* ed. Shawki Daif (Cairo, 1947). The text dates from A.D. 1180.

way of interpretation: there can be no strict meaning, no control
over what words in fact say, no responsibility toward the words.
The Zahirite effort was to restore and rationalize a system of
reading a text in which attention was focused on the words
themselves, not on hidden meanings they might contain. The
Cordovan Zahirites in particular went very far in trying to provide a reading system placing the tightest possible control over
the reader and his circumstances by means of a theory of the
text.

I can not here go into this theory in detail. What I can do,
however, is indicate how the controversy itself is endemic to a
circumstantial, or if you like, a worldly notion of the sacred text,
a notion that essentially puts a line of demarcation between Islamic ideas and the main Judeo-Christian textual traditions.
There is a brilliant and concise account of this difference in
Roger Arnaldez's book on Ibn Hazm, and I can do little better
than paraphrase some of his observations. The Judeo-Christian
text, at whose center is Revelation, cannot be reduced to a specific point of impact by which the Word of God entered the
world; rather the Word enters human history, all along that
history, continually, and therefore a very important place is
given to what Arnaldez calls "human factors" in the reception,
transmission, and understanding of such a text.[5] By contrast the
Koran is the result of a unique event, the "descent" into worldliness of a text, whose language and form are thereafter to be
viewed as stable, complete, unchanging; the language of the text
is Arabic, therefore a greatly privileged language, and its vessel,
the messenger Mohammed, similarly privileged. Such a text is
an absolute and cannot be referred back to any particular interpreter or interpretation, although this is clearly what the
Batinites tried to do (perhaps, it is suggested, under the influence of Judeo-Christian exegetical techniques). Arnaldez puts
his description of the Koran in the following terms: the Koran
speaks of historical events, yet is not itself historical. It repeats
past events, which it condenses and particularizes, yet it is not

[5]*Grammaire et théologie chez Ibn Hazm de Cordoue* (Paris: J. Vrin, 1956), pp. 12
and passim. There is a clear, somewhat schematic account of Ibn Ginni, Ibn
Mada, and others in Anis Fraiha, *Nathariyat fil Lugha* (Beirut: Al-Maktaba al
Jamiya, 1973).

itself an actually lived experience; it ruptures the human continuity of life; God does not enter temporality by a sustained and/or concerted act. The Koran evokes the memory of actions whose content repeats itself eternally in ways identical with itself, as warnings, orders, imperatives, punishments, rewards.[6] In short, the Zahirite position adopts a view of the Koran that is absolutely circumstantial and worldly, without at the same time making that worldliness *dominate* the actual sense of the text—this is the ultimate avoidance of vulgar determinism in the Zahirite position.

Hence Ibn Hazm's linguistic theory is based upon an analysis of the *imperative* mode since, in its most radical and verbal form, the Koran, according to Ibn Hazm, is a text controlled by two paradigmatic imperatives, *iqra*: read, or recite, and *qul*: tell.[7] Since those imperatives obviously control the circumstantial, worldly, and historical appearance of the Koran (and its uniqueness as an event), and since they must also control uses (that is, readings) of the text thereafter, Ibn Hazm connects his analysis of the imperative mode with a juridical notion of *hadd,* a word meaning both a logico-grammatical definition and a limit. What transpires in the imperative mode, between the injunctions to read and write, is the delivery of an utterance (*khabar* in Arabic, translated by Arnaldez as *énoncé*), which is the verbal realization of a signifying intention, *niyah.* Now the signifying intention is synonymous not with a psychological intention, but exclusively with a verbal intention, itself something highly worldly—that is, it takes place exclusively in the world, it is occasional and circumstantial in both a very precise and wholly pertinent way. To signify is only to use language, and to use language is to do so according to certain rules, lexical and syntactic, by which language is in and of the world; by that the Zahirite means that language is regulated by real usage, and neither by abstract prescription nor by speculative freedom. Above all, language stands between man and a vast indefiniteness: if the world is a gigantic system of correspondences, then it is verbal form—language in actual grammatical use—that allows us to isolate from among these

[6]Arnaldez, *Grammaire et théologie,* p. 12.
[7]Ibid., p. 69.

correspondences the denominated object. Thus, as Arnaldez puts it, fidelity to such true aspects of language is an *askesis* of the imagination.[8] A word has a strict meaning understood as an imperative, and with that meaning also a strictly ordained series of resemblances (correspondences) to other words and meanings, which play, strictly, around the first word. Thus figurative language (as it occurs even in the Koran), otherwise elusive and at the mercy of the virtuosic interpreter, is part of the actual, not virtual, structure of language, is a resource therefore of the collectivity of language users.

What Ibn Hazm does, Arnaldez reminds us, is to view language as possessing two seemingly antithetical characteristics: first, that of a divinely ordained institution, unchanging, immutable, logical, rational, intelligible; and second, that of an instrument existing as pure contingency, that is, as an institution signifying meanings anchored in specific utterances.[9] It is exactly because the Zahirite sees language in this double perspective that he rejects reading techniques that reduce words and their meanings back to radicals from which (in Arabic at least) they may be seen grammatically to derive. Each utterance is its own occasion and, as such, is firmly anchored in the worldly context in which it is applied. And because the Koran, which is the paradigmatic case of divine-and-human language, is a text that incorporates speaking and writing, reading and telling, Zahirite interpretation itself accepts as inevitable not the separation between speech and writing, nor the disjunction between a text and its circumstantiality, but rather their necessary interplay. It is this field of interaction that generates meaning, indeed that makes meaning (in the severe Zahirite sense of the word) at all possible.

I have summarized very quickly an enormously complex theory, in relation to which my own position is still that of an uncertain novice. I cannot claim any particular influence for such a theory, certainly not in Western European literature since the Renaissance, perhaps not even in Arabic literature since the Middle Ages. But what has struck me forcibly about this whole

[8] Ibid., p. 77.
[9] Ibid., p. 80.

theory is that it represents a considerably articulated thesis for dealing with a text as significant form, in which—and I put this as carefully as I can—worldliness, circumstantiality, the text's status as an event having sensuous particularity as well as historical contingency, are incorporated in the text, are an infrangible part of its capacity for conveying and producing meaning. This means that a text has a specific situation, a situation that places restraints upon the interpreter and his interpretation not because the situation is hidden within the text as a mystery, but rather because the situation exists at the same level of more or less surface particularity as the textual object itself. There are many ways for conveying such a situation, and I shall consider some examples presently. But what I will be drawing attention to is an ambition on the part of a writer to deliver his text as an object whose interpretation—by virtue of the exactness of its situation in the world—*has already commenced* and is therefore already constrained in, and constraining, its interpretation. Such a text can thereafter be construed as needing at most complementary, as opposed to supplementary, reading.

My principal task now is to discuss ways by which texts impose constraints and limits upon their interpretation. Recent critical theory has placed undue emphasis upon the limitlessness of interpretation. Part of this emphasis has been due to a conception of the text as existing entirely within a hermetic, Alexandrian textual universe, having no connection with actuality. This is a view I oppose, not simply because texts are in the world, but also because as texts they *place* themselves—that is, one of their functions as texts is to place themselves—and they *are* themselves by acting, in the world. Moreover, their manner of doing this is to place restraints upon what can be done with (and to) them interpretively.

Modern literary history gives us a number of examples of writers whose text, as a text, incorporates quite explicitly the circumstances of its very concretely imagined, and even described, situation. One type of author—exemplified by Hopkins, Wilde, and Conrad—conceives his text as supported explicitly by a discursive situation involving speaker and audience; the designed interplay between speech and reception, between verbal-ity and textuality *is* the text's situation, its placing of itself in the world.

The three authors I mentioned wrote their major works between 1875 and 1915. The subject matter of their writing varies so widely that similarities among the three have to be looked for elsewhere. Let me begin with a journal entry by Hopkins:

> The winter was called severe. There were three spells of frost with skating, the third beginning on Feb. 9. No snow to speak of till that day. Some days before Feb. 7 I saw catkins hanging. On the 9th there was snow but not lying on the roads. On the grass it became a crust lifted on the heads of the blades. As we went down a field near Caesar's Camp I noticed it before me *squalentem,* coat below coat, sketched in intersecting edges bearing 'idiom', all down the slope:—I have no other word yet for that which takes the eye or mind in a bold hand or effective sketching or in marked features or again in graphic writing, which not being beauty nor true inscape yet gives interest and makes ugliness even better than meaninglessness.[10]

Hopkins's earliest writing attempts in this manner to render scenes from nature as exactly as possible. Yet he is never a passive transcriber since for him "this world then is word, expression, news of God."[11] Every phenomenon in nature, he wrote in the sonnet "As kingfishers catch fire," *tells* itself in the world as a sort of lexical unit:

> Each mortal thing does one thing and the same:
> Deals out that being indoors each one dwells;
> Selves—goes itself; *myself* it speaks and spells,
> Crying *What I do is me: for that I came.*[12]

So in the notebook entry Hopkins's observation of nature is dynamic. He sees in the frost an intention to speak or mean, its layered coats *taking* one's attention because of the idiom it bears toward meaning or expression. The writer is as much a respondent as he is a describer: similarly the reader is a full participant in the production of meaning, being obliged, as a mortal thing,

---

[10] *The Journals and Papers of Gerard Manley Hopkins,* ed. Humphry House and Graham Storey (London: Oxford University Press, 1959), p. 195.
[11] Ibid., p. 129.
[12] *The Poems of Gerard Manley Hopkins,* ed. W. H. Gardner and N. H. Mackenzie (London: Oxford University Press, 1967), p. 90.

to do—that is, to act—himself, to produce the sense that, even though ugly, is better than meaninglessness.

This dialectic of production is everywhere present in Hopkins's work. Writing is telling; nature is telling; reading is telling. He wrote to Robert Bridges on May 21, 1878 that in order to do a certain poem justice, "you must not slovenly read it with the eyes but with your ears, as if the paper were declaiming it at you.... Stress is the life of it."[13] Seven years later he specified more strictly that "poetry is the darling child of speech, of lips and spoken utterance: it must be spoken; *till it is spoken it is not performed,* it does not perform, it is not itself. Sprung rhythm gives back to poetry its true soul and self. As poetry is emphatically speech, speech purged of dross like gold in the furnace, so it must have emphatically the essential elements of speech."[14] So close is the identification in Hopkins's mind between world, word, and the utterance, the three coming alive together as a moment of performance, that there is no need of critical intervention. It is the written text that provides the immediate circumstantial reality for the poem's "play" (the word is Hopkins's). So far from being a document associated with other lifeless, worldless texts, Hopkins's own text was for him his child; when he destroyed his poems he spoke of the slaughter of the innocents, and everywhere in his career he speaks of writing as the exercise of his male gift. At the moment of greatest desolation in his career, in such a poem as "To R. B.," the urgency of his feeling of poetic aridity is expressed biologically throughout. When he comes to describe finally what it is he now writes he says:

> O then if in my lagging lines you miss
> The roll, the rise, the carol, the creation,
> My winter world, that scarcely breathes that bliss
> Now, yields you, with some sighs, our explanation.[15]

Because his text has lost its ability to incorporate the stress of creation, and because it is no longer performance but what in

---

[13]*The Letters of Gerard Manley Hopkins to Robert Bridges,* ed. Claude Colleer Abbott (Oxford: Oxford University Press, 1955), pp. 51-52.

[14]Quoted in Anthony Bisshof, S. J., "Hopkins' Letters to His Brother," *Times Literary Supplement,* December 8, 1972, p. 1511.

[15]*Poems of Hopkins,* p. 108.

another poem he calls "dead letters," he now can write only an explanation, which is lifeless speech "bending towards a real reference" (*pace* Ricoeur).

It was said of Wilde by one of his contemporaries that everything he spoke sounded as if it were enclosed in quotation marks. This is no less true of everything he wrote, for such was the consequence of having a pose, which Wilde defined as "a formal recognition of the importance of treating life from a definite reasoned standpoint."[16] Or as Algernon retorts to Jack's accusation that "you always want to argue about things" in *The Importance of Being Earnest:* "That's exactly what things were originally made for."[17] Always ready with a quotable comment, Wilde filled his manuscripts with epigrams on every conceivable subject. Everything he wrote was intended either for more comment or for quotation or, most important, for tracing back to him. There are obvious social reasons for some of this egoism, which Wilde made no attempt to conceal in his quip "To love oneself is the beginning of a life-long romance," but they do not exhaust the speech of Wilde's style. Having forsworn action, life, and nature for their incompleteness and diffusion, Wilde took as his province a theoretical, ideal world in which, as he told Alfred Douglas in *De Profundis,* conversation was the basis of all human relations.[18] Since conflict inhibited conversation as Wilde understood it from the Platonic dialogue, the mode of interchange was to be by epigram. This epigram is Wilde's radical of presentation: a compact utterance capable of the utmost range of subject matter, the greatest authority, and the least equivocation as to its author. When he invaded other forms of art Wilde converted them into longer epigrams. As he said of drama: "I took the drama, the most objective form known to art, and made it as personal a mode of expression as the lyric or the sonnet, at the same time that I widened its range and enriched its characterization."[19] No wonder he could say: "I summed up all systems in a phrase, and all existence in an epigram."[20]

[16] *The Artist as Critic: Critical Writings of Oscar Wilde,* ed. Richard Ellmann (New York: Vintage, 1970), p. 386.
[17] *Complete Works of Oscar Wilde,* ed. J. B. Foreman (London: Collins, 1971), p. 335.
[18] *De Profundis* (New York: Vintage, 1964), p. 18.
[19] Ibid., p. 80.
[20] Ibid., p. 81.

De Profundis records the destruction of the utopia whose individualism and unselfish selfishness Wilde has adumbrated in
The Soul of Man under Socialism. From a free world to a prison
and a circle of suffering: how is the change accomplished?
Wilde's conception of freedom was to be found in *The Importance
of Being Earnest,* where conflicting characters turn out to be
brothers after all just because they say they are. What is written
down (for example, the army lists consulted by Jack) merely
confirms what all along has been capriciously, but stylistically,
said. This transformation, from opponent into brother, is what
Wilde had in mind in connecting the intensification of personality with its multiplication. When the communication between
men no longer possesses the freedom of conversation, when it is
confined to the merely legal liability of print, which is not in-
genuously quotable but, because it has been signed, is now crim-
inally actionable, the utopia crumbles. As he reconsidered his
life in *De Profundis,* Wilde's imagination was transfixed by the
effects of one text upon his life. But he uses it to show how in
going from speech to print, which in a sense all of his other more
fortunate texts had managed somehow to avoid by virtue of
their epigrammatic individuality, he had been ruined. Wilde's
lament in what follows is that a text has too much, not too little,
circumstantial reality, and hence, the Wildean paradox, its vul-
nerability:

> You send me a very nice poem, of the undergraduate school of
> verse, for my approval: I reply by a letter of fantastic literary
> conceits. . . . Look at the history of that letter! It passes from you
> into the hands of a loathsome companion: from him to a gang of
> blackmailers: copies of it are sent about London to my friends, and
> to the manager of the theatre where my work is being performed:
> every construction but the right one is put on it: Society is thrilled
> with the absurd rumours that I have had to pay a huge sum of
> money for having written an infamous letter to you: this forms the
> basis of your father's worst attack: I produce the original letter
> myself in Court to show what it really is: it is denounced by your
> father's counsel as a revolting and insidious attempt to corrupt
> Innocence: ultimately it forms part of a criminal charge: the
> Crown takes it up: the Judge sums up on it with little learning and
> much morality: I go to prison for it at last. That is the result of
> writing you a charming letter.[21]

[21]Ibid., pp. 34-35.

In a world described by George Eliot as a "huge whispering gallery," the effects of writing can be grave indeed: "As the stone which has been kicked by generations of clowns may come by curious little links of effect under the eyes of a scholar, through whose labours it may at last fix the date of invasions and unlock religions, so a bit of ink and paper which has long been an innocent wrapping or stop-gap may at last be laid open under the one pair of eyes which have knowledge enough to turn it into the opening of a catastrophe."[22] If Dr. Casaubon's caution has a purpose, it is by rigid secrecy and an endlessly postponing scriptive will to forestall "the opening of a catastrophe." Yet he cannot succeed, since Eliot is at pains to show that even his tremendously nursed *Key* is a text, and therefore in the world. Unlike Wilde's, Casaubon's disgrace is posthumous, but their textual implication takes place for the same reason, which is their commitment to what Eliot calls an "embroiled medium."

Last let me consider Conrad. Elsewhere I have described the extraordinary *presentational* mode of his narratives, how each of them, almost without exception, dramatizes, motivates, and circumstances the occasion of its telling, how all of Conrad's work is really made out of secondary, reported speech, and how the interplay between appeals to the eye and the ear is highly organized and subtle and constitutes that work's meaning.[23] The Conradian encounter is not simply between a man and his destiny embodied in a moment of extremity but, just as persistently, it is the encounter between speaker and hearer. Marlow is Conrad's chief invention for this encounter, Marlow with his haunting knowledge that a man such as Kurtz or Jim "existed for me, and after all it is only through me that he exists for you."[24] The chain of humanity—"we exist only in so far as we hang together"[25]—is the transmission of actual speech, and existence, from one mouth, and then after that, from one eye, to another. Every text that Conrad wrote, whether formally, aesthetically, or thematically considered, presents itself as unfinished and still in

[22]*Middlemarch*, ed. Gordon S. Haight (Boston: Houghton Mifflin, 1956), p. 302.
[23]See Edward W. Said, "Conrad: The Presentation of Narrative," *Novel*, 7 (Winter 1974), 116–132.
[24]*Lord Jim* (Boston: Houghton Mifflin, 1958), p. 161.
[25]Ibid., p. 160.

the making. "And besides, the last word is not said—probably shall never be said. Are not our lives too short for that full utterance which through all our stammerings is of course our only and abiding intention?"[26] Texts convey the stammerings, but that full utterance, the statement of wholly satisfactory presence, remains distant, attenuated somewhat by a grand gesture like Jim's self-sacrifice, which closes off a text circumstantially without in any way emptying it of its actual urgency. Quite the contrary.

This is a good time to remark that the Western novelistic tradition, from *Don Quixote* on, is full of examples of texts insisting not only upon their circumstantial reality but also upon their status as *already* fulfilling a function, a reference, or a meaning *in the world.* Cervantes and Cide Hamete come immediately to mind. More impressive is Richardson playing the role of mere editor for *Clarissa,* "simply" placing those letters in successive order after they have done what they have done, arranging to fill the text with printer's devices, reader's aids, analytical contents, retrospective meditations, commentary, so that a collection of letters grows to fill the world and occupy all space, to become a circumstance as large and as engrossing as the reader's understanding itself. Surely the novelistic imagination has always included this unwillingness to cede control over the text in the world, or to release it from the discursive and human obligations of all human presence; hence the desire, which is almost a principal action of many novels, to turn the text back, if not directly into speech, then at least into circumstantial, as opposed to meditative, duration.

No novelist, however, can be quite as explicit about circumstances as Marx is in *The Eighteenth Brumaire of Louis Bonaparte.* To my mind no other work is as brilliant and as compelling in the exactness with which circumstances (the German word is *Umstände*) are shown to have made the nephew possible, not as an innovator, but as a farcical repetition of the uncle. What Marx attacks are the atextual theses (1) that history is made up of free events, and (2) that history is guided by superior individuals.[27]

[26]Ibid., p. 161.
[27]Marx, *Der Achtzehnte Brumaire des Louis Bonaparte* (1852; Berlin: Dietz Verlag, 1947), p. 8.

By inserting Louis Bonaparte in a whole intricate system of repetitions, by which first Hegel, then the ancient Romans, then
the 1789 revolutionaries, then Napoleon I, then the bourgeois
interpreters, then finally the fiascos of 1848–51 are all seen in a
pseudoanalogical order of descending worth, increasing deriva-
tiveness, and deceptively harmless masquerading, Marx effectively circumstances, *textualizes,* the random appearance of a new
Caesar. Here we have the case of a text itself providing a world
historical situation with circumstances otherwise hidden in the
deception of a *roi des drôles.* What is ironic—and to be sure in
need of extensive analysis—is how a text, by being a text, by
insisting upon and employing all the devices of textuality,
preeminent among them *repetition,* historicizes and prob-
lematizes all the fugitive significance that has chosen Louis
Bonaparte as its representative.

There is another aspect to what I have been saying about
the novel generally, and about Hopkins, Wilde, and Conrad.
In producing texts with either a firm claim on, or an explicit
will to worldliness, these writers and genres have valorized
speech, making it the tentacle by which an otherwise silent
text ties itself into the world of discourse. By the valorization
of speech I mean that the discursive, circumstantially dense interchange of speaker facing hearer is made to stand—sometimes
misleadingly—for a democratic equality and copresence in actuality between speaker and hearer. Not only is the discursive relation far from equal in actuality (as I shall argue presently), but
also the text's attempt to dissemble, by seeming to be open dem-
ocratically to anyone who might read it, is an act of bad faith.
(Incidentally, one of the strengths of Zahirite theory is that it
dispels the illusion that a surface reading, which is the Zahirite
ambition, is anything but difficult.) Texts of such a length as
Tom Jones aim to occupy leisure time of a quality not available to
just anyone. Moreover, all texts essentially displace, dislodge
other texts or, more frequently, they take the place of something
else. As Nietzsche had the perspicacity to see, texts are fundamentally facts of power, not of democratic exchange.[28] They

[28] Nietzsche's analyses of texts in this light are to be found everywhere in his
work, but especially in *The Genealogy of Morals* and *The Will to Power.*

compel attention away from the world even as their beginning intention as texts, coupled with the inherent authoritarianism of the authorial authority (the repetition in this phrase is a deliberate emphasis on some tautology within all texts, since all texts are in some way self-confirmatory), makes for sustained power.

Yet in the patrimony of texts there is a first text, a sacred prototype, a scripture, which the reader is always approaching through the text before him either as petitioning suppliant or as an initiate among many in a sacred chorus supporting the central patriarchal text. Northrop Frye's theory of literature makes it apparent that the displacing power in all texts derives finally from the displacing power of the Bible, whose centrality, potency, and dominating anteriority inform all Western literature. The same is no less true, in the different modes I discussed earlier, of the Koran and its priority. Both in the Judeo-Christian and in the Islamic traditions these hierarchies repose upon a solidly divine, or quasi-divine, language, a language whose uniqueness is that it is theologically and humanly circumstantial.

It is too often forgotten that modern Western philology, which begins in the early nineteenth century, undertook to revise commonly accepted ideas about language and its divine origins. That revision tried first to determine which was the first language and then, failing to achieve that ambition, proceeded thereafter to reduce language to specific circumstances: language-groups, historical and racial theories, geographical and anthropological theses. A particularly interesting example of how such investigations went is Ernest Renan's career as a philologist; *that* was his real profession, and not that of the boring sage. His first serious work was his 1847 analysis of Semitic languages, revised and published in 1855 as the *Histoire générale et système comparé des langues sémitiques.* Without this study, the *Vie de Jésus* could not have been written. The accomplishment of the *Histoire générale* was scientifically to describe the *inferiority* of Semitic languages, principally Hebrew, Aramaic, and Arabic, the medium of three purportedly sacred, spoken (by God) texts, the Torah, the Koran, and later, the derivative Gospels. Thus in the *Vie de Jésus* Renan would be able to insinuate that the so-called sacred texts, delivered by Moses, Jesus, and Mohammed, could not have anything divine in them if the very medium of their supposed divinity, as well as the body of their message to and in the world, was made up of such comparatively poor worldly stuff. Renan argued that even if these texts were prior to all others in the West, they held nonetheless only a primitive, not a theologically dominant, position.

Renan first reduced texts from objects of divine intervention in the world's business to objects of historical materiality; God as author-authority had little value after Renan's philological and textual revisionism. Yet in dispensing with divine authority, Renan put philological power in its place. What is born to replace divine authority is the textual authority of the philological critic who has the effective skill to separate Semitic, that is, Oriental, languages from the languages of Indo-European culture. Not only therefore did Renan kill off the extratextual validity of the great Semitic sacred texts, he confined them as objects of European study to a scholarly field thereafter to be known as Oriental, and ruled by the Orientalist.[29] The Orientalist is a Renan, or a Gobineau, Renan's contemporary quoted here and there in the 1855 edition of the *Histoire générale et système comparé des langues sémitiques,* for whom the old hierarchy of sacred Semitic texts has been destroyed as if by an act of parricide; the passing of divine authority makes possible the appearance of European ethnocentrism, whereby the methods and the discourse of Western scholarship analyze and characterize as inferior non-European cultures so as to confine them to a position of subordination. Oriental texts come to inhabit a realm without development or power—it is a realm that corresponds exactly to the position of a colony for European texts and culture. All this takes place at the same time that the great European colonial empires in the East are emerging or, in some cases, flourishing.

I have introduced this brief account of the twin origin of the Higher Criticism and of Orientalism as a European scholarly discipline in order to be able to speak about the fallacy of imagining the life of texts as being pleasantly ideal and without force or

---

[29]See in particular Renan, *Histoire générale et système comparé des langues sémitiques,* in *Oeuvres complètes,* Vol. 8, ed. Henriette Psichari (Paris: Calmann-Lévy, 1947–1961), pp. 147–157 and *passim.*

conflict, and conversely, the fallacy of imagining the discursive relations in actual speech to be, as Ricoeur would have it, a relation of equal copresence between hearer and speaker.

Texts incorporate discourse, sometimes violently, in the ways I have been discussing. There are other ways, too. Michel Foucault's archeological analyses of what he calls systems of discourse are premised on the thesis, originally adumbrated by Marx and Engels in *The German Ideology,* that "in every society the production of discourse is at once controlled, selected, organized and redistributed according to a certain number of procedures, whose role is to avert its powers and dangers, to cope with chance events, to evade its ponderous, awesome materiality."[30] Discourse in this passage means what is written as well as what is spoken. Foucault's contention is that the fact of writing itself is a systematic conversion of the power relationship between the controller and the controlled into mere written words; the reason this happens is to let it seem that writing is only writing, whereas writing is one way of disguising the awesome materiality of so tightly controlled and managed a production. Foucault continues:

> In a society such as our own we all know the rules of *exclusion.* The most obvious and familiar of these concerns what is *prohibited.* We know perfectly well that we are not free to say just anything. We have three types of prohibition, covering objects, ritual with its surrounding circumstances, the privileged or exclusive right to speak of a particular subject; these prohibitions interrelate, reinforce and complement each other, forming a complex web, continually subject to modification. I will note simply that the areas where this web is most tightly woven today, where the danger spots are most numerous, are those dealing with politics and sexuality.... In appearance, speech may well be of little account, but the prohibitions surrounding it soon reveal its links with desire and power... speech is no mere verbalization of conflicts and systems of domination, but that it is the very object of man's conflicts.[31]

The discursive situation, despite Ricoeur's simplification of it, far from being a type of idyllic conversation between equals, is

[30]Michel Foucault, "The Discourse on Language," in *The Archeology of Knowledge,* trans. A. M. Sheridan Smith (New York: Pantheon, 1972), p. 216.
[31]Ibid.

more usually of a kind typefied by the relation between colonizer
and colonized, the oppressor and the oppressed. It is too little
recalled that the great modernists (Proust and Joyce are instances) had an acute understanding of this fact; their representations of the discursive situation always show it in this
power-political light. A formative moment in Stephen Dedalus's
rebellious consciousness occurs as he converses with the English
dean of studies:

> What is that beauty which the artist struggles to express from
> lumps of earth, said Stephen coldly.
>   The little word seemed to have turned a rapier point of his
> sensitiveness against this courteous and vigilant foe. He felt with a
> smart of dejection that the man to whom he was speaking was a
> countryman of Ben Jonson. He thought:—The language in which
> we are speaking is his before it is mine. How different are the
> words *home, Christ, ale, master,* on his lips and on mine! I cannot
> speak or write these words without unrest of spirit. His language,
> so familiar and so foreign, will always be for me an acquired
> speech. I have not made or accepted its words. My voice holds
> them at bay. My soul frets in the shadow of his language.[32]

Joyce's oeuvre is a recapitulation of those political and racial
separations, exclusions, prohibitions instituted ethnocentrically
by the ascendant European culture throughout the nineteenth
century. The situation of discourse, Stephen Dedalus knows,
hardly puts equals across from each other. Rather, discourse
places one interlocutor above another or, as Fanon brilliantly
described it in *The Wretched of the Earth,* discourse reenacts the
geography of the colonial city, "this world cut in two is inhabited
by two different species . . . where the agents of government
speak the language of pure force":

> The zone where the natives live is not complementary to the zone
> inhabited by the settlers. The two zones are opposed, but not in the
> service of a higher unity. Obedient to the rules of pure Aristotelian
> logic, they both follow the principle of reciprocal exclusivity. No
> conciliation is possible, for of the two terms, one is superfluous.
> The settlers' town is a strongly-built town, all made of stone and
> steel. It is a brightly-lit town; the streets are covered with asphalt,

[32] Joyce, *A Portrait of the Artist as a Young Man* (New York: Viking, 1964), p. 189.

and the garbage-cans swallow all the leavings, unseen, unknown and hardly thought about. The settler's feet are never visible, except perhaps in the sea; but there you're never close enough to see them. His feet are protected by strong shoes although the streets of his town are clean and even, with no holes or stones. The settler's town is a well-fed town, an easygoing town; its belly is always full of good things. The settler's town is a town of white people, of foreigners.

The town belonging to the colonized people, or at least the native town, the negro village, the medina, the reservation, is a place of ill fame, peopled by men of evil repute. They are born there, it matters little where or how; they die there, it matters not where, nor how. It is a world without spaciousness; men live there on top of each other, and their huts are built on top of the other. The native town is a hungry town, starved of bread, of meat, of shoes, of coal, of light. The native town is a crouching village, a town on its knees, a town wallowing in the mire. It is a town of niggers and dirty arabs. The look that the native turns on the settler's town is a look of lust, a look of envy; it expresses his dreams of possession—all manner of possession: to sit at the settler's table, to sleep in the settler's bed, with his wife if possible. The colonised man is an envious man. And this the settler knows very well; when their glances meet he ascertains bitterly, always on the defensive, "They want to take our place." It is true, for there is no native who does not dream at least once a day of setting himself up in the settler's place.[33]

No wonder that the Fanonist solution to such discourse is violence.

My choice of examples, extreme though most of them may have been, has done for me the job of rejecting simple oppositions between texts and the world, or between texts and speech. Too many exceptions, too many historical, ideological, and formal circumstances implicate the text in actuality, even if a text may also be considered a silent printed object with its own unheard melodies which play "not to the sensual ear, but, more endeared, / Pipe to the spirit ditties of no tone." The play of forces by which a text is engendered and maintained as a fact not of mute ideality but of *production* completely dispels the symmetry of even heuristic oppositions. Moreover the textual utopia

[33]*The Wretched of the Earth,* trans. Constance Farrington (New York: Grove, 1966), pp. 31-32.

that T. S. Eliot and Northrop Frye envisioned each in his own way, whose nightmarish converse is Borges's library, is at complete odds with the *eccentric*, dialectical intermingling of history with form in texts. My thesis is that any centrist, exclusivist conception of the text, or for that matter of the discursive situation as defined wrongly by Paul Ricoeur, ignores the ethnocentrism and the erratic will to power from which texts can spring.

But where in all this is the critic and *his* text?

Scholarship, commentary, exegesis, *explication de texte,* history of ideas, rhetorical or semiological analyses: all these are modes of pertinence, of attention, to the textual matter usually presented to the critic as already at hand. I shall concentrate now on the essay, the traditional form in which criticism has expressed itself. The central problematic of the essay as a form is its *place,* by which I mean a series of three different but connected ways the essay has of being the form the critic takes, and locates himself in, to do his work. Place therefore involves relations the critic fashions with the texts he addresses and the audience he addresses; it also involves the dynamic *taking place* of his own text as it produces itself.

The first mode of place is the essay's relation to the text it attempts to approach. How does it come to the text of its choice? How does it enter that text? What is the concluding definition of its relation to the text it has dealt with? The second mode of place is the essay's intention (and the intention, presumed or perhaps created by the essay, that its audience has) in attempting an approach. Is the critical essay an attempt *to identify* or *to identify with* the text of its choice? Does it stand between the text and the reader, or to one side of one of them? How great, or how little, is the ironic disparity between its essential formal incompleteness, because it is *an essay,* and the formal completion of the text it treats? The third mode of place concerns the essay as a zone in which certain kinds of occurrences, events, happen as an aspect of the essay's production. What is the essay's consciousness of its marginality to the text it discusses? What is the method by which the essay permits history a role during the making of its own history, that is, as the essay moves from beginning to development to conclusion? What is the quality of the essay's speech, toward, away from, into the *actuality,* the arena of nontextual historical vitality and presence that is taking place simultaneously with the essay itself? Finally is the essay a text, an intervention between texts, an intensification of the notion of textuality, or a dispersion of language away from a contingent page to occasions, tendencies, currents, or movements in and for history?

Put as jaggedly and as abstractly as this, these questions are not immediately answerable. It is entirely possible that my scattering, grapeshot manner of formulating them prevents, rather than encourages, answers from appearing; also one is tempted perhaps to be impatient and say that these questions are fairly abstruse solipsisms that take the critic away from his real business, which is writing criticism *tout court.* Perhaps I would argue, however, that a juster response to these questions is a realization of how unfamiliar and how rare such questions are in the general discussion of contemporary criticism. It is not that the problems of criticism are undiscussed, but rather that criticism is considered essentially as defined once and for all by its secondariness, by its temporal misfortune of having come *after* the text (or texts) it is supposed to be treating. Just as it is all too often true that texts are thought of as monolithic objects of the past, to which criticism is a despondent appendage in the present, then the very conception of criticism symbolizes being outdated, being dated *from* the past rather than *by* the present. Everything I tried earlier to say about a text—its dialectic of engagement in time and the senses, the paradoxes in a text by which discourse is shown to be immutable and yet contingent, as fraught and politically intransigeant as the struggle between dominant and dominated—all this was an implicit rejection of the secondary after-role usually assigned to criticism. For if we assume instead that texts make up what Foucault calls archival facts, the archive being defined as the text's social discursive presence in the world, then criticism, too, is another aspect of that present. In other words, one should prefer to say that rather than being defined by the silent past, commanded by it to speak in the present, criticism, no less than any other text, is the present in the course of its articulation, struggles for definition, attempts at overcoming.

We must not forget that the critic does not, cannot speak without the mediation of writing, the ambivalent *pharmakon* so suggestively portrayed by Derrida as the constituted milieu where the oppositions are opposed: this is where the movement and the play occur that bring the oppositions into direct contact with each other, that overturn oppositions and transform one pole into another, soul and body, good and evil, inside and outside, memory and oblivion, speech and writing.[34] In particular the critic is committed to the essay, whose metaphysics were sketched by Lukács in the first chapter of his *Die Seele und die Formen*. There Lukács said that as a form the essay allows, and indeed is, the coincidence of inchoate soul with exigent material form.[35] Essays are concerned with the relations between things, with values and concepts, in fine, with significance.[36] Whereas poetry deals in images, the essay is the abandonment of images; this abandonment the essay ideally shares with Platonism and mysticism.[37] If, Lukács continues, the various forms of literature are compared with sunlight refracted in a prism, then the essay is ultraviolet light.[38] What the essay expresses is a yearning for conceptuality and intellectuality, as well as for great ultimate questions such as what is life or man and destiny.[39] (Throughout his analysis Lukás refers to the Platonic Socrates as the typical essayistic figure, always talking of immediate mundane matters while at the same time through his life there sounds the purest, the most profound, and the most concealed yearning—*Die tiefste, die verborgenste Sehnsucht ertönt aus diesem Leben*.)[40]

Thus the essay's mode is ironic, which means, first, that the form is patently insufficient in its intellectuality with regard to living experience and, second, that the very form of the essay, its being an essay, is an ironic destiny with regard to the great questions of life.[41] Socrates' death perfectly symbolizes, in its arbitrariness and irrelevance to those questions he debates, the

[34]Derrida, "La Pharmacie de Platon," in *La Dissémination* (Paris: Seuil, 1972), pp. 145 and *passim*.
[35]*Die Seele und die Formen* (1911; reprinted Berlin: Luchterhand, 1971), p. 17.
[36]Ibid., p. 12.
[37]Ibid., p. 13.
[38]Ibid., p. 15.
[39]Ibid., p. 15.
[40]Ibid., p. 25.
[41]Ibid., p. 16.

essayistic destiny, or rather the absence of real (that is, tragic) destiny in the essay; there is no internal conclusion for an essay, for only something outside it can interrupt or end it, as Socrates' death is decreed offstage and ends his life of questioning. Form fills the function in an essay that images do in poetry: form is the reality of the essay, and form gives the essayist a voice with which to ask questions of life, even if that form must always make use of art—a book, a painting, a piece of music—as the initial subject matter of its investigations.[42]

Lukács, in his analysis of the essay, a small part of which I have summarized only to indicate the kind of thought available to the critic about his extremely complex relations with the world and with his medium, holds in common with Wilde the view that criticism in general, and the essay in particular, is rarely what it seems, not least in its form. Criticism adopts the mode of commentary on and evaluation of art; yet in reality criticism matters more as a necessarily incomplete and preparatory *process toward* judgement and evaluation. What the critical essay does is *to begin* to create the values by which art is judged. I said earlier that a major inhibition on the critic is that his function as critic is often dated and circumscribed for him by the past, that is, by an already created work of art. Lukács acknowledges the inhibition, but he shows how in fact the critic appropriates for himself the function of starting to make values, and therefore the work he is judging. Wilde said it more flamboyantly: criticism "treats the work of art as a starting point for a new creation."[43] Lukács put it more cautiously: "the essayist is a pure instance of the precursor" (*[Der Essayist] ist der reine Typus des Vorläufers*).[44]

I prefer the latter description, for as Lukács develops it the critic's position is vulnerable because he awaits and prepares for a great aesthetic revolution whose result, ironically enough, will render him marginal. Of course this idea, this consciousness of the possibility of the future, as well as the need in consciousness for a constant conversion of thought from static to dynamic, itself prefigures Lukács's later ideas about the role of the proletariat dynamic class consciousness which will bring about the

[42]Ibid., p. 17.
[43]*The Artist as Critic*, p. 367.
[44]*Die Seele und die Formen*, p. 29.

overthrow of bourgeois reification.[45] What I wish to emphasize here in conclusion is not so much the critic's role in writing as dialectically creating the values by which art might be judged and understood, but the critic's role in creating the processes of the *present*, as process and inauguration, the actual conditions by means of which art and writing bear significance. By this I mean not only what R. P. Blackmur, following Hopkins, called the bringing of literature to performance, but more explicitly, the articulation of those voices dominated, displaced, or silenced by the textuality of texts. Texts are a system of forces institutionalized at some expense by the reigning culture, not an ideal cosmos of ideally equal poems. Looking at the Grecian urn, Keats *sees* graceful figures adorning its exterior, and also he actualizes in language (and perhaps nowhere else) the little town "emptied of this folk, this pious morn." The critic's attitude to some extent is restorative in a similar way; it should in addition and more often be frankly inventive, in the traditional rhetorical sense of *inventio* employed so fruitfully by Vico, finding and exposing things that otherwise lie hidden beneath piety, heedlessness, or routine. Most of all, I think, criticism is worldly and in the world so long as it opposes *monocentrism* in the narrowest as well as the widest sense of that too infrequently considered notion: for monocentrism is a concept I take in conjunction with ethnocentrism, the assumption that culture masks itself as the sovereignty of *this* one and *this* human, whereas culture is the process of dominion and struggle always dissembling, always deceiving. Monocentrism is practiced when we mistake one idea as the only idea, instead of recognizing that an idea in history is always one among many. Monocentrism denies plurality, it totalizes structure, it sees profit where there is waste, it decrees the concentricity of Western culture instead of its eccentricity, it believes continuity to be given and will not try to understand, instead, how continuity as much as discontinuity is made.

My inclinations now are to say that worldliness—as expressed in such denials and affirmations as the ones I have examined—is enough for criticism: for if this worldliness prepares for a still more liberating one to come after it, then so much the better.

[45]See Lukács, *History and Class Consciousness: Studies in Marxist Dialectics*, trans. Rodney Livingstone (London: Merlin Press, 1971) pp. 178-209.

René Girard

Myth and Ritual in Shakespeare:
A Midsummer Night's Dream

I have considered, our whole life is like a *Play:* wherein every man, forgetfull of himselfe, is in travaile with expression of another. Nay, wee so insist in imitating others, as wee cannot (when it is necessary) returne to ourselves: like Children, that imitate the vices of *Stammerers* so long, till at last they become such; and make the habit to another nature, as it is never forgotten.

—Ben Jonson, *Timber of Discoveries*

The opening scene of *A Midsummer Night's Dream* leads the audience to expect an ordinary comedy plot. Boy and girl love each other. A mean old father is trying to separate them, with the help of the highest authority in the land, Theseus, duke of Athens. Unless she gives up Lysander, Hermia will have no choice but death or the traditional convent. As soon as this formidable edict is proclaimed, the father figures depart, leaving the lovers to their own devices. They launch into a duet on the impediments of love: age difference, social conditions, and, last but not least, coercion by those in authority.

The two victimized youngsters leisurely and chattingly prepare to flee their ferocious tyrants; they plunge into the woods; Hermia is pursued by Demetrius, himself pursued by Helena, Hermia's best friend, whom, of course, he spurns. The first couple's happiness appears threatened from the outside, but the second couple, even from the start, insist on being unhappy by themselves, always falling in love with the wrong person. We soon realize that Shakespeare is more interested in this systematically self-defeating type of passion than in the initial theme of "true love," something unconquerable by definition and always in need of villainous enemies if it is to provide any semblance of dramatic plot.

It quickly turns out that self-defeating passion dominates the relationship of not just one but both couples, involving them in a fourway merry-go-round that never seems to allow any amorous reciprocity even though partners are continually exchanged. At first the two young men are in love with Hermia; then, during the night, both abandon that girl and fall in love with the other. The only constant element in the configuration is the convergence of more than one desire on a single object, as if perpetual rivalries were more important to the four characters than their changing pretexts.

Although the theme of outside interference is not forgotten, it becomes even more flimsy. In the absence of the father figures, the role is entrusted to Puck, who keeps pouring his magical love juice into the "wrong" eyes. When Oberon rebukes Puck for his mistake, he does so with a show of emotion, in a precipitous monologue that ironically reflects the confusion it pretends to clear, thereby casting doubt upon the reality of the distinctions it pretends to restore:

> What hast thou done? Thou hast mistaken quite,
> And laid the love juice on some true love's sight:
> Of thy misprision must perforce ensue
> Some true love turned, and not a false turned true.
>
> [III.ii.88–91]

Who will tell the difference between *some true love turned* and *a false turned true*? We may suspect a more serious rationale for the four protagonists' miseries, for the growing hysteria of the midsummer night. A close look reveals something quite systematic about the behavior of the four, underlined by more than a few ironic suggestions. The author is hinting at something which is never made fully explicit, but which seems cogent and coherent enough to call for a precise formulation.

The midsummer night is a process of increasing violence. Demetrius and Lysander end up in a duel; the violence of the girls' rivalry almost matches that of the boys. Their fierce quarreling certainly contradicts—or does it?—Helena's earlier expression of unbounded admiration for her friend Hermia:

> Your eyes are lodestars, and your tongue's sweet air,
> More tunable than lark to shepherd's ear,

When wheat is green, when hawthorn buds appear.
Sickness is catching. O! were favor so,
Yours would I catch, fair Hermia, ere I go;
My ear should catch your voice, my eye your eye,
My tongue should catch your tongue's sweet melody.
Were the world mine, Demetrius being bated,
The rest I'd give to be to you translated.

[I.i.183–191]

This is a strange mixture of quasi-religious and yet sensuous worship. The last line admirably sums up the significance of the passage. Desire speaks here, and it is desire for another's *being*. Helena would like to be *translated*, metamorphosed into Hermia, because Hermia enjoys the love of Demetrius. Demetrius, however, is hardly mentioned. The desire for him appears less pressing than the desire for Hermia's being. In that desire, what truly stands out is the irresistible sexual dominance that Hermia is supposed to exert upon Demetrius and all those who approach her. It is this sexual dominance that Helena envies: "O teach me how you look and with what art / You sway the motion of Demetrius' heart" (I.i.192–193). Helena sees Hermia as the magnetic pole of desires in their common little world, and she would like to be that. The other three characters are no different; they all worship the same erotic absolute, the same ideal image of seduction which each girl and boy in turn appears to embody in the eyes of the others. This absolute has nothing to do with concrete qualities; it is properly metaphysical. Even though obsessed with the flesh, desire is divorced from it; it is not instinctive and spontaneous; it never seems to know directly and immediately where its object lies; in order to locate that object, it cannot rely on such things as the pleasure of the eyes and the other senses. In its perpetual *noche oscura*, metaphysical desire must therefore trust in another and supposedly more enlightened desire on which it patterns itself. As a consequence, desire, in *A Midsummer Night's Dream*, perpetually runs to desire just as money runs to money in the capitalistic system. We may say, of course, that the four characters are in love with love. That would not be inaccurate; but there is no such thing as love or desire in general, and such a formulation obscures the most crucial point, the necessarily jealous and conflictual nature of mimetic convergence on a single object. If we keep borrowing each other's desires, if we allow our respective desires to agree on the same object, we, as individuals, are bound to disagree. The erotic absolute will inevitably be embodied in a successful rival. Helena cannot fail to be torn between worship and hatred of Hermia. Imitative desire makes all reciprocal rapports impossible. Shakespeare makes this point very clear, but for some reason no one wants to hear. The audience resembles the lovers themselves, who talk ceaselessly about "true love" but obviously do not care to understand the mechanism of their own feelings.

Metaphysical desire is mimetic, and mimetic desire cannot be let loose without breeding a midsummer night of jealousy and strife. Yet the protagonists never feel responsible for the state of their affairs; they never hesitate to place the blame where it does not belong, on an unfavorable fate, on reactionary parents, on mischievous fairies, and on other such causes. Throughout the play, the theme of outside interference provides much of the obvious dramatic structure; and we must suspect that it is not simply juxtaposed to the midsummer night which, in a sense, it contradicts: the two may well be in a more complex relationship of disguise and reality, never clearly spelled out and formalized, allowing enough juxtaposition and imbrication so that the play, at least in some important respects, can really function as two plays at once. On one level it is a traditional comedy, destined for courtly audiences and their modern successors; but, underneath, mimetic desire holds sway, responsible not only for the delirium and frenzy of the midsummer night but also for all the mythical themes which reign supreme at the upper level.

The real obstacles are not outside the enchanted circle of the lovers: each of them is an obstacle to the others in a game of imitation and rivalry that is their mode of alienation, and this alienation finally verges on trancelike possession. The outside obstacle is an illusion, often a transparent one, a telltale disguise of the real situation, constructed so that it can serve as an allegory. It even happens that absolutely nothing has to be changed in order to pass from the truth to the lie and back again to the truth: the same words mean both the one and the other. Shakespeare loves to play on these ambiguities. I have already mentioned the love duet between Lysander and Hermia: most critics would agree that it constitutes a parody of fashionable clichés, and they are no doubt correct; but we cannot view this parodic character as sufficient justification in itself. The real purpose cannot be parody for parody's sake. There must be something more, something which Shakespeare definitely wants to say and which we are likely to miss because it will appear in the form of "rhetoric." In the duet part of that love scene, the first seven lines seem to mark a gradation which leads up to the eighth, on which the emphasis falls:

LYSANDER: The course of true love never did run smooth;
            But either it was different in blood—
HERMIA: O cross! Too high to be enthralled to low.
LYSANDER: Or else misgraffed in respect of years—
HERMIA: O spite! Too old to be engaged to young.
LYSANDER: Or else it stood upon the choice of friends—
HERMIA: O hell! To choose love by another's eyes.
                                             [I.i.134–140]

The last two lines can be read as only one more "cross," the most relevant really, the one we would expect to see mentioned first in the present context. The reference to "friends" is somewhat unexpected, but not so strange as to merit a second thought for most listeners. But if we isolate these last two lines, if we replace the love mystique in the spirit of which they are uttered with the present context, the context of the preceding remarks and of countless Shakespearean scenes (not only in *A Midsummer Night's Dream* but also in almost every other play), another meaning will appear, a meaning more evident and infinitely more significant.

Everywhere in Shakespeare there is a passion which is primarily the copy of a model, a passion that is destructive not only because of its sterile rivalries but because it dissolves reality: it tends to the abstract, the merely representational. The model may be present in the flesh and strut on the stage of the theater; and it may also rise from the pages of a book, come out of the frame of a picture, turn into the worship of a phantom, verbal or iconic. The model is always a text. It is Othello's heroic language, the real object of fascination for Desdemona rather than Othello himself. It is the portrait of Portia which her lover chooses to contemplate in preference to the original. This metaphysical passion is a corruption of life, always open to the corruptive suggestions of mediators and go-betweens, such as the Pandarus of *Troilus and Cressida*. The paramount role that Shakespeare attributes to such desire, in an obviously calculated way, even in relationships where we may least expect it, is matched only in the works of such writers as Cervantes, Molière, or Dostoevsky. *O hell! To choose love by another's eyes.* Since the phrase is uttered in conformity with the ideology of "true love," surely appropriate to a royal wedding (the occasion of *A Midsummer Night's Dream*), the true Shakespearean meaning must dawn upon us, prompted not only by the events that follow but by a thousand echoes from all the other plays.

Mimetic desire remains unperceived even when it is most obvious. In the very process of being denied, displaced, reified, it still manages to proclaim its own truth. Almost every time they open their mouths, the lovers unwittingly proclaim what at the same time they ignore, and we generally go on ignoring it along with them. The midsummer night is a hell of the lovers' own choosing, a hell into which they all avidly plunge, insofar as they all choose to choose love by another's eyes. Hermia, talking about the turn her love affair with Lysander has given her own life, naively recognizes that the hell is all hers, and that it was already there before the appearance of the parental and supernatural bugaboos that are supposed to be its cause:

> Before the time I did Lysander see,
> Seemed Athens as a paradise to me.
> O then, what graces in my love do dwell,
> That he hath turned a heaven into a hell!
>
> [I.i.204–207]

Shakespeare is making fun of us, of course. He seems intent on proving that you can say almost anything in a play as long as you provide the audience with the habitual props of comedy, the conventional expressions of "true love," even in minimal amounts, adding, of course, a ferocious father figure or two to satisfy the eternal Freudian in us. As long as the standard plot is vaguely outlined, even in the crudest and least believable fashion, the author can subvert his own myths and state the truth at every turn, with no consequences whatsoever. The audience will instinctively and automatically rally around the old clichés, so completely blind and deaf to everything which may contradict them that the presence of this truth will not even be noticed. The continued misunderstanding of the play throughout the centuries gives added resonance to the point Shakespeare is secretly making, providing ironic confirmation that the most worn-out myth will always triumph over the most explicit demythification.

If the subject persists in his self-defeating path, the rivalries into which mimetic desire inevitably runs must logically be viewed as glorious signs and heralds of the absolute that keeps eluding him. Mimetic desire breeds rejection and failure; it is rejection and failure that it must ultimately seek. The impossible is always preferred to the possible, the unreal to the real, the hostile and unwilling to the willing and available. This self-destructive character flows directly and automatically from the mechanical consequences of the first definition: *to choose love by another's eyes.* Are these consequences really spelled out in the play? They are in the most specific fashion, in perfectly unambiguous statements that somehow never manage to be heard; and even when they are noticed, a label is immediately placed on them, canceling out their effectiveness. The following lines, for example, will be labeled "rhetorical," which means that they can be dismissed at will, treated as insignificant. Recall that when Helena seeks the secret of Hermia's power over Demetrius, Hermia answers:

>   I frown upon him, yet he loves me still.
> HELENA: O that your frowns would teach my smiles such skill!
> HERMIA: I give him curses, yet he gives me love.
> HELENA: O that my prayers could such affection move!
> HERMIA: The more I hate, the more he follows me.
> HELENA: The more I love, the more he hateth me.
>   [I.i.194–199]

It cannot be denied that there is a great deal of rhetoric in *A Midsummer Night's Dream.* Rhetoric in the pejorative sense means that certain figures of speech are repeated unthinkingly by people who do not even notice their meaning. The four protagonists of *A Midsummer Night's Dream* certainly are unthinking repeaters of modish formulas. But mere parodies of rhetorical vacuity would be themselves vacuous, and Shakespeare does not indulge in them. With him the most exhausted clichés can become bolts of lightning. When Helena calls Demetrius a "hard-hearted adamant," she speaks the most literal truth. Harshness and cruelty draw her and her friends as a magnet draws iron. The supposedly artificial figures of speech really describe the truth of desire with amazing exactitude. When an impeccably educated reader comes upon the lines, "Where is Lysander and fair Hermia? / The one I'll slay, the other slayeth me" (II.i.189–190), he feels a secret anxiety at the thought that a cultural monument like Shakespeare may be lapsing into less than impeccable taste. These lines are satirical; but, in order to be completely reassured, we have to know what the satirical intent is about. Shakespeare is not mocking a particular "rhetoric" and a particular "bad taste." Considerations of "style" are mainly relevant to professors of literature. It is rather the whole language of passion, with its constant borrowings from the fields of war, murder, and destruction, that Shakespeare is commenting upon. A book like De Rougemont's *Love in the Western World* throws more light on the type of meditation that nourishes Shakespearean satire than all stylistics put together. Shakespeare is almost contemporary in his recourse to the debased language of degraded human relations. With us, however, debased language generally remains just what it is and nothing more; the work never rises above the mire it pretends to stigmatize, or else it immediately sinks gently back into it. Not so with Shakespeare. The interest of the so-called rhetoric is its frightening pertinence; the destiny it spells for the four lovers, the destiny they unthinkingly announce, is really the one that they are busily forging for themselves; it is a tragic destiny from which they escape only by the sheer luck of being in a comedy.

This ambiguous nature of "rhetoric" is essential to the twofold nature of the play. As long as we listen as unthinkingly as the protagonists speak, we remain in the superficial play which is made up of "figures of speech," as well as of fairies and father figures. At the purely aesthetic and thematic level of "poetic imagination," we operate with the same conceptual tools as Theseus and the lovers; good and bad metaphors, true love turned false and false turned true. We understand little more than the lovers themselves. If, on the contrary, we stop long enough to hear what is being said, a pattern begins to emerge: the disquieting infrastructure of mimetic desire, which will erupt into hysterical violence a little later.

One of the most striking features in the amorous discourse of the protagonists is the abundance of animal images. These images express the self-abasement of the lover in front of his idol. As he vainly tries to reach for the absolute that appears incarnated in the model, the lover exalts his successful rival to greater and greater heights; as a result, he feels degraded to lower and lower depths. The first animal images appear immediately after Helena's hysterical celebration of her rival's beauty:

> No, no, I am as ugly as a bear.
> For beasts that meet me run away for fear ....
> What wicked and dissembling glass of mine
> Made me compare with Hermia's sphery eyne?
>
> [II.ii.94–99]

We will be told once again that such images are "pure rhetoric"; their source has been identified: most of them, it appears, come from Ovid. This is true, but the existence of a literary source for a figure of speech does not necessarily imply that it is used in a purely formal and inconsequential manner, that it cannot be given a vital significance by the second writer. It can be shown, I believe, that the animal images are part of the process which leads from mimetic desire to myth; this process is a continuous one, but a certain number of steps can be distinguished which have an existential as well as a functional significance. Far from raising himself to the state of a superman, a god, as he seeks to do, the subject of mimetic desire sinks to the level of animality. The animal images are the price the self has to pay for its idolatrous worship of otherness. This idolatry is really "selfish" in the sense that it is meant for the sake of the self; the self wants to appropriate the absolute that it perceives, but its extreme thirst for self-elevation results in extreme self-contempt, quite logically if paradoxically, since this self always meets and invites its own defeat at the hands of a successful rival.

Animal images are thus a direct consequence of the inordinate metaphysical ambition that makes desire mimetic. They are an integral part of the rigorous pattern I am trying to unravel; the law of that pattern could be defined by Pascal's aphorism, *Qui fait l'ange fait la bête.* The whole midsummer night looks like a dramatization of that aphorism. Here again is Helena, who *fait la bête* with Demetrius:

> I am your spaniel, and, Demetrius,
> The more you beat me, I will fawn on you.
> Use me but as your spaniel, spurn me, strike me,
> Neglect me, lose me—only give me leave,
> Unworthy as I am, to follow you.
> What worser place can I beg in your love—
> And yet a place of high respect with me—
> Than to be used as you use your dog?
>
> [II.i.203–210]

Partners in mimetic desire cannot think of each other as equal human beings; their relationship becomes less and less human; they are condemned to an angel-beast or superman-slave relationship. Helena's near worship of Hermia might be described, today, in terms of an "inferiority complex." But psychiatrists view their so-called complexes almost as physical entities, almost as independent and stable as the self they are supposed to affect. Shakespeare is alien to this substantial thinking; he sees everything in terms of relations. Helena's "inferiority complex," for example, is only the "wrong" or the "beast" end of her relationship with Hermia and Demetrius. Ultimately, everyone ends up with the same "inferiority complex," since everyone feels deprived of an absolute superiority that always appears to belong to someone else.

Being purely mimetic, this relationship is anchored in no stable reality; it is therefore bound to be unstable. The metaphysical absolute seems to shift from character to character. With each shift the entire configuration is reorganized, still on the basis of the same polarities, but reversed. The beast becomes a god and the god becomes a beast. Inferiority becomes superiority and vice versa. Up is down and down is up.

During the first scenes, Hermia, being worshiped by everyone, appears to be and feel divine. Helena, being truly rejected and despised, feels despicable. But then it is Helena's turn to be worshiped and Hermia feels like a despicable beast. After the initial moment of relative stability, the four lovers enter a world of more and more rapid reversals and inversions. The necessities of dramatic presentation force Shakespeare to be selective and somewhat schematic in his description of the process, but the principles at work are obvious. As soon as the midsummer night crisis begins in earnest, the animal metaphors are not only multiplied but turned upside down and jumbled together. As the reversals become more and more precipitous, we obviously move toward complete chaos. All this, of course, to the renewed chagrin of our guardians of "good taste," who do not see any purpose to this unseemly spectacle and view it as mere stylistic self-indulgence on the part of the author. The "rhetoric" was bad enough before, but now it is going out of its rhetorical mind. Here is Helena, once more, getting ready to chase Demetrius through the woods:

> Run when you will, the story shall be changed.
> Apollo flies, and Daphne holds the chase;
> The dove pursues the griffin; the mild hind
> Makes speed to catch the tiger.
>
> [II.i.230–233]

Reversal is so pervasive a theme in *A Midsummer Night's Dream*, as in most of Shakespeare's plays, that it finally extends to the whole of nature. Titania tells us, for example, that the seasons are out of turn. Scholars assume that the weather must have been particularly bad in the year Shakespeare wrote the play; this, in turn, gives some clues to the dating of the play. It must be true, indeed, that Shakespeare needed some really inclement weather to write what he did; however, the bad weather serves a specifically Shakespearean purpose, providing still another opportunity for more variations on the major theme of the play, the theme of differences reversed and inverted:

> ... The spring, the summer,
> The childing autumn, angry winter, change
> Their wonted liveries, and the mazed world,
> By their increase now knows not which is which.
>
> [II.i.111 –114]

The very pervasiveness of reversal makes it impossible for commentators not to acknowledge the theme, but it also provides a means of minimizing its significance by shifting the emphasis where it should not be shifted, onto nature and the cosmos. This, of course, is exactly what myth itself does in its constant projection and expulsion of human violence. The nineteenth- and twentieth-century mythologists who asserted and still assert that myth is mostly a misreading of natural phenomena really perpetuate the mythical dissimulation and disguise of human violence. Shakespeare seems to be doing the same thing when he inserts his midsummer night into the poetic frame of a crisis of quasi-comic proportions. In that vast macrocosm, our four protagonists' antics appear as a tiny dot moved by forces beyond its own control, automatically relieved, once more, of all responsibility for whatever harm its even tinier components may be doing to one another and to themselves. Nature, in other words, must be included among the other mythical excuses, such as the mean father and the fairies. Shakespeare certainly gives it a major poetic and dramatic role, in keeping with the principles of what I earlier called the surface play. This is true; but, as in the other instances, he also makes sure that the truth becomes explicit. The real Shakespearean perspective is clearly suggested immediately below the lines just quoted. Titania ascribes disarray neither to herself nor to Oberon nor even to both, insofar as they would remain serene divinities manipulating humanity from outside, but to the *conflict* between them, a very human conflict, to be sure, which implies the same reversals of roles as the midsummer night and which duplicates perfectly the strife among the four lovers:

> And this same progeny of evils comes
> From our debate, from our dissensions;
> We are their parents and original.
>
> [II.i.115–117]

Reversals in nature are only reflections, metaphoric expressions, and poetic orchestrations of the mimetic crisis. Instead of viewing myth as a humanization of nature, as we always tend to do, Shakespeare views it as the naturalization as well as the supernaturalization of a very human violence. Specialists on the subject might be well advised to take a close look at this Shakespearean view; what if it turned out to be less mythical than their own!

The lopsided view that the lovers take of their own relationships keeps reversing itself with increasing speed. This constant exchange of the relative positions within the total picture is the cause of the vertigo, the loss of balance which the four characters experience. That feeling is inseparable from the sense of extreme difference to which the same characters never cease to cling, even as this difference keeps shifting around at a constantly accelerating tempo. It is a fact, to be sure, that two characters who face each other in fascination and rivalry can never occupy the same position together, since they themselves constitute the polarity that oscillates between them. They resemble a seesaw, with one rider always going up when the other is going down and vice versa. Never, therefore, do they cease to feel out of tune with each other, radically different from each other. In reality, of course, the positions successively occupied are the same; whatever difference remains is a purely *temporal* one which must become smaller and, as the movement keeps accelerating, even tend to zero, though without actually reaching it.

Even though they persevere in difference (an ever more vertiginous difference to be sure, but difference nevertheless), the protagonists become more and more undifferentiated. We have seen that the seasons lose their relative specificity, but the true loss of differentiation comes from the crisis among men who are caught in the vicious circle of mimetic desire. Progressive undifferentiation is not an illusion but the objective truth of the whole process, in the sense that reciprocity becomes more and more perfect. There is never anything on one side of a rivalry which, sooner or later, will not be found on the other. Here and there it is exactly the same mixture of fascination and hatred, the same curses, the same everything. It can be said that mimetic desire *really works:* it really achieves the goal it has set for itself, which is the *translation* of the follower into his model, the metamorphosis of one into the other, the absolute identity of all. As the climax of the midsummer night approaches, the four protagonists lose whatever individuality they formerly appeared to have; they wander like brutes in the forest, trading the same insults and finally the same physical blows, all drugged with the same drug, all bitten by the same serpent.

The more our characters tend to see one another in terms of black and white, the more alike they really *make* one another. Every slightest move, every single reaction becomes more and more immediately self-defeating. The more these characters deny the reciprocity among them, the more they bring it about, each denial being immediately reciprocated.

At the moment when difference should be most formidable, it begins to elude not one protagonist but the four of them all at once. Characters dissolve and personalities disintegrate. Glaring contradictions multiply, no firm judgment will hold. Each protagonist becomes a masked monster in the eyes of the other three, hiding his true being behind deceptive and shifting appearances. Each points at the hypocrite and the cheat in the others, partly in order not to feel that the ground is also slipping from under him. Helena, for example, accuses Hermia of being untrue to her real self: "Fie, fie! You counterfeit, you puppet, you!" (III.ii.288). Hermia misunderstands and thinks Helena is making fun of her shortness:

> Puppet? Why so? Aye, that way goes the game.
> Now I perceive that she hath made compare
> Between our statures, she hath urged her height.
> And with her personage, her tall personage,
> Her height, forsooth, she hath prevailed with him.
> And are you grown so high in his esteem
> Because I am so dwarfish and so low?
> How low am I, thou painted maypole?
> How low am I? I am not yet so low
> But that my nails can reach unto thine eyes.
>
> [III.ii.289–298]

C. L. Barber correctly observes that the four young people vainly try to interpret their conflicts through something "manageably related to their individual identities," but they never achieve their purpose:

> Only accidental differences can be exhibited. Helena tall, Hermia short. Although the men think that "reason says" now Helena is

"the worthier maid," personalities have nothing to do with the case. . . . The life in the lovers' part is not to be caught in individual speeches, but by regarding the whole movement of the farce, which swings and spins each in turn through a common pattern, an evolution that seems to have an impersonal power of its own.[1]

The time comes when the antagonists literally no longer know who they are: "Am I not Hermia? Are you not Lysander?" (III.ii.273).

Here it is no exaggeration or undue modernization to speak of a "crisis of identity." To Shakespeare, however, the crisis is primarily one of differentiation. The four characters lose a self-identity which they and the philosophers would like to turn into an absolute and which becomes relative for that very reason; it is made to depend upon the otherness of a model. When Barber points out that Shakespeare fully intends for his characters, in the course of the play, to lose whatever distinctiveness they had or appeared to have at the beginning (which wasn't much anyway), he runs counter to a long tradition of criticism, the whole tradition of "realism" and of "psychology." Many critics do not find it conceivable that a writer like Shakespeare might be more interested in the undoing and dissolving of "characters" than in their creation, viewing as they do the latter task as the one assigned to all artists of all eternity. Only the most honest will face squarely their own malaise and formulate the obvious consequences of their own inadequate principles: they blame Shakespeare for "insufficient characterization."

The question is truly fundamental. The whole orientation of criticism depends on it. It is usually the wrong solution that is adopted, all the more blindly because it remains implicit. I personally believe that the conflictual undifferentiation of the four lovers is the basic Shakespearean relationship in both his tragedies and comedies.[2] It is the relationship of the four *doubles* in *A Comedy of Errors;* it is the relationship of the Montagues and the Capulets, of course, but also of Caesar, Brutus, and his coconspirators, of Shylock and Bassanio, of all the great tragic

---

[1] *Shakespeare's Festive Comedy* (Cleveland: Meridian, 1963), p. 128.
[2] See my *Violence and the Sacred,* trans. Patrick Gregory (Baltimore: Johns Hopkins University Press, 1977), pp. 43–49.

and comic characters. There is no great theater without a grip-
ping awareness that, far from sharpening our differences, as we
like to believe, our violence obliterates them, dissolving them
into that reciprocity of vengeance which becomes its own self-
inflicted punishment. Shakespeare is fully aware, at the same
time, that no theater audience can assume the full force of this
revelation. Its impact must and will necessarily be blunted. Some
violence will be made "good" and the rest "bad" at the expense
of some sacrificial victim, with or without the complicity of the
writer. There is no doubt that, in many instances, Shakespeare is
a willing accomplice; but his is never an absolute betrayal of his
own vision, because the differences he provides are always at the
same time undermined and treated as quasi-allegories. An ex-
cessive appetite for "characterization" and catharsis will take
nothing of this into account: it will systematically choose as most
Shakespearean what really is least so, at least in the form in
which it is chosen. It will thus provide not only our realistic
stodginess but also our romantic self-righteousness with the only
type of nourishment they can absorb.

It is in a comedy like *A Midsummer Night's Dream,* if we only
agree to read through the transparence of the "airy nothing,"
that the truth will stare us most openly in the face. Far from
lacking substance and profundity, as even George Orwell inexplicably maintained, this play provides a quintessence of the
Shakespearean spirit.

Am I not "going too far" when I assimilate the midsummer
night to the tragic crisis; am I not running the risk of betraying
the real Shakespeare? The language of differences and undifferentiation is not Shakespeare's own, after all. This is true if we
take the matter quite literally; but it is also true that Shakespeare, in some of his writing, comes close to using that same
language. A case in point is the famous speech of Ulysses in
Troilus and Cressida: it describes that very same crisis, but does so
in purely theoretical language and on as vast a scale as the most
ambitious tragedies, as the crisis of an entire culture. The speech
is built around one single word, *degree,* which would certainly be
condemned as too "abstract," too "philosophical," if it were
applied to Shakespeare by anyone but Shakespeare himself. And

obviously Shakespeare applies it to himself as well as to the
Greeks: it is the social framework of tragedy which is at stake.[3]

> ... O when degree is shaked,
> Which is the ladder to all high designs,
> The enterprise is sick! How could communities,
> Degrees in schools, and brotherhoods in cities,
> Peaceful commerce from dividable shores,
> The primogenitive and due of birth,
> Prerogative of age, crowns, sceptres, laurels,
> But by degree, stand in authentic place?
> Take but degree away, untune that string,
> And, hark, what discord follows! Each thing meets
> In mere oppugnancy. The bounded waters
> Should lift their bosoms higher than the shores,
> And make a sop of all this solid globe;
> Strength should be lord of imbecility,
> And the rude son should strike his father dead;
> Force should be right, or rather, right and wrong,
> Between whose endless jar justice resides,
> Should lose their names, and so should justice too.
> Then every thing include itself in power,
> Power into will, will into appetite;
> And appetite, an universal wolf,
> So doubly seconded with will and power,
> Must make perforce an universal prey,
> And last eat up himself.

> [I.iii.101–124]

The word *degree,* from the Latin *gradus* (step, degree, measure of distance), means exactly what is meant here by difference. Culture is conceived not as a mere collection of unrelated objects, but as a totality, or, if we prefer, a structure, a
system of people and institutions always related to one another
in such a way that a single differentiating principle is at work.
This social transcendence does not exist as an object, of course.
That is why, as soon as an individual member, overcome by
hubris, tries to usurp Degree, he finds imitators; more and more
people are affected by the contagion of mimetic rivalry, and
Degree collapses, being nothing more than the mysterious ab-

[3]Ibid., pp. 49–51.

sence of such rivalry in a functional society. The crisis is described as the "shaking," the "vizarding," or the taking away of Degree; all cultural specificities vanish, all identities disintegrate. Conflict is everywhere, and everywhere meaningless: *Each thing meets in mere oppugnancy.* We must note this use of the word "thing," the least determined, perhaps, in the English language. The meaningless conflict is that of the *doubles.* Unable to find a way out, men err and clash stupidly, full of hatred but deprived of real purpose; they resemble objects loose on the deck of a ship tossed about in a storm, destroying one another as they collide endlessly and mindlessly.

In the light of the above remarks, a precise analysis of the midsummer crisis becomes possible. The four protagonists do not see one another as *doubles;* they misunderstand their relationship as one of extreme if unstable differentiation. A point must finally be reached where all of these illusory differences oscillate so rapidly that the contrasting specificities they define are no longer perceived separately; they begin to impinge on one another, they appear to merge. Beyond a certain threshold, in other words, the dizziness mentioned earlier will make normal perception impossible; hallucination must prevail, of a type that can be ascertained with some precision, being not purely capricious and random but predetermined by the nature of the crisis.

When polarities such as the ones described earlier between the "beast" and the "angel" oscillate so fast that they become one, the elements involved remain too incompatible for a harmonious "synthesis," and they will simply be juxtaposed or superimposed on each other. A composite picture should emerge which will include fragments of the former "opposites" in a disorderly mosaic. Instead of a god and a beast facing each other as two independent and irreducible entities, we are going to have a mixture and a confusion of the two, a god that is a beast or a beast that is a god. When the polarities revolve fast enough, all antithetic images must be viewed simultaneously, through a kind of cinematic effect that will produce the illusion of a more or less single being in the form or rather the formlessness of "some monstrous shape."

What *A Midsummer Night's Dream* suggests, in other words, is that the mythical monster, as a conjunction of elements which normally specify different beings, automatically results from the more and more rapid turnover of animal and metaphysical images, a turnover which depends on the constantly self-reinforcing process of mimetic desire. We are not simply invited to witness the dramatic but insignificant birth of bizarre mythical creatures; rather we are confronted with a truly fascinating and important view of mythical genesis.

In a centaur, elements specific to man and to horse are inexplicably conjoined, just as elements specific to man and ass are conjoined in the monstrous metamorphosis of Bottom. Since there is no limit to the differences that can be jumbled together, since the picture will necessarily remain blurred, the diversity of monsters will appear properly limitless and the infinite seems to be at hand. Insofar as separate entities can be distinguished within the monstrous whole, there will be individual monsters; but they will have no stability: they will constantly appear to merge and marry one another. The birth of monsters, their scandalous commingling with human beings, and the wedding of the one with the other, all these mythical phenomena are part of one and the same experience. The wedding of Titania with the ass-headed Bottom, under the influence of that same "love juice" that makes the lovers crazy, can take place only because the difference between the natural and the supernatural is gone; haughty Titania finds to her dismay that the barrier between her and ordinary mortals is down:

> Tell me how it came this night
> That I sleeping there was found
> With these mortals on the ground.
>
> [IV.i.103–105]

The conjunction of man, god, and beast takes place at the climax of the crisis and is the result of a process which began with the play itself. It is the ultimate metamorphosis, the supreme *translation*.

In that process the animal images play a pivotal role. I noted earlier that their perfect integration into the disquieting symphony conducted by Shakespeare was not at all incompatible with their identification as literary reminiscences. We must now go further. To say that these images are compatible with the role that Shakespeare himself wants them to play in his own work is no longer enough. It is evident that these animal images are especially appropriate to that role and that Shakespeare has selected them for that reason. Most of them come from Ovid's *Metamorphoses.* They are directly implicated in an earlier genesis of myth, still quite mythical, and far removed from the obviously psychosocial interpretation implicitly proposed by Shakespeare. It is no exaggeration to assert that *A Midsummer Night's Dream,* because it is a powerful reinterpretation of Ovid, also provides, at least in outline, Shakespeare's own genetic theory of myth. It is a mistake, therefore, to view the animal images as if they were suspended in midair between the matter-of-fact interplay of desires on the one hand and purely fantastic shapes on the other. They are the connecting link between the two. Thus we can no longer see the play as a collage of heterogeneous elements, as another monstrosity; it is a continuous development, a series of logically related steps that will account even for the monsters in its own midst if they are only followed to the end, if enough trust is placed in the consistency of the author.

At the climax of the crisis, Demetrius and Lysander are about to kill each other, but Puck, on Oberon's orders, substitutes himself for the *doubles* and puts the four lovers to sleep. When they wake up the next morning, they find themselves reconciled, neatly arranged this time in well-assorted couples. Good weather is back, everything is in order once more. Degree is restored. Theseus appears upon the scene. He and his future wife hear an account of the midsummer night, and it is for the duke to pronounce the final word, to draw the official conclusion of the whole episode in response to a slightly anxious question asked by Hippolyta. Then comes the most famous passage of the entire play. Theseus dismisses the entire midsummer night as the inconsequential fruit of a gratuitous and disembodied imagination. He seems to believe that the real question is whether or not to believe in the fairies. Hippolyta's later words will reveal that her concern is of an entirely different sort; but, like all rationalists of a certain type, Theseus has a marvelous capacity for simplifying the issues and displacing a debate toward his favorite stomping ground. Much of what he says is true, of course; but it is beside the point. To believe or not to believe, that is *not* the question; and, by trumpeting his fatuous skepticism, Theseus dispenses himself from looking at the remarkable pattern of the midsummer night and the disturbing clues it may contain concerning the nature of all social beliefs, including his own. Who knows if the crisis and its cathartic resolution are responsible only for the monsters of the night? Who knows if the peace and order of the morning after, if even the majestic confidence of the unchallenged ruler are not equally in their debt? Theseus' casual dismissal of myth is itself mythical in the sense that it will not ask such questions. There is irony in the choice of a great mythical figure to embody this rationalistic dismissal. Here Theseus acts as the high priest of a benign casting-out of all disturbing phenomena under the triple heading of poetry, lunacy, and love. This neat operation frees respectable men of all responsibility for whatever tricks, past, present, and future, their own desires and mimetic violence might play on them, thus perfectly duplicating the primary genesis of myth, the one that I have just noted.

HIPPOLYTA: 'Tis strange, my Theseus, that these lovers speak of.
THESEUS: More strange than true. I never may believe
These antique fables, nor these fairy toys.
Lovers and madmen have such seething brains,
Such shaping fantasies, that apprehend
More than cool reason ever comprehend.
The lunatic, the lover, and the poet
Are of imagination all compact.
One sees more devils than vast Hell can hold,
That is the madman. The lover, all as frantic,
Sees Helen's beauty in a brow of Egypt.
The poet's eye, in a fine frenzy rolling,
Doth glance from heaven to earth, from earth to heaven,
And as imagination bodies forth
The form of things unknown, the poet's pen
Turns them to shapes, and gives to airy nothings
A local habitation and a name.
Such tricks hath strong imagination

> That if it would but apprehend some joy,
> It comprehends some bringer of that joy;
> Or in the night, imagining some fear,
> How easy is a bush supposed a bear!
>
> [V.i.1–22]

This positivism *avant la lettre* seems to contradict much of what I have said so far. Evidence so laboriously assembled seems scattered once more. Where are the half-concealed yet blatant disclosures, the allusive ambiguities artfully disposed by the author (or so I supposed) for our enlightenment? Long before I came to it, I am sure, many skeptical readers had the passage in mind, and they will rightly want to know how it fits into my reading. Here it is, finally, an obvious ally of the traditional readings that quite naturally regard it as the unshakable rock upon which they are founded. As such, it must constitute a formidable stumbling block for my own intricate revisionism.

The lead is provided by Shakespeare himself, and the present status of the passage as a piece of anthology, a *lieu commun* of modern aestheticism, testifies to the willingness of posterity to take up that lead. The reading provided by Theseus is certainly the most pleasant, the one which conforms to the wishes of the heart and to the tendency of the human mind not to be disturbed. We must note, besides, that the text is centrally located, placed in the mouth of the most distinguished character, couched in sonorous and memorable phrases, well fit to adorn academic dissertations on the so-called "imaginative faculty."

This speech has been so successful, indeed, that no one ever pays any attention to the five quiet lines that follow. Hippolyta's response does not have the same resounding eloquence, but the dissatisfaction she expresses with the slightly pompous and irrelevant *postmortem* of Theseus *was written by Shakespeare himself*. It cannot fail to be of immense significance:

> But the story of the night told over,
> And all their minds transfigured so together,
> More witnesseth than fancy's images,
> And grows to something of great constancy,
> But howsoever strange and admirable.
>
> [V.i.23–27]

Hippolyta clearly perceives Theseus' failure to come up with the holistic interpretation that is necessary. He and his innumerable followers deal with the play as if it were a collection of separate cock-and-bull stories. To them imagination is a purely individual activity, unrelated to the interplay of the four lovers. They themselves are the true inheritors of myth when they confidently believe in their simplistic objectivity. They see myth as something they have already left behind with the greatest of ease, as an object of passing amusement, perhaps, when the occasion arises to watch some light entertainment such as *A Midsummer Night's Dream.*

There is no doubt that we are dealing with two critical attitudes and that Shakespeare himself vindicates the one that has always been least popular. When I suggest that *A Midsummer Night's Dream,* behind all the frills, is a serious genetic theory of myth, I am only translating the five lines of Hippolita into contemporary parlance. It is not I but Shakespeare who writes that the midsummer night is more than a few graceful arabesques about English folklore and Elizabethan lovers. It is not I but Shakespeare who draws our attention to *all their minds transfigured so together* and to the final result as *something of great constancy,* in other words, a common structure of mythical meaning.

I have suggested that *A Midsummer Night's Dream* might well be two plays in one. This hypothesis is now strengthened. At this point, the two plays are coming to life as individuals; they are speaking to us and to each other, one through Theseus, the other through Hippolyta. The exchange between the bridegroom and his acutely perceptive but eternally overshadowed bride amounts to the first critical discussion of the play. Representing as he does blissful ignorance and the decorum of Degree enthroned, Theseus must hold the stage longer, speaking with a brilliance and finality that confirms the dramatic preeminence of the surface play, a preeminence that is maintained throughout. Since he gives a voice to all those—the immense majority— who want nothing more in such an affair than "airy nothings," Theseus must be as deaf and blind to his bride's arguments as Shakespeare's audiences and critics seem to have been ever since. The debate seems onesided in the duke's favor, but how could we fail, at this juncture, to realize that the real last word belongs to Hippolyta, both literally and figuratively? In the context of the evidence gathered earlier, how could we doubt that Hippolyta's words are the decisive ones, that they represent Shakespeare's own view of how the play really hangs together? If we really understand that context, we cannot be surprised that Shakespeare makes his correction of Theseus as discreet and unobstrusive as it is illuminating, visible only to the same thoughtful attention already needed to appreciate such pregnant ambiguities as "to choose love by another's eyes" and other similar gems of exquisitely direct, yet almost imperceptible revelation.

Hippolyta is gently tugging at Theseus' sleeve, but Theseus hears nothing. Posterity hears nothing. Hippolyta has been tugging at that sleeve for close to four hundred years now, with no consequence whatever, her words forever buried under the impressive scaffoldings of Degree once more triumphant in the guise of rationalism, eternally silenced by that need for reassurance which is answered first by belief in myths, then by a certain kind of disbelief. Shakespeare seems to give his blessing to both, ironically confounded in the person of Theseus. He places in the hands of his pious and admiring betrayers the instruments best designed to blunt the otherwise intolerably sharp edge of their favorite bard's genius.

EUGENIO DONATO

The Museum's Furnace: Notes toward a Contextual Reading *of* Bouvard and Pécuchet

Le feu est chez vous.

—Flaubert

Nous sommes embarqués sur un microcosme volcan, prêt à s'abîmer. Pascal revu par Nietzsche pour les amateurs d'émotions cérébrales fortes.

—Michel Serres

The Library

Flaubert's *Bouvard and Pécuchet* describes the systematic pursuit by two office clerks of a number of activities—agriculture, arboriculture, garden architecture, chemistry, anatomy, physiology, geology, archeology, and others—which span the totality of human knowledge by systematically exhausting its various domains. Yet neither the well-meant, systematic enterprises of the two clerks nor their immense resiliency in the face of failure allows them ever to gain mastery over any of the regions of the encyclopedia. The encyclopedia, assumed to be the ultimate principle of reality, turns out to be a constantly elusive mirage. The odyssey of the two asexual bachelors stages the concept of an encyclopedic knowledge both as that which preexists and determines the various activities in which the two clerks engage and also as the teleological end point which they indefatigably attempt to attain, without its ever being at any time present to them.

The office clerks systematically fail in each and every one of their endeavors; each field of knowledge reveals itself to be contradictory, unsystematic, or simply unable to give an adequate representation of the objects it is supposed to describe. A bookish knowledge of agriculture in no way permits them to grow crops, archeology is full of contradictions, the writing of history impossible. Having finally recognized the failure of their enterprise, they return to their original activity of copying; however, this time they simply copy anything and everything that comes to hand. Having begun with the dream and hope of a total, finite, rational domain of knowledge, they come to realize that not only is knowledge as a given totality unavailable but that also any act of totalization is by definition incomplete, infinite, and everywhere marked by accident, chance, and randomness:

> They copy papers haphazardly, everything they find, tobacco pouches, old newspapers, posters, torn books, etc. (real items and their imitations. Typical of each category).
> Then, they feel the need for a taxonomy. They make tables, antithetical oppositions such as "crimes of the kings and crimes of the people"—blessings of religion, crimes of religion. Beauties of history, etc.; sometimes, however, they have real problems putting each thing in its proper place and suffer great anxieties about it.
> —Onward! Enough speculation! Keep on copying! The page must be filled. Everything is equal, the good and the evil. The farcical and the sublime—the beautiful and the ugly—the insignificant and the typical, they all become an exaltation of the statistical. There are nothing but facts—and phenomena.
> Final bliss.[1]

Most readings of *Bouvard and Pécuchet* take their point of departure from Flaubert's remarks about the composition and significance of the work. The result of the author's meanderings through the library: "I'm aghast at what I have to do for *Bouvard and Pécuchet*. I read catalogues of books that I annotate" (1324);[2]

[1] In *Oeuvres complètes de Gustave Flaubert* (Paris: Club de l'Honnête Homme, 1971), VI, 607. Flaubert died before finishing *Bouvard and Pécuchet* but left a number of scenarios for the ending of the novel. I have slightly modified the text and have not taken into account words or expressions erased by Flaubert nor reproduced the diacritical marks the editors have used to indicate words and expressions added by Flaubert at a later date.

[2] All quotes followed by a number refer to the Conard edition of Flaubert's *Correspondance* in *Oeuvres complètes de Gustave Flaubert* (Paris: Conard, 1923–1933).

"I am, sir, *inside a labyrinth!*" (550); "I have gotten indigestion from books. I burp in-folio" (537); "Reading is an abyss; one never gets out of it. I am becoming as dumb as a pot" (397). The novel is to portray "the story of these two men who copy a kind of farcical version of a critical encyclopedia" (1318).

Flaubert's comments could hardly have passed unnoticed by critics such as Foucault and Kenner, who—after Seznec but without acknowledging him[3]—make *Bouvard and Pécuchet* emblematic of the metaphor of the *Library-Encyclopedia,* which for them governs the modern developments of fiction's textuality, from Hegel's *Encyclopedia of Philosophic Sciences* to Borges's "Library of Babel." For Kenner, "The mark of the Encyclopedia," which is its fragmentation of all knowledge into little pieces so arranged that they can be found one at a time, points only to the "burlesque . . . of fiction," to "the incompetence . . . of fiction itself which is endlessly *arranging* things."[4] For Foucault, *Bouvard and Pécuchet,* along with *The Temptation of Saint Anthony,* belongs to "a literature that exists only inside and as a result of the web of the already written: the book in which is played out the fiction of all books." Hence *The Temptation,* but also implicitly *Bouvard and Pécuchet,* "is not only a book that Flaubert had long dreamed of writing; it is the dream of other books: all those other dreaming and dreamt-of books—fragmented, taken up again, displaced, combined, distanced by the dream but also brought back by it to the imaginary and scintillating satisfaction of desire. After *The Book* Mallarmé will become possible, then Joyce, Roussel, Kafka, Pound, Borges. The library is aflame." Bouvard and Pécuchet "are tempted by books, by their indefinite multiplicity, by the rippling of works in the colorless space of the Library."[5]

Both Kenner's and Foucault's readings underscore the critical importance of the metaphor of the *Encyclopedia-Library* and its importance to the development of the Flaubertian canon. For

[3]See in particular his *Nouvelles Etudes sur "La Tentation de Saint Antoine"* (London: Warburg Institute, 1949), in which he writes, for example, "To understand the worker Flaubert . . . it is necessary to lose one's way with him in the labyrinth of libraries" (p. 11).
[4]Kenner, *The Stoic Comedians: Flaubert, Joyce and Beckett* (Boston: Beacon, 1962), pp. 12–13.
[5]Foucault, "La Bibliothèque fantastique," introduction to Flaubert, *La Tentation de Saint Antoine,* ed. Henri Ronse (Paris: Gallimard, 1967), p. 11.

both, *Bouvard and Pécuchet* is a book constructed out of fragments of other books; the book presupposes, then, the *Library* as
its genetic memory. Such a memory, however, is neither the
"constructive memory" of the interiorized world which Hegel
writes about[6] and which guarantees the ontological status of representation, nor a Divine Book of Nature that the modern writer
might have inherited from an earlier theological tradition. If the
Library makes *Bouvard and Pécuchet* possible, in no way does it
provide it with a privileged origin which might guarantee the
mimetic or representational veracity of fiction, or the capacity of
the world to fictionalize itself in an unequivocal fashion. What
the *Library* imposes on the two unfortunate heroes of Flaubert's
novel is the impossibility of reaching its order, its totality, or its
truth. The library dooms the characters—but the author and the
reader as well[7]—to an indefinite wandering in a labyrinthine
space not unlike that described by the narrator of Borges's "Library of Babel." The characters' plight, as Flaubert so often
indicated, is also the author's: the novel, then, stages the impossibility of its authorship and of its inscription. Flaubert, like his
characters Bouvard and Pécuchet, is reduced to the role of a
scribe; their failure is his failure. Through Flaubert's signature,

[6]On this question of the relationship of memory to representation, see Derrida's "Le Puits et la pyramide" in *Marges de la philosophie* (Paris: Minuit, 1972). In
the example of the Abbé Faria in *Le Comte de Monte-Cristo,* the nineteenth century
has provided us also with the literary example of an internalized "constructive
memory" which is not only the internalization of the outside world, but the
internalization of the outside world through the internalization of a library: "In
Rome, I had approximately five thousand volumes in my library. By dint of
reading and rereading them, I discovered that with one hundred fifty well-
chosen works, one has, if not a complete summary of human knowledge, at least
all that is useful for a man to know. I devoted three years of my life to reading
and rereading these one hundred fifty volumes, with the result that I knew them
almost by heart when I was arrested. In prison, with a slight effort of memory I
was able to recall them in their entirety."
[7]Claude Mouchard, in a recent article entitled "Terre, technologie, roman: A
propos du deuxième chapitre de *Bouvard et Pécuchet*" in *Littérature,* 15 (1974), 67,
has, again, after Seznec, further expanded the problem of the dilemma of the
reader: "The reader who really wants to 'comprehend' what the text of the novel
deals with should refer to the manuals mentioned by Flaubert. But this would
involve the risk of entering into an unending game of cross-references, which is
one of the temptations of technological discourse despite its claims to immediate
and effective clarity . . . . And this movement toward a knowledge that must
always be clarified further would make reading the novel even more problematic
than the immediate obscurity of the quotations."

it is fiction which signs the dramatization of its impossible quest for privileged origins.

The final scene of the two clerks copying whatever happens to fall into their hands might then be read as an allegory of the way literature unfolds its representational texture. Flaubert's addition to the earlier scenario for the ending of the novel, quoted above and incorporated in a later, more extended version of "Give as being true bibliographical information which is false," becomes, then, the emblem of that allegory. Literature, having shed its onto-theological illusions, shamelessly parades its fictions as "truths" to hide the staging of its hopeless quest for a privileged origin, a quest which invariably ends in fiction's dispersion into the infinite, non-natural labyrinthine web of textuality.

Such a reading of *Bouvard and Pécuchet,* besides having the merit of accounting for the way the text inscribes its own genesis and showing how this inscription is isomorphic to the way Flaubert himself described the textual construction of the novel, permits one to read specific passages as a precise critique of linguistic representation. As I have tried to show elsewhere,[8] the clerks' failure at agriculture can be derived from the failure of nominalization and rhetorical signification to sustain a stable system. Their failure at writing history can be analyzed to show the generalized failure of symbolization in reaching any signified beyond the open-ended play of signifiers. In summary, it is difficult, after *Bouvard and Pécuchet,* not to arrive at the conclusion that Flaubert is a linguistic nihilist, and that in his descriptions of the two office clerks' failures, he undertook a critique of representation not unlike to that of Nietzsche in texts such as "Truth and Illusion in an Extra-Moral Sense."

The Museum

The reading of *Bouvard and Pécuchet* in terms of the metaphor of the *Encyclopedia-Library,* despite its relating the novel to a

[8]See my "'A Mere Labyrinth of Letters'/Flaubert and the Quest for Fiction/A Montage" in *MLN,* 89 (1974). C. Bernheimer's "Linguistic Realism in Flaubert's *Bouvard et Pécuchet*" in *Novel,* 7 (Winter 1974), provides an interesting discussion, in spite of the different conclusions at which he arrives, of the problems of linguistic representation and symbolization in *Bouvard and Pécuchet.*

crucial textual problematic and allowing for the reading of certain passages in terms of primarily linguistic or representational considerations, falls short, however, of being completely satisfactory. The reason for this is twofold. On the one hand, the *Encyclopedia-Library* is never thematized as a master-term that explicitly controls the deployment of the various regions of knowledge; on the contrary Flaubert systematically stages the *Encyclopedia-Library* as one nonprivileged term in an indifferent series. On the other hand, a good number of the failures of Bouvard and Pécuchet cannot be attributed to the incapacity of linguistic or symbolic representation to account for reality. For example, when wind and rain destroy their fruit crops, or when a storm destroys their wheat crop, there is no way of accounting for the storm within any representational system. The forces at play within nature are absolutely other than those at work in the deconstruction of taxonomies, rhetoric, and semiology.

The clerks' original dream of a pastoral existence excludes the activity of writing, that is to say, of the most complex and resistant of language's representational forms: "Waking with the lark, they would follow the plough, go out with a basket to gather apples, watch the butter being made, the corn threshed, the sheep sheared, the beehives tended, and they would revel in the mooing of cows and the scent of fresh-mown hay. No more copying!" (*BP,* 30).[9] Carried away by their illusion, they also reject from the start any need for books. Flaubert in the *Dictionnaire des idées reçues* writes: "Library—always have one in one's home, especially when living in the country." Bouvard, on the contrary, on the verge of his new rural life decides that "we'll have no library." In their pastoral dream, Bouvard and Pécuchet dismiss the mediation of books and aspire instead to the mastery of a science which acts directly on nature. Significantly, they start their adventures equipped with an odd assortment of scientific instruments: "They purchased gardening implements and a mass of things 'which might come in useful,' such as a tool-box (every house should have one), followed by a pair of scales, a

---

[9] All quotes from *Bouvard and Pécuchet* are from the translation of T. W. Earp and G. W. Stoner (New York: New Directions, 1954), indicated by "*BP*" and the page number in parentheses.

land-chain, a bath-tub in case of illness, a thermometer, and even a barometer, 'on the Gay-Lussac system,' for meteorological experiments, should the fancy take them" (*BP*, 30–31).

The odd assortment of books that belonged to Pécuchet before he undertook his rural adventure hardly amounts to a library. The books, in fact, are part of a group of heterogeneous objects that anticipate the "*bric-a-brac* shops" they will later visit: "and in the corners were scattered a number of volumes of the Roret Encyclopaedia, the Mesmerist's Handbook, a Fenelon, and other old tomes, as well as a pile of papers, two coconuts, various medallions, a Turkish fez, and shells brought from Le Havre by Dumouchel" (*BP*, 21). It can be argued, of course, that Bouvard and Pécuchet are defeated by the very thing whose importance they fail to account for in the first place. As I suggested earlier, there is no doubt that such a remark is regionally correct and that the efforts of the two clerks are sometimes undone by an unstable representational or symbolical system that they fail fully to understand or to recognize. Nevertheless, when the theme of the *Encyclopedia-Library* appears in the novel, it is thematized in such a way as to require a separate set of remarks. To return to the passage quoted above, the clerks' library—if one can call it that—is on the one hand contrasted with their scientific instruments, that is, with an otherness which is not obviously inscribed in the texture of representation; but more important, it appears in a series of heterogeneous elements. The difficulty resides, precisely, in reading a series of heterogeneous elements, since through their heterogeneity they offer what is absolutely other to the homogeneous representational space of the *Encyclopedia-Library*.

Later in the novel, when Flaubert describes the various buildings and public collections that Bouvard and Pécuchet visit, the library is again placed in a heterogeneous series:

> They sauntered past the old *bric-a-brac* shops. They visited the Conservatoire des Arts et Métiers, Saint-Denis, the Gobelins, the Invalides and all the public collections.
>
> In the galleries of the Museum they viewed the stuffed quadrupeds with astonishment, the butterflies with pleasure, the metals with indifference; fossils fired their imagination, conchology bored them. They peered into hot-houses, and shuddered at the

thought of so many foliages distilling poison. What struck them
most about the cedar was that it had been brought over in a hat.

They worked up an enthusiasm at the Louvre for Raphael. At
the Central Library they would have liked to know the exact
number of volumes. [*BP*, 25–26]

The bric-a-brac is emblematic of the whole series. Again, it is
not the bric-a-brac which is in the library; it is the latter that
belongs to a series which can be characterized as bric-a-brac.
Interestingly, however, the series contains one term that itself
contains a heterogeneous series, namely the *Museum* (the
Museum of Natural History). The term which is then repre-
sentationally privileged, which allegorizes the series, is the
museum and not the library, since the former contains a series of
which the latter is only a term. It is then perhaps in the concept
of the *Museum* that we must search for an encyclopedic totality.

If Bouvard and Pécuchet never assemble what can amount to
a library, they nevertheless manage to constitute for themselves
a private museum. The museum, in fact, occupies a central position in the novel; it is connected to the characters' interest in
archeology, geology, and history and it is thus through the
Museum that questions of origin, causality, representation, and
symbolization are most clearly stated. The *Museum,* as well as the
questions it tries to answer, depends upon an archeological epistemology. Its representational and historical pretensions are
based upon a number of metaphysical assumptions about
origins—archeology intends, after all, to be a science of the
archēs. Archeological origins are important in two ways: each
archeological artifact has to be an original artifact, and these
original artifacts must in turn explain the "meaning" of a subsequent larger history. Thus, in Flaubert's caricatural example,
the baptismal font that Bouvard and Pécuchet discover has to be
a Celtic sacrificial stone, and Celtic culture has in turn to act as
an original master pattern for cultural history:

> . . . whence it must be concluded that the religion of the Gauls had
> the same principles as that of the Jews.
>   Their society was very well organized. . . . Some uttered prophe-
> sies, others chanted, others taught botany, medicine, history and
> literature: in short, "all the arts of their epoch." Pythagoras

and Plato were their pupils. They instructed the Greeks in metaphysics, the Persians in sorcery, the Etruscans in augury, and the Romans in plating copper and trading in ham.

But of this people which dominated the ancient world, there remain only a few stones. [*BP*, 127–128]

These stones will become the archival material displayed in the museums which are the outward manifestation of an implicit archeological knowledge or essence.

The outstanding characteristic of the Flaubertian *Museum* is its irreducible heterogeneity. This heterogeneity becomes, in fact, caricatural in Flaubert's early scenarios for the novel. To quote from one of them:

> Six months later the house looked entirely different. They possessed a collection. *Museum*.
>
> Old junk, pottery of all sorts, shaving cups, butter plates, earthenware lamps, wardrobes, a halberd, one of a kind! Bludgeons, panoplies of primitive origins. Works of spun glass. Chest of drawers and Chippendale trunks, prison hampers. Saint-Allyre's petrified objects: a cat with a mouse in its jaws, stuffed birds. Various curios: chauffeur's cap, a madman's shoe. Objects drawn from rivers and people, etc.[10]

I have quoted this early draft because of its brevity; the lengthy description of the Museum of Bouvard and Pécuchet contains as heterogeneous a collection of objects as that of the draft, and interestingly enough contains also a library as one of the objects of the Museum.

A parenthesis might be in order here. The ideology that governs the *Museum* in the nineteenth century and down to the present has often been equated with that of the *Library,* namely, to give by the ordered display of selected artifacts a total representation of human reality and history. Museums are taken to exist only inasmuch as they can erase the heterogeneity of the objects displayed in their cases, and it is only the hypothesis of the possibility of homogenizing the diversity of various artifacts which makes them possible in the first place.

As late as 1929, W. J. Holland, director of the Carnegie Insti-

---

[10] *Oeuvres complètes de Gustave Flaubert* (1971), VI, 662.

tute and president of the American Association of Museums, wrote: "The ideal museum should cover the whole field of human knowledge. It should teach the truths of all the sciences, including anthropology, the science which deals with man and all his works in every age. All the sciences and all the arts are correlated." The critique of early museums is done in terms of bric-a-brac. Lord Balcarres, trustee of the National Portrait Gallery, wrote: "The modern museum of art differs essentially from its earlier prototypes. The aimless collection of curiosities and bric-a-brac, brought together without method or system, was the feature of certain famous collections in by-gone days." The success of the modern museum again depends upon the order in which the objects are displayed: "To be of teaching value, museum arrangement and classification must be carefully studied.... Attention must be given to the proper display and cataloguing of the exhibits.... Great progress has been made in the classification of objects."[11] To give one more example, in 1930, Sir Frederic Kenyon, then director and principal librarian of the British Museum, wrote:

> In the galleries of these museums are gathered together examples of the art and craftsmanship of man, from the most remote stone age to the present day. The study of such objects teaches us how man has reacted to his surroundings, what products of art or industry he has achieved, how he has used or misused his opportunities. They are at once the material and the illustrations of written history, and to a generation becoming daily more dependent on the picture than on the written word their importance is increasing.
>
> The study of history not only widens our mind by increasing our interests, but contributes to the stability of our civilisation by its record of the actions of men, and their results, in conditions more or less analogous to our own. History is vicarious experience, and the neglect of it leads to rash ventures and disastrous experiments.[12]

These pronouncements seem to indicate as naive a faith as that of the two clerks in the capacity of giving an adequate repre-

---

[11] In "Museums of Science" and "Museums of Art," *Encyclopedia Britannica,* 11th ed. (1911), XIX, 64–65, 60.

[12] *Libraries and Museums* (London: E. Benn, 1930), pp. 69–70.

sentation of reality as it was or as it is. The onto-theological temptation to equate the *Encyclopedia-Library* with the *Museum* is as understandable as it is surprising. The *Encyclopedia-Library* is a lay version of the medieval metaphor of the *Book of Nature.* Implicit in that metaphor is the assumption that the world can be completely textualized and, vice versa, that any element of the world can be treated as a textual element. Borges, for example, significantly begins his "Library of Babel" with the words: "The Universe (which others call the Library). . . ." A linguistic critique of the onto-theological pretensions of the *Library* accentuates the open-ended boundaries of the web of language to which the *Library* tries to give a center and a limit. If the *Library* is not the mirror of a presumed World or Nature, then the *Library* is the emblem of the infinite autoreferentiality of language. Such critiques, while underscoring the open-ended play of language and its uncentered labyrinthine structure, nevertheless often maintain a nostalgia for the center—witness Mallarmé's quest for *The Book,* or Borges's search for the "Catalogue of Catalogues." This is hardly the case for the *Museum.* The set of objects the Museum displays is sustained only by the fiction that they somehow constitute a coherent representational universe. The fiction is that a repeated metonymic displacement of fragment for totality, object to label, series of objects to series of labels, can still produce a representation which is somehow adequate to a nonlinguistic universe. Such a fiction is the result of an uncritical belief in the notion that ordering and classifying, that is to say, the spatial juxtaposition of fragments, can produce a representational understanding of the world. Should the fiction disappear, there is nothing left of the *Museum* but "bric-a-brac," a heap of meaningless and valueless fragments of objects which are incapable of substituting themselves either metonymically for the original objects or metaphorically for their representations.

Flaubert's critique seems radical enough to question, by means of the *Museum,* the possibility of reaching any truth, essence, or origin through a representational mode. If the *Museum* as concept has at its origin the same metaphysical ambition that the *Library* has in other contexts, namely, to give an adequate ordered rational representation of reality, nevertheless its project is doomed from the start because representation within the concept of the museum is intrinsically impossible. The museum can only display objects metonymically at least twice removed from that which they are originally supposed to represent or signify. The objects displayed as a series are of necessity only part of the totality to which they originally belonged. Spatially and temporally detached from their origin and function, they signify only by arbitrary and derived associations. The series in which the individual pieces and fragments are displayed is also arbitrary and incapable of investing the particular object with anything but irrelevant fabulations.[13] Again, the critique implied here goes beyond a critique which would limit itself to linguistic representation, even though it includes it. Linguistic representation carries within itself, in the *Library,* its own memory, its own origin, its own *archē*—displaced or hidden as it may be. The *Museum,* on the other hand, testifies to an archeological memory that cannot be recovered except through fabulation. The chapter on Bouvard and Pécuchet's museum, in fact, repeats other statements by Flaubert to the same effect. For example, in a chapter in *Par les champs et par les grèves,* he described the ruins of Carnac, ironizing all attempts to understand them:

> Thus we find this famous field of Carnac that has occasioned the writing of more stupidities than it contains rocks, and one certainly does not come across such rocky paths every day. But, in spite of our natural penchant for admiring everything, we saw in it only a hardy joke, left there by an unknown age to excite the spirit of antiquarians and stupefy travelers. In front of it one opens naive eyes and, all the while finding it quite uncommon, must admit at the same time that it is not very pretty. We understood then the

[13]To the best of my knowledge, the first to underscore the epistemological importance of archeology and of museums is Raymond Schwab in *La Renaissance orientale* (Paris: Payot, 1950). In particular, he writes: "the scriptural document . . . ceases to have sole and absolute reign. The advent of the archeological method forcefully heightens the authority and efficiency of history . . . . The museum is no longer so much a conservatory of models as a storehouse of information; the masterpiece, formerly a source only of pleasure and a standard of taste, now must share the same room with household artifacts; it is placed side by side with the commercial object on an exhibit table; it is removed from the class of aeroliths in order to become a number in these series . . . . The object is contrasted to the text, the inscription to the chronical, the statue or the vase to the narrative, the king's deeds to his legend" (p. 410).

irony of these granite boulders that, since the age of the Druids, have laughed in their green lichen beards at seeing all the imbeciles that came to stare at them. Scholars' lives have been spent in an attempt to determine their past usages; don't you admire this eternal preoccupation of the unfeathered biped with finding some sort of usefulness for everything? Not content with distilling the ocean to salt his stew, and assassinating elephants to make knife-handles out of them, his egotism is again provoked when he is faced with some debris or other whose utility he can't figure out.[14]

It should be obvious from such a passage that the cornerstone of Flaubert's critique is in a way remarkably similar to Nietzsche's critique of representation—namely, the anthropocentrism of meaning. If the *Museum* fails at reaching the nature and essence of the objects it displays, it is because it tries to understand them in relation to the spectator rather than in relation to the objects themselves. "Meaning," the result of metonymic or metaphoric displacements, is anthropomorphic and anthropocentric, and it is because of its anthropocentrism that it is necessarily doomed to failure. Archeology, ultimately, is not an objective science but a fantasy of the perceiving subject.[15]

Another parenthetical remark may be in order here.

[14]*Oeuvres complètes de Gustave Flaubert* (1971), X, 99.
[15]The metonymic displacement of the archeological objects of the museum which makes them unsuitable for an objective science makes them, on the contrary, very suggestive to the literary imagination. The archeologist's loss is the novelist's gain; witness *Salammbô*.
In 1851, Flaubert went to England with his mother to visit the "Great Exhibition of the Works of Industry of All Nations." There is no particular rationale to the objects that caught Flaubert's fancy. Seznec notes, for example, that in the Indian section Flaubert "pauses for a long time in front of a harnessed elephant; then examines a chariot, then instruments of music, a canon on a camel's saddle, a coat of mail, a divan, a vest, some fans, three Indian dancing girl dresses, and some turbans." Even taking into account the "unusual nature of the Exposition," the question remains as to why Flaubert chose to describe one object rather than another. I believe Seznec's answer to be very convincing. The function of the objects chosen by the novelist is to permit him to reconstruct a *fictional image* of a particular culture: "I am inclined to believe that an object is chosen on account of its special power of evocation. This knick-knack, that accessory, is the fragment of a civilization which, by itself, it is capable of suggesting. 'Is not *all of China* contained in a Chinese woman's slipper decorated with damask roses and having embroidered cats on its vamp' (421). In basing itself on objects, the imagination reconstructs that universe whose quintessence they express." (Jean Seznec, *Flaubert à l'Exposition de 1851* [Oxford: Clarendon Press, 1951], pp. 16–17.)

Flaubert's critique is of consequence for us. Archeology is still a discipline unlike others not only because it pretends to deal with origin and meaning, but because, today as for the nineteenth century, it offers a possible epistemological master pattern. Take, for example, Foucault's *Les Mots et les choses* and *L'Archéologie du savoir:* both books claim an epistemology based upon an archeological master pattern. Foucault hopes, through the treatment of linguistic entities by archeological metaphors, to avoid what he considers the implicit idealism of a problematic rooted in linguistic representation. If, however, Flaubert's critique is correct, then the whole enterprise is a fabulation unable to recognize itself as such.

Foucault describes the *épistémè*, the epistemological invariant, of the Enlightenment as being governed by a quest for a perfect representation. The taxonomies of Linnaeus and Buffon are, for the twentieth-century thinker, quests for a well-constructed language that would provide an adequate representation of Nature. The isomorphism between the order of Nature and the order of Language is rooted, somehow, in their discontinuity. The relationship between the order of Words and the order of Things is presumably problematical neither for the eighteenth century nor for Foucault. Things, of course, are slightly more complicated. The botanical and zoological taxonomies did not, as the author of *Les Mots et les choses* argues, originate in or through any presumed space between the order of Nature and the order of Words which is assumed to have governed Classical representation. The eighteenth century generated its botanical nomenclatures by a procedure based upon the same epistemology that would later on be applied to archeological artifacts. The botanical and zoological taxonomies assumed that a single specimen could stand for a species, that part of a specimen could stand for a specimen, that the parts could be related and named, and finally that they could be seen to stand to each other in a contiguous ordered fashion. The possibility of a perfect representation of Nature rests then on a complex series of metonymies and metaphors bridging the gap between the natural object and its representation. Assuming such a *continuous* representation the Enlightenment could then originate the idea of giving an ordered representation of Nature in various botanical gardens. It is in this idea of an ordered spectacle of

Nature, supplemented by an ordered language that would describe the spectacle, that the idea of the *Museum* was born.

At the beginning of the nineteenth century the development of an archeological method, and an archeological idea of the *Museum,* was simply the displacement onto human history of what was until then considered "natural history." This displacement guaranteed archeology a metaphysical basis by providing it with a "natural" master pattern. Such a metaphysical basis was all the more necessary in that the passage from the fragments of archeology to the discourse of history is much more problematical than the passage from "Nature" to the language of botanical and zoological taxonomies. At any rate, Foucault's epistemology is rooted in the epistemology of the Enlightenment he describes so well and, like it, is vulnerable to a critique that takes as its point of departure the questioning, through representation, of the continuity between Word and Thing, Taxonomy and Nature, and Language and Stone.

To return to *Bouvard and Pécuchet,* if the *Museum* as both theme and concept is important, then it ought to account for more than the central chapters related to archeology and history.

In *Bouvard and Pécuchet,* and in the nineteenth century generally, the archeological metaphor is closely linked with geology and its specific epistemology. It is, in fact, the scientific nature of geology which guarantees the displacement of its metaphors toward archeology. The central name in geology is that of Cuvier, whom the two clerks, of course, had read: "Cuvier ... had appeared to them in the brilliance of an aureole, on the peak of a science beyond dispute" (*BP,* 108). This is not surprising, since Cuvier's *Discours sur les révolutions de la surface du globe* was a very widely read text whose influence in the earlier part of the century was comparable to that of Claude Bernard's *Introduction à la médecine expérimentale* in the latter part. Cuvier described his enterprise as that of an archeological antiquarian:

Antiquarian of a new type, I found it necessary to learn at the same time to restore these monuments of past revolutions and to decode their sense; it was my task to collect and to put together in their original order the fragments which composed them, to reconstruct the antique creatures to which these fragments belonged; to reproduce them conserving their proportions and their characteris-

tics; to compare them finally to those which live today at the earth's
surface. . . . I was sustained, in this double work by the fact that it
promised to be of equal import both to the general science of
anatomy, the essential basis of all those sciences which deal with
organized bodies, and to the physical history of the earth, the
foundation of mineralogy, of geography, and even, one could say,
of the history of men, and of everything that it is most important
for them to know concerning themselves.

    If it is of interest to us to track down in the childhood of our
species the nearly eradicated traces of so many extinct nations,
would it not be of greater interest to search in the darkness of the
childhood of the earth for the traces of revolutions that took place
prior to the existence of all nations? . . . Would there not be some
glory for man in knowing how to overstep the limits of time, and in
rediscovering, by means of a few observations, the history of this
world and a series of events which preceded the birth of the
human race?[16]

    Cuvier's text is exemplary; for him, geology is a form of ar-
cheology. The function of the geologist is to reconstruct a continuous temporal history out of the fragments handed down to
him. His task, like that of the archeologist, is twofold: to reconstruct the entities to which the fragments belonged and then to
arrange those same entities in a series so as to discover the history of the globe—a history which, incidentally, is of necessity as
anthropocentric as that proposed by archeology: "All of these
ages have been separated from each other by cataclysms, of
which our deluge was the last. It was like a fairy-tale in several
acts, having man for the finale" (*BP,* 98). To the geologist, the
earth in its entirety is a museum.

    When Bouvard and Pécuchet, their fancy having been caught
by geology, attempt such a reconstruction in imitation of Cuvier,
they fail, but their failure is the failure of the epistemology of the
Museum to offer an adequate continuous representation between
Words and Things. That is to say, attempting to understand the
history of the globe through geological fragments is as futile as
trying to understand human history through archeology. Disor-
dered fragments lead only to a multitude of contradictory fabulations, something that even the two clerks seem to understand,

---

    [16]In Georges Cuvier, *Recherches sur les ossemens fossiles* . . . (Paris: E. d'Ocagne,
1834–1836), I, 93–95.

since to Bouvard's "Geology is too restricted!" Pécuchet replies, "Creation takes place in an up-and-down and haphazard manner. We should do better to start on something else" (*BP*, 112). Their only blindness is in not seeing that what they will pursue next through archeology is the same thing they attempted to find in geology, namely, a continual temporal order where there are actually only disconnected fragments.

The figure of the *Museum* is so pervasive that Bouvard and Pécuchet's failure at the various branches of agriculture can also be read as a failure of the *Museum,* or, more exactly, their failure at agriculture should signal to the reader from the start the failure of the *Museum.* Mouchard had already put forth the argument that the two clerks' concern with agriculture, being aesthetic, deals primarily with the question of selecting and ordering, that is to say with precisely the activities upon which the *Museum* is based.[17] I believe the argument can be generalized, and that perhaps the fact is that we still have a theological nostalgia for the *Museum* that has in part prevented us from seeing the obvious. If the Museum of Natural History is singled out, it is because, as I stated earlier, the ideology of the *Museum* was first applied to Nature. The Museum of Natural History was, strictly speaking, the first French museum.[18] Its function was to give an

[17]Specifically Mouchard writes: " 'Pécuchet spent ... delightful hours there unpodding the seeds, writing tickets, arranging his little pots. He used to rest on a box at the door and meditate improvements' [*BP*, 46]. From Rousseau to Goethe or Jünger, we note the contemplative meticulousness of botany and the charms of manipulating the plant kingdom. The concerns of classifying and conserving plants are very close, in the nineteenth century, to those which regard the library. In this way, these few lines enter into a game of mirrors with many other passages of *Bouvard and Pécuchet,* and even with the entire book in its ever-present tendency to classify" ("Terre, Technologie," p. 68).

[18]For a history of the Museum of Natural History, see Joseph Philippe François Deleuze, *Histoire et description du Muséum royal d'histoire naturelle* (Paris: A. Royer, 1823). Michelet in a curious passage gives a good illustration of how for his generation the first museum with a pedagogical function that comes to mind is the Museum of Natural History: "The young people from the provinces, who arrived trembling with excitement, found the immense creation of the museums and of the libraries ready to welcome them. . . . These museums, these gardens, were our education for us, the children of Paris. When from dreary neighborhoods, from dark streets, we went there to dream before so many beautiful enigmas, what things did we not feel instinctively, from our hearts! Did we understand? Not everything. . . . It was there and nowhere else that history first made a deep impression on me" (quoted by Schwab, *La Renaissance orientale,* pp. 412–413).

ordered representation, a spectacle of Nature. By displaying
plants, metonymically selected and metonymically ordered, it
meant to produce a *tableau* of Nature. The botanical failure of
Bouvard and Pécuchet points directly to the failure of understanding Nature. In spite of our hopes and wishes, Nature will
always escape any attempt on our part to comprehend it through
the representation we give of it to ourselves, in our cultured,
cultivated, tame fields and gardens.

Soon after their failure in the various branches of botany,
Bouvard and Pécuchet undertake a study of anatomy. The
order of succession seems random only if one does not take the
Museum into account. Edward Said has already perceptively
pointed out how anatomy in the eighteenth century epistemologically belongs to the realm of the laboratory and the
museum:

> Both linguists and anatomists purport to be speaking about mat-
> ters not directly obtainable or observable in nature. . . . The text of
> a linguistic or an anatomical work bears the same general relation
> to nature (or actuality) that a museum case exhibiting a speci-
> men mammal or organ does. What is given on the page and in the
> museum case is a truncated exaggeration. . . whose purpose is to
> exhibit a relationship between the science (or scientist) and the
> object, not one between the object and nature.[19]

This is also true, in a caricatural way, of the anatomical episode
in *Bouvard and Pécuchet*. In the first place, the two clerks do not
study the anatomy of a "natural specimen" but of a mannequin,
that is to say, a representation: "It was brick-coloured, hairless,
skinless, striped with numerous blue, red and white filaments.
This was not so much a corpse as a kind of toy, horrible-looking,
very spick-and-span, and smelling of varnish" (*BP*, 76–77). The
function of each part of the mannequin, instead of having any
relation to a presumed nature, is the cause of imaginary fabulations; for example, "the brain inspired them with philosophical
reflections" (*BP*, 78). More important, however, throughout the
eighteenth and beginning of the nineteenth centuries anatomy
was, along with botany, very much a part of the *Museum*.

---

[19]*Orientalism* (New York: Pantheon, 1978), p. 142.

Anatomy stands in the same relation to animals and humans that botany does to plants. Significantly, the Museum of Natural History had from its very beginnings a chair of anatomy attached to it.[20] By taking up anatomy after the various branches of botany, Bouvard and Pécuchet in fact exhaust what were the domains of knowledge associated with the Museum of Natural History and its major epistemological ideology from approximately the time of Buffon to that of Cuvier.

In summary, then, *Bouvard and Pécuchet* retraces the changes, the evolution, the archeological metaphor on which the *Museum* is based. Representation of Nature, representation of the globe, representation of history, the *Museum* believed it possible to make visible the implicit order of Nature and of History. It failed. It failed not only at its pretense of displaying the order of Nature and History, but in comprehending them as well. Behind our gardens and our fields hides a Nature to which we cannot have access. As for the past of our globe or of human societies, it is given to us only in the form of senseless fragments without a memory, and any attempt of ours to reconstruct a history is nothing but vain fabulation. We are irrevocably cut off spatially from Nature and temporally from our past. There is no continuity between Nature and us, any more than between our past and us. And in this sense, beyond language, Flaubert is an epistemological nihilist.

The Furnace

Bouvard and Pécuchet fail systematically: they fail in their dealings with Nature, with the world, with society, and, up to a

[20]A nineteenth-century description of the gallery of anatomy attached to the Museum of Natural History gives a clear illustration of its similarity to collections of bric-a-brac: "the gallery of comparative anatomy, established by Cuvier, . . . is made up of several rooms; the first of them presents bones and skeletons of gigantic fossils, skeletons of cetaceans and of whales; then come skeletons of all the human races, of heads of birds, of reptiles, of fish, of mammals, etc., etc. Other rooms are devoted to ovology, to phrenology, to teratology. The anatomy gallery contains approximately twenty-five thousand specimens, six thousand of which are stuffed, five thousand preserved in alcohol, the rest in wax or in plaster." (In Pierre Larousse, "Jardin des plantes de Paris," *Grand Dictionnaire universel du XIXe siècle* [Paris, 1865–1890], IX, 906–907.)

point, in their private lives. Some of the failures seem to be
intrinsic to their pursuits; if they fail at history, geology, or archeology it is because these enterprises are epistemologically
doomed from the start. Their botanical failures seem to be of a
different kind. If our cultured nature has no epistemological
privilege, it nevertheless need not fail as long as our concerns,
like those of the count of Faverges or of the peasants who sur-
round Bouvard and Pécuchet, are pragmatic rather than
theoretical. However, as we mentioned earlier, their botanical
enterprises fail in part because of storms, wind, and rain.
Storms, wind, and rain belong to Nature proper, and not to the
spectacle of Nature that the cultured botanical museum and
garden offer. Storms, in fact, are there to remind us that the two
are discontinuous. Once, when Flaubert's own garden at Crois-
set was badly damaged by a storm, he wrote in a letter to Louise
Colet:

> Not without some pleasure, I beheld my destroyed espalier trees,
> all my flowers cut to pieces, and the vegetable garden in total
> disarray. In beholding all these little artificial arrangements
> created by man which five minutes of Nature sufficed to overturn,
> I admired true order reestablishing itself within false order. These
> things tormented by us—sculptured trees, flowers growing where
> they have no desire to, vegetables from other lands, got a type of
> revenge in this atmospheric rebuff. All this has a *farcical side* to it
> which overcomes us. Is there anything more ridiculous than bell-
> glass covers for melons? So, these poor bell-glass covers have had
> quite a time of it! Ah! Ah! To what fantasies of little useful purpose
> this Nature whom we exploit pitilessly, whom we make ugly with so
> much impudence, whom we disdain with such fine speeches,
> abandons herself when the temptation seizes her! This is right. It is
> widely believed that the sun has no other useful purpose on earth
> except to make cabbages grow. [407]

An essential form of our contact with Nature is through the
forces it brings into play which cannot be understood as such,
but which wreak havoc with our ordinary representations of
Nature.

If we were to search for other instances of the unaccountable
manifestations of such a force in the novel, we should easily find
them in the way the two clerks encounter, time and again, fire

and heat and all of their literary and historical metaphors without ever realizing exactly what it is they face, nor ever knowing how to come to terms with it.

Their first encounter with fire occurs when the hay spontaneously ignites. As in the case of the storm, they no more have a way of understanding this event's origin than of coping with its results. Their second encounter, this time in the form of an explosion, is far more significant. During their experiment at distillation, the container explodes:

> Suddenly, with the detonation of a shell, the still burst into a score of pieces which leapt to the ceiling, cracking the pots, knocking over the ladles, shivering the glasses; the coals were scattered, the stove demolished . . . .
> The pressure of the steam had broken the apparatus—naturally so, as the cucurbit turned out to be blocked at the mouth . . . .
> When they recovered their speech, they asked themselves what could be the cause of so much ill-luck, especially the last? And they could make nothing of it, except that they had escaped death. Finally, Pécuchet said: "Perhaps it is because we never studied chemistry!" [*BP*, 72–73]

What is particularly relevant, of course, is Pécuchet's inability to determine the cause of the explosion. Steam is a concern not of chemistry but of thermodynamics. Thermodynamics, on the other hand, is the one science they are not capable of recognizing, because it constitutes the new science which will sweep away the old Newtonian physics as well as all the epistemologies based upon the temporality it predicates. The tools that Bouvard and Pécuchet take with them to the country are in themselves significant. They are tools that belong to the old physics of mechanical devices and not to the new physics of heat and fire.

The point, of course, is not to make Flaubert the proponent of one system as opposed to the other. The case for Flaubert's knowledge of the new physics and what it entailed could easily be stated and is rather uninteresting—the hasty extrapolation of the second law of thermodynamics, according to which the solar system will cool down and our universe will die a frozen death, an idea that the nineteenth-century imagination found striking, is even mentioned in *Bouvard and Pécuchet*. What is at stake is something different. The new physics brought with it a new

concept of time and history, differing from and subverting the
one postulated by archeology and the *Museum.* What is significant is the fact that Flaubert subscribes to a view of history which
assumes a temporality similar to that predicated by the new
physics.

Before we turn to that subject, however, a remark is in order.
Heat, as the object of thermodynamics, possesses in the literary
imagination of the nineteenth century a number of metaphorical equivalents, in particular, revolutions, gold, and sexuality. It
is interesting to note that Bouvard and Pécuchet encounter all
three of these metaphors without understanding them. They
live through the revolution of 1848 without realizing its historical implications. They disperse, through their financial failures,
a fortune in gold without realizing it. Finally, their attempts at
integrating sexuality into their lives are resounding failures.

Let us return to the problem of history. The Newtonian model
of time displays its object as forever identical to itself, based
upon an eternal, circular, and recurring movement. Time, the
clock as an emblem, moves from point to point, each point considered identical to the others. In this sense, the Newtonian
model moves from point of presence to point of presence and
does not have, intrinsically, a temporality that describes systems
as changing. As Laplace would have it, given Newtonian
mechanics:

> An intelligence that, at a given instant was acquainted with all the
> forces by which Nature is animated and with the state of the bodies
> of which it is composed would—if it were vast enough to submit
> these data to analysis—embrace in the same formula the
> movements of the largest bodies in the Universe and those of the
> lightest atoms: nothing would be uncertain for such an intelli-
> gence, and the future like the past would be present to its eyes.[21]

[21]Quoted in David Layzer, "The Arrow of Time," in *Scientific American,* December 1975, p. 69. The opposition between a geological history and a thermodynamic history runs throughout the nineteenth century. The opposition is
made even more evident by curious attempts, such as Renan's, at synthesizing
the two. For Renan there are three histories: the history of the universe before
the creation of the earth (Laplace's history), the history of the world before the
advent of man (geological history—the history of Cuvier), and finally the history
of man (the history of the sun—thermodynamic history): "The history of our
planet before the advent of man and of life is in some respects beyond our reach

It is easy to see how the model of Newtonian physics and the *Museum* depend epistemologically on the same temporal scheme, for the *Museum* also makes of time a spatial continuum in which each point is equivalent to each other point.

The revolution introduced by thermodynamics is a revolution at the very heart of history. The second principle, so striking to the romantic imagination, states that energy goes from a differentiated to an undifferentiated state. The consequences are enormous; henceforth, systems will move inexorably in a given direction. The process of a history patterned after the new science will be an abolition of differences. Finally, the system has no memory. From the state of the system at a given moment, it is impossible to deduce what conditions were at its origin. In Michel Serres's characterization:

> The final equilibrium à la Fourier or Boltzmann implies an ignorance of initial conditions and of duration. Whatever the origin of history may be, its end is unequivocal, determined, everywhere identical and necessary, no matter what the length of the process is. Universal equilibrium, monotonous distribution, maximum entropy . . . Inevitable, the boltzmanian world is without individualizing memory, it wipes out progressively both memory banks and differences. It has its discrete events, without causal preconditions; it is subject to this single linear law which gives a distribution over an orderless space as the end-point of history. And no matter how long the time necessary, one only need wait; and whatever one may do . . .[22]

---

for it hinges on a less delicate order of things. It is the geologist who, in this context becomes a historian. With the help of general physics, he narrates the transformations that the earth has undergone since the first day it existed as an independent globe . . . . One can truthfully say that the geologist holds the secrets of history. . . .

The *System of the World* of Laplace is the history of a preterrestrial era, the history of the world before the formation of the planet Earth, or if one prefers, of the Earth in its unity with the Sun. In fact, we have reached a point in our reasoning where the history of the world is the history of the sun" (Letter to Marcellin Berthelot in Ernest Renan, *Oeuvres complètes* (Paris: Calmann-Lévy, 1947), I, 638–639.

[22] *Hermes III: La Traduction* (Paris: Minuit, 1974), p. 62. Serres has most convincingly argued for the importance of understanding thermodynamics in order to understand the nineteenth century. My argument is derived entirely from his analysis. On this same subject, see also his *Jouvences sur Jules Verne* (Paris: Minuit, 1974). For a less analytic but more descriptive treatment of the influence of thermodynamics on the romantic imagination, see S. Brush, "Thermodynamics and History," in *The Graduate Journal,* 7 (1967), 477–566.

What thermodynamics makes impossible is a history conceived as archeology. In the long run, the metaphors of thermodynamics will rob Cuvier's geology, as well as the museums of natural or human artifacts, of any epistemological privilege, reducing them to the status of a bric-a-brac collection of disparate objects, which they always were and had remained for the author of *Bouvard and Pécuchet,* despite the illusions of an archeological history.

In contrast to Newtonian history, based upon points of presence, thermodynamics will substitute a notion of history based upon the metaphors of decay, decadence, corruption; in a word, a notion of history based upon any metaphor that can be read as abolishing differences.

Bouvard at one point is overtaken by a "frenzy for manure," and furiously begins to produce fertilizer out of manure, excrement, and anything else he can find that is in an advanced state of decomposition.

> In the compost-trench were flung together boughs, blood, entrails, feathers—everything that could be found. He employed Belgian dressing, Swiss fertilizer, lye, pickled herrings, seaweed, rags; he sent for guano, and tried to manufacture it; then, pushing his tenets to the extreme, would not let any urine be wasted. He suppressed the privies. Dead animals were brought into the yard with which he treated the soil. Their carcasses were scattered over the country in fragments. Bouvard smiled in the midst of the stench. [*BP,* 50]

Bouvard, who was unable to recognize the forces which ushered in the new science, is unable to recognize his emblematic fabrication of the metaphor of the very history in which he is caught and which determines his failures. What escapes the characters does not escape the author, who recognizes in the products of Bouvard the very metaphors of the history in which his work is inscribed: "We are not dancing on a volcano, but on the floorboard of a latrine that seems to me quite rotten. Pretty soon society will go drown itself in nineteen centuries of excrement and they'll scream themselves hoarse."[23] It is then precisely

---

[23]From a letter to Louis Bouilhet in Flaubert's *Correspondance,* ed. Jean Bruneau (Paris: Gallimard, 1973), I, 708.

at the level of the metaphors of decomposition that we must localize the lucid irony that constitutes the distance between the characters and the author, who can but write from where he stands and compose with what history has handed down to him.

> But finally is it not necessary to recognize all the rooms of the heart and the social body, from the cellar to the attic, not even leaving out the latrines; above all not forgetting the latrines! In them are worked out a magical chemistry, fertilizing decompositions are made in them. Who knows to what excremental ooze we owe the perfume of roses and the taste of melons? Has anyone ever counted how many contemptible actions must be contemplated to build the greatness of a soul? How much nauseating pollution one must have swallowed, how much chagrin one must have felt, how many tortures one must have endured, to write one good page? [446]

It is with the rotting by-products of history that one grows tasty melons, not with the botanical taxonomies cherished by Bouvard who "had grown different species next to one another, the sweet variety got mixed with the bitter, the big Portuguese with the great Mongolian, and the presence of tomatoes completing the anarchy, there resulted abominable hybrids of a pumpkin flavour" (*BP*, 48).[24] In the same way that it takes excrement to grow proper melons, it takes the rotting by-products of history and the ruins of the Museum to construct a book such as *Bouvard and Pécuchet*.

In conclusion, then, *Bouvard and Pécuchet* stages within itself the conflict of two epistemologies, one characterized by the *Museum*, the other by a *Force* that escapes the domain of representation, and the undoing of one by the other.

Bouvard and Pécuchet does not so much argue for one system as opposed to the other; rather it denounces the optimism of the first system in the name of the implicit nihilism of the latter. In part an epistemological nihilism that denounces the possibility of ever attaining an essential knowledge of the world, it manifests itself more explicitly as a historical nihilism. The *Museum* displayed history as an eternally present spectacle with transparent

[24]For a reading of this passage in terms of linguistic taxonomies, see my "A Mere Labyrinth of Letters," p. 892.

origins and anthropocentric ends. The history ushered in by thermodynamics is a different one. Origins are forever erased, differences disappear, and the end foreseen is an indifferent universe governed by the laws of chance and statistics. More important, in this perspective, nihilism becomes an event at the end of time, and as such, *Bouvard and Pécuchet* is a book at the end of time about the end of time.

This permits us, perhaps, to read the ending of the novel, from whence we began, as the final state of indifferent events governed purely by chance: "Everything is equal . . . exaltation of the statistical. There are nothing but facts—and phenomena." In this sense the ending of *Bouvard and Pécuchet* and the creation of *The Copy*,[25] "the orderless space" of the text, rather than being emblematic of a literature yet to come, intends, instead, to be damningly prophetic.

[25]Flaubert had projected a second volume for *Bouvard and Pécuchet* which was to be made up of a collage of quotations and was to constitute the "Book" composed by Bouvard and Pécuchet.

LOUIS MARIN

On the Interpretation of Ordinary
Language: A Parable of Pascal

By gathering together in one volume, essays that differ as
much in content as in methods of analysis, the editor of this book
aimed "in concreto" at a theory of the interpretation of literary
texts which includes, as one of its essential propositions, an
axiom regarding the plurality of meaning. This axiom must be
clearly understood: it does not imply that there are *several meanings* and that the truth of the interpretation is dependent upon
the contingency of critical approaches, the arbitrary choice of a
point of view, procedure, or method of analysis, or the oppor-
tuneness (not to say the opportunism) of a historical, social, and
cultural position of critical discourse. It signifies rather that
meaning is plural, that the possible, the latent, and the divergent
enter into its very definition—not just into its speculative definition, but also into its concrete production, be it that of the writer
or that of the reader, of the emitter or the receiver of the message at different moments of history and at different places in
the world and in culture. A truly fundamental theory of interpretation must therefore find its impetus in the elaboration of
a logic of the possible and the plural, a logic of diversity and
divergence in which meaning is not assignable to a closed system
of univocal signs, but in which it is produced and indicates its
processes of production by the displacement of signifiers.

In order to give a sketch of this theory, I have chosen to
analyze some of Pascal's fragments, in which a production of
meaning [*pratique du sens*] seems to be clearly indicated, and in

which, at the same time, we can elaborate the pragmatics that corresponds to this production in interpretative discourse. It is a question here of ordinary language, of the discourse of the "people." The people speak the truth—"their opinions are sound"—but they do not know what they say: "the people are vain, although their opinions are sound, because they do not see the truth when it is there, and assume things to be true when they are not, with the result that their opinions are always thoroughly wrong and unsound" (93).[1] They do not know how to discern "the cause of the effects" [*la raison des effets*] of meaning in their discourse. "Astute men" [*les habiles*][2] and learned men speak like the people, but they know what they say. Still, their knowledge is ignorance, and, in this respect, they find themselves in the same ignorance as the people. They "run through the whole range of human knowledge, only to find that they know nothing and come back to the same ignorance from which they set out, but it is a wise ignorance which knows itself" (83). The dialogic play between the people and the learned men allows Pascal simultaneously to describe ordinary language through the utterance of a political maxim—"we should honour the gentry" (92)—and to criticize this language as a general form of discourse and as a political discourse. From here on, the questions that we will ask starting with the fragments on "the cause of the effects"—questions that seem to lead directly to a specific theory of interpretation—are the following: what is the "true" content (*illusorily* true) of ordinary language and how does the passage from natural ignorance to "knowing ignorance" allow one to discover the truth of the illusion? How and why is it not possible to *speak* this truth, to *construct* the theory of ordinary

[1]This and all further quotations followed by a simple number in parentheses are taken from Pascal, *Pensées*, trans. A. J. Krailsheimer (Harmondsworth, England: Penguin, 1966). The numbers are those of the individual *pensées* and follow the order of the Lafuma edition. Brackets indicate necessary adjustments in the translation by the editor.

[2]The seventeenth-century concept of *l'habile* is extremely complicated; no one English word expresses its full meaning. Gaston Cayrou's *Le Français classique* defines the concept, in part, as follows: *l'habile* has "not only facility of assimilation, but also a judgment that is both quick and profound, as well as a sharp and extensive discernment." For the purposes of this translation, "astute man" will be employed for *habile*.—Ed.

language while unveiling its structure? How and why will this structure appear to us as a structure of *referral* [*renvoi*] or *displacement* toward a discourse, a text that is always "other," resembling in this the structure of the biblical parable, a genre that might well constitute the "model" of Pascalian discourse, and whose characteristic is to offer itself immediately to interpretation while making it impossible to confine it to a univocal allegorization.

The Parabolic Narrative of the
First Discourse on the Condition of the Great

Let us examine the political example: what does the astute man discern which the people do not recognize and which yet allows him to use their language? "We should honour the gentry but not because gentle birth is a real advantage, etc." (92). It so happens that Pascal occupies the astute man's discursive position, and practices his discourse of discernment by putting on stage a character who, in the circumstances of fiction in which he finds himself, necessarily discovers what the people and the gentry dissimulate in their ordinary discourses while letting a truth surface in the formula of the maxim that they utter. It is in the exercise of astute discourse undertaken by Pascal as subject of the speech-act that the unformulable theory of discourse is indicated. The *Three Discourses on the Condition of the Great* provide the text of this theory:

> A man was cast by a tempest upon an unknown island the inhabitants of which were [anxious] to find their king who was lost; and [bearing] a strong resemblance both [corporally and facially] to this king, he was taken for him and acknowledged in this capacity by all the people. At first he knew not what course to take; but he finally resolved to give himself up to his good fortune. He received all the homage that they chose to render, and suffered himself to be treated as a king. [*Discourse*, p. 382][3]

---

[3]This and all further quotations followed by *Discourse* and a page number are taken from Pascal, *Discourses on the Condition of the Great,* in *Blaise Pascal,* the Harvard Classics, ed. Charles W. Eliot (New York: P. F. Collier, 1910). Brackets indicate necessary adjustments in the translation by the editor.

The castaway—in this exceptional circumstance—thinks and acts
in a state of separation: he acts as a king but he thinks as a man
by recognizing his true state and the hazardous contingency of
his royal position. "He concealed the latter thought, and revealed the other. It was by the former that he [dealt] with the
people, and by the latter that he [dealt] with himself" (*Discourse,*
p. 383). If this is the initial parable, one must nevertheless note
that in its second part the narrative continually shifts toward its
own interpretation: as narration, it already encompasses the
constituent elements of its code, since the fictive character is
analyzed by the narrator and presented in his motivations and
behavior as an astute man. Even at this point, Pascal's interlocutor is no longer fictively one of the island's subjects, an in-
habitant of this kingdom whose king has vanished; from now on,
he shares the secret of a political and social behavior, since he
sees the castaway act as a king. He also shares the secret of the
castaway's judgment on his own behavior, the thought the castaway hides from the people. Nevertheless, this thought is also a
thought that hides and dissimulates. Indeed, from here on the
decoding of the narrative (which is presented as an "image") is at
work in the narrative itself, and it is this code and its rules that,
quite naturally, the text presents: "Do not imagine that it is less
an accident by which *you* find yourself master of the wealth
which you possess" (*Discourse,* p. 383). This code is precisely the
one that suits the interlocutor (the young duke addressed by
Pascal in the second person) as an "other" who enters into a
dialogic situation with an "I" who, for the moment, appears in
the utterance only through this "other" whom he addresses.
This dialogic situation defined in its sociopolitical specificity
masks, at the same time, the other possible codes, the "potential
of meaning" generated by the fictive narrative—and also masks
speculative or theoretical discourses (or even theological or
spiritual ones) that could, by the rigorous play of comparisons
and *rapprochements,* articulate other codes of the narrative.

In effect, however, in the passage from the narrative third
person to the first person of the cosmological imagination, does
not the speculative discourse appear in the parable, as well as in
the following fragments? "I see the terrifying spaces of the universe hemming me in, and I find myself attached to one corner

of this vast expanse.... I only see infinity on every side, hemming me in like an atom" (427, para. 13); "When I consider the brief span of my life absorbed into the eternity which comes before and after ... the small space I occupy and which I see swallowed up in the infinite immensity of spaces of which I know nothing,... I ... am amazed to see myself here rather than there" (68); "let him regard himself as lost [in this canton turned away from nature] and in this little dungeon, in which he finds himself lodged, I mean the universe, let him take the earth, its realms, its cities ... and himself at their proper value" (199, para. 4). The tempest that casts the man upon the unknown island could well be the theoretical cosmological "tempest" that, by breaking the stable certitudes of a closed world for a universe with neither limits nor center,[4] has put the subject of knowledge in a position of total contingency.[5] Is not the lost king Man, who was formerly the center of the world and who finds himself dispossessed of this center in an epistemological situation that Pascal perceives tragically? "All these examples of wretchedness prove [man's] greatness. It is the wretchedness of a great lord, the wretchedness of a dispossessed king" (116).

At another level, however, is not the true lost king God himself, who withdrew from men, who hid himself from their knowledge as manifested by the very name that He gave himself in the Scriptures, *Deus absconditus* (427, para. 1)? Pascal says that Nature is "the presence of a God [who hides himself from the eyes of those who try to see God in it]" (449, paras. 13–16). In addition, is the man cast upon the unknown island not a return of the hidden God? "He remained concealed under the veil of Nature that [hid him from us until] the Incarnation; and when it was necessary that he should appear, he concealed himself still the more in covering himself with humanity.... All things cover

[4]Cf. A. Koyré, *From the Closed World to the Infinite Universe* (New York: Harper Torchbooks, 1958).
[5]*Pensée* 198: "When I see the blind and wretched state of man, when I survey the whole universe in its dumbness and man left to himself with no light, as though lost in this corner of the universe, without knowing who put him there, what he has come to do, what will become of him when he dies, incapable of knowing anything, I am moved to terror, *like a man transported in his sleep to some terrifying desert island,* who wakes up quite lost and with no means to escape" (my emphasis).

some mystery; all things have veils that cover God."[6] In this way another discourse is superimposed upon the first in order to overdetermine the parable, and to convey still another meaning: the three discourses of knowledge, power, and "charity" (or desire) become implicit simultaneously in the same narrative. Because the plurality of meaning has been produced in this way, the dialogic situation limits this plurality to a single decoding, while still conserving it in the narrative itself. At the end of the discourse addressed by Pascal to the young duke, the dialogue opens the text to its other possibilities of meaning: "We should honour the gentry but not because gentle birth is a real advantage, etc." (92). One must act as a king and think as a man, but not because the sociopolitical order, even an upright one, is the truth of man, the place of judgment. . . .

The Sociopolitical Code

One must obey the injunctions of Pascalian discourse in its dialogic situation and recognize the first articulation of discourse in the parabolic narrative as political discourse. Pascal carries out a very careful "decoding" of the "image." The chance occurrence by which this man finds himself owner of the kingdom is no different from the one that makes the young duke a master of wealth. Neither the castaway nor the nobleman has a natural right over these things. In other words, the right of neither has a natural foundation; both are based only upon the arbitrariness of imagination and the chance occurrences of the tempest and of circumstances. The duke's ownership of his possessions is doubtless legitimate, since the legitimacy of possession is in no way identified with a natural right, but is founded on that very law by which this ownership is made legitimate.[7] Thus, the argument of the narrative—"this man possessed his kingdom only through

[6]Pascal, *Letters to Mademoiselle de Roannez,* in *Blaise Pascal,* pp. 354–355.

[7]*Pensée* 60: " . . . Nothing is so defective as those laws which correct defects. Anyone obeying them because they are just is obeying an imaginary justice, not the essence of the law which is completely self-contained: it is law and nothing more. . . . The truth about the usurpation must not be made apparent: it came about originally without reason and has become reasonable. We must see that it is regarded as authentic and eternal, and its origins must be hidden if we do not want it soon to end."

the error of the people" (*Discourse,* p. 384)—describes only a situation of "beginning," while the duke's ownership of his own goods is, in reality, founded in all legitimacy. God's authorization only concerns the regulation of societies by laws and, very precisely, by the law of ownership. It permits their validation; it does not establish their value rationally.

One last nuance is introduced between the code and the narrative: the double thought by which the castaway behaves as king and man is a factual necessity in the narrative—"as *he could not forget* his [natural] condition" (*Discourse,* p. 382)—for otherwise he would have been prey to madness or stupidity. This factual necessity is that of the fictive situation—in the narrative—but it is also a situation of "beginning" in the code. On the other hand, this double thought is a rule or norm for the young duke to observe: "you *should* have a double thought" (*Discourse,* p. 384). It is the passage from *fact* to *right* like that from the parabolic narrative fiction of the beginning to the present reality of a sociopolitical situation that can no longer admit anything other than injunctions and prescriptions.

One perceives how narrative and code function in relation to each other in the construction of Pascalian discourse: the first narrative is (in its textual manifestation) the figural development of the notion of chance occurrence contained in the second code. This notion appears in the narrative only in the form of an "image," without being expressly manifested: the tempest, the disappearance of the island's king, the shipwreck, and finally the castaway's corporal and facial resemblance to the lost king, are all so many figures of contingency, the notion of which permits the deciphering of the parabolic narrative by another narrative which is unveiled in its turn, as it comes into contact with the "parable," at a point of articulation marked by the term "chance occurrence." This other narrative is the biographical "structure" of the interlocutor: his birth as son of a duke, his finding himself "in" the world, the marriage of his parents and all those of his ancestors, a thousand unforeseen events which left their mark on his family and whose narration would constitute the family tradition (*Discourse,* p. 384). This real biographical structure becomes, in turn, a figurative narrative, through its relation to the figures of the parabolic narrative that precedes it textually; in its essence, the biographical structure is fiction. The function of the parabolic narrative therefore appears through an ambiguity which gives it a great practical efficacy: the parable designates in its fiction a real narrative (situation, position) that it assimilates to itself in the process of showing that this narrative is the revealing figure of one term of the code by which the parable was encoded into a fictive narrative. The parable functions as an explanation, but a figurative one; it shows, it designates, but as *figure;* it introduces into this explanation a "play" of the imaginary that provokes new explanations.

The mechanism must be taken apart in order to exhibit the operation of the astute man's discourse. What is he showing? That "the right which you have [to your possessions] is not founded ... upon any quality or any merit in yourself which renders you worthy of it. Your soul and your body are, of themselves, equally indifferent to the state of boatman or to that of duke; and there is no natural bond that attaches them to one condition rather than to another" (*Discourse,* p. 384). This is the astute man's thesis, the object of his discernment whose nature neither the people nor the nobleman grasps; he perceives that there is no bond between body and soul on the one hand and social condition on the other, neither resemblance nor difference, but rather a lack of difference which is the sign of a natural difference prohibiting, by definition, any type of natural bond. Furthermore, in the parable itself, the island castaway *corporally and facially resembles* the lost king so much that he is taken for him and recognized in this capacity by all the people. The parable therefore bases its own commentary on a factual resemblance; it signifies first that a king is a body and a face, that he is defined by exteriority (*Discourse,* p. 384). The fact that there is no structural or causal, no rational or rationally justifiable relationship between merit (stemming from a natural quality) and the mastery of wealth on the one hand and of external power in sociopolitical reality on the other, is shown by the mimetic relationship that permits the castaway to be king: it is the relationship of resemblance which, in fiction, authorizes the criticism and negation of the relationship, in reality, of proportion and congruence [*adéquation*]. In other words, it is because the notion of representation articulates the whole of the astute man's discourse that this discourse can turn the notion of representation back against itself in its contents. If there is a relationship of resemblance between the castaway and the king, if there is a relationship of analogy between the situation recounted by the parabolic narrative and that of the duke's son, if representation functions as fiction at the origin of discourse, this signifies, in the end, that the true king is a false king, that the true and real son of a duke cannot and must not be honored under the pretense that gentle birth is a real advantage, that the real mastery of wealth does not refer to a natural merit, and, in short, that representation is without value in reality. The fictive or figurative use of representation is the other side of the critique of representation in the discourse on social and political reality.

But it is necessary to pursue further the parabolic narrative's "provocations." The people honor the castaway because he corporally and facially resembles the king they sought; they actually posit the relation of resemblance, even if by mistake they transform the representational relationship to one of identity, even if they take the representer for the represented, in the visibility of his perfect resemblance. Therefore, the people *believe* that nobility is a real greatness; as a consequence, they consider noblemen to be of *another nature* than their own (*Discourse,* p. 384). The nobleman himself in turn believes that *his being* is in essence superior to that of others (ibid.). These beliefs, these opinions—which link the people and the noblemen in the same order of respect and "legitimate" domination—are all real, all effective. Better still, the discourse that expresses these opinions states "a truth, but one which is not where [the people] imagine it to be": an illusion of truth whose truth is established by the astute man's discourse, a critical discourse that unveils an ideology still unaware of itself and demonstrates through its discursive practice how this ideology is produced. We say "through its discursive practice" because the role and function of the parable will be to trace this production in the play of parabolic fiction.

The people believe that nobility is a real and heterogeneous greatness. The nobleman believes that his own being is somehow superior to that of others: in other words, the people posit a relationship of equivalence between nobility and real greatness, a relationship which the noble brings about or reifies: it is *his being* that is somehow superior. One must stress how, in the discursive expression itself, the structural or causal relation—which is *false,* but *really* posited by an act of belief—is transformed into an ontological identity, how the copula "to be" in the utterance formulated by the people is transformed into an ontological affirmation. In addition, the nobleman's *being* results from the interiorization of a relationship posited in the social setting: it is this relationship that constitutes the self by determining its position. *Being* itself is therefore defined as the metaphor or the interiorization of a relationship. As a result, the nobleman is engaged in a double process of misunderstanding and illusion (*Discourse,* p. 384): misunderstanding of the movement of interiorizing, of making his own, a social relation defined by the irreducible exteriority of an other to the self, and the illusion that results from this misunderstanding, that his being is his own, while it is merely a relation external to him seized in the discourse and behavior of the other. Is this not a remarkable approach to ideology?

The Production of Ideology and the Function of Representation

The parabolic narrative is the fictive mediation between two heterogeneities, one normative or ideal, which would define *honnêteté*[8] in the sociopolitical field, the other factual and real, which articulates this same field concretely. The first is the object and goal of the astute man's discourse; there is no natural link between the social status of duke or boatman and their respective merits, that is, the qualities of body and soul. The second is the real situation, the object of Pascalian discourse, the content of the people's utterance, the real attitude of the people and the noblemen: a duke's corporal and spiritual qualities and those of a boatman are different in nature; they are heterogeneous and, simultaneously, there is between the duke and the boatman a

---

[8]Cayrou's *Le Français classique* defines *l'honnête* as "a nobleman who possessed not only the gifts of noble birth, but also those of the body and of a cultivated mind." *L'honnêteté* (the quality of being *honnête*) was the social ideal of the aristocracy in seventeenth-century France.—Ed.

difference naturally founded on their own merits. The diagram shows these two opposed models.

$$
\begin{array}{c}
\text{A} \\
\text{(II) C} \quad
\dfrac{\text{Social status: duke} \quad \Big| \quad \text{Qualities of the body and the soul: merit}}{\text{Social status: boatman} \quad \Big| \quad \text{Qualities of the body and the soul: merit}} \quad \text{D} \\
\text{B} \\
\text{(I)}
\end{array}
$$

The line AB is a line of heterogeneity which shows the break between two orders of greatness, the natural and the institutional. This is a normative model of the ordered conception of real society, of its true discourse: such is the object of the astute man's discernment in his instructive discourse addressed to the duke's son. On the other hand, the line CD is the line of another heterogeneity which articulates not only real society according to the distance between two classes or two social conditions, but also the real valorizations of these conditions, that is, the individual merits and the corporal and spiritual qualities attached to them. The instructive critical discourse must effect the rotation of CD onto AB, or to be more exact, it must make apparent in model II (CD) the oversight or miscognizance of model I (that is, of the heterogeneity inscribed by AB); it must permit the discernment of I in II. It does not, however, transform—how could it through a simple discursive practice?—the model schematized in II into that which model I "represents": critical discernment is not a practical transformation, and the incisive discovery of the ideology of a society or of a social group may well remain, in practice, caught up in this ideology, although the discourse that produces the ideology keeps its distance from it.

The corporal and facial resemblance that makes of the castaway the *portrait* of the king, his "representation," allows the people to *have* a (false) king or the castaway to *be* a (false) king; but at the same time, the play of the same mimetic representation permits the castaway to *think* of himself not as a (true) king but as a (true) man. Mimetic representation simultaneously authorizes not only the "simulation" of the real situation by the model, but also the ideal normative operation which puts, although only in the model, being and function, the natural situation and the role, at a distance from each other. From then on, the model functions not only as an epistemological instrument, but also as an ethical and normative example. This double game of representation, which on the one hand "translates" reality into the model, and which on the other transforms only the representation and not the reality that it represents, constitutes the astute critical discourse that Pascal uses when speaking to the young duc de Chevreuse. In this discourse, the role of the transforming practice, of the real criticism of society, is held by the parabolic narrative, by the narrative fiction which, because it is the image of reality and only its image, is the locus of operations that are certain only in this locus of fiction. These transformations will become, in the pedagogic discourse, a rhetorical exhortation to a subjective moral conversion.[9] Yet there is something in addition which, in our care to stress the ideological character of the astute man's discourse that criticizes ideology, we risked not recognizing.

We must return to the corporal and facial resemblance between the castaway and the lost king which is the pivotal point of the fiction and which allows for the astute man's discourse of discernment: because the castaway's body and face reproduce those of the king, he becomes king. The violence that consists in taking a sign as the reproduction of the being it represents escapes unnoticed, and the people receive this false king with the same marks of respect that they would have shown to the true one. Here then is signaled, in the fiction itself, the ideological operation of representation by which the idea of reality, its reproduced sign, is taken for reality itself. This is a violent operation whose violence is dissimulated by the operation itself in that this operation remains only reproductive. If model II (CD) is the model of ideology, the parabolic narrative is then the model of the production of ideology. This model shows that reality (the true king) is reproduced in the form of a sign (the castaway who resembles him) which, substituting itself for reality, becomes reality (the false king accepted as true).

In order to understand the importance of this transformation, let us vary the narrative freely on this point: we could then read

---

[9] *Discourse,* p. 384; in the *Third Discourse* we also find a collection of "exhortative imperatives" (p. 387).

here what we read in many historical tales and narratives: "A man was cast by a tempest upon an unknown island, the inhabitants of which were anxious to find their king, who was lost; and as this man was very good and very virtuous, he was taken for king and recognized in this capacity by all the people." The narrative would continue to function as a model, but a weakened one, not of reality, certainly, but of moral exhortation: "It is by being very good and very virtuous that the castaway was able to become king in place of the true one. In the same way, you yourself...." In fact, the parabolic narrative is not only in a structural, but also in a mimetic proximity to the two models that articulate the two poles of the discursive situation: reality and the rational norm. First, a continuity of content exists between the narrative and the discourse that interprets it; both deal with force, usurpation of power, respect, and attitudes toward the institution. Still, if no pure and simple repetition exists between the two levels of the narrative and its interpretation, it is because the form of perfect reproduction, of visible and faithful representation embodied in the "castaway," introduces an effective displacement of signification with regard to the two models produced by this analysis: that of the real situation and that of sociopolitical *honnêteté*. As "look-alike" [*sosie*], the castaway is automatically king; as double, he is immediately the other-as-same; this is certainly representation, but indicated only in order to show how representation in its purity functions ideologically. The signifier takes the place of the referent and hides it: there is a usurpation of power by the initial violence of the substitution. The signifier (the castaway as body and face) takes the place of the lost king.

One final remark must be made on this point. We have said that the parabolic narrative mediates between two heterogeneities; still, this mediation precedes that which it mediates, since the text, when read, opens onto the "image" of the castaway. Model I (AB) is the "originary" truth of the text's content, the heterogeneity between states and conditions on the one hand, and between qualities and merits on the other. Model II (CD) is the "present" reality of the sociopolitical situation: the image precedes its original, and the simulacrum the situation whose simulation it makes possible. Still, is it not fiction which makes

252   *Louis Marin*

possible the "construction," the articulation of the original, and also permits it to be treated as a signifier? Inversely, however, the fictive narrative can only appear retroactively in its explicative and normative efficacy in relation to the ideal of *honnêteté* I (AB) and the real situation II (CD), since only the opening parable shows what this ideal effaces in its perfect discernment, in the peaceful separation of the nobleman and the man. Only the parable shows what the real situation dissimulates in the real experience of institutional power and of its external signs: that the nobleman is a man whose power is not founded naturally. The parable therefore appears fundamental to us: it opens the text and makes it work with a view toward producing a plural meaning. Through fiction as a discursive equivalent of the transforming process, the parabolic discourse shows how ideology conceals truth or misconstrues it.

The Thought in the Back of the Mind: The Effect of the Infinite

Here then the discourse of the astute man, whose position Pascal occupies in his dialogue with the young duke, terminates. The parabolic narrative permits us to understand simultaneously the illusion of truth shared by the people and the noblemen in their discourse, and the truth of the illusion of this same discourse, which is spoken as a true discourse, truth being constituted by the very possibility of *speaking* it: it is the very fact of saying and being able to say "we must honour the gentry" that makes truth appear in the relation (transposed into discourse) of master to subject, of dominator to dominated. Still, we also know that the astute man knows nothing, or rather that he knows he knows nothing (83) and that, in this way, speculatively, he resembles the people in their ignorance. In other words, it is the contents of knowledge in the astute man's discourse that give way to the form of his knowledge, that is, to his discourse. The astute man's only knowledge is that he knows nothing; this knowledge is form without meaningful content, pure discourse, not empty but with its contents continually being eroded at the very moment they are uttered. The parabolic narrative of the *First Discourse on the Condition of the Great* indicates this: the castaway-become-king is a representation of the politically astute man who is simultaneously *honnête* and effective; he is a figure of this man. What then does this narrative which is the "image" of the discourse that corresponds to it and that it transposes reveal? It shows us that the thought by which the castaway deals with himself *annuls* and *invalidates* the action by which he deals with others. It does not annul his action in itself: the castaway continues to act, but his thought invalidates his action as the action of a king, effacing its intrinsic value, since he can perceive it only as the action of a false king, a usurper. "The thought in the back of his mind" (*Discourse,* p. 383) is the center of this corrosive action, but it is a thought, a form, and not an action. It is a judgment which leaves action, and in particular political action, intact: he acts as a king and receives all the respect that the people want to give him, but he knows that he is not king, that he is nothing but a castaway, thrown by chance upon an unknown island.

This knowledge of the usurper's true state, knowledge of being-nothing, is—in the speculative discourse into which it becomes transposed—a knowledge of nonknowledge, a science of nonscience acquired at the extremity of judgment, at a point where the latter reverts, in an instant, to its contrary: ignorance (ibid.). This movement defines the condition which governs the possibility of meaning in ordinary discourse in general, by a negative designation of its locus, that is, a thought in the back of the mind which tends to make all determined *contents* of knowledge equal to zero. This thought is that of the infinite, by which the formal identity between knowledge and nonknowledge operates:[10] just as, on the level of political practice as represented in fiction, the astute usurper continues to act as king, so the learned man, on the speculative level, continues to augment his knowledge quantitatively; in thinking about the infinite, however, he discovers that he has not left (that he cannot leave) the state of natural ignorance which he had seemed to have left so long ago. The semi-learned man knows no less than the learned man. Like the duke's companions in the realm of power and its natural legitimation, the semi-learned man thinks and believes that in

[10]Pascal, *Of the Geometrical Spirit,* in *Blaise Pascal,* p. 444; *Pensée* 199.

the realm of learning it is possible—and it is, in fact, possible—
for knowledge to develop in a linear and cumulative progression
(199, para. 11). This progress by accumulation is the *real* situation of science and knowledge (which Pascal heralds in the *Preface to the Treatise on the Vacuum*[11]) just as the nobleman's situation
of power and mastery is real through institutional rights. In an
instant, however, the "thought of the infinite" converts this
knowledge into ignorance. The astute man's learned ignorance
is nothing other than a form of knowledge (the "knowledge of
the infinite") that makes all content of knowledge equal to zero;
in the same way, the thought in the back of the castaway's mind,
without ever keeping him from acting as a king, transforms in an
instant his kingly action into that of a usurper and invalidates the
action. But do politics deal essentially with values? Does knowledge deal essentially with the infinite? Quite obviously not: consequently, the castaway, in his secret thoughts, deals with the
man that he is, and not with the king that he seems to be. This is
also why the geometrician strives—even if it entails using everyday language—to constitute certain principles as "ultimate,
which seem so to our reason, as in material things [when] we call
a point indivisible when our senses can perceive nothing beyond
it, although by its nature it is infinitely divisible" (199, para. 14).
Therefore semi-learned people are not a dialectic mediation between the two manifestations of knowledge: zero-knowledge at
one extreme, and the infinite form of knowledge at the other;
they represent neither a dialectic synthesis nor a progressive
totalization. The same ignorance which was present at the point
of departure is rediscovered at the end but, in truth, there is
neither point of departure nor end; the quest has always already
begun. The "thought of the infinite" (the thought that makes all
content of knowledge equal to zero) transcends the realm in
which the quest for knowledge is pursued: it is other, of another
realm.[12]

The truth or the illusion of truth contained by the ordinary
discourse of the people resides here, at this point of the infinite
(or at infinity) that makes all the utterances of the discourse

[11] In *Blaise Pascal*, pp. 51, 53–54.
[12] *Of the Geometrical Spirit*, pp. 442–443.

equal, that is, equal to zero and yet all stating this point, but without knowing it. Pascal also refers to this destruction of the discourse in its contents as mockery: "To mock philosophy is to philosophize truly" (513). Thus, in the fragment "We always picture Plato and Aristotle . . .," which deals directly with politics, play, laughter, and diversion constitute the truth of the attitude of great minds in philosophy and in politics. False appearances, a superior mockery in which one plays at not laughing, introduce the interlocutor into this truth of the illusion of truth inherent in philosophical discourse: "If they [Plato and Aristotle] wrote about politics, it was as if to lay down rules [to govern] a madhouse. And if they pretended to treat it as something really important, it was because they knew that the madmen they were addressing believed themselves to be kings and emperors. They humoured these beliefs in order to calm down [the madmen] with as little harm [to them] as possible" (533). This is why living simply and tranquilly is, by a new twist, "the most philosophical part" of their lives (ibid.). Immediate and naive existence provides the very form of zero-knowledge, the natural ignorance that, "at the end" of the discourse of learning annuls its contents by the mockery of the infinite, by the fulgurating action of the judgment pronounced at this "point": one must think about everything starting from a thought in the back of the mind.

"*The cause of the effects.* One must have a thought in the back [of one's mind] and judge everything accordingly, but go on talking like an ordinary person" (91). Alien to ordinary discourse, the thought in the back of the mind is also its truth, since it judges it. But it is equally *in* the discourse as what is uttered, since it is possible to speak like the people (91). Such is the paradox encountered from the start, which appears again here in a new form: the meaning is certainly in the words, since it is their meaning, and yet it is "other," elsewhere, displaced in relation to their enunciation. Otherwise ordinary discourse would be the very discourse of truth, which it is not. Instead, it is merely the "opinions of vain people." The thought in the back of the mind, in this way, hollows out ordinary discourse, in its spoken immediacy, creating an internal distance which makes its utterance alien to its enunciation, decentering it from the subject who formulates it, disappropriating it from the self who offers it as an expression of himself, of his beliefs, and of his opinions, in order to make ordinary discourse into a speech "totally other" without modifying its form; in this "otherness," in this distancing [*retrait*] of the discourse in relation to itself, its true meaning appears.

Judgment

This distancing is the very operation of "judgment," the act of the thought in the back of the mind. Yet the judgment whose locus is the thought in the back of the mind is a unitary, indivisible, unanalyzable act. As such, it is radically opposed to reasoning, which is articulated in a logical sequence of principles and consequences (512). Judgment is not and cannot be analyzed as a comparison of two ideas, as the attribution of a predicate to a subject, as an operation of synthesis. "The [object of judgment] must be seen all at once, at a glance, and not as a result of progressive reasoning, at least up to a point" (512, para. 4; also 751). However, those principles which make up this object, that is, its elements or parts, "are in common usage and before everyone's eyes." All that is needed is good vision, but it must be good. Why? Because "the principles are so intricate and numerous that it is almost impossible not to miss some" (512, para. 2). Judgment is therefore first of all feeling, the "immediate and with one glance" apprehension of the multitude of principles in the oneness of the object, and then the sharp penetration into the consequences of these principles by *one* act which in the same movement reconciles the contrary qualities of the sociopolitical order (512).

Judgment that grasps the object in its oneness is the "position of the infinite" as the dynamic constituent of this thought. The thought in the back of the mind is, in judgment, the position, the point or indivisible locus—but is it actually discernible?—from which "one must... judge everything" (91), from which thoughts are annulled, leaving room only for simple and naive existence and for its discourse, ordinary discourse. Pascal will therefore regard the "style of... Solomon de Tultie [as] the commonest... because it consists entirely of thoughts deriving from everyday conversations" (746). Judgment therefore discovers that the ordinary discourses of men are true in their illusion, their errors, and their falseness, to the extent that they are the immediate "language of real life." It discovers this negatively, however, by discovering that a theory of the language of real life is impossible because the infinite is not a speculative object: this impossibility grounds the truth of ordinary discourse (as form) in the language of daily existence, that is, as an ignorance which is the *true* locus of man.[13] In its behavior and in its discourse, the mind ordinarily *acts*[14] in accord with units and totalities which are never exhaustively analyzed. It is not possible to transpose this action of natural existence into a speculative discourse that would reflect it according to geometric order and reconstruct its meaning and its psycho-physiological mechanisms *partes extra partes:* "*Descartes.* In general terms one must say: 'that is the result of figure and motion,' because it is true, but to name them and assemble the machine is quite ridiculous" (84). To express this is beyond all men. It is possible, however—and this is the astute man's role—to know that it is impossible and why, and at the same time to discover that the most philosophical part of life is to live simply and tranquilly.

The beginning of the *First Discourse* (*Discourse,* pp. 382–383), as we have seen, presents an "image" on which the rest of the text is a commentary. By dealing thus with the political example of the condition of Great Men which the fragments of the *Pensées* did not include in the typology of ordinary discourses, Pascal employs in his own discourse, and reveals through it, the very essence of ordinary discourse in general, namely, its signifying structure in the form of a parable. His narrative announces a

---

[13]*Pensée* 512, and notably: "Thus it is rare for mathematicians to be intuitive or for the intuitive to be mathematicians, because mathematicians try to treat these intuitive matters mathematically, and make themselves ridiculous, by trying to begin with definitions followed by principles, which is not the way to proceed in this kind of reasoning. It is not that the mind does not do this, but it does so *tacitly, naturally and artlessly, for it is beyond any man to express it and given to very few even to apprehend it*" (my emphasis).

[14]*Pensée* 821, and particularly: "Reason works slowly, looking so often at so many principles which must always be present, that it is constantly nodding or straying . . . . Feeling does not work like that, but works instantly, and is always ready."

truth which it totally encloses in the fiction of narration. Its commentary on this truth does not constitute a definitive interpretation; rather its explanation of it is still a sort of veiling, since true understanding of the narrative begins at the moment when the discourse ceases. Pascal's narrative is an encoded one that opens the *discourses* that will simultaneously explain and obscure it. It is a narrative whose code is given and carefully analyzed, but which is powerless to make this code's meaning appear; its meaning will appear when we know at the end of the given explanations that our ignorance is total: "learned ignorance, which knows itself, but which is the same as that of the people" from which we started. By analyzing the Pascalian practice of ordinary discourse as parabolic discourse in this political text, we have tried to bring out what Pascal left to the intradiscursive process alone, the dialogic relationship between himself and the young duc de Chevreuse. We have tried to formulate a set of theoretical propositions which, by explicitly uncovering this dialogic structure and its implications, will constitute it as a pragmatics of discourse.

By carefully decoding the political meaning of the "parable-image," Pascal offers his interlocutor the choice of a meaning, but in perceiving this meaning from the injunctions of the Pascalian discourse, the young duke dissimulates from himself the other meanings, that plurality of meaning which the political meaning conceals yet indicates, without making it possible for the discourse itself or its speaker to state, outside of fiction, this multiple meaning, to fix it in a meaning that would be *the* meaning. The discourse becomes in itself an opaque object and, by a new twist, this very opacity, this secret, is—if not meaning—at least the instrument of meaning. "[Jesus Christ and St. Paul possess an organization guided by charity, not by the mind, for they wished to humble, not to teach. The same with St. Augustine. The principal function of this organization consists in digressing upon each point which relates to the end, in order to point constantly to this end]" (298). A striking paradox closes the explanatory commentary on the "parable-image." Everything has been said, the political meaning explored and made explicit, the code of the fiction unveiled with precision, and the theoretical models traced with exactitude in their representational function. Pascal adds: "What I tell you does not go very far; and if you stop there you will not save yourself from being [damned]: but at least you will be [damned like an *honnête homme*]. . . . The way which I open to you [to damn yourself] is doubtless the most honorable; but in truth it is always a great folly for a man to expose himself to damnation; and therefore he must not stop at this. . . . Others than I will show you the way to this" (*Discourse*, p. 387). The perception of meaning was a dissimulation of another meaning, a meaning that the parable already told in telling the first, but without knowing that it was saying it. Such is, briefly sketched, the movement of discernment that traverses the learned man's discourse; to speak the fiction, the narrative, then to state yet another meaning encoded in the narrative's primitive meaning—this is the astute man's role—then, this meaning unveiled, to indicate that this unveiling is still a concealment of meaning, though a practical one ("you will expose yourself to damnation"), a simultaneous opening-up and distancing in which there appears yet another meaning that was already stated but only in the *language* of the parable—and this is the role of Pascalian discourse. "I *too* will have thoughts in the back of my mind" (797).

> "Why do you speak to them in parables?" And then he answered them, "To you it has been given to know the secrets of the kingdom of heaven, but to them it has not been given. For to him who has, will more be given, and he will have abundance; but from him who has not, even what he has will be taken away. This is why I speak to them in parables, because seeing they do not see, and hearing they do not hear, nor do they understand." [Matthew 13:10–13]

MICHEL SERRES

The Algebra of Literature: The Wolf's Game

THE WOLF AND THE LAMB

The reason of the strongest is always the best.[1]
We will show this shortly.
A Lamb quenched his thirst
In the current of a pure stream,
A fasting Wolf arrives, looking for adventure,
And whom hunger draws to this place.
"Who makes you so bold as to muddy my drink?"
Said the animal, full of rage:
"You will be punished for your temerity."
"Sire," answers the Lamb, "may it please Your Majesty
Not to become angry;
But rather let Him consider
That I am quenching my thirst
In the stream,
More than twenty steps below Him;
And that, as a result, in no way
Can I muddy His drink."
"You muddy it," responded this cruel beast;
"And I know that you slandered me last year."
"How could I have done so, if I had not yet been born?"
Responded the Lamb; "I am not yet weaned."
"If it is not you, then it is your brother."
"I do not have any." "Then it is one of your clan;
For you hardly spare me,
You, your shepherds, and your dogs.
I have been told: I must avenge myself."
Upon which, deep into the woods
The Wolf carries him off, and then eats him,
Without any other form of *procès*.

[1]As Serres's article will show, "La raison du *plus fort* est toujours la *meilleure*" can also be understood as meaning "the reason of the stronger is always better."—Ed.

The notion of structure, recently discovered in the realm of methodology, has an algebraic origin. It designates a set of elements whose number and nature are not specified, a set provided with one or more operations, one or more relations which possess well-defined characteristics. If one specifies the number and nature of the elements of the structure and the nature of the operations, then its model becomes evident. Perhaps the simplest example is that of an *ordered structure*. It designates a set of elements provided with an *ordering relation*. Let there be for example three points *A, B,* and *C* on a line *D,* and a direction defined by the arrow. The ordering relation between these three points, which are elements of the set, can be one of "predecession" or of succession. *A* precedes *B,* which precedes *C. C,* in

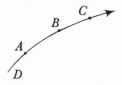

turn, is the successor of B, which succeeds A. One sees immediately that no point is its own predecessor or successor: the relation is irreflexive. If, on the other hand, *A* precedes *B,* it is impossible for *B* to precede *A*; the relation is antisymmetric. Finally, if *A* precedes *B* and if *B* precedes *C,* then *A* precedes *C*: the relation is transitive. An ordering relation is irreflexive, antisymmetric and transitive. An ordered structure is a set provided with such a relation. The reader must excuse these prolegomena, which come from basic mathematics.

We are in the countryside, beside a stream; but let us forget all this for a moment—except the fable's last words: the "form of the *procès*." This term has at least two meanings: the judicial meaning (trial), and the etymological meaning (process). A process includes a predecession and a succession: it is an order. Question: what is, first of all, the form of the trial, to wit, and the form of the process? Here the form is a reason, a ratio, a connection, a relation.

"The reason of the stronger" is definitely an ordering relation. *A* cannot be stronger than itself. *A*'s being stronger than *B* excludes *B*'s being stronger than *A,* and if *A* is stronger than *B,* and *B* is stronger than *C,* it follows that *A* is stronger than *C.* In the set of animals present, being stronger clearly defines an ordered structure. This is the first (we will call it the biological) model. The whole question will soon become one of finding the strongest, he who will have no predecessor in the order, but only successors.

Being "better" is also an ordering relation. *A* cannot be better than itself. *A*'s being better than *B* excludes *B*'s being better than *A*; if *A* is better than *B* and *B* is better than *C,* then *A* is better than *C.* We will call this second model of the ordered structure ethical. The whole question will soon become one of passing from the relative (an ordering relation) to the absolute, of finding the best, he who will have no predecessor in the order, only successors. The movement of the transitive relation is therefore blocked in order to arrive at stability, invariance: *always.* Finally, the use of *is* ("The reason of the strongest *is* always the best") indicates the invariance of the models in the structure, and therefore there is no need for demonstration: it is *always* a matter of the same process.

Let there be "the current of a pure stream." This is a third, topographical model of the same structure. It deals with an irreversible process which can, nevertheless, be determined at any point using an "upstream-downstream" type of relation. I shall no longer verify the axioms, because they are self-evident: no point is upstream of itself, the upstream's upstream is still upstream, and so forth. The wolf "whom hunger drew to this place," and not thirst, is farther up than the lamb, who drinks, in the stream, "more than twenty steps below Him."

In the fourth place, in an irreversible stream, one can define a process of causality. The cause precedes the effect, which succeeds the cause, without any possible reversal, without moving against the current. The third model was sequential; this one is consequential: "Who makes you so bold as to muddy my drink?" Since the cause is upstream from the effect, the lamb replies: "And that, *as a result,* in no way / Can I muddy His drink." One finds here a demonstration. The demonstration by cause and effect is only one particular model of the global structural chain. The lamb demonstrates and La Fontaine shows. Whereas the latter shows the structural invariance using the model's variance, the former demonstrates his point by using only one of the structure's models. Hence the idea, which can help us understand Descartes: the order of reason is only a particular exemplar of order in general. And this result has immense consequences.

One can construct a phenomenon on a spatial-type sequence or on a chain of consequences. Geometry, algebra, and physics constitute the Cartesian construct of the real. As Descartes wrote to R. P. Bourdin, the simplest of these phenomena can be seen in a basket of apples; if one of them is rotten, it diffuses rottenness around it by an irreversible process. In other words, and contrary to certain cosmogonies, the chaotic mixture succeeds separation, and impurity succeeds purity. We have since learned that this belongs to the irreversibility principle of thermodynamics (the law of entropy). The chain of purity or separation followed by mixture is the physical model of the ordered structure. For us, it is isomorphic to the relation of the strongest: maximal energy is always upstream in an irreversible process. It is always a wolf, and not a lamb, who quenches his thirst in the transparent stream of a pure reason.

Now let us choose a political hierarchy, such as that of the Classical age. Mark two points on our drawing and name them king and subject. This is a new model of the ordered structure: "Sire," answers the Lamb, "may it please Your Majesty / Not to become angry; / But rather let Him consider / That I am quenching my thirst / In the stream, / More than twenty steps below Him." Here there is something new. It is no longer the case of a strong individual who can find a still stronger one, of a "betterable better," an upstream that is downstream from another spot, a cause which can be an effect, or a purifiable energy; it is not, in short, the case of a *greater,* but of a *maximum.* There is nothing above the king. Is this the answer to our previous question?

In seventh place, as Rousseau—and many others—would say, none of these chains and none of these processes can be thought of outside of time. This is a new, temporal model of the ordered structure. On its flow, mark the before and the after, then verify the axioms. "And I know that you slandered me last year." But two events block the continuing movement of the flow: birth and death. "How could I have done so, if I had not yet been born?" If you kill me and then eat me, my time freezes and its order disappears. Relative relation and absolute limits: the wolf, upstream from time, is looking for adventure; he is the master of the future.

Now let us deal with the parental relation. This set is now well known, provided with several ordering relations. Either the ancestor-descendant (parent-child) relation: "I am not yet weaned," or the older child-younger child relation: "If it is not you, then it is your brother." The latter is the elder, since the encounter occurred last year. Or finally the general relation on the irreversible genealogical tree: "Then it is one of your clan." These are the complete models of kinship for the ordered structure.

Finally, let us try a social organization and its various roles. Mark two points on its flow chart and call them (seriously, now) protector and protected. Designated in this way, the relation clearly verifies all the axioms. One thereby obtains the ninth model: "You, your shepherds, and your dogs."

The trial is a process whose global balance sheet can easily be recorded. It consists of an ordered structure with given axioms, a structure that branches out in several models: the social tree, the genealogical tree, the tree of time and history, the political tree, the tree of the production of energy, of entropy, and of pollution, the tree of causes, the hydrographic tree, the tree of the "better," the tree of good, evil, and knowledge, the tree of the distribution of forces—and a tree in general. So many trees make a forest, into which "The Wolf carries him [the lamb] off, and then eats him."

This is not demonstrated by an order between that which precedes and that which follows, but shown as a forest of models, a forest of symbols. The proof is only one process among others: there exist philosophers from whom a whole forest is hidden by a single tree.

In this way one obtains something like a space, a very general space organized by the ordered structure. All of the fable's model-spaces are deducible from very elementary properties of the ordering relation. Let us take the most general case, the very form of the process. And let us say that this space, organized in this way—a space in which there always exist pairs like upstream-downstream, cause-effect, mother-son—is that of a *game-space*. Now the process becomes a trial. What is its form? What are the rules of the game?

Absolute limit	Ordering relation	Model
the strongest	stronger-weaker	biological
the best	better-worse	ethical
source	upstream-downstream	spatial
	cause-effect	rational
	purity-mixture	physical
king	dominator-subject	political
birth-death	before-after	temporal
	ancestor-descendant	genealogical
	protector-protected	social
Maximum	*Greater-Lesser*	*Ordered Structure*

A trial (as elementary jurisdiction) first of all tries to establish a responsibility. Let there be a wrong-doing that a plaintiff claims to have suffered: before evaluating the vengeance (the punishment that the accused must incur), it is necessary to show at least the possibility of injury. The set of possibilities includes physical, moral, temporal, sociopolitical, and other possibilities. Now, possibility is always the higher point on the tree, whatever that tree might be. If an order is strict, he who occupies the lower position, let us call him the *minorant,* has no control over the *majorant,* who, on the contrary, has complete control over the former. Hence the fable's strategies.

They are all engendered by the wolf's first word: "*Who* makes you so bold as to muddy my drink?" Until now we only knew two terms, which defined an order in the game-space: wolf and lamb. It is necessary to define a third one, namely that which makes the lamb so bold. As a consequence we have the *rule of the game* and the trial's law: the wolf plays, in the order, either the lamb or the third man upstream of himself, the lamb on the contrary plays himself downstream. The term *who?* is a reference to the majorant (the upper position's occupant). Now, he who is upstream, he who is greater, is responsible and loses. The

minorant wins and eats the other. Whether dealing with drink-
ing, eating, or dying, the *succession of moves* in the game follows
the ordering relation: you are the stronger, I am the weaker;
you are upstream, I am downstream; you are the cause, I am the
effect; you muddy it, I cannot muddy it; you slandered me last
year, I had not yet been born; it must be your brother, I do not
have any, and so on. The lamb shows, at every move, that he (or
the third man) is absent from the upper position where his adversary places him. In short, the wolf "majorizes" or maximizes
the lamb, who "minorizes" or minimizes himself. Everything is
played upstream from the wolf: however, are the places there
occupied or vacant? And how is this going to determine the
results of the game? Theorem I: the lamb wins. The number of
moves is almost infinite. There are as many of them as there are
models of the ordered structure and as a result, the game would
never end: it would be necessary to show at every move, that the
place is vacant. This is what the lamb does. But, in addition, in
the ultimate instance, he no longer proves the place's vacancy,
but rather its inexistence, and the game is over. Not only is the
place vacant, but there is no place. If the wolf is the king, "Sire,"
and "Majesty," he does not have a majorant. He is in an absolute
position like an absolute monarch. Not only is there no third
man, but it is impossible to conceive of one: *quo nihil majus
cogitari potest.* Therefore the lamb has won, and the wolf has no
majorant. He is himself the maximum. But then there is
theorem II: the wolf carries him off, nonetheless, and he does it
according to the rule of the game. He succeeds in showing the
existence of a third man, upstream from himself, in the lamb's
social group. This is because the shepherds and the dogs, protec-
tors of the flock, are, in reality, much stronger than the wolf;
they retain, upstream, the constant possibility of doing him
harm. "I have been told": *quo nihil majus dici potest.* In the ordering relation, they are clearly majorants. The place preceding the
wolf's place is occupied by the shepherd, who is the strongest.
The shepherd and his watchdogs are above the "king-wolf." The
fable is a perfect operational definition—perfect in that it is free
of all psychologism—of hypocrisy. In fact, the term *hypocrisy*
comes from the verb to judge, to choose, to decide, and from the
prefix underneath. In other words, if you want to win, play the

role of the minorant. I imagine that all the *Fables,* by the meta-morphosis that they represent, function in a similar fashion.

Structure organizes only the game-space. Without a set provided with an ordering relation, there would be no game. But the structure by itself is not the game. There is a tree space, and then active and mortal choices associated with each location on the tree, whatever that tree may be. Stable structures and dialectical processes are inseparable.

Besides, let us note the circle: *A* is upstream from *B*. *A* must place *B* or a third person upstream from himself in order to have the right to eat or kill the adversary. Let us, for the moment, retain the three results: ordered structure, fight to the death, and circularity.

The seventeenth century founded experimental and mathematical physics as well as the calculus of probability. Pascal discovered the equilibrium of liquids; Leibniz developed an acoustics, a game theory and his logical calculus; Bernoulli dealt with mechanics when he wrote his *Ars Conjectandi.* This simultaneity has a meaning, even though, in the details of the demonstrations and of the works, the relationships are not easily visible. I do not know if historians have ever described these two births as contemporaneous, or if they have even questioned their "twinness."

If we define nature as the set of objects with which the exact sciences are concerned at a given moment in history, viewed synchronically (which is a restrictive but operational definition), the emergence of physics, in particular, can be thought of only in the global framework of our relations to nature. Now, ever since Francis Bacon's work, these relations have been described, from the heights of his social situation, by the command-obedience couplet. One commands nature only by obeying it. This is probably a political ideology—betrayed by the prosopopeia—which implies practices of ruse and subtlety: in short, a whole strategy. Since nature is stronger than we are, we must bend to its law, and it is through this subterfuge that we dominate it. We are under its orders and turn its forces back against order. This is the circle of ruse and productive hypocrisy: nature is a majorant; we try, ourselves, downstream, to majorize ourselves in relation to it.

Here one finds again, intact, an ordered structure, a game, its rule (and how best to implement it), the struggle to seize power, and the closed cycle outlined by these moves.

Descartes, after Bacon, picks up the precept: he calls for us to become the masters and possessors of nature. *The impulse to obey has just disappeared.* Baconian physics made science into a duel, a combat, a struggle for domination; it gave it an agonistic model, proposing a form of ruse for it so that the *weak one* would triumph. It transformed science into a game of strategy, with its rules and its moves. But Baconian reason is a weak reason which loses at least the first round, because it first resigns itself to obedience. Descartes rejects this, and, consequently, he suppresses the loss. In the relationship of agonistic forces between ourselves and the exterior world, he seeks the means that will permit us to win at every move. "The reason of the strongest is *always* the best." The best reason *always* permits a winning game. The foundation of modern science is in this word, *always.* Science is a game, an infinite game, in which we always win. Reason is an absolute and constant "optimization."

In a contest, a competitor is not always assured of winning. A player stronger at a given moment because of a given move, can later fail when his opponent discovers the means or obtains the power to pass upstream from him. The dichotomy then appears to reverse itself; the weaker has taken the stronger's place. In fact, it is the entire couplet which is displaced in the game-space structured by the ordering relation. This displacement is infinite, and does not stop—as long as one stays in the same space—since it is relative. It is the infernal time of hierarchical struggle, the time of human unhappiness. There are two, and only two strategies that can give a final turn to the sequence of moves. First, one stays with the *dialectical game* and tries to discover a martingale[2] in order to win, whatever the move might be: then the game is over and there is a definitive dominant. Old times are over and struggles stop under the insurmountable power of one of the contestants. With a maximal move, one freezes the game-space in a single pattern of order and hierarchy. It is the

[2]A martingale is any system by which one tries to make up one's losses in previous bets by doubling or increasing the amount bet.—Ed.

end of a slice of history. Second, one attacks *the ordered structure itself*—which is the condition for the game's existence, or rather, without which the game can have neither space nor time—in order to shatter it. This move would mark the beginning of a new history. Philosophers have rarely taken the second path: they have always tried to find the maximum and the minimum points at the edge of the space organized by the couplet of the majorant and the minorant. As soon as it is discovered, one can say: *always*. And it is always the time of the wolf.

Look at Rousseau, for example. He repeats, after many others: the stronger is *never* strong enough *always* to be the master, unless he transforms his might into right and obedience into duty. As we indicated earlier, this kind of transformation is the shift from one model to the other: another move, same game. The second move is as unstable as the first: jurisprudence and ethics are relative to a cultural space organized by the ordering relation. At times a radical, at others a tiny change in the ordering relation is sufficient to make an entire group overthrow its morals and its laws. The trial's dialectics remain, based on the majorant's and the minorant's relationships, with the division of the stakes left to the balanced distribution of forces and to the recuperation of ruse. It is therefore necessary to recognize an infinity of moves in the relative field of the "more" and the "less." As in the fable, one must maximize the "more" and minimize the "less." *One must maximize in an absolute fashion;* in such a way that there may not exist, that one may not conceive, a majorant to a maximum and a minorant to a minimum. One must transform force into factual necessity and obedience into an inevitable law. One may cut off the king's head, kill the dog, or eat the shepherd, yet one cannot do without Reason's verdicts. And this is why, since Rousseau, *one no longer hesitates to invoke science in the realm of law, power, and politics. It is because science has already pointed the way to the winning strategy.* For it must be remembered that the foundation of science—whether it be the pure sciences at the Hellenic dawn or the experimental sciences in the Classical age—had taken place in an agonistic field.

I could be accused of forcing the answer. And yet, one can show that abstract mathematics and axiomatics owe their emergence to the Sophists' discussions and paradoxes, as well as to Plato's dialogue techniques. Agonistics is there, in the background. And yet, the purest positivist cannot challenge Auguste Comte's analysis, which defines the birth of geometry (in his eyes a natural science) as a ruse or set of ruses: to be able to measure inaccessible things, to find indirect means for man to perform that which he does not have the means to do. Once again, this is a strategy. And as soon as laws are written, they allow man *always* to have access to the inaccessible. The stability and constancy of certitudes or precisions are conceived in the beginning as the end of a prior game.

Another founding word was that of Galileo: nature is written, it is drafted in a language; everyone agrees that this is a mathematical language. But this writing is not obvious, it is hidden, concealed under the phenomenal appearance of the material world. One must force open the secret, find the key to the logogriph, and decode this writing. Now, in this game of decoding or deciphering, nature defends itself. It is subtle, it is hidden, it is secret. One must therefore employ subtler strategies in order to make its defenses fail. Once the key is discovered, the world surrenders. The isomorphic relation between force and writing, recognized elsewhere,[3] is again brought into play here.

Just as in Plato's work there abound traces of this state of affairs necessary for the founding of the rigorous sciences, so, in the same way, Descartes's work shows such traces at the dawn of exact sciences (conceived, since the Classical age, as the optimal relationship from subject to object). I have recalled this founding word at the end of which we should have made ourselves the masters and possessors of nature. And I expressed it in terms of a game: Baconian obedience having been suppressed, the project became one of *always* winning. Reason is optimized, it is the best, it is always invincible. From La Fontaine spring Descartes and the game, or vice versa; it matters little. The three elements located in the fable should then be found in the *Metaphysical Meditations:* a space structured by the ordering relation, a circle, a game with its moves, its end and its winner. Two and only two have been recognized by the commentators; the third, which is the most visible—since it concerns action—remains hidden. I

---

[3]Cf. Jacques Derrida's *De la grammatologie* (Paris: Minuit, 1967).—Ed.

have suggested elsewhere a static type of solution[4] to the problem of the Cartesian circle framed in a historical context. Another solution is possible through the strategy of the game.

First of all, there exists in the text an ordering relation, the famous order of reason, the long chain of the geometricians, such that a link *A* precedes *B*, its successor, which proceeds from *A,* its predecessor, and such that it is impossible that *A* derive from *B*. The order of reason is therefore irreflexive, antisymmetric, and transitive, according to the axioms of the relation. Transitivity remains a constant preoccupation with Descartes, who suggests time and again that we reconsider the ordered set in its totality. But, as we have seen in the fable, the demonstrative (or deductive, if one wishes) sequence is only one tree in the forest of model-sequences. One tree alone must not hide the forest from us. Behind, or besides, the premises-consequences couplet, there exist other simple couplets, other models of the ordering relation present in the text: predecessor-successor, upstream-downstream, older-younger, and so forth. Moreover, the demonstrative order, taken from the Greek geometricians, links together relationships or proportions, as is noted throughout Descartes's *Regulae.* The geometric sequence is a series of relationships and analogies. These relationships quantify very different things: relationships of size, height, ruse, and power. Even, occasionally, relationships of sovereignty and slavery, since the first *Meditation* closes with the representation of a slave who, while sleeping, dreams that he is free. From this results an ordered space and no longer just a linear chain whose list of model-relations would be quite long: more powerful/less powerful, better/worse, before/after, more wily/less wily, more or less true, more or less false, etc., and in which the cause-effect pair is only one particular relation. The set of these models, and not just one of them, makes the ordered structure visible. This is because the word "structure" was taken by commentators in the Latin sense commonly used until the end of the nineteenth century, that is, in the etymological sense of architecture, meaning logical architecture.

If one takes it in the sense defined above, everything changes:

[4]Serres, *Hermes ou la communication* (Paris: Seuil, 1968).—Ed.

the ordered structure is common to several relations. One need only choose a parallel text, such as Leibniz's *Meditationes,* in order to understand the question clearly. These meditations are constructed by pairs, such as light-dark, confused-distinct, aligned so that they constitute a simple filter. The ordered structure being relative, the pluralist method makes it function iteratively, until it finds one or several remainders. If, in Descartes (or in the Cartesian method), there was only order, and order alone, then Leibniz's text would be Cartesian. Reciprocally, Descartes's text would be Leibnizian, since it posits a maximum and minimum strategy in an ordered space. This switch is exactly what happens. On the ordered structure considered as a game-space, one can, of course, construct a game. And this, again, Leibniz had seen, since he accuses Descartes of staging a whole spectacle, that is, an action in a game. "I would . . . believe myself at fault, if I spent in deliberation the time that remains to me for action."[5] Action: characters or prosopopeias, God, the ego, the evil spirit, defined as opposing elements in a regulated global strategy. In the fable, one saw, quite simply, that if the direction of the moves remained at the level of the formal pair majorant-minorant, the game was endless and without a stable victor. It is therefore necessary to put an end to this once and for all; one of the adversaries must be assured of always winning. That is possible only if one passes from the position of majorant to a maximum without conceivable predecessor, and from the position of minorant to a minimum without any imaginable successor. There is no place above the king, there is no place above the shepherd assisted by his dogs, and there is no place below the lamb. From this comes the global theorem: in the Cartesian *Meditations,* all the moves are maximized.

The syntax confirms this without exception: comparatives of order, superlatives of maxima. Descartes speaks of his age: "*so* ripe, *that* I could *not hope* for another after it, in which I could be adequate to execute [this enterprise]" (p. 404); of his project: "it made me defer *so* long *that* I would henceforth believe myself at

[5]Descartes, *Oeuvres philosophiques* (Paris: Garnier, 1963) II, 404. All further page references will be to this volume of the Garnier edition. Given the technical nature of Serres's demonstration, the editor has chosen to translate all of Descartes's quotes from the French original.

fault, if I spent in deliberation the time that remains to me . . . " (ibid.). Optimal age, optimal time, such that there no longer remains any better. Descartes again, speaking of doubt: "as much as reason persuades me already that I should no *less carefully* keep myself from believing in things that are *not entirely* certain and indubitable, *any more than* in those that appear to us to be *manifestly* false" (p. 405). Result: the universal quantificator. A constant repetition of: all, always, never, absolutely, etc. Appearances of *always,* the key word, "I shall *always* follow this path" (p. 414).

Quantification, until now, has been rather indefinite. Observe the progression from the first *Meditation* to the second: "*Any* subject for doubt that I find will suffice to make me reject *all* [opinions]" (p. 405); "it is *never entirely* prudent to trust those who have deceived us *once*" (ibid.); and "distancing myself from *everything* in which I will be able to imagine the *least* doubt" (p. 414). First we move from the universal (*all*) to the particular (*any*), then, to the reduction of the particular to a single case, (*once*), and finally, to the reduction of unicity to the minimum (*the least*). This is clearly the final move.

God's position and that of the atheists establish the rule: "the *less powerful* the author that they assigned to my origin will be, the *more* probable it is that I am *so* imperfect that I am *always* in error" (p. 410). It will suffice to envisage the extreme case in order to invert the result, to find the *quo nihil cogitari possit,* sovereignly omnipotent, veracious. As far as I know, "perfect" signifies "optimal."

The global description of the procedure follows: "having *so* balanced my [new and old] prejudices that they can *no longer* sway my opinion" (p. 411). With the model of a simple machine, taken up again, later, at Archimedes' point (p. 414) (thus the minimum, to move the earth, the maximum), one obtains the static comparison of relationships. In this space, the optimized move is precisely the Archimedian fixed point. The progression is the same.

Speaking of the evil spirit, Cartesian progression is still the same: first called "*no less* wily and deceiving *than* powerful" (p. 412), the evil spirit is called later in the second *Meditation* "a *very* powerful and *very* wily deceiver, who employs *all* his energy

to deceive me *always*" (p. 415). We move again from the comparison of relationships to the maximal relationship such that
nothing can exist beyond it. Here is the strategy in relation to
this spirit: "I shall prepare my mind *so* well against *all* of this
great deceiver's ruses, that, *no matter how* powerful and wily he
may be, he will *never* be able to impose *anything* on me" (p. 412).
And the final move as Descartes sees it: "let him deceive me *as
much as* he wishes, he will *never* manage to turn me into *nothing*,
as long as I think that I am *something*" (p. 415). This doubt is
called hyperbolic, but no effort is made to understand the hyperbole's function. The word must be analyzed as I have done
for the fable's hypocrisy. *Hypocritical ruse and hyperbolic doubt are
operators totally devoid of psychologism.*

   "My meditation of yesterday has filled my mind with *so many*
doubts, that it is *no longer* in my power to forget them . . . " (p.
414); "I am *so* surprised, that I can*not* fix my feet on the bottom
nor swim . . . " (ibid.). The existence of the "I," "I am," "I exist,"
is clearly uncovered by a minimum-maximum move: it is the
minimal remainder of a maximized strategy or ruse. At the end
of which, as soon as *everything* that can be in *any way* disputed has
been dismissed, I [Descartes] obtain "a *more* certain and *more*
evident knowledge than *all* the knowledge I had earlier" (p.
416). Once again, the universal quantificator is the final move in
the quantification of a relationship followed to its limit.

   One could continue the demonstration. The syntax is constructed entirely in this way. The process is everywhere quantified, tactics are everywhere maximized, the final move is on the
maximum *maximorum,* and even more on the *quo nihil.* . . . Not
only is there no one in the places upstream, but there is no
longer any upstream locus. To give oneself an adversary and
defeat him with the help of an all-powerful and truthful associate, God Himself: this is a game between two players, between three, in which nature disappears; burned, melted,
minimized, destroyed. The malleable wax and I become one;
thus I always win. God is a point without an upstream, the wax a
point without a downstream, and myself in the center, hence the
circle; I can no longer lose at this game.

   Then everything becomes possible: optics and dioptics, the
world and its system, medicine and everything that follows from

it. In the game of truth, error has been checkmated; in the game of domination, all is reduced to slavery, including the body. Metaphysics is operatory, it is the strategic set without which physics and the exact sciences are nothing but partial and dispersed tactics. Einstein rediscovered Descartes by turning around a parable: God is subtle, but he does not cheat. To know nature is a game. Not a futile amusement, but a deadly dangerous game. Nature's secret lies in the fact that one sees only the backs of the cards, and that one must play carefully and cautiously, in order to uncover this secret and read the faces of the cards, that is to say, to read them mathematically. Experimentation is a game in which the more one cheats, the less one knows (hence morals and deontology), a game one can lose and win, but in which there exists a guaranteed winning strategy. The development of mathematics, independent of experimentation is another result: one must try to refine strategies, which are useful against an adversary whose strategies are also extremely refined. "Game," then, is not just a word of science, it is the model of all exact knowledge. Information theory, the daughter of physics and probabilities, has discovered this model once again. But during the Classical age, it is a martial game. Like many other philosophers, Descartes pursued his military calling in metaphysics.

It is often said that probability theory and the art of conjecture were born, in a given economic context, from the idea of life annuities, before the large banks and companies thought of insuring against death. This is probable, although not proven by the facts. Leibniz, among others, computed life annuities. Even supposing that one proved it, one would only have affirmed in one case an already established theory which had sometimes proved itself useful. The more significant idea is that of the wager, a wager that is not very specific, since every martial game is a game to the death, a wager on death. If it is a question of dates, you have insurance and annuities; if it is a question of stakes, you have Pascal. Thus it is that the relation between theory and practice, the relation of metaphysics to knowledge, and the relation of the latter to domination, come together in the same place, *at the outcome provided by death.*

For Plato and a tradition which lasted throughout the Classical age, knowledge is a hunt. To know is to put to death—to kill the lamb, deep in the woods, in order to eat it. Moving from combat with prey outside the species to killing inside the species, knowledge now becomes military, a martial art. It is then more than a game; it is, literally, a strategy. These epistemologies are not innocent: at the critical tribunal they are calling for executions. They are policies promulgated by military strategists. To know is to kill, to rely on death, as in the case of the master and the slave.

Today we live out the major results of these wolfish actions. For the "I," who played the role of the lamb by minimizing his powers and placing the declared powers upstream from himself, this "I" is the wolf. In the ordering relation, in the game-space, the "I" is clearly in the middle, between the victorious sheepdog and the defeated devil or the wax. It has taken the wolf's place, its true place. The reason of the strongest is reason *by itself.* *Western man is a wolf of science.*

GILLES DELEUZE

The Schizophrenic and Language:
Surface and Depth in
Lewis Carroll and Antonin Artaud

The presence of esoteric words and portmanteau words has been pointed out in the rhyming chants of little girls, in poetry, and in the language of madness. Such an amalgamation is troubling, however. A great poet can write in a direct relation to the child that he was and the children that he loves; a madman can produce a great body of poetry in direct relation to the poet that he was and has not ceased to be. This in no way justifies the grotesque trinity of child, poet, and madman. We must be attentive to the displacements which reveal a profound difference beneath superficial resemblances. We must note the different functions and depths of *non-sense* and the heterogeneity of portmanteau words, which do not authorize grouping together those who invent them or even those who employ them. A little girl can sing "pimpanicaille" (in French, a mixture of "pimpant" + "nique" + "canaille"), a poet write "frumious" (furious + fuming) or "slithy" (lithe + slimy), and a schizophrenic say "perspendicacious" (perpendicular + perspicacious)[1]: we have no reason to believe that the problem is the same because of superficially analogous results. There can be no serious association of the little elephant Babar's song with Artaud's breath-screams, "Ratara ratara ratara Atara tatara rara Otara otara

---

[1] "Perspendicacious" is a portmanteau word used by a schizophrenic to designate spirits that are suspended above the subject's head (*perpendicular*) and that are very *perspicacious*. Mentioned in Georges Dumas, *Le Surnaturel et les dieux d'après les maladies mentales* (Paris: Presses Universitaires de France, 1946), p. 303.

277

katara. . . ."[2] Let us add that the logicians' error when speaking of
non-sense, is to give disembodied examples which they construct
laboriously for the needs of their demonstration, as if they had
never heard a little girl sing, a great poet recite, or a schizophrenic speak. Such is the poverty of these "logical" examples
(except in the case of Russell, who was inspired by Lewis Carroll). Here, again, the inadequacies of the logicians do not authorize us to construct a new trinity in opposition to theirs, however. The problem is a clinical one: that of the displacement from
one mode of organization to another, or of the formation of a
progressive and creative disorganization. The problem is also
one of criticism, that is, of determining differential levels at
which change occurs in the form of non-sense, in the nature of
portmanteau words, in the dimension of language as a whole.

We would like to consider two great poetic texts containing
such traps of resemblance: Antonin Artaud confronts Lewis
Carroll first in an extraordinary transcription—a counterequiv-
alence—of Carroll's "Jabberwocky" and then in one of his letters
written from the insane asylum in Rodez. Reading the opening
stanza of "Jabberwocky" as it was rendered into French by Artaud, one has the impression that the first two lines still correspond to Carroll's criteria, and conform to the rules of other
French translations of Carroll.[3] Beginning with the last word
of the second line, however, a displacement, and even a central, creative breakdown, occurs, one which transports us to
another world and to a completely different language. In fright
we recognize this language without difficulty: it is the language
of schizophrenia. Caught up in grammatical syncopes and over-
burdened with gutturals, even the portmanteau words seem to
have another function. At the same time, we see the distance
separating Carroll's language, which is emitted at the surface,
from Artaud's language, which is hewn from the depths of

---

[2]Antonin Artaud, *Oeuvres complètes* (Paris: Gallimard, 1970), IX, 188. Henceforth, references will be to the volume and page of this edition. All translations
are the editor's. Breath-screams are used in Artaud's theater of cruelty as a
means of preventing spectators from relating to the "intellectual" content of
language. (The scream is a specific system of breathing derived from the Kab-
bala, and is designed to free the feminine or repressed side of the self.)—Ed.

[3]The original text of "Jabberwocky" which Humpty Dumpty explicates is
found in *Through the Looking Glass* (Lewis Carroll, *Complete Works*, Modern Li-

bodies—a distance which reflects the difference between their problems. We then understand the full significance of Artaud's declarations in one of the letters from Rodez:

> I did not do a translation of "Jabberwocky." I tried to translate a fragment of it, but it bored me. I never liked the poem, which always seemed to me to smack of affected infantilism. . . . *I do not like surface poems or languages* which smell of happy leisure moments and intellectual triumphs. . . . One can invent one's language and make pure language speak with an a-grammatical meaning, but this meaning must be valid in itself, it must come from anguish. . . . "Jabberwocky" is the work of a profiteer who wanted— while filled with a well-served meal—to fill up intellectually on others' suffering. . . . When one digs into the shit of the individual being and his language, the poem must necessarily smell bad; "Jabberwocky" is a poem that its author has taken special pains to keep outside the uterine being of suffering into which all great poets have dipped, and from which, delivering themselves into the world, they smell bad. In "Jabberwocky" there are passages of fecality, but it is the fecality of an English snob who curls the obscene in himself like ringlets around a hot curling iron. . . . It is the work of a man who ate well, and you can smell it in his writing.
> [IX, 184–186]

In short, Artaud considers Lewis Carroll a pervert, a minor pervert, who limits himself to the creation of a surface language and

---

brary ed., p. 215. Henceforth, all references will be to this edition) and goes as follows:
> 'Twas brillig, and the slithy toves
> Did gyre and gymble in the wabe
> All mimsy were the borogoves,
> And the mome raths outgrabe.

Artaud's version (taken from "L'Arve et l'aume, tentative anti-grammaticale contre Lewis Carroll," IX, 156–174) is as follows:
> Il était roparant, et les vliqueux tarands
> Allaient en gibroyant et en brimbulkdriquant
> Jusque là où la rourghe est à rouarghe à rangmbde et rangmbde à rouarghambde:
> Tous les falomitards étaient les chats-huants
> Et les Ghoré Uk'hatis dans le grabugeument.

Whereas Henri Parisot's translation (cf. *Lewis Carroll,* Seghers ed.) reads:
> Il était grilheure; les slictueux toves
> Gyraient sur l'alloinde et vriblaient;
> Tout flivoreux allaient les borogoves;
> Les verchons fourgus bourniflaient.
> —Ed.

does not sense the true problem of language in its depth—the schizophrenic problem of suffering, of death, and of life. Carroll's games seem puerile to him, his nourishment too worldly, even his fecality hypocritical and too well-bred.

Let us briefly consider *Alice*. A strange evolution takes place throughout all of Alice's adventures. One can sum it up as the conquest or discovery of surfaces. At the beginning of *Alice in Wonderland*, the search for the secret of things and events goes on in the depths of the earth: in deeply dug wells and rabbit holes, as well as in the mixtures of bodies which penetrate each other and coexist. As one advances in the narrative, however, the sinking and burrowing movements give way to lateral, sliding movements: from left to right and right to left. The animals of the depths become secondary, and are replaced by playing card characters, characters without thickness. One might say that the former depth has spread itself out, has become breadth. Here lies the secret of the stammerer [Carroll]—it no longer consists in sinking into the depths, but in sliding along in such a way that depth is reduced to nothing but the reverse side of the surface. If there is nothing to see behind the curtain, it is because everything visible (or rather, all possible knowledge) is found along the surface of the curtain. It suffices to follow the curtain far enough and closely enough—which is to say superficially enough—in order to turn it inside out so that right becomes left, and vice versa. Consequently, there are no adventures of Alice; there is but *one* adventure: her rising to the surface, her disavowal of the false depths, and her discovery that everything happens at the borderline. For this reason, Carroll abandoned the first title that he had in mind, *Alice's Adventures Underground*.

This is even more true of *Alice's* sequel, *Through the Looking Glass*. Events, in their radical difference from things, are no longer sought in the depths, but at the surface: a mirror that reflects them, a chess-board that "flattens" them to a two-dimensional plane. By running along the surface, along the edge, one passes to the other side; from bodies to incorporeal events. The continuity of front and back replaces all levels of depth. In *Sylvia and Bruno*, Carroll's major novel, one witnesses the completion of this evolution: a stretching machine elongates even songs; the barometer neither rises nor falls, but moves sideways, giving horizontal weather; Bruno learns his lessons backward and forward, up and down, but never in depth; and Fortunatus' purse, presented as a Moebius strip, is made of handkerchiefs sewn together "in the wrong way," so that its external surface is in continuity with its internal surface, and inside and outside become one.

This discovery that the strangest things are on the surface or, as Valéry would say, that "the skin is deepmost" [*le plus profond, c'est la peau*], would be unimportant if it did not carry with it an entire organization of language: Carrollian language. It is clear that, throughout his literary work, Carroll speaks of a very particular type of thing, of *events* (of growing, shrinking, eating, cutting, and so on), and he interprets the nature of these events in a strange manner whose equivalent one finds only in the logic of the Stoics.

[The privileged position of the Stoics comes from the fact that they were the initiators of a paradoxical theory of meaning which imposed a new division between beings and things on the one hand, and concepts on the other.[4] The Stoics distinguished between two states of *being:* (1) real beings, that is, *bodies* with their depth, their physical qualities, their interrelationships, their *actions* and *passions;* (2) the *effects* that take place on the surface of beings. Effects are not states of things, but *incorporeal events;* they are not physical qualities, but logical attributes. Emile Bréhier, for instance, explains incorporeal events in these terms: "When a scalpel slices into the flesh, the first agent produces, not a new property in the second body, but a new attribute, that of having been cut. The *attribute* does not designate a real *qual-*

---

[9]Editor's note: My long interpolation here about the Stoics attempts to define: (1) the parameters within which Deleuze's essay was written; (2) the concepts Deleuze develops and uses further on in his study. In order to facilitate the reader's task, brief definitions of the key Stoic concepts at work in Deleuze's text follow: *Action* and *Passion:* in the interaction among bodies, *actions* are the active principles by which bodies act, and passions are the *passive* principles by which bodies are acted upon. This establishes the duality agent-body versus patient-body. *Proposition:* that which allows the expression of *events* (or *effects*) in language. *Designation* and *expression:* two dimensions of the proposition. The first, *designation* (consisting of nouns and adjectives), is what links the proposition to physical things (bodies or consumable objects) which are exterior to it. The second, *expression* (consisting of verbs), links the proposition to incorporeal events and logical attributes; it *expresses* them and thus represents the conceptual link between the proposition and meaning.

ity . . ., on the contrary, it is always expressed by a verb, which means that it is not a being, but a *manner of being.*"[5]

It is in this sense that we must understand the events of which Carroll speaks. "To grow," "to shrink," "to cut," or "to be cut" are not states of things, but incorporeal events that occur on the surface of things. Carroll's entire work consists precisely in marking this difference between events on the one hand, and corporeal beings, things, and states of things on the other.

The first great duality of Stoic origin is therefore the opposition between causes and effects, between corporeal things and incorporeal events. But to the extent that the event-effect does not exist outside the *proposition* that expresses it, the duality body/event is carried over into the duality things/propositions, that is, bodies/language. From this comes the alternative which recurs throughout Carroll's work: to eat or to speak. In *Sylvia and Bruno,* the choice is between "bits of things," and "bits of Shakespeare." Eating is the operational model for bodies, for their actions and passions, and for their modes of coexistence with(in) each other. Speaking, on the other hand, is the movement of the surface; it is the operational model for incorporeal events.

The second duality, body/language or eating/speaking, is not sufficient for an understanding of Carroll. We know that although meaning does not exist outside of the proposition that expresses it, it is nevertheless an attribute of things (bodies) or states of things (physical qualities) and not of the proposition. Things and propositions are positioned not so much in a radical duality as on the two sides of the borderline constituted by meaning.[6] This borderline neither mixes nor unites them. It is rather the articulation of their difference: body versus language, things versus propositions. This duality is reflected on both sides, in each of the two terms. On the side of things, there are, on the

---

[5]*La Théorie des incorporels dans l'ancien stoïcisme* (Paris: Vrin, 1928), p. 11.

[6]On the one hand, meaning doesn't exist outside of the proposition that expresses it. But, on the other hand, it is not to be equated with the proposition; it has its own completely distinct "objectivity." The *expressed* does not resemble the *expression* at all. Meaning is not an attribute of the proposition; it is the attribute of a thing or of the state of a thing. It deals, on the one hand, with things, and, on the other, with propositions. But is is no more to be equated with the proposition that expresses it than with either the state of things or the physical quality that the proposition designates. Meaning is exactly on the borderline between propositions and things.—Ed.

one hand, physical qualities and real relationships; on the other hand are logical attributes indicating incorporeal events. And, on the side of propositions, there are, on the one hand, nouns and adjectives which *designate* the state of things, and on the other, verbs which *express* events or logical attributes.

The duality in the proposition is thus between two levels of the proposition itself: between *designation* and *expression,* that is the designation of things (bodies and consumable objects) and the expression of meaning. We have here something similar to the two sides of a mirror except that what is on one side does not resemble what is on the other. To pass to the other side of the mirror is to move from a relationship of designation to one of expression, to enter a region in which language no longer has any relationship to bodies or designated objects (which are always consumable) but only to meanings (which are always expressible).]

This abstractly presented schema of the logic of the Stoics comes to life in Carroll's work. As he said in an article entitled "The Dynamics of a Parti-cle," "*plain superficiality* is the character of a speech." Throughout Carroll's work, the reader will encounter: (1) exits from tunnels in order to discover surfaces and the incorporeal events that are spread out on these surfaces; (2) the essential affinity of events with language; (3) the constant organization of the two surface series into the dualities eating/speaking, consumption/proposition, and designation/expression; and (4) the manner in which these series are organized around a paradoxical element, which is expressed sometimes by a hollow word, sometimes by an esoteric word, and sometimes by a portmanteau word whose function is to fuse and ramify these heterogeneous series.[7] In this way "snark" ramifies an alimentary series ("snark" is of animalish origin, and belongs therefore

---

[7]An esoteric word can be defined as the point of convergence of two different series of propositions. A first type of esoteric word is limited to a contraction of the syllabic elements of a proposition ("y'reince" for "your royal highness"). Another type is concerned with affirming, within the esoteric word, the conjunction and the coexistence of two series of heterogeneous propositions. (Snark = shark + snake). Finally, there exists a third type of esoteric word—the portmanteau word—which is the contraction of several words and thus englobes several meanings. The essential characteristic of the portmanteau word is that is is based on a strict *disjunctive synthesis.* Its function always consists of ramifying the series in which it is placed (frumious = fuming + furious *or* furious + fuming).—Ed.

to the class of consumable objects) and a linguistic series ("snark" is an incorporeal meaning); "Jabberwocky" subsumes an animal and a conversation at the same time; and finally, there is the admirable gardener's song in *Sylvia and Bruno,* in which each couplet brings into play two different types of terms that elicit two distinct perceptions: "He thought he saw ... He looked again, and found it was. ... " The couplets develop two heterogeneous series: one of animals, of beings, or of consumable objects described according to physical and sensory (sonorous) qualities; the other, of symbolic objects and characters, defined by logical attributes which are bearers of meaning.[8]

The organization of language described above must be called poetic, because it reflects that which makes language possible. One will not be surprised to discover that events make language possible, even though the event does not exist outside of the proposition that expresses it, since as an "expressed" it does not mix with its expression. It does not exist prior to it and has no existence by itself, but possesses an "insistence" which is peculiar to it. "To make language possible" has a very particular meaning. It signifies to "distinguish" language, to prevent sounds from becoming confused with the sonorous qualities of things, with the noisiness of bodies, with their actions and passions, and with their so-called "oral-anal" determinations. What makes language possible is that which separates sounds from bodies, organizes them into propositions, and thus makes them available to assume an expressive function. Without this surface that distinguishes itself from the depths of bodies, without this line that separates things from propositions, sounds would become inseparable from bodies, becoming simple physical qualities con-

---

[8]The song of the gardener, in *Sylvia and Bruno,* is made up of nine verses, eight of which are in the first volume, the ninth appearing in *Sylvia and Bruno Concluded,* chapter 20. We quote here two of the verses.—Ed.

He thought he saw an Albatross
   That fluttered round the lamp;
He looked again, and found it was
   A Penny-Postage-Stamp.   [p. 347]

He thought he saw an Argument
   That proved he was the Pope:
He looked again, and found it was
   A Bar of Mottled Soap.   [p. 701]

tiguous with them, and propositions would be impossible. This is why *the organization of language is not separable from the poetic discovery of surface,* or from Alice's adventure. The greatness of language consists in speaking only at the surface of things, and thereby in capturing the pure event and the combinations of events that take place on the surface. It becomes a question of reascending to the surface, of discovering surface entities and their games of meaning and of non-sense, of expressing these games in portmanteau words, and of resisting the vertigo of the bodies' depths and their alimentary, poisonous mixtures.

Let us consider another text, far removed from the genius of Artaud and the surface games of Carroll, one whose beauty and density lie in the clinical realm.[9] This text concerns a schizophrenic language student who experiences an eating/speaking duality, and who transposes it into propositions, or rather, into two sorts of language: his mother tongue (English), which is essentially *alimentary* and excremental, and foreign languages, which are essentially *expressive* and which he strives to acquire. In order to hinder the progress of his study of foreign languages, his mother threatens him in two equivalent ways: either she waves before him tempting but indigestible foods packaged in cans, or else she jumps out at him suddenly and abruptly speaks English to him before he has time to plug his ears.

He fends off this double threat with a set of ever more perfected procedures. He eats like a glutton, stuffs himself with food, and stomps on the cans, all the while repeating several foreign words. At a deeper level, he establishes a resonance between the alimentary and the expressive series, and a conversion from one to the other, by translating English words into foreign words according to their phonetic elements (consonants being the most important). For example, *tree* is converted by use of the *R* that reappears in the French vocable (*arbre*), and then by use of the *T* which reappears in the Hebrew term. Finally, since the

[9]Louis Wolfson, *Le Schizo et les langues* (Paris: Gallimard, 1971). On this subject see the introduction written by Deleuze to Wolfson's book and the articles by Alain Rey ("Le Schizolexe" in *Critique,* Nos. 279–80 [1970]) and Jeffrey Mehlman ("Portnoy in Paris" in *Diacritics,* 2 [Winter 1972]).—Ed.

Russians say *devero* (tree), one can equally transform *tree* into *tere*, *T* then becoming *D*. This already complex procedure gives way to a more generalized one when the idea occurs to the schizophrenic student to employ certain associations: *early,* whose consonants (*R* and *L*) raise particularly delicate problems, is transformed into French expressions dealing with time like "*suR Le champ,*" "*de bonne heuRe,*" "*matinaLement,*" "*dévoRer L'es-pace,*" or even into an esoteric and fictive word of German con-sonance, "*uRLich.*"

Here, again, what is it that gives us the impression that this language is both very close to, and yet totally different from, Carroll's? Are we talking of a different organization of language, or something worse and more dangerous? One is reminded of Artaud's vehement denunciation of Carroll: "I do not like sur-face poems or languages. . . . " Consequently, how could Carroll appear to Artaud as anything but a well-mannered little girl, sheltered from all the problems of the depths?

 The discovery that *there is no more surface* is familiar to and experienced by any schizophrenic. The great problem, the first evidence of schizophrenia, is that the surface is punctured. Bodies no longer have a surface. The schizophrenic body ap-pears as a kind of body-sieve. Freud emphasized this schizo-phrenic aptitude for perceiving the surface and the skin as if each were pierced by an infinite number of little holes.[10] As a result, the entire body is nothing but depth; it snatches and carries off all things in this gaping depth, which represents a fundamental involution. Everything is body and corporeal. Everything is a mixture of bodies and, within the body, telescoping, nesting in and penetrating each other. It is all a question of physics, as Artaud says: "We have in the back filled vertebra, which are pierced by the nail of pain, and which through walking and the effort of lifting, become cans by being encased upon each other."[11] A tree, a column, a flower, a cane pushes through the body; other bodies always penetrate into our body and coexist

---

[10]"The Unconscious," in *Metapsychology* (1915). Citing the cases of two patients, one of whom perceives his skin, and the other his sock, as systems of small holes in continual risk of expansion, Freud shows that this symptom is peculiar to schizophrenia, and could belong neither to a hysteric nor to an obsessional neurotic.

[11]In *La Tour de feu,* April 1961.

with its parts. As there is no surface, interior and exterior, container and content no longer have precise limits; they plunge into universal depth. From this comes the schizophrenic way of living contradictions: either in the deep cleavage that traverses the body, or in the fragmented parts of the body which are nested in each other and whirl around. Body-sieve, fragmented body, and dissociated body form the first three dimensions of the schizophrenic body—they give evidence of the general breakdown of surfaces.

In this breakdown of the surface, all words lose their meaning. They may retain a certain power of designation, but one which is experienced as empty; a certain power of manifestation, but experienced as indifferent; a certain signification, but experienced as "false." But words, in any case, lose their meaning, their power to set down or express incorporeal effects (events) distinct from the body's actions and passions. All words become physical and affect the body immediately. The process is of the following type: a word, often of an alimentary nature, appears in capital letters printed as in a collage that fixes it and divests it of its meaning. Yet as the pinned word loses its meaning, it bursts into fragments, decomposes into syllables, letters, and above all into consonants which act directly on the body, penetrating it and bruising it. We have seen this in the case of the schizophrenic language student: the mother tongue is emptied of its meaning at the same time that its *phonetic elements* gain an uncommon power to inflict pain. Words cease to express attributes of the state of things. Their fragments mix with unbearable sonorous qualities and break into parts of the body where they form a mixture, a new state of things, as if they themselves were noisy, poisonous foods and encased excrements. The organs of the body become defined and determined as a function of the decomposed elements which affect and attack them.[12] In this process of passion, a pure *language-affect* is substituted for the *language-effect:* "All Writing is Pig-Shit," says Artaud (I, 120); that is, all fixed, written words are decomposed into noisy, alimentary, and excremental fragments.

In this way an awesome primary order, namely, language-

[12]On the subject of organ-letters, see Artaud, "Le Rite de Peyotl," in *Les Tarahumaras* (IX, 32–38)—Ed.

affect, replaces the organization of language. It is within this primary order that the schizophrenic fights and strives to affirm the rights of another sort of word over the passion-word. It is henceforth less a matter for the schizophrenic of recuperating meaning than of destroying words, of warding off affects, or of transforming the body's painful passion into a triumphant action. All this takes place in the depths beneath the punctured surface. The language student offers an example of the means by which the painful splinters of words in the mother tongue are converted into actions through foreign languages. Just as, earlier, the power of wounding was in the phonetic elements affecting the encased or dislocated parts of the body, so victory now can be obtained only by establishing breath-words, scream-words in which all values are exclusively tonic and nonwritten. To these values corresponds a superior body, a new dimension of the schizophrenic body. The body has become a superior organism without parts, one that functions entirely by insufflation, inhaling, evaporation, and transmission of fluids.[13]

This determination of the active process, in opposition to the process of passion, doubtless seems insufficient at first. Indeed, fluids seem no less maleficent than fragments. But they seem so only because of the action/passion ambivalence. It is here that the contradiction experienced in schizophrenia finds its true point of application: passion and action are the inseparable poles of an ambivalence only because the two languages that they form belong inseparably to the body, to the depths of bodies. One is therefore never sure that the ideal fluids of a partless organism do not carry with them parasitic worms, fragments of organs and solid foods, and remnants of excrements; one can even be certain that maleficent powers use fluids and insufflations in order to make fragments of passion pass into the body. The fluid is necessarily corrupted, but not by itself—only by the other pole, from which it is inseparable. Nevertheless, the fact remains that it represents the active pole, or the state of perfect mixture, in opposition to the encasing and bruising of imperfect mix-

---

[13]Cf. Artaud's superior, or "organless" body made only of bone and blood: "No mouth No tongue No teeth No larynx No esophagus No stomach No belly No anus I will reconstruct the man that I am" (*84,* November 1947, p. 102).

tures, which constitute the passive pole. In schizophrenia there is a way of living the distinction between two corporeal mixtures, the partial mixture, which corrupts, and the total and liquid mixture, which leaves the body intact. In the insufflated fluid or liquid element there is the unwritten secret of an active mixture that is like the liquefying "principle of the Sea," in opposition to the passive mixtures of the encased parts. It is in this sense that Artaud transforms the Humpty Dumpty poem about the sea and the fishes into a poem about the problem of obedience and command.[14]

This second language, this process of action, is defined in

[14]Compare Carroll's and Artaud's versions of the same poem—Ed.

But he was very stiff and proud:
He said, 'You needn't shout so loud!'

And he was very proud and stiff:
He said, 'I'd go and wake them, if—'

I took a corkscrew from the shelf:
I went to wake them up myself.

And when I found the door was locked,
I pulled and pushed and kicked and knocked.

And when I found the door was shut,
I tried to turn the handle, but—   [Carroll, p. 220]

He who is not does not know
The obedient one does not suffer.

It is for him who is to know
Why total obedience
Is that which has never suffered

When the being is what disintegrates
Like the mass of the sea.

.   .   .

God only is that which obeys not,
All other beings do not yet exist,
And they suffer.

.   .   .

The being is he who imagines himself to be
To be enough to dispense with himself
From learning what the sea wants . . .

But every little fish knows it.   [Artaud, IX, 171–172; Editor's translation]

practice by an overload of consonants, gutturals, and aspirates, as well as interior apostrophes and accents, breaths and scansions, and a modulation which replaces all the syllabic and even literal values. It is a matter of making an action out of a word by rendering it indecomposable, impossible to disintegrate: language without articulation. Here, however, the bond is a palatalized, an-organic principle, a block or mass of sea. In the case of the Russian word *devero* (tree), the language student rejoices over the existence of a plural—*derev'ya*—in which the interior apostrophe ("yod," the linguists' soft sign) seems to assure him of a fusion of the consonants. Instead of separating them and making them pronounceable, one could say that the vowel reduced to the "yod" makes the consonants indissociable by liquefying them, that it leaves them unreadable, and even unpronounceable, but it turns them into vocal outbursts in a continuous breath. The outbursts are welded together in the breath, like the consonants in the sign which liquefies them, like the fish in the mass of the sea, like the bones in the blood of the organless body, or like a sign of fire, a wave "that hesitates between gas and water," as Artaud said.[15] These outbursts become sputterings in the breath.

When Antonin Artaud says in his "Jabberwocky": "Up to the point where rourghe is to rouarghe to rangmbde and rangmbde to rouarghambde," it is precisely a question of articulating, insufflating, or palatalizing a word, causing it to blaze out so that it becomes the action of a partless body, rather than the passion of a fragmented organism. It is a question of turning the word into a consolidated, indecomposable mass of consonants by using soft signs. In this language one can always find equivalents for portmanteau words. For "rourghe" and "rouarghe," Artaud himself indicates *ruée* (onslaught), *roue* (wheel), *route* (route), *règle* (rule), *route à régler* (a route to be regulated). (One can add

[15]"One feels as if one is inside a gaseous wave which emits an incessant crackling from all sides. Things are released, as from what was your spleen, your liver, your heart, or your lungs; they escape untiringly, and burst in this atmosphere which hesitates between gas and water, but which seems to call things to itself and to command them to regroup.

"What escaped from my spleen or my liver was in the shape of letters from a very ancient and mysterious alphabet chewed by an enormous mouth" (IX, 32–33).—Ed.

le Rouergue, the region of Rodez in which Artaud happened to be.) In the same way, when he says "Uk'hatis" (with the interior apostrophe), he indicates *ukhase* (ukase), *hâte* (haste), and *abruti* (idiot), and adds "a nocturnal jolt beneath Hecate which means the moon pigs thrown off the straight path" (IX, 167).

However, at the very moment in which the word appears to be a portmanteau word, its structure and the commentary adjoined to it persuade us of something entirely different: Artaud's "Ghoré Uk'hatis" are not equivalent to the "pigs who have lost their way," to Carroll's "mome raths," or to Parisot's "verchons fourgus." They do not function on the same level. Far from assuring a ramification of series according to meaning, they bring about a chain of associations between tonic and consonantal elements, in a region of infra-meaning, according to a fluid and burning principle that absorbs or actually resorbs the meaning as it is produced: Uk'hatis (or the strayed moon pigs), is K'H (*cahot*—jolt), 'KT (*nocturne*—nocturnal), H'KT (*Hécate*—Hecate).

The duality of schizophrenic words has not received adequate attention. It consists of *passion-words which explode in wounding phonetic values,* and *action-words which weld together inarticulated tonic values.* These two types of words develop in relation to the state of the body, which is either fragmented or organless. They also refer to two types of theater—the theater of terror and passion, and the theater of cruelty, which is essentially active—as well as to two types of non-sense, passive and active: the nonsense of words emptied of meaning, which decompose into phonetic elements, and the non-sense of tonic elements which form indecomposable words that are no less empty. In both these cases everything happens below meaning, far from the surface. It is here a matter of under-meaning [*sous-sens*], of un-meaning [*insens*], of *Untersinn,* which must be distinguished from the nonsense at the surface. In both of its aspects, language is, to quote Hölderlin, "a sign empty of meaning." It is still a sign, but one that merges with an action or passion of the body. This is why it is insufficient to say that schizophrenic language is defined by an incessant and mad sliding of the signifying series onto the signified series. In fact, no series remains at all; both have disappeared.

They now exist only in appearance. "Speaking" has collapsed onto "eating," and into all the imitations of a "chewing mouth," of a primitive oral depth. Non-sense has ceased to give meaning at the surface; it absorbs, it engulfs all meaning from both sides, that of the signifier and that of the signified. Artaud says that Being, which is nonsense, has teeth.

In the surface organization which we described earlier as secondary, physical bodies and sonorous words were at the same time separated and articulated by an incorporeal borderline—that of meaning, which represents the pure "expressed" of words, on the one side, and logical attributes of bodies on the other. It follows then, that although meaning results from the body's actions and passions, it is a result that is different in nature (is neither action nor passion), and that protects sonorous language against being confused with the physical body. In the primary order of schizophrenia, on the contrary, there is no duality except that between the actions and passions of the body; language is both of these at the same time and is entirely re-sorbed into the body's gaping depths. There is no longer anything to prevent propositions from collapsing onto bodies and mixing their sonorous elements with the olfactive, gustative, digestive, and excremental affects of bodies. Not only is there no longer any meaning, but there is no longer any grammar or syntax, nor even any articulated syllabic, literal, or phonetic elements. Antonin Artaud can entitle his essay "An Antigrammatical Endeavor against Lewis Carroll."[16] Carroll needs a very strict grammar, one responsible for preserving the inflexion and articulation of words as separated from the flexion and articulation of bodies, if only by mirrors that reflect these words and "send" a meaning back to them. For this reason we can oppose Artaud and Carroll, point by point—the primary order in opposition to the secondary organization. Surface series of the "eating/speaking" type really have nothing in common with those poles of the depths that apparently resemble them. The two configurations of non-sense which, at the surface, distribute meaning between

---

[16]"And I will add that I have always despised Lewis Carroll (see my letters from Rodez concerning the 'Jabberwocky'): for me this was an antigrammatical endeavor not *following* Carroll, but *against* him" (IX, 273–274).—Ed.

different series have nothing to do with the two descents of non-sense (*Untersinn*) that pull, engulf, and resorb meaning. The two forms of stuttering—clonic and tonic—have only the most super-ficial analogy with the two schizophrenic languages. The break at the surface has nothing in common with the deep cleavage (*Spaltung*). Even portmanteau words have entirely heterogene-ous functions.

One can find a schizoid "position" in the child before he rises to or conquers the surface. In addition, one can always find schizoid fragments at the surface itself, since its role is precisely that of organizing and displaying elements that have come from the depths. Still, it is no less erroneous and condemnable to confuse the conquest of the surface in the child, the breakdown of the surface in the schizophrenic, and the mastery of surfaces by a "minor pervert." Lewis Carroll's work can always be turned into a kind of schizophrenic tale. Some English psychoanalysts have rashly done so, pointing out the telescopings and encasings of Alice's body, her manifest alimentary (and latent excremen-tal) obsessions, the fragments that designate morsels of food as well as "choice morsels," the collages and labels of alimentary words that are quick to decompose, the losses of identity, the fishes in the sea, and so on. One may also ask what sort of madness is represented clinically by the Mad Hatter, the March Hare, and the Dormouse. In the opposition between Alice and Humpty Dumpty,[17] one can always recognize the two ambivalent poles: fragmented organs/organless body, body-sieve/superior body. Artaud himself had no other reason at first for confront-ing the Humpty Dumpty text. But it is at this moment that Artaud's warning rings out: "I did not do a translation.... I never liked the poem.... I do not like surface poems or lan-guages."

Bad psychoanalysis has two ways of deceiving itself: it can believe that it has discovered identical subject matters, which necessarily can be found everywhere, or it can believe that is has found analogous forms which create false differences. In doing

[17]Cf. *Through the Looking Glass,* in which Humpty Dumpty introduces himself as an egg, or a body without organs, and reproaches Alice for the organic differentiation of her face, which he judges to be too ordinary.

either, psychoanalysis fails on both grounds: those of clinical psychiatry and literary criticism. Structuralism is right in reminding us that form and content matter only within the original and irreducible structures in which they are organized. Psychoanalysis should have geometric dimensions rather than merely consisting of personal anecdotes. It is first of all the organization and the orientation of these geometric dimensions, rather than reproductive materials or reproduced forms, that constitute both life and sexuality. Psychoanalysis should not be content with designating cases, analyzing personal histories, or diagnosing complexes. As a psychoanalysis of meaning, it should be geographic before being anecdotal: it should distinguish between different regions. Artaud is neither Carroll nor Alice, Carroll is not Artaud, Carroll is not even Alice. Artaud plunges the child into an extremely violent alternative between corporeal passion and action that conforms to the two languages of depth. Either the child must not be born, which is to say, must not leave the chambers of his future spinal column, upon which his parents fornicate (which amounts to an inverse suicide)—or else he must become a fluid, "superior," flaming body, without organs or parents (like those whom Artaud called his "daughters" yet-to-be-born).

Carroll, on the contrary, awaits the child in accordance with his language of incorporeal meaning. He awaits her at the moment at which the child leaves the depths of the maternal body without yet having discovered the depths of her own body, that brief moment of surface when the little girl breaks the surface of the water, like Alice in the pool of her own tears. Carroll and Artaud are worlds apart. We may believe that the surface has its monsters (the Snark and the Jabberwock), its terrors and its cruelties which, though not from the depths, nevertheless have claws and can snatch laterally, or even pull us back into the depths whose dangers we thought we had averted. Carroll and Artaud are nonetheless different; at no point do their worlds coincide. Only the commentator can move from one dimension to the other, and that is his great weakness, the sign that he himself inhabits neither. We would not give one page of Antonin Artaud for all of Carroll; Artaud is the only person to have experienced absolute depth in literature, to have discovered a "vital" body and its prodigious language (through suffering, as he says). He explored the infra-meaning, which today is still unknown. Carroll, on the other hand, remains the master or the surveyor of surfaces we thought we knew so well that we never explored them. Yet it is on these surfaces that the entire logic of meaning is held.

NEIL HERTZ

Freud and the Sandman

For my old age I have chosen the theme of death; I have stumbled on a remarkable notion based on my theory of the instincts, and now must read all kinds of things relevant to it, e.g. Schopenhauer, for the first time. But I am not fond of reading.

—Freud to Lou Andreas-Salomé, August 1919

"I invented psychoanalysis because it had no literature," Freud once remarked,[1] joking about what is now lugubriously known as The Burden of the Past or The Anxiety of Influence. "Literature," of course, meant the writings of other investigators in his field—his predecessors, the contemporaries he saw as rivals, or more benignly, as disciples and colleagues—but we have only to let the word drift a bit, until "literature" means just "literature," for the joke to become still more suggestive. That, at any rate, will be the drift of what follows: the question of "literary priority" and the concerns that cling to it (the wish to be original, the fear of plagiarism, the rivalry among writers) will be brought into touch with some topics commonly grouped under the rubric Psychoanalysis-and-Literature (the overlapping of the two fields, the rivalry between them, the power of one to interpret and neutralize the other). My chief text will be Freud's essay "The Uncanny"[2]—in particular the reading he offers there of E. T. A. Hoffmann's story "The Sandman," and the links he establishes between the sentiment of the uncanny and his newly elaborated theory of the repetition-compulsion—but I shall also

[1] Cited by Paul Roazen in *Brother Animal: The Story of Freud and Tausk* (New York: Knopf, 1969), p. 92.

[2] *The Standard Edition of the Complete Psychological Works of Sigmund Freud*, trans. James Strachey (London: Hogarth, 1953–73), vol. XVII. References to this and other writings of Freud will be given by volume and page in the *Standard Edition*, accompanying the citations.

be examining some recently published biographical material which suggests that the motifs of the uncanny, of repetition, and of literary priority were playing themselves out in Freud's relations with one of his younger colleagues at about the same time that he was bringing them into prominence in his writing. My hope is to quilt together these scraps of verbal material, each with a somewhat different feel to it—a work of fiction, a psychoanalytic account of its structure, the formulation of a metapsychological theory, some biographical anecdotes—and to comment on their power, collectively or when working at odds with one another, to fix and fascinate our attention.

I

Even the simple facts concerning the writing and publication of "The Uncanny" seem designed to raise questions about repetition. The essay came out in the fall of 1919, and a letter of Freud's indicates that it was written in May of that year, or, rather, rewritten, for the letter speaks of his going back to an old manuscript that he had set aside, for how long isn't clear—perhaps as long as a dozen years. However old the manuscript, it is usually assumed that Freud was prompted to return to it by his reformulation, in March or April of 1919, of his understanding of the repetition-compulsion, in the course of producing a first draft of *Beyond the Pleasure Principle*. I have seen no account of the contents of that draft, which may no longer exist, but it is customarily thought to have been a considerably less developed version of the text Freud finally published as *Beyond the Pleasure Principle* late in 1920. That it contained a new and powerful theory of repetition is a safe guess, since that theory was available for publication in "The Uncanny," but scholars have also reasoned that it made no mention of the other remarkable notion included in the published version, Freud's postulation of the death instincts (XVIII, 3-4). That notion, it is assumed, was what Freud was working his way toward in the summer of 1919, when he wrote the letter quoted above, a letter which mentions the "theme of death" and a "theory of the instincts," but in which the compound noun *Todestriebe* does not appear; according to the editors of the Standard Edition, the death instinct is not mentioned as such until February 1920. An interval, then, is generally imagined, during which the theory of an autonomous compulsion to repeat existed in Freud's mind and on paper, as yet ungrounded in any more fundamental metapsychological explanation; and it was in that interval, and rather early on, that "The Uncanny" was rewritten.

If one then asks what relationship the essay bears to the theory it announces, the customary answer is that it represents an application of a general explanatory principle to a particular, though by no means central, case. "In the famous 'compulsion to repeat,'" Philip Rieff writes, "Freud found the concept that was to give unity and truth to an essay which, without such a transfusion of theory, would have remained a relatively pale piece of erudition."[3] And that seems reasonable, until one looks more closely at the essay and at the theory. For the essay's "unity" is anything but patent—if it is there at all, it must be tracked down through a rambling and intriguingly oblique presentation[4]—and the theory of the compulsion to repeat is so strange that its explanatory power is not the first thing one is likely to respond to when one comes across it. The impulse to rewrite "The Uncanny" may have been Freud's wish to test out the value of his theory, as Rieff suggests, but it might also have been his exclamatory response ("*Unheimlich!*") to the theory's strangeness.

If one follows the course of Freud's thinking about repetition, one finds him, in 1919, granting an oddly autonomous status, and an emphatic priority, to what had previously been thought of as a secondary and explainable element within the system of psychoanalytic theory.[5] From the first, Freud was bound to at-

[3]In his introduction to S. Freud, *Studies in Parapsychology* (New York: Collier-Macmillan, 1963), p. 7.

[4]See Hélène Cixous, "Fiction and Its Phantoms: A Reading of Freud's *Das Unheimliche*" in *New Literary History*, 7 (Spring 1976), 525–548, a translation of an article originally published in *Poétique*, 10 (1972), 199–216. "The Uncanny" has drawn to it a series of remarkably acute interpretations in the last few years. See Jacques Derrida, "La Double Séance," in *La Dissémination* (Paris: Seuil, 1972), pp. 300–301; Samuel Weber, "The Sideshow, or: Remarks on A Canny Moment," in *MLN*, 88 (1973), 1102–1133; Jeffrey Mehlman, "Poe Pourri: Lacan's Purloined Letter," *Semiotext(e)*, 1 (1975), 51–68; and Sarah Kofman, "Le Double e(s)t le diable" in *Quatre Romans analytiques* (Paris: Galilée, 1974), pp. 135–181.

[5]For clarification of psychoanalytic theory, see J. Laplanche and J. B. Pontalis, *The Language of Psycho-Analysis*, trans. Donald Nicholson-Smith (New York: Norton, 1973), in particular, the entries "Compulsion to Repeat," and "Death Instincts."

tend to a variety of repeated and repeating phenomena—the recurrence of infantile material in dreams and in neurotic symptoms, the rehearsal of behavior patterns that came to be known as "acting-out," the revivification and transference of unconscious wishes that a patient experienced in relation to his analyst, and so on. The word "repetition" could be used to designate all these without purporting to explain why any of them should occur; that, Freud believed, was the task of his two interacting principles of mental functioning—the pleasure principle, and its more sober partner, the reality principle. Even in 1914, when he wrote of a patient's "compulsion to repeat" certain forgotten, because repressed, material, the attribution of power implicit in the term "compulsion" was still relative and, above all, still explicable through reference to forces other than itself. In 1919, however, Freud felt obliged (compelled?) by certain new data to acknowledge the independence of the compulsion to repeat, and, for at least several months, to address himself to its apparently irreducible inexplicability. The repetition-compulsion "itself"— or was it merely Freud's theory of repetition?—may then have seemed to its discoverer to have taken on an uncanny life of its own; indeed, the very uncertainty as to whether it was the force "itself" or its theoretical formulation that was claiming attention would contribute to the effect of strangeness.

How does one come to terms with a force that seems at once mobile and concealed in its operation? When, in *Beyond the Pleasure Principle,* Freud developed his more abstract conception of a compulsion to repeat and argued for the existence of "death instincts," the mythical *Triebe* (drives) underlying (constituting? informing?) the *Zwang* (compulsion), he was obliged to acknowledge that evidence for such an instinctive force was hard to find: the drive was, in his words, never "visible," it "eluded perception" except (he added in *Civilization and Its Discontents* [XXI, 120]) when it was "tinged or colored" by sexuality. The metaphor has been taken as a means of suggesting something about the nature of instinctual forces—that they were always encountered in some mixture with each other, never in a state of "purity." But, with only a slight shift of emphasis, it can also be read as a way of describing an epistemological difficulty: like certain substances that must be prepared before they can be

examined under a microscope, it is only when stained that the
death instinct can be brought into focus. Taken in this latter
sense, the relation between the erotic instincts and the death
instinct comes to sound very much like the relationship Freud
described, elsewhere in *Beyond the Pleasure Principle*, between his
own figurative language and the "bewildering and obscure processes" with which he was concerned:[6]

> We need not feel greatly disturbed in judging our speculations
> upon the life and death instincts by the fact that so many bewilder-
> ing and obscure processes occur in it—such as one instinct being
> driven out by another, or an instinct turning from the ego to an
> object, and so on. This is merely due to our being obliged to operate
> with the scientific terms, that is to say with the figurative language,
> peculiar to psychology (or, more precisely, to depth psychology).
> We could not otherwise describe the processes in question at all,
> and indeed we could not have become aware of them. [XVIII, 60]

Freud sees his figurative language as a means of lending color to
what is otherwise imperceptible. We may wish, later, to question
the appropriateness of this analogy, but for the moment let us
accept it and explore its possible elaborations: can we press the
point and say that the figures of psychoanalytic discourse are
"like" the erotic instincts, color codings of a sort that allow one to
trace the paths of concealed energy? Or, alternately, that the
visible signs of desire are "like" figures of speech? The interest
of these questions will become apparent when we rephrase them
in the terms of "The Uncanny," in which the invisible energies
are thought of as those of the repetition-compulsion, and the
glimpses one gets of them are felt as disturbing and strange:

> It must be explained that we are able to postulate the principle of a
> repetition-compulsion in the unconscious mind, based upon in-
> stinctual activity and probably inherent in the very nature of the
> instincts—a principle powerful enough to overrule the pleasure-
> principle, lending to certain aspects of the mind their daemonic
> character, and still very clearly expressed in the tendencies of small
> children; a principle, too, which is responsible for a part of the

[6]On the relation between Freud's theorizing and his figurative language, see
the superb reading of *Beyond the Pleasure Principle* provided by Rodolphe
Gasché in "La Sorcière métapsychologique," *Digraphe*, 3 (1974), 83–122.

course taken by the analysis of neurotic patients. Taken in all, the
foregoing prepares us for the discovery that whatever reminds us
of this inner repetition-compulsion is perceived as uncanny. [XVII,
238]

The feeling of the uncanny would seem to be generated by
being-reminded-of-the-repetition-compulsion, not by being-
reminded-of-whatever-it-is-that-is-repeated. It is the becoming
aware of the process that is felt as eerie, not the becoming aware
of some particular item in the unconscious, once familiar, then
repressed, now coming back into consciousness. Elsewhere in
the essay, Freud seems to be saying something easier to understand. When he quotes Schelling's formulation: "Everything is
uncanny that ought to have remained hidden and secret yet
comes to light," (XVII, 224) or even when he describes the effect
produced by "The Sandman" as bound up with the reactivation
of a repressed infantile dread of castration, it would seem to be
the something-that-is-repeated that is the determining factor, not
the reminder of compulsive repetition itself. But it is the bolder
and more puzzling hypothesis that Freud stresses once more in
Beyond the Pleasure Principle: "It may be presumed that when
people unfamiliar with analysis feel an obscure fear—a dread
of rousing something that, so they feel, is better left sleeping—
what they are afraid of is the emergence of this compulsion with
its hint of possession by some daemonic power" (XVIII, 36). It is
the emergence of the compulsion that they fear, as much as the
reappearance of a particular fear or desire. It may seem like a
quibble to dwell on this difference: surely the awareness of the
process of repetition is inseparable from the awareness of something being repeated, for there can be no such thing as sheer
repetition. Of course: repetition becomes "visible" when it is
colored or tinged by something being repeated, which itself
functions like vivid or heightened language, lending a kind of
rhetorical consistency to what is otherwise quite literally unspeakable. Whatever it is that is repeated—an obsessive ritual,
perhaps, or a bit of acting-out in relation to one's analyst—will,
then, feel most compellingly uncanny when it is seen as *merely*
coloring, that is, when it comes to seem most gratuitously
rhetorical. So much for "people unfamiliar with analysis," or for

patients recognizing the uncanny effects generated by the transference. But what of the investigator "obliged to operate with
the scientific terms, that is to say with the figurative language,
peculiar to depth psychology?" Mightn't he, too, experience effects of the uncanny at those moments when the figurativeness
of his figurative language was brought home to him in some
connection with the repetition-compulsion? That is a question
we shall return to after considering Freud's reading of "The
Sandman."

II

> I was most strongly compelled to tell you about Nathanael's dis-
> astrous life.
> —Narrator of "The Sandman"

Freud offers, in fact, two readings of the story: the first is of its
manifest surface, given in the form of a rapid, selective paraphrase of the plot, moving sequentially from the childhood recollections of the hero, Nathanael, on through his attacks of madness to his eventual suicide. The nursery tale of the Sandman
who tears out children's eyes, the terror Nathanael experiences
when the lawyer Coppelius threatens his own eyes, the death of
Nathanael's father—these early experiences, and their subsequent reprise in slightly altered forms, with Coppola the optician standing in for Coppelius—these are the elements that
Freud strings together with a minimum of interpretive comment, in the interest of showing that what is uncanny about the
story is, as he puts it, "directly attached to the figure of the
Sandman, that is, to the idea of being robbed of one's eyes." E.
Jentsch, the psychologist whose 1906 article may have drawn
Freud's attention to "The Sandman," had located the source of
the uncanny in effects of intellectual uncertainty—doubts
whether apparently inanimate beings are really alive, for
example—but Freud is insistent in rejecting this notion. He
grants that a kind of uncertainty is created in the reader in the
opening pages of the story, uncertainty whether he is being
taken into a real world or a fantastic one of Hoffmann's own
creation, but he argues that by the end of the story, those doubts
have been removed, and one is convinced "that Coppola the

optician really is the lawyer Coppelius and thus also the Sandman." In other words, Nathanael's sense that he is "the horrible plaything of dark powers" is, within the fiction of the story, correct. "We are not supposed to be looking on at the products of a madman's imagination," Freud comments sardonically, "behind which we, with the superiority of rational minds, are able to detect the sober truth" (XVII, 230).

And yet Freud's second account of the story, offered in a long and stunningly condensed footnote (XVII, 232–233), is precisely that: the sober truth detected behind the products of a madman's imagination, the latent substructure, or what Freud calls the "original arrangement" of the elements of the story. Here, instead of a line of narrative—the unfolding in time of Nathanael's fate—what Freud presents is a series of repeated structures arranged so as to display the forces within Nathanael's mind that generated them. The child's ambivalence toward his father splits that character into two figures, a loving father who is killed off and the threatening Coppelius who can be blamed for this violence, and this pairing is reproduced later in the characters of Spalanzani (the mechanician who is called the father of the doll Olympia) and Coppola (who destroys the doll): linked to this is a series of triangular relationships, in which the Sandman blocks Nathanael's attempts at love, first in the form of Coppelius coming between Nathanael and his fiancée Klara, then in the form of Coppola taking Olympia away from Nathanael, finally once again as Coppelius, driving Nathanael to suicide just as he is about to marry Klara. The structures are accounted for dynamically, and the story is taken as illustrating, in Freud's words, "the psychological truth of the situation in which the young man, fixated upon his father by his castration-complex, is incapable of loving a woman." The footnote concludes with a glancing remark about Hoffmann's childhood, but it is clear that Freud is not interested in biographical speculation: indeed, his point is that the castration-complex is not peculiar to Hoffmann but is universal, and it is because of this universality that its veiled presence in the story is capable of creating the effect of the uncanny, of something that ought to have remained hidden and secret and yet comes to light.

Someone suspicious of psychoanalysis might find these two

accounts contradictory, and argue that Freud cannot have it both ways—either the story is about Nathanael's being driven to suicide by an evil external power, the Sandman, or it is about the progressive deterioration of someone "fixated upon his father by his castration-complex"—but Freud would have no difficulty answering this objection. The two accounts, he would say, are linked to each other as latent to manifest, the castration-complex generates the fiction of the Sandman; the reader, even when he is most convinced of the reality of the Sandman, indeed especially when he is most convinced, senses as uncanny the imminent return of the repressed.

But a more interesting and, I think, more serious objection can be raised to Freud's reading of Hoffmann, and that is that Freud has overstabilized his first account of the story, that there is, indeed, more cause for doubt and uncertainty as one moves through "The Sandman" than Freud allows. Looking back at his paraphrasing of the story we can see one way in which this overstabilization has been accomplished. Freud retells the story, occasionally quoting from the text, but what is remarkable is that everything he includes within quotation marks has already appeared within quotation marks in "The Sandman": that is, he quotes nothing but dialogue, things said by Nathanael or by some other character; the words of the narrator have completely disappeared, replaced by Freud's own, and we have the illusion of watching Nathanael's actions through a medium considerably more transparent than Hoffmann's text. For Hoffmann's narration is anything but unobtrusive: it is, rather, vivid, shifty, and extravagant, full of assonances, verbal repetitions, literary allusions and startling changes in the pace, in the mood, and in the quasi-musical dynamics of its unfolding. What is more, this narrative exuberance is, at certain moments, rendered thematically important within the story in ways that make Freud's decision to set it aside seem more puzzling. For it may be that what is unsettling, if not uncanny, about "The Sandman" is as much a function of its surface as of the depths it conceals.

Consider one such moment where narrative technique and thematic concerns are intertwined, a moment about which Freud has nothing to say. "The Sandman" opens as if it were going to be an epistolary novel: without introduction or interspersed commentary, we are offered three letters headed simply "Nathanael to Lothar," "Klara to Nathanael," "Nathanael to Lothar."[7] It is in the first of these that Nathanael describes his "dark forebodings of . . . impending doom," then interrupts himself to exclaim: "Oh, my dearest Lothar, how can I begin to make you realize, even vaguely, that what happened a few days ago really could have so fatal and disruptive an effect on my life? If you were here you could see for yourself; but now you will certainly think I am a crazy man who sees ghosts . . . " (137). The letter then goes on at length, describing his childhood, his terror of the Sandman, the death of his father, and his certainty at having recognized in Coppola his father's murderer, Coppelius. Two shorter letters are exchanged, then there is a slight spacing of the printed text, and a narrator emerges:

> Gentle reader, nothing can be imagined that is stranger and more extraordinary than the fate which befell my poor friend, the young student Nathanael, which I have undertaken to relate to you. Have you, gentle reader, ever experienced anything that totally possessed your heart, your thoughts and your senses to the exclusion of all else? Everything seethed and roiled within you; heated blood surged through your veins and inflamed your cheeks. Your gaze was peculiar, as if seeking forms in empty space invisible to other eyes, and speech dissolved into gloomy sighs. Then your friends asked you "What is it, dear friend? What is the matter?" And wishing to describe the picture in your mind with all its vivid colors, the light and the shade, you struggled vainly to find words. But it seemed to you that you had to gather together all that had occurred—the wonderful, the magnificent, the heinous, the joyous, the ghastly—and express it in the very first word so that it would strike like lightning. Yet every word, everything within the realm of speech, seemed colorless, frigid, dead. [148]

Somewhere along the way, the gentle reader is likely to realize that the torment he is being asked to imagine is not that of Nathanael, though it sounds so much like it, but rather that of the narrator faced with the problem of telling Nathanael's story. Or, more specifically, faced with that classic problem of the Romantic writer: how to begin. On the next page the narrator

---

[7] *Selected Writings of E. T. A. Hoffmann,* ed. and trans. Leonard J. Kent and Elizabeth C. Knight, 2 vols. (Chicago: University of Chicago Press, 1969). "The Sandman" is printed in I, 137–167. Henceforth, references to the story will be given parenthetically after each citation.

mentions some possible opening lines he had tried and rejected, then adds: "There were no words I could find which were appropriate to describe, even in the most feeble way, the brilliant colors of my inner vision. I resolved not to begin at all. So, gentle reader, do accept the three letters, which my friend Lothar has been kind enough to communicate, as the outline of the picture to which I will endeavor to add ever more color as I continue the story" (149).

The point is not that a narrative persona is being elaborated with a character or "point of view" of his own—that would not be very interesting if it were the case, and it is not the case here; nor is it simply that Hoffmann is a supple and entertaining virtuoso of narrative. Rather, his virtuosity is productive of certain very specific and interesting effects, two of which I would like to examine in some detail.

To begin with, consider the structuring of the story: Hoffmann's feint in the direction of epistolary fiction confers an odd status on those three opening letters. Like any supposedly documentary evidence embedded in a narrative, a greater degree of authenticity seems to be claimed for them, and the reader is inclined to go along with the illusion and accept them as underwriting the narrator's account. That would be so wherever the letters were placed; as it is, though, because the letters precede the appearance of the narrator, what he says of them has the effect of requiring the reader to make a funny retroactive adjustment, granting them a kind of documentary reality just as he is being most strongly reminded both of their fictitiousness and, more important, of how badly the narrator seems to need them to initiate and impel his own writing. The effect is playful but nonetheless complex: in fact, its particular structural complexity—a temporal lag which produces, retroactively, a situation in which a text cannot be characterized as unequivocally "real" or unequivocally "fictitious"—is remarkably close to that of Freud's own notion of the workings of what he termed *Nachträglichkeit* ("deferred action") in conferring meaning and pathogenic power on infantile experiences and fantasies.[8] Nor is it simply the tem-

---

[8]For an account of the use of this term by Freud and, in its French version—*après-coup*—by Jacques Lacan, see the entry "Deferred Action" in Laplanche and Pontalis, pp. 111–114.

poral structure of the opening pages of "The Sandman" that seems Freudian *avant la lettre*. The content of Nathanael's first letter—his account of his quasi-castration at the hands of Coppelius and of the subsequent trauma of his father's death—is precisely the sort of childhood material with which Freud's concept of *Nachträglichkeit* was concerned.

But here an important difference is worth remarking. Freud looks to Nathanael's story—as it is presented in his letters—for the signs of his having revised an early traumatic experience, recasting it in the form of a primal scene and drawing it out into an explanatory narrative. The differences he discerns are between a hypothetical early version—some experience (real or fantasmatic) taken in by the child but numbly unassimilated at the time and hence unspeakable—and its subsequent expression in a reassuring, if lurid, form. The forces at play are a complex of Nathanael's wishes (for instance, his "death-wish against the father") that are repressed only to resurface, transformed and acceptably disguised in Nathanael's prose (for example, Coppelius' murder of the father). But while Hoffmann's story could offer Freud material for just such an account of the workings of *Nachträglichkeit*, it also adds an instance of its own of a similar revisionary process, one that is not so easily aligned with Freud's intrapsychic model. When the narrator retroactively produces Nathanael's letters, it is *his* ambivalent desire, not Nathanael's, that is being momentarily displayed: and, I should add, only momentarily, for a reader's interest in the narrator is allowed to fade rapidly; the rest of the story is recounted with practically no traces of his comically anguished self-consciousness. But for the length of the several paragraphs in which the narrator's desire to write occupies our attention, we are obliged to consider a compulsion that has been slightly dislocated, for it seems to be neither exactly exterior and "daemonic" (in the sense that Nathanael imagines himself to be "the horrible plaything of dark powers") nor exactly inner and psychological (in the sense that Klara intends when she reassures Nathanael that "if there is a dark power . . . it must form inside us, form part of us, must be identical with ourselves"), but something else again.

This is not the only point in "The Sandman" where one is teased with the likeness between the unfolding of Nathanael's fate and the elaboration of a narrative, between the forces driving Nathanael and whatever is impelling the narrator. A similar effect is created by Hoffmann's choice and manipulation of diction. The story consistently presents the pathos (and, almost as often, the comedy) of the psychological/daemonic in language that draws on the vocabulary and topics of Romantic aesthetics. It is as if Hoffmann had begun with the commonplace equation of poets, lovers, and madmen, and then clustered together fragmentary versions of that analogy so that the semantic overlapping and sheer accumulation of instances would dazzle his readers, as Nathanael is dazzled by Coppola's display of eyeglasses: "Myriad eyes peered and blinked and stared up at Nathanael, who could not look away from the table, while Coppola continued putting down more and more eyeglasses; and flaming glances criss-crossed each other ever more wildly and shot their blood-red rays into Nathanael's breast" (156).

If we are curious about the effect of such effects, there is no better place to start than with that image of the blood-red rays that shoot into Nathanael's breast: it turns out to be an element in a long series that includes the glowing grains of coal that Coppelius threatens to sprinkle on Nathanael's eyes, the "rays of the mysterious" that can't find their way into Klara's cold heart, that "very first word" that the narrator hoped would "strike like lightning," the music that flows into Klara's admirers when they look at her, penetrating them "to the very soul," Olympia's voice as she sings, that scorches Nathanael to *his* very soul, the bloody eyes that Spalanzani flings at Nathanael's breast, and so on. And this series itself is linked to another, one based on a combination of two aesthetic motifs—the conventional analogy between poetry and painting, and the likening of communication and perception to inscribing or imprinting: to convey in warm and penetrating language is to find words that color in the outlines. That was the narrator's hope in the passage I quoted above: the three authentic letters will serve as the "outline of the picture" to which he will "add ever more color" as the story goes on; it is linked to the mock-allegorical description of Klara in terms of paintings by Battoni and Ruisdael; to the fading of the colors in Nathanael's mental image of Coppelius; to Nathanael's contradictory insistence, earlier in the story, that the image of Coppelius was permanently imprinted on his memory; as well as to a similar play between the vividness and permanence of Nathanael's image of Klara and its subsequent fading when he falls in love with Olympia.

The images and allusions that go to make up these series occur often enough and in sufficiently different tonalities—lyrical, melodramatic, ironic, and others—so that their most immediate effect is to create the sense of excess I mentioned, felt sometimes as fatefully enigmatic and burdensome, sometimes as the token of the storyteller's exuberant virtuosity. But this appearance of compulsive or haphazard plurality is slightly misleading, for the series are organized in other ways as well, so as to produce a particular configuration of the themes of power, duration, and what could be called the desire for representation. Briefly we could say that the interaction of any pair of characters in "The Sandman" is figured less as an exchange of meaningful signs (conversation, gestures, letters, and so on) than as a passage of energy, sometimes benign, sometimes baneful, between them (warm glances, penetrating words, scorching missiles) and that the effectiveness of such "communication" ought to be measurable by its power to leave a lasting mark. If we take this as a characteristically Gothic rendering of experience, we can see that Hoffmann has complicated this model in at least four respects. (1) He offers conflicting accounts of the source of the energy that circulates through the story, impelling characters into action or expression: is it a creation of the self, or does it come beaming in from some exterior point? Is the tale psychological or daemonic? (2) He insists now on the deep and lasting colors or inscriptions left by these exchanges of energy, now on the odd impermanence of those same marks. (3) He blurs the boundaries between the fields where such marking goes on, the fields of action and expression, of primary event and subsequent representation. And (4) he links the wish to make a mark, the wish for the power to produce durable representations, to the uncertainties generated by (1), (2), and (3). It is, for example, the fading of "the ugly image of Coppelius" in Nathanael's imagination that leads him "to make his gloomy presentiment that Coppelius would destroy his happiness the subject of a poem." As a result of Hoffmann's manipulations a reader is made to feel, confusedly, that Nathanael's life, his writings, the narrator's storytelling, Hoffmann's writing, and the reader's own fascinated acquiescence in it, are all impelled by the same energy, and impelled precisely, to represent that energy, to color in its barely discerned outlines, to oblige it, if possible, to leave an unfading mark. Nathanael's letters, of course, qualify as such an attempt on his part, but the poem I have just alluded to is a still more condensed instance of this desire for representation. It is an episode which is best approached once again by way of Freud's reading of the story.

At the story's end, when Nathanael, in a frenzy, is about to leap from a tower to his death, he is heard shrieking, "Ring of fire! Whirl about!" This is one of the passages Freud quotes, adding that these are "words whose origin we know" (XVII, 229). He is alluding to his own retelling of an earlier episode: "Nathanael succumbs to a fresh attack of madness, and in his delirium his recollection of his father's death is mingled with this new experience. He cries, 'Faster—faster—faster—rings of fire—rings of fire—Whirl about—rings of fire—round and round! . . . '" That is, Freud is tracing the origins of those words from the suicide scene back through the earlier moment of Nathanael's madness to the initiating childhood trauma. But, oddly enough, if we look back to those early scenes for the "ring of fire" (the expression translates the word *Feuerkreis*—an unusual one in German) we find none. There is certainly fire, and a sort of semicircular hearth where Nathanael is tormented, but no *Feuerkreis*. The origin of the word turns out to be elsewhere, in a passage Freud ignores, the poem Nathanael composes and reads to Klara:

> Finally it occurred to him to make his gloomy presentiment that Coppelius would destroy his happiness the subject of a poem. He portrayed himself and Klara as united in true love but plagued by some dark hand which occasionally intruded into their lives, snatching away incipient joy. Finally, as they stood at the altar, the sinister Coppelius appeared and touched Klara's lovely eyes, which sprang into Nathanael's own breast, burning and scorching like bleeding sparks. Then Coppelius grabbed him and flung him into a blazing circle of fire which spun round with the speed of a whirlwind and, with a rush, carried him away. The awesome noise was like a hurricane furiously whipping up the waves so that they rose up like

white-headed black giants in a raging inferno. But through this savage tumult he could hear Klara's voice: "Can't you see me, dear one? Coppelius has deceived you. That which burned in your breast was not my eyes. Those were fiery drops of your own heart's blood. Look at me. I have still got my own eyes." Nathanael thought: "It is Klara: I am hers forever." Then, it was as though this thought had grasped the fiery circle and forced it to stop turning, while the raging noise died away in the black abyss. Nathanael looked into Klara's eyes; but it was death that, with Klara's eyes, looked upon him kindly. While Nathanael was composing his poem he was very calm and serene; he reworked and polished every line, and, since he had fettered himself with meter, he did not pause until everything in the poem was perfect and euphonious. But when it was finally completed and he read the poem aloud to himself, he was stricken with fear and a wild horror and he cried out "Whose horrible voice is this?" Soon, however, he once more came to understand that it was really nothing more than a very successful poem. [152–153]

There is no term in English for what French critics call a *mise en abîme*—a casting into the abyss—but the effect itself is familiar enough: an illusion of infinite regress can be created by a writer or painter by incorporating within his own work a work that duplicates in miniature the larger structure, setting up an apparently unending metonymic series. This *mise en abîme* simulates wildly uncontrollable repetition, and it is just that, I believe, that is imaged here in the whirling *Feuerkreis,* carrying Nathanael away into the black abyss. Earlier in the story, the narrator had dreamed of creating images whose coloring was so deep and intense that "the multifarious crowd of living shapes" would sweep his audience away until they saw themselves in the midst of the scene that had issued from his soul. The *Feuerkreis* in Nathanael's poem is the daemonic complement to the narrator's literary ambitions—and not only the narrator's: the unobtrusive fluidity with which Hoffmann's prose sweeps the reader into the scene (although not into the text) of Nathanael's poem ("He portrayed himself . . .") and then out again ("Nathanael looked into Klara's eyes; but it was death that, with Klara's eyes, looked upon him kindly. While Nathanael was composing his poem. . . .") sets up an indeterminate play between Coppelius' victim and someone expressing a grandiose wish for rhetorical power, for a power that would capture and represent the energies figured in the *Feuerkreis* itself.[9]

The poem, then—or, more accurately, the prose that stands in for the poem—demands to be read in two quite different ways. One, which I have referred to as the psychological/ daemonic, is entirely compatible with Freud's reading of the story as a whole, and in this respect his choosing to ignore the poem is unimportant: it could be easily enough assimilated to his description of both the manifest and the latent structures of the story. The Oedipal anxiety associated with Coppelius, the allusions to bleeding eyes, the final image of Klara as death—Freud could explain all these elements and string the episode onto the narrative thread he constructs leading from Nathanael's childhood to his suicide. In another reading, however, a reading I shall label—somewhat willfully—the literary, the poem resists any attempts to situate it in the temporal structures implicit in either of Freud's accounts (that is, in either the fantastic sequential narrative of Nathanael's being driven to his death by the Sandman, or in its psychoanalytic reconstruction as the story of Nathanael's progressive insanity). In this other reading, Nathanael's writings about his fate—his letters, his poem—are linked to the fading of the image of Coppelius, to the narrator's impulsive wish to tell Nathanael's story and, beyond this, to Hoffmann's own work on "The Sandman." But these instances cannot be organized chronologically or in any genetic fashion—it is only in a banal metaphor that we can speak of Hoffmann as Nathanael's "father" (though we can properly, in Freud's scheme, speak of Coppelius as a figure of the father), and just as the question of Oedipal priority no longer applies, so the possibility of seeing in Nathanael's writing about himself an example of narcissistic regression (a diagnosis applicable, within Freud's framework, to his falling in love with Olympia) is equally irrelevant. My point is not that Freud's reading should yield to this other scheme, but

[9]Hoffmann's account of the plot and scenic effects of Nathanael's poem, like Freud's account of "The Sandman," serves as a powerfully convincing substitute for a text, in this case a poem in meter which we never get to read. Unlike Freud, however, Hoffmann calls attention to this play between a literary object and its lurid double by stressing the wild alternation in Nathanael's response to what he had written.

rather that a sign of the story's power—what makes it an instance of Romantic irony at its most unsettling or, if you like, of the un-canny—is its availability to both these schemes, its shifting be-tween the registers of the psychological/daemonic and the literary, thereby dramatizing the differences as well as the complici-ties between the two.[10] When Freud turns aside from these more literary aspects of the story he is making a legitimate interpretive move, but it has the effect of domesticating the story precisely by emphasizing its dark, daemonic side.

III

The professor of poetry and rhetoric took a pinch of snuff, snapped the lid shut, cleared his throat, and solemnly de-clared: "Most honorable ladies and gentlemen, do you not see the point of it all? It is all an allegory, an extended metaphor."
But many honorable gentlemen were not reassured by this. The story of the automaton had very deeply impressed them, and horrible distrust of human figures in general arose.
—Narrator of "The Sandman"

The claims I have been making for Hoffmann's well-known levity and extravagance may seem beside the point, and I can imagine someone objecting to my characterizing those aspects of the story—its rhetorical range, its shifting narrative modes and frameworks—as "unsettling." They may indeed produce a sort of pleasurable dizziness, like a roller-coaster ride, but surely their effects are not of the same order of emotional seriousness as what Freud's analysis disclosed? So the objection might run: Hoffmann's bizarre playfulness would seem considerably less important than "the theme of the Sandman who tears out chil-dren's eyes," a theme, as Freud pointed out, that draws its inten-sity from the "peculiarly violent and obscure emotion" excited by the "threat of being castrated." Given that intensity, given the concealed power of that threat, does the counteremphasis I have been placing on "The Sandman" "as literature" represent a seri-ous qualification of Freud's critique?
I would like to meet that objection, and take up the question of

[10]On the conflict of psychoanalytic and "literary" texts, see Jacques Derrida, "Le Facteur de la vérité," *Poétique,* 21 (1975), 96–147.

emotional seriousness, in a roundabout way, by first setting another narrative down in juxtaposition with "The Sandman" and with Freud's retelling of it. What I shall offer is a summary of a book by Paul Roazen, published several years ago, called *Brother Animal: The Story of Freud and Tausk,* an account of Freud's relationship with one of his followers. Roazen's book has provoked a good deal of criticism, much of it justifiable: his analysis of his material is sometimes naive, and his writing is often thin and overexcited (he is given to saying things like "These three brilliant people were playing with human dynamite"). But the book's documentation seems to have been done carefully, and it is possible to verify the accuracy of much of his material in other collections of letters and journals.[11] Roazen's story is of interest here for two reasons: first, its dénouement takes place during the early months of 1919, just before Freud set to work on *Beyond the Pleasure Principle* and "The Uncanny," and, second, because, although Roazen never alludes to Hoffmann's story, his own tale comes out sounding remarkably like it with Tausk playing the part of Nathanael and Freud in the role of the Sandman. The story goes like this:

In 1912, Lou Andreas-Salomé, the friend of Nietzsche and of Rilke, came to Vienna to learn about psychoanalysis. Freud seems to have welcomed her into his circle, which by then included Victor Tausk, whom she was to characterize as both the most loyal and the most intellectually impressive of Freud's disciples. She was invited to attend what had become the traditional Wednesday meetings of the Psychoanalytic Society and to sit in on Freud's and Tausk's courses of lectures. The journal she kept that year—partly gossip, partly recorded discussions, public and

[11] I say this despite the objections raised by K. R. Eissler in *Talent and Genius: A Psychoanalytic Reply to a Defamation of Freud* (New York: Quadrangle, 1971). Eissler corrects Roazen on a number of points of detail, and objects, often quite rightly, to the tone and the tendentiousness of Roazen's account, but Eissler's own interpretations are hardly compelling. Other material on Freud and Tausk can be found in Ernst Pfeiffer, ed., *Sigmund Freud and Lou Andreas-Salomé: Letters*, trans. W. and E. Robson-Scott (New York, 1972), and in *The Freud Journal of Lou Andreas-Salomé,* ed. Stanley A. Leavy (New York: Basic Books, 1964). For other interpretations of the Freud-Tausk affair, see the essays by Th. Neyraut-Sutterman and Jean Gillibert accompanying the French translation of Tausk's articles, *Oeuvres psychanalytiques* (Paris: Payot, 1975).

private, about psychoanalytic theory—has been published, along with her correspondence with Freud. From this material Roazen has been able to postulate, convincingly I think, a triangular relationship among Freud, Tausk, and Lou Salomé. Her journals record long conversations with Tausk, and their editor takes it as common knowledge that she became his mistress for some months; they also record talks with Freud about what the two of them came to refer to as "the Tausk-problem," that is, about Tausk's complicated feelings of rivalry with Freud and Freud's reciprocal uneasiness. Toward the end of the following summer there is a long journal entry analyzing Tausk's character, seeing him as repetitively placing himself in the role of the thwarted son vis-à-vis Freud, and, "as if by thought-transference . . .always busy with the same thing as Freud, never taking one step aside to make room for himself."

Roazen's next focal point is the winter of 1918–19, when Tausk, after serving in the army and managing, nevertheless, to write a number of psychoanalytic papers, had returned to Vienna. He asked Freud to take him on as a patient but Freud refused; instead Tausk entered analysis with a younger and less distinguished colleague, Helene Deutsch, who was already, as it happened, several months into her own training analysis with Freud. Roazen's recent interviews with Deutsch convinced him that Freud's motives for refusing Tausk were bound up with fears of plagiarism: Freud spoke of Tausk's making an "uncanny" impression on him, of the impossible complications that would result if Tausk became his patient, for he (Tausk) would be likely to imagine that ideas he had picked up in his hours with Freud were actually his own, and so on. Roazen is rather incautiously willing to attribute motives, but, whatever Freud's motives, Roazen is right to see this newly constituted pattern—of Tausk spending five hours a week with Deutsch while Deutsch was engaged in a similarly intensive analysis with Freud—as a repetition of the earlier triangle, with Deutsch this time substituted for Lou Andreas-Salomé.

This arrangement lasted for about three months; then (again according to Deutsch) the analytic hours began to interpenetrate—Tausk would talk to her mostly about Freud and she, in turn, found herself drawn into talking more and more about

Tausk to Freud. Freud finally (in March 1919) moved to break out of the triangle, insisting that Deutsch choose between continuing as his patient or continuing as Tausk's analyst. Roazen interprets this as coercive, no choice at all, given what Freud knew to be Deutsch's investment in her work with him. However that may have been, Tausk's analysis was terminated immediately. Three months later, on the eve of his marriage, he killed himself, leaving a note for Freud full of expressions of gratitude and respect.

Roazen's story may not be as well told as Hoffmann's but it exercises some of the same lurid fascination and holds out some of the same teasingly uncertain possibilities for interpretation, all the more so when one considers the number of ways the story is intertwined chronologically and thematically with what we know to have been Freud's theoretical concerns in 1919. Roazen speculates on the coincidence of Tausk's suicide (in July) and Freud's "simultaneous . . . explicit postulation of an instinct of primitive destructiveness"; as he points out, the letter in which Freud reports Tausk's death to Lou Salomé is also the letter in which he mentions the "theme of death" and writes of having "stumbled on a remarkable notion based on my theory of the instincts." "The very same letter," as Roazen characteristically writes; and if we would dissociate ourselves from that particular tone, it is less easy to deny the feeling of being intrigued that underlies it. "Could Tausk have been acting out Freud's newest, or even just barely burgeoning, idea?" Roazen asks. "Or perhaps the notion of a death instinct represented another way for Freud to deny any responsibility for Tausk's suicide?" Well, we know the notion of a death instinct represents considerably more than that in the economy of Freud's thought, and we may find it easier, at this point, to pull free: there is nothing like a reductive interpretation to break the spell of a fascinating anecdote. But let me invoke that spell once more, this time with another series of apparent coincidences, which I think can lead to some more interesting conclusions.

Freud's removing himself from a triangular relation with Tausk and Deutsch (for whatever reasons, with whatever motives—there is no need to follow Roazen in his speculations here) coincides with his beginning work on the first draft of

Beyond the Pleasure Principle, that is, on the text in which he first
formulates a puzzling theory of repetition. In the interval between the conception of that theory and its working-out in terms
of the death instinct, he turns back to a manuscript on the uncanny and rewrites it, proposing "the discovery that whatever
reminds us of this inner repetition-compulsion is perceived as
uncanny," and delineating, as an instance of the activity of that
compulsion, a sequence of triangular relations in "The Sandman"—*Coppelius/Nathanael/Klara* followed by its parodic repetition *Coppola/Nathanael/Olympia.* Here again, one may begin to feel
the pull of the interpreter's temptation: can we superimpose Roazen's sequence of triangles (*Freud/Tausk/Salomé, Freud/Tausk/
Deutsch*) on Freud's? And if we think we can—or wish we could—
what then? Can we make a story out of it? Might we not feel
"most strongly compelled" to do so, to arrange these elements in
temporal and causal sequences? For example, could we say that
the theory of repetition Freud worked out in March 1919 followed close upon—was a consequence of—his realization that he
was once again caught in a certain relationship to Tausk? Could
we add that Freud was bound to perceive that relation as uncanny—not quite literary, but no longer quite real, either, the workings of the compulsion glimpsed "through" an awareness of
something-being-repeated? Could we go on to suggest that it was
this experience of a repetitive triangular relationship that under-
writes his analysis of "The Sandman" in May? That is, that the
glimpse of his relationship to Tausk has the same "documentary" status vis-à-vis Freud's retelling of "The Sandman" that
Nathanael's letters have for Hoffmann's narrator, that it serves
as both a source of energy and a quasi-fictitious pretext for
writing?

Suppose this were the story one put together. Mightn't one
then, like Nathanael crying out "Whose voice is this?" after he
had finished his poem, still feel impelled to ask: *Whose story is
this?* Is it one's own? Is it Roazen's? Is it Hoffmann's? Is it *The
Story of Freud and Tausk* "as told to" Paul Roazen, chiefly by
Helene Deutsch?

To the degree that such questions still solicit us and still resist
solution, we are kept in a state somewhere between "emotional
seriousness" and literary forepleasure, conscious of vacillating

between literature and "nonfiction," our sense of repetition-at-
work colored in with the lurid shades of aggression, madness,
and violent death. At such moments we can say we are experiencing the uncanny; we might just as well say we are puzzled by
a question of literary priority.

IV

I am not fond of reading.
                           —Freud to Lou Andreas-Salomé

I invented psychoanalysis because it had no literature.
                                —Freud to Helene Deutsch

   The Anxiety of Influence: when Roazen describes the tensions between Freud and Tausk as generated by fears of
plagiarism, he takes his place among an increasing number of
American critics who put Freud's Oedipal model to work accounting for the relations among writers. There is evidence
enough in Freud's own texts to suggest that he was not immune
to such anxieties. At the beginning of "The Uncanny," for
example, he apologetically introduces what he calls "this present
modest contribution of mine," confessing that he could not—
because of the restrictions imposed on him by the war—make "a
very thorough examination of the bibliography, especially the
foreign literature" (XVII, 219–220) so that, he goes on, his "paper is presented to the reader without any claim of priority."
Beyond the Pleasure Principle, too, opens with a firm announcement that "priority and originality are not among the aims that
psycho-analysis sets itself" (XVIII, 7), but some sixty pages later
we come across a qualm about originality expressed at an in-
triguing point in the argument, and in an odd verbal formula.
Freud is about to move from his discussion of the compulsion to
repeat to a concept he hopes will help explain its relation to the
rest of his theory, the concept of the death instinct, and he
begins his paragraph with a question: "But how is the predicate
of being instinctual related to the compulsion to repeat?" He
then produces, italicized for emphasis, a preliminary statement:
"*It seems that an instinct is an urge inherent in organic life to restore an
earlier state of things,*" a sentence to which he appends the following footnote: "I have no doubt that similar notions as to the

nature of the 'instincts' have already been put forward repeatedly" (XVIII, 36). It is the word "repeatedly" that is striking;
here the twinge about priority seems in some relation to Freud's
subject matter: it is as if, at the very moment of grounding the
repetition-compulsion in a theory he hoped would have biological validity, he was drawn to gesture once more to the un-
groundable nature of repetition.[12]

A similar instance can be found in the case history of the
"Wolf Man," where Freud again is engaged with questions of
origins and their subsequent rehearsals. This time what is at
stake is the degree of reality to be attributed to the primal scene
and the limit of the effects of *Nachträglichkeit* in constituting,
retroactively, that scene's importance and meaning. Freud had
revised his first draft of the case so as to counter the rival claims
of Jung and Adler, and, after arguing his own reconsidered
position carefully and at length, he adds this testy footnote:

> I admit that this is the most ticklish question in the whole domain
> of psychoanalysis. I did not require the contributions of Adler and
> Jung to induce me to consider the matter with a critical eye, and to
> bear in mind the possibility that what analysis puts forward as
> being forgotten experiences of childhood (and of improbably early
> childhood) may on the contrary be based upon phantasies brought
> about upon occasions occurring late in life. . . . On the contrary, no
> doubt has troubled me more; no other uncertainty has been more
> decisive in holding me back from publishing my conclusions. I was
> the first—a point to which none of my opponents have referred—
> to recognize the part played by phantasies in symptom formation
> and also the phantasying-back of late impressions into childhood
> and their sexualization after the event. (See *Traumdeutung,* First
> Edition, 1900 . . . and "Notes upon a Case of Obsessional
> Neurosis," 1908.) [XVII, 103]

[12]A comparable gesture can be found in Tocqueville's account of the events of
1848 in France. Writing of the February Revolution he states, "This was something completely new in our history. It is true that similar revolutions had taken
place in other countries at other times; however new and unexpected contemporaries may find the particular events of any age, including our own, they are
always part of the age-old history of humanity." His editors note the following
words marked for omission in the manuscript: *"For what we call new facts are
most often only forgotten ones,"* next to which, in the margin, Tocqueville had added
"Has not this been said by others?" The passage is translated by George Lawrence in
J. P. Mayer's and A. P. Kerr's edition of the *Recollections* (New York: Anchor-
Doubleday, 1971), pp. 89–90.

Whatever anxiety Freud may be imagined to have felt about his own originality, then, may not be exactly illusory, but displaced. These passages suggest that more fundamental "doubts" and "uncertainties"—doubts about the grasp any figurative language has on first principles, especially when the first principles include a principle of repetition—may be at work generating the anxiety that is then acted out in the register of literary priority. The specificity of that range of wishes and fears—the wish to be original, the fear of plagiarizing or of being plagiarized—would act to structure and render more manageable, in however melodramatic a fashion, the more indeterminate affect associated with repetition, marking or coloring it, conferring "visibility" on the forces of repetition and at the same time disguising the activity of those forces from the subject himself.

But here, I think, I should turn back to the doubts I mentioned earlier, doubts about the appropriateness of the compound analogy I proposed between that-which-is-repeated, coloring matter, and figurative language. All three, I suggested, could be thought of as means of representing processes and energies that might otherwise go unnoticed. But this model seems unsatisfactory and wishful in at least two ways. First, it depends upon the notion of a real preexistent force (call it sheer repetition, the death instinct, or whatever) that is merely rendered more *discernible* by that-which-is-repeated, or by the lurid colors of the erotic, or by some helpful figure of speech; and, second, it suggests that the workings of figurative language (like acting-out or coloring-in) do indeed have the effect of rendering that force "visible." But we know that the relation between figurative language and what it figures cannot be adequately grasped in metaphors of vision; and we might well doubt that the forces of repetition can be isolated—even ideally—from that-which-is-repeated. The wishfulness inherent in the model is not simply in its isolating the *forces* of repetition from their representations, but in its seeking to isolate the *question* of repetition from the question of figurative language itself. But suppose, as Gilles Deleuze has suggested,[13] that implicit in Freud's theory of repe-

---

[13]In *Différence et répétition* (Paris: Presses Universitaires de France, 1968), pp. 1–30 and 128–168.

tition is the discovery that these two questions are impossible to disentangle, that in trying to come to terms with the repetition-compulsion one discovers that the irreducible figurativeness of one's language is indistinguishable from the ungrounded and apparently inexplicable notion of the compulsion itself. At such moments the wish to put aside the question of figurative language might assert itself as a counterforce to one's most powerful apprehension of the compulsion to repeat, and it might take the form it does in Freud's reading of "The Sandman," the form of a wish to find "no literature" there.

JOSEPH RIDDEL

Decentering the Image: The "Project" of "American" Poetics?

> Our debt to tradition through reading and conversation is so
> massive, our protest or private additions so rare and insignifi-
> cant . . . that, in a large sense, one would say there is no pure
> originality. All minds quote. Old and new make the warp and
> woof of every moment. There is no thread that is not a twist
> of these two strands.
>
> —Ralph Waldo Emerson

> The whole of great art is a struggle for communica-
> tion. . . . And this communication is not a levelling, it is not an
> elimination of differences. It is a recognition of differences.
>
> —Ezra Pound

I begin by putting the question in quotation marks. "American
literature" is an oxymoron—a notion of the belated original, of
the immaculate opening of an old closure. "American literature"
has always been inscribed in such a questioning parenthesis, because its dream of "making it new," of realizing itself originally,
begins with the contradiction inherent in the notion of original
or creative "literature," of an original secondariness. What is
called the modern, and "American literature" has always been
"modern"—that is, inscribed as both an end and a beginning
between two notions of history—is always an "event" that is logically anterior yet historically posterior to that literature we call
traditional or classical. "American literature" has always played
in the paradoxical margins of the "new." One has only to mention the double sense of "tradition" that obsesses our modernist
experimenters, the makers of the modern Image, to understand
the contradiction Paul de Man finds in the privileged notion of
the "modern." To "make it new" means in one sense (for example, T. S. Eliot's) to supplement the tradition, to add something

to an already completed whole; but it also means to repeat the moment of some pure origin that has been obscured by history's lengthened shadow, and hence to rewrite the whole. "American literature," we might say, is a search which repeatedly suspends the dream of literature, the dream of totalization, of poetic closure. In this, of course, it simply makes explicit, by repetition, the subversive element in all literature, the "double sense" contained in every "sense of an ending." Once achieved, The Great American Novel would be the end of "American literature"; that is why we have so many of them, and why it is always "to be written."

William Carlos Williams's long poem *Paterson* puts the question of the "American" crisis most directly: how can a new beginning be original? "How to begin to find a shape—to begin to begin again, / turning the inside out: to find one phrase that will / lie married beside another for delight?" In its context this question leads directly to a quotation, a statement once made by the British poet George Barker: "*American poetry is a very easy subject to discuss for the simple reason that it does not exist*" (Book Three, *Paterson*). It is always situated in a borrowed language, and in a tradition that, as Emerson saw, would not close. To "exist," an American poetry would have to write that closure, and repeat an opening that had already always begun. In Emerson's sense, the poet of the present must be the genius: "Next to the originator of a good sentence is the first quoter of it. . . . there are great ways of borrowing. Genius borrows nobly" ("Quotation and Originality"). Williams and his poem compose one figure, one more repetition, in a line of so-called American Adamic poets, running, let us say for historical convenience, from Emerson's call for a purely American idiom to Charles Olson's announcement of the forward thrust of "Projective Verse." This is a somewhat arbitrary line, not a "history" at all, but a metaphor for all the new beginnings that dot the "development" of an "American poetry" which does not yet exist.

Indeed, we might explore one sequence of those repetitions, where the historical possibility of an unbroken, continuous development does seem present, as the measure of the "project." I am referring to what literary history calls the "Imagist movement," obviously an international rather than an American revolution, but a movement nevertheless indirectly tied to Emerson. For Imagism led successively to movements with counternames— Vorticism, Objectivism, even Objectism—and to in-mixtures with continental movements like Dadaism, Surrealism, and Cubism. From Emerson to Olson, there is not a straight line but a movement of appropriations, of decenterings, of repetitions that manage to keep the possibility of an "American" poetry open. That possibility is perhaps most vividly inscribed in the wonderful figure by which Olson defines the American: "We are the last 'first' people."[1]

"I take SPACE," Olson writes in *Call Me Ishmael*, "to be the central fact to man born in America, from Folsom cave to now" (*CMI,* 11). Space, he says, is "prime," is of the beginning; it is an origin which "history" necessarily erases and cannot recall, except in its utopian fiction of perfection. But for Olson, space is neither absence nor plenitude. It is original homelessness, or restlessness (Hegelian?), of the self which awakes to itself as already bound in the other, in geo-graphy. Space is what was violated in the "Original Act . . . the First Murder." For Melville, as Olson puts it, Shame takes precedence "to any Eden." Shame is "of Prime." In the beginning was the act, and in the knowledge of that act the "concord of Space . . . was curdled" (*CMI,* 83). Yet, the Olson/Melville myth is not a teleological myth of *felix culpa,* of an original Unity violated and a redemption tentatively promised. Shame already preceded Eden. What was shattered with the First Murder was the "concord" of Space, original difference. In the "Original Act," space was displaced as history, the hierarchical and authoritarian history of the West, logocentrism. Man arrogated to himself centrality or priority, of which Emerson's central man is a last, late repetition.

For Olson, man's original state was always already Shame, the

---

[1]Charles Olson, *Call Me Ishmael* (New York: Reynal and Hitchcock, 1947), p. 14. Because of the number of quotations from Olson, I use the following code, noting sources and pages in the text: *CMI—Call Me Ishmael; HU—Human Universe and Other Essays,* ed. Donald Allen (New York: New Directions, 1967); *LO—Letters for Origin: 1950-1955,* ed. Albert Glover (London: Cape Goliard/Grossman, 1969); *MP—The Maximus Poems* (New York: Jargon/Corinth, 1960); *SVH—The Special View of History,* ed. Ann Charters (Berkeley: Oyez, 1970); *SW—Selected Writings of Charles Olson,* ed. Robert Creeley (New York: New Directions, 1966).

condition of need. Man is a secondary condition, prefigured as the wanderer who has always repeated the primordial "First Murder," itself a figural event inscribed in the moment of all writing. As Olson says, the "tale of the Great Tower [of Babel] is as ultimate a legend as the Flood, Eden, Adam" (*CMI*, 96). In the beginning was random distribution, space as difference. "Man" is an "outrider," a wanderer, in space; his first knowledge is of himself as other. His first need is for community, communication. Thus Olson's figure for the (original) writer is the "figure of outward" or "figure of forward." "Man" is forever deprived of his sources, is never central. His belated discovery, or insinuation, of his centrality, therefore, which Olson identifies with humanism, becomes evident in the very invention of metaphysics and radiates through the literature of the West, particularly in its preoccupation with epic or "narrative." For Olson, Melville's crisis, realized both thematically and psychologically in his radical and obsessive questioning of narrative, repeats the structure of "mythic consciousness": he "agonized over paternity" and "demanded to know the father" (*CMI*, 82), leading him to a displacement of the "father" that permeates his whole canon. His mythopoeic imagination lured him toward an origin that was originally violated. The author/writer is originally a foundling. And Olson sees Melville's late capitulation to Christianity as coincidental with his refusal to write, his abandonment of a narrative that was directed against the history of narrative. Melville reembraced the "white guilt" and a "promise of a future life" (*CMI*, 92, 100), but this false return to a symbolic father stifled the "myth power" and with it the guilt implicated in writing, since writing *is* murder, the "First Murder," the displacement of the father, and the projection or elongation of "space." This "First Murder," then, is not an event from which everything following derives, but the sign of an originally impure origin. It is, in Olson's figures, irreducibly a scene of writing, a beginning without origin.

Call Me Ishmael is the first of Olson's manifestoes of a new writing that would repeat, yet be different from, a first writing, considering that the very notion of a first writing can only be represented in writing. His essay, "Projective Verse," is a second. In the history of modern poetry, he once speculated, the year

1950 would align with the year 1910, to bracket Modernism. The advent of "Projective Verse" would complete and supplement the experiments of Imagism, and begin again the invention of poetry. Olson's "project," like Melville's, goes back to come forward, repeating and displacing the Image, repeating the succession of openings and closings that mark the spatial history of cultures, of cities, and thus of writing. Hence Olson's interest in a nonphonetic writing, in what preceded logocentrism. Hence his reading of Melville's double career: of writing as a murder of the father, and the guilt that led to silence, Melville's late capitulation to the "promise of a future life" or a return to the father.

Melville goes back, as Olson says, behind the great Hellenic elevation of the *logos,* in order to know "the great deed and misdeed of primitive time" (*CMI,* 85). He is a "Beginner—and interested in beginnings. Melville had a way of reading back through time until he got history pushed back so far he turned time into space" (*CMI,* 14). For Olson, this origin is (was) multiple, a chaos, and not an origin at all. To go back is not to seize the origin, to recuperate some paradisal space, but to begin again the "deed and misdeed" signified by writing. Olson's new beginning rejects (figuratively) everything that lay between Homer's writing and Melville's.[2] That is, it rejects (or at least puts in question) representation, humanism, and history. What Olson comes to call projective (and also con-jectural, in the sense of throwing together) writing would reinscribe a spatial doubleness into the linearity or narrativity of Western literature, thus re-marking the problematics of representation which Olson feels has been silently suppressed with the appropriations of Homer (and mythic consciousness) by the rational, humanist literatures of the "tradition." Homer and Melville, then, bracket the epoch of humanism; they are both inside and outside the "history" their art opens and closes. Olson's Melville, as he suggests in his *Mayan Letters,* repeats Homer's deconstruction of the Mediterra-

---

[2]One should doubly emphasize here that Olson does not exclude all writers who fall within the period of Western literature, since Shakespeare is his model of the "mythic" and universal imagination never containable in this "history." *Call Me Ishmael* is a pioneering, speculative study of Melville's appropriation of Shakespeare.

nean myth with his own deconstruction of the Pacific myth. Melville writes an end to humanism, to the Emersonian dream of the "central man," just as Homer writes an end to the myth of wandering (writing) and makes possible, if not inevitable, the era of the hero, of return and redemption (the closed circle of representation).

It must be the project of a postmodern poetry, says Olson, to repeat the "figure of outward," to go back behind Homer in order to come forward beyond Melville and Romanticism, and thus to open up once more the possibility of generative repetition. To be posthistorical, however, is to be a contradiction. Original writing repeats the violent moment that marks the rupture between prehistory and history, that is, the space or scene of writing itself, and reveals the artifice of those historical categories. Olson's Melville wants to "go back" to (to repeat) the founding of prehistorical cities, where the invention of writing marks the selection that is "culture," an origin that is never pure and simple. To "go back" to these places is to repeat and reappropriate their act of first writing, an archeological adventure that is also archeo-clastic, since the writer does not reappropriate the old signs (as in grave robbing) so much as he repeats the violence of opening a site. He therefore goes for the center, as into a pyramid (*CMI*, 99), not to retrieve a meaning lost or buried in past forms, but to effect a new writing, a pro-jecting and con-jecturing of old signs that is the "beginning" of writing. Olson gives us the figure of the poet, in Gilles Deleuze's phrase, as Egyptologist, who descends into the crypts in order to read the secret language of hieroglyphs.[3] The "archeologist of morning" (it is the metaphorical title posthumously given to Olson's collected shorter poems) dismantles the myth of origins, only to construct another, a fiction of impure origins. He produces, in Deleuze's terms, a "literary machine," an "anti-logos." Olson reads out of Melville's writing, his worrying over the father/center, the whole history of Imagism, and the need for a "Projective Verse" as the next radical decentering of "modernism."

[3]Deleuze, *Proust and Signs,* trans. Richard Howard (New York: Braziller, 1972), pp. 91, 167. The book was first published in France in 1964, revised and supplemented in 1970.

Olson, of course, is rewriting a particular chapter of American literature, or better, displacing that chapter from its position as the conclusion, the final repetition, in the history of Western literature to the position of yet another "beginning." He needs to displace the origins of an "American literature" from Emersonian logocentrism to an even more original notion of beginning, and this involves him in nothing less than rewriting or doubling the concepts of "beginning" and "re-presentation," that is, erasing them.[4] Olson's appeal to Melville's "mythopoeic" imagination may appear to compromise his entire project, particularly if one traces the notion of mythopoeisis to its Jungian formulations, as Olson seems elsewhere to do. But in Olson the mythopoeic is never inscribed in the power of some arche-type, some universal center, that governs the continuity between origin and image. On the contrary, the site of the mythopoeic is a place of violence, of the great "deed and mis-deed" which underscores the need for creative discontinuity. Olson rewrites, as it were, the genealogical fable of Western literature.[5]

Olson's privileged text is *Moby Dick,* a protean work for anyone ready to extend Olson's arguments to a commentary on the "scene of writing."[6] Had he extended his inquiry to *Pierre,* however, he might have viewed Melville's worrying over the

[4]The reference here is to Jacques Derrida's deconstruction of Husserl's presentational phenomenology: "somehow everything 'begins' by 're-presentation,'" which "means that there is no 'beginning' and that the 're-presentation' we are talking about is not the modification of a 're' that has *befallen* a primordial presentation." See Derrida, *Speech and Phenomena,* trans. David Allison (Evanston, Ill.: Northwestern University Press, 1973), p. 45n. This is a translation of Derrida's *La Voix et le phénomène* (1967).

[5]In his "Nietzsche, Genealogy, History," in *Language, Counter-Memory, Practice,* trans. Donald Bouchard and Sherry Simon (Ithaca: Cornell University Press, 1977), pp. 139–164. Michel Foucault distinguishes between a nostalgia for origins and the concerns of genealogy: "The genealogist [of morals] needs history to dispel the chimeras of origin" (p. 144). The Nietzschean genealogist is concerned with the gaps, the lapses, the intensities, the agitations, in short the discontinuities and not some thread that links history with an ideal, simple origin. Thus Foucault reads the Nietzschean genealogy as an indifference to the "father." Melville, even as Olson reads him, worries over the question of identifying the father/origin, and of deriving an identity from "him." The author, then, always lives in the uncertainty marked by genealogy.

[6]See, for example, Rodolphe Gasché, "The Scene of Writing: A Deferred Outset," *Glyph I* (Baltimore: Johns Hopkins University Press, 1977), pp. 150–171.

"father," as it is inscribed in the genealogical and representational metaphor and the question of original writing (indeed the very question of the possibility of "American" literature), as even more radical and problematical than *Call Me Ishmael* admits. I will restrict my commentary here to one brief part of that novel, which has been the subject of a brilliant essay by Edgar Dryden, precisely on this same problem: of the entanglement of the metaphors of genealogy and representation in an American novelist's efforts to articulate his tainted originality.[7] There is a chapter in *Pierre* entitled "Young America in Literature" where Melville deals satirically with the prevailing notion that a young country might begin again, in all innocence, to produce an art, at once nationalistic and universal, out of something as spontaneous as "poetic nature." The youthful Pierre has written a number of things, juvenilia, marked by the "pervading symmetry of his general style," but he has not composed a "mature" work nor anything like a "book." When he finally decides to become a writer in seriousness, he finds a pair of editors who have recently switched professions, from tailoring to publishing, and who arrange for him to produce his first book, in the "Library Form," as they put it. What they project for Pierre is a canon, but cut to the whole cloth, made on the "Sample of a coat."[8]

If the satire is directed at anything other than Emerson and his original quotings or appropriations of Carlyle, it is surely a reminder that writing has always been implicated in a series of conventions and complications which preclude any access to its origin in the "poetic nature." Pierre discovers the project of his Collected Works to involve the "Library Form: an Illustrated Edition" and a whole series of productive constraints and economic demands that made the notion of author fairly anonymous. Pierre finds himself embroiled in an economy of production where there is always a remainder; he is an author, literally, without a distinct "signature."

[7] "The Entangled Text: Melville's *Pierre* and the Problem of Reading," *Boundary 2*, 7:3(1979).
[8] This and subsequent quotations from *Pierre* are from the Northwestern/Newberry edition, ed. H. Hayford, H. Parker, and G. T. Tanselle (Evanston and Chicago, 1971).

The theme is entangled with Pierre's obsessive questioning of his identity, and as Dryden shows, is complicated throughout with the question of his name (whether, indeed, he takes his proper name from a living or dead rock, from the sacred origin of the Bible and its living ground or a dead nature). Publishers repeatedly ask of him a "biography" which he cannot deliver, reminding us, perhaps, that Emerson had always claimed that history is "biography," the "lengthened shadow of a man," in Eliot's acid phrase. Writing, Pierre discovers, implicates him in the worldly economy of textuality. The author becomes a "sort of publisher"; "the age of authors is passing," Pierre declares. Young America usurps the innocent's dream of originality, of radical innocence, and implicates its authors in a chain of fraternal complications, a capitalist enterprise of textual production that abolishes the romantic dream of the "author" and subordinates his originality to the collective designs of the "tailor." From this mortgaging of his innocence Pierre draws a bitter lesson: "Youth must wholly quit, then, the quarry, for awhile, and not only go forth, and get tools to use in the quarry, but must go and thoroughly study architecture." He must give up Nature, and study craft, but when he turns to method, to architecture, he must learn another ironic lesson: that architecture reveals the artifice of the construction of origins. Once again, Pierre finds the self to be defined by an artificially constructed house. His identity, as author, is not naturally derived, nor is it singular: "Never was a child born of one parent."

Still later, when Pierre attempts his first "mature" or "comprehensive work," he must come to terms with this democratic economy of production, in which every text has not one but many authors. Only now he must contemplate "originality" in terms of his implication in both a paternal and a fraternal nexus of production: "most grand productions of the best human intellects ever are built round a circle, as atolls (i.e. the primitive coral islets which, raising themselves in the depths of profoundest seas, rise funnel-like to the surface ...)"; a "book," then, composed out of "reading," of heterogeneous materials acquired by a "random but lynx-eyed mind, in the course of ... multifarious, incidental, bibliographic encounterings." Pierre "would climb Parnassus with a pile of folios on his back"; he would layer his book out of the compilations of other books, so that no master book might command his production, or be represented in it as master, since "all existing great works must be federated in the fancy." Federal production not only abolishes the notion of author, but it disturbs the logocentric notion of an orderly movement between origin and image. As several commentators on this remarkable chapter of the novel have observed, none more convincingly than Dryden, any idea of the natural origins of art is suspended.

At the end of a series of reflections, which began in the figure of the "book" as an "atoll," or the sedimentation of skeletal forms into the shape of a mountain, the narrator elaborates yet another figure of the book as the exterior of the "soul" of man, cast in the architectural shape of the pyramid, itself a composition of heterogeneous elements, a tomb that is produced to house the body of the king, the "mummy which lies buried in cloth on cloth." The explorer or reader of the pyramid or book seeks its center, moving through and removing layer upon layer, seeking the "unlayered substance." But a stratified reading does not uncover the unstratified. The "central room," and I will not repeat the whole of this famous passage, is empty, "No body is there!" Neither the king nor the author. The pyramid, which Melville elsewhere notes, is made on the model of natural mountains, represents instead the "atoll." Neither nature nor its representation is anything more than a representation; neither house their origin. Neither atoll nor pyramid is natural. The "book," then, is not a representation of nature, but a text, the texture of a representation, of nature as always already an archi-tecture, a technic, a text, a construct. And it is interesting that in the one paragraph separating these opposing yet complementary metaphors of the "book" (as circle upon circle, as atoll) and the "sarcophagus," Melville poses the figure of the traveler in Switzerland who can never see, let alone achieve, the peak of his Alps. The traveler comes "at last to gain his Mont Blanc" only by paying a severe price, a "tithe" he cannot calculate. The mountaintop (itself an obsessive Romantic figure of remote, inaccessible origins, and hence not representable, as Eugenio Donato has revealed in a recent essay)[9] is as absent as

[9]"The Ruins of Memory: Archeological Fragments and Textual Artifacts," *MLN,* 93 (1978), 575-596.

the king in the pyramid. And "far over the invisible Atlantic, the Rocky Mountains and the Andes are yet unbeheld." It is just this natural origin that is never beheld, except in a belated image that can never represent it fully but can only stand for its absence, like a textual construct.

So American literature begins, not by inventing or recuperating an authentic origin, but by repeating in radical innocence the double vision of Romanticism, a Romanticism obscured, as Paul de Man has shown, in those idealized readings of its recuperation of nature, of immediacy.[10] In Wallace Stevens's figure, the poem has always already taken the place of a mountain. The problematic that de Man and Donato find in the Romantic Image— that the image not only signifies the murder of the "natural object" but makes unthinkable its natural origin—lies at the very heart of the question of "beginnings" which "American literature" poses to itself: that it can never, in the language of *Pierre,* take an "overtopping view of these Alps," but must build a machine to bridge the abyss its questioning repeatedly opens up, a machine that turns out to be the sign itself of the abyss.

I turn now to one of those curious paradoxes of literary history: to a text which may be said to tie together a movement of "American poetics" from Emerson through Pound to Charles Olson. It is also a text inscribed in the discontinuity of that movement: a text composed only as lecture notes by its author, but revised and published in a collection of essays by the poet (Ezra Pound) who made the most effective use of it and whose own poetry turns upon the double sense of what it elaborates. The text is Ernest Fenollosa's (non-)essay, "The Chinese Written Character as a Medium for Poetry."[11] Its centrality to the modernist experiment is all the more illuminating because of what Hugh Kenner has called its "history of interesting mistakes."[12]

In *The Pound Era,* Kenner submits the essay to extensive ex-

[10]See his early, more phenomenologically oriented essay, "Intentional Structure of the Romantic Image," in *Romanticism and Consciousness,* ed. Harold Bloom (New York: Norton, 1970). The essay first appeared in 1960.

[11]First published in Pound, *Instigations* (New York: Boni & Liveright, 1920), pp. 357–387, reprinted in 1967. Quotations are not further noted.

[12]*The Pound Era* (Berkeley: University of California Press, 1971), pp. 192–231, esp. p. 230.

amination, but he focuses on two crucial aspects of its argument: (1) Fenollosa's discovery in the Chinese written character of a vital relation between language and reality, or between culture and nature; and (2) his curiously limited understanding of Chinese writing, particularly his assumption that Chinese writing is nonphonetic. Fenollosa had gone to Japan to teach philosophy; he was a student of Hegel and Emerson but not a linguist. His interpretation of Chinese writing is refracted through Transcendentalism: "A true noun . . . ," he writes, "does not exist in nature," nor does a "true verb." Language, like nature, is therefore only apparently marked by the grammar of the *logos,* by dualism. Nature is not made up of things (nouns) and motions (verbs), but of things which move and a motion which is only that of moving things. Similarly, Chinese language is not constituted by "parts" of speech with discrete functions. And Fenollosa opposes to this the abstract structure of Western grammar, which legislates the priority of subject to object and heightens the arbitrary relation between signs and facts, or abstractions and concretions. (The terminology, of course, is riddled with problems, since facts and concretions here would be in effect signifieds.)

Thus Fenollosa identifies what modern linguistics has recognized as the irreducible doubleness of the sign (accentuated by the mark of a written language and repressed in spoken language), and at the same time interprets Chinese writing as a primordial script that preceded the dualisms of the West, as they are manifest in phonetic writing. To put it in terms which would perplex a contemporary philosopher of language, he gives nonphonetic writing the status of primordiality and associates phonetic writing with secondariness and abstraction. The neo-Hegelian rewrites not only Aristotle, but Hegel. The Chinese written character reminds Fenollosa of what Emerson had always claimed nature to be: vital and thus verbal. All words were originally charged with transitive power. Western nominalization, its elevation of the subject, was for Fenollosa a rupture of language from its natural origins. Most interestingly, in Fenollosa's writing of a history of language's westering and fall, its loss of primordial (and natural) power, his interpretation locates itself in the full authority of Transcendental idealism, for which Nature is both God and grammar.

"Things," Fenollosa writes, "are only the terminal points, or rather the meeting points of actions." Nouns are both formal and transitive; all language is verbal, thus temporalizing, though it temporalizes in the sense of unfolding or explicating. Form and power are one in nature, as Emerson had argued. Fenollosa remarks that our tendency to isolate either the motion or the location (verb or noun) reveals the limit of conceptuality already built into Western grammatology. But he conceived of an original language which transcended that limit, not in its adequation with nature but in its own graphic naturalness. Ideogrammic writing, he claimed, is neither purely pictorial nor purely abstract, neither a representation nor an arbitrary substitution, but the very law of nature itself. Like a hieroglyph—and unlike other writers, Fenollosa does not distinguish between ideographic and hieroglyphic writing—it is not an "arbitrary symbol," not a sign that displaces what it signifies, but a "vivid shorthand picture of the operations of Nature," a synecdoche. The Western degradation of writing beneath speech does not trouble Fenollosa. In its Orient, language was at once speech and writing, the power and the law folded in one. As "vivid shorthand," at once visual and nonrepresentational, this writing is "close" to, yet not identical with, nature. It is the truth of nature, then, its idea as action. Here he gives a certain unique twist to Hegel. Language is the becoming of nature, nature as becoming. But the grammar of nature—which as we will see has no grammar— excludes the negative. In Chinese writing, strangely, Fenollosa finds the ever-presence of becoming, a writing which bears on its face the entire history of presence.

The double sense of his theory shows up in Kenner's analysis of Fenollosa's "misinterpretation": the view that all Chinese writing is nonphonetic. According to Kenner, that is a common mistake of Western scholars who tend to study only a limited number of radicals. And Kenner offers a corrective, while praising Fenollosa's discovery of the ground "truth" that relates natural language and nature: the continuity of "process." Fenollosa "needed to suppose," Kenner writes, "that all ideograms followed one principle so that by gazing into them as into living monads he could expand, miraculously concentrated, the Emersonian organicism he had brought to Tokyo from Cambridge."[13]

[13]Ibid., p. 230.

(Parenthetically, I should note here that Kenner never questions the adequacy of the organic metaphor, nor its Emersonian authority. A deconstruction of Emerson's theory of language might reveal, indeed, that nature is always thought on the model of language rather than the reverse. If we heed the wisdom of Harold Bloom's view that "deconstructing Emerson is . . . impossible, since no discourse ever has been so overtly aware of its own status as rhetoricity,"[14] then we have to conclude that nature arises, indeed originates, only in a text. But for Bloom, rhetoric remains primarily speech, located or oriented in the trope of will, in the power of a "psyche" or a subject, which though irreducibly a trope, originates by and in its turn. Kenner, on the other hand, never feels the need to question either the metaphor of natural origin or the problematical notion of an Image through which is translated, with exactness and clarity, the otherwise unseen laws of nature, an Image simultaneously representational and presentational. If Emerson cannot be deconstructed, however, it is nonetheless possible to show that nowhere in his writing can Nature, or God, or Unity, appear outside of a linguistic chain. One brief example: in the early essay *Nature*, the chapter on "Language" appears as the third stage of a circular or dialectical movement, translating nature as commodity into idealism, a circuit that Spirit must traverse to fulfill itself, yet a circuit that is itself Spirit. And the stage of language repeats and completes the entire circuit: "(1) Words are signs of natural facts; (2) Particular natural facts are symbols of particular spiritual facts; (3) Nature is the symbol of the spirit." There is no distinction between signs and symbols. There is a continuity between origin and difference, one and many, idea and representation: "A Fact is the end or last issue of spirit." In Derrida's terms, Emerson's siting of language, and Kenner's use of it to explain the Fenollosa/Pound derivation of ideographic precision, is "pneumatological" and not grammatological:[15] "material facts" must preserve an "exact relation to their first origin," the "substantial thoughts of the Creator." No deconstruction of Emerson

[14] *Wallace Stevens: The Poems of Our Climate* (Ithaca: Cornell University Press, 1977), p. 12.
[15] *Of Grammatology*, trans. Gayatri Spivak (Baltimore: Johns Hopkins University Press, 1976), p. 17.

is necessary to reveal that any importation of the Emersonian circle to the Orient is a doubled dream of recuperation by supplementation. If Fenollosa needed to recover the power lost when the West forfeited Eastern graphism, his separation of the circle necessitates the importation of idealism, of language as spirit and breath, of the soul back into the abstract body, as Leibniz saw it, of the Chinese written character, a restoration of the organic roots to the body of the radical. Like Hegel, Fenollosa celebrates the triumph of the very Western language that has divided up Eastern nature, a nature whose totality, we have seen, is thinkable only as an organic and logocentric circle.)

As a "shorthand" picture, Fenollosa's radical would at first appear to be a privileged representation. Yet he (and Pound) insist on calling it "presentational" and productive. It is, therefore, an interpretation, productive of equations, of laws that govern culture's relation to nature. Indeed, it signifies the orderly transformation from nature to culture. As a "shorthand" system, language is a figuration of force which produces and maintains a field of differences or, like a transistor in an electrical circuit, it signifies the order of a discontinuous repetition. Pound, in a footnote to the essay, and again in his Vorticist book, *Gaudier-Brzeska,* calls both Image and Ideogram the "language of exploration" or "interpretative metaphor" and employs the metaphors of electrical circuits and cinemato*graphic* projection to exemplify the new organicism. Writing, then, occupies a space of origin (of complex rather than simple origin) which maintains differences by producing or multiplying them. This nature (this grammar) will not close. Its writing is not simple, is never a nondifference.

Fenollosa's nature is a grid or graph that inscribes only "objective lines of relations." And "relations are more real and more important than the things which they relate." The forces of nature function as resistances; they are unequivocal; they branch rather than reunite, producing a kind of doubling or disseminating effect that refuses any return to equivocity. And Fenollosa employs a metaphor which will become familiar in modern poetry—the concept of potentiality held within the seed of an acorn. The seed, however, is a figure for culture, for cultivation, for the "city." Thus Fenollosa blindly collapses culture and nature into one organic figure: the city is a body, like the ideographic sign, of spirit. Systems of nerves, he argues, grow like a culture, like roadways connecting towns, ports, and the like. Every system is literally a radical, and thus rooted in what Fenollosa calls an "identity of structure." "Had the world not been full of homologies, sympathies, and identities," he says, "thought would have been starved and language chained to the obvious." "Thought" precedes language, which expresses or exteriorizes that true origin, natural law. But the circularity of Fenollosa's argument undoes itself. Rather than uncovering the unity of ancient roots, it reveals a branching of the origin. If as Fenollosa argues, "Nature has no grammar," then nature cannot be conceived of in terms of unity. We recall Nietzsche's identification of God and grammar in *Twilight of the Idols:* "I fear we are not getting rid of God because we still believe in grammar."

Fenollosa employs still another problematic metaphor of the "history" of language: that it develops through "quasi-geological strata," of metaphor upon metaphor, a geo-arche-ology. Nature is kind of palimpsest. Moreover, nature is, as he says, a myth, the spatial interpretation (*āletheia*) of the invisible, the movement from invisible to visible. Thus, language explicates. But Fenollosa must preserve this appearance of nature from its death. A geological unlayering, an archeological excavation, would reveal, he argues, that the text of nature is grounded in a primordial life that sustains a continuity between original language and its historical repetitions. Thus Chinese radicals, these "visible hieroglyphics," bear on their face their whole "etymological history" while Western languages (characterized by the discontinuous representations of phonetic writing) have imposed upon our poets the need to "feel painfully back along the thread of our etymologies and piece together our diction."

On this point, the essay becomes aberrant. Ideograms are concrete, and thus natural symbols, yet abstract, like Hegel's hieroglyphs, in that they are a "shorthand" of a nature which is a law. They are graphs, a shorthand, of nature's "clues." Thus nature is a system, a structure; the "relation" of its "clues," the presence of "homologies" and "identities," afford man a "bridge" between the visible (or empirical) and the invisible (truth or *logos*). Ideogram, and by extension, an ideogrammic poetry, would be a "bridge" between visible and invisible, but only because the poem, or art, is a graph (interpretation) of nature's visible model. Language cannot properly have its origin in either the visible or invisible, in either nature or spirit. The ideogram as bridge has no foundation, but is itself the ground. It is therefore *radical* in two senses, of a root that will not return to its root, an originary force that is not, as such, original.

The modern reader of Hegel, that is to say, of Derrida's readings of Hegel, cannot help remarking that Fenollosa's privileging of the "visible hieroglyphics" of Chinese writing against the secondary and arbitrary signs of phonetic writing, and hence his privileging of poetry over philosophy, is something more than a simple misreading of Hegel, Hegel Emersonized as it were. In a sense one might even say that this version of Emerson anticipates Heidegger, both in its treatment of poetry as the language of unconcealment and in its disruption of the thinking of metaphysics it seems everywhere to confirm. Derrida himself suggests that it was modern literature, before even the analytics of philosophy or science, which began the systematic dislocation or decentering of the "founding categories" of metaphysics, the representational order of speech/writing. As Kenner points out, Fenollosa seems to ignore the fact that phonetic writing was never absolutely excluded from ideographic writing (though in the essay he does acknowledge some phonetic radicals). But as Derrida shows, the rebus-like effect of Oriental writing breaks or constellates the sign into an irreducible double which can never allow the unity of sound and mark: thus a language "structurally dominated by the ideogram," gives "testimony of a powerful movement of civilization developing outside of all logocentrism,"[16] since this language can never presume to encounter "reality." Fenollosa, however, celebrates the "graphic symbol" because it is not representational but a "force." Yet he continues to think historically: Chinese language retains its primordial power, the power of direct, innocent observation, while Western language has grown "pale," losing contact with its natural origin, so that a recuperation of Chinese graphism will close a circle and complete a history. His

[16]Ibid., p. 90; also, p. 91.

fable of the origin of language as writing rather than speech employs the figure of its being primordially "verbal" rather than "nominal": "The sentence form was forced upon primitive man by nature." Strangely enough, this syntax is the order of causation. Yet, causation is figured as a discontinuity, the sentence not as complete thought but as the "*transference of power*": "The type of sentence in nature is a flash of lightning," a unit of redistributed force. The syntactical force of nature is open-ended. Nothing returns to a subject. Process branches into a discontinuous play of forces.

At this point, what seems like an incoherent argument for the natural origin of language produces the possibility (or necessity) of a double reading: Kenner's or Derrida's. On the one hand, all the elements of organicism or logocentrism are there; in the notion of language as a "metaphoric advance," and poetry, particularly the "graphic symbol," as a "centre" throwing "about it a nimbus of meanings." The "graphic symbol" is presentational and interpretative at the same time, marking the continuity between culture and nature, the origin of culture in nature. Kenner reads Pound's faith in the classical precisions of graphic language as an efficient archeology, a recuperation of primordial language or proper naming. Derrida, on the other hand, cites Pound and Fenollosa, in *Of Grammatology,* because of their "irreducibly graphic poetics [which] was with that of Mallarmé, the first break in the most entrenched Western tradition." Like Nietzsche, he adds, they "at first destroyed and caused to vacillate the transcendental authority and dominant category of the *épistémè*: being."[17] If the "graphic symbol" is Fenollosa's "centre," then it is a noncentered noncentering center, irreducibly multiple. And nature is not an agent, but already a play of forces, a constellated and constellating field.

Fenollosa's concluding example of the triumph of ideographic precision is the graph for the English sentence, "The sun rises in the east." He explains it as follows: "The [ideograph of the] sun, shining, on one side, on the other the sign of the east, which is the sun entangled in the branches of a tree. And in the middle sign, the verb 'rise,' we have further homology; the sun is above

17Ibid., p. 92.

the horizon, but beyond the single upright line is the growing trunk-line of the tree sign." Derrida must have been illuminated by the very precision of this placement of Western metaphor, the "sun" as origin entangled in the branches of a tree, eclipsed in its origin, distributed across the branchings of a text which is its origin, the site of it. Fenollosa would hardly have understood this unnatural and perverse reading, this textualizing of nature, even if we see it in his own inscription.

What we call today the movement of Imagism—and even Vorticism—is not a method deriving from Fenollosa's text, any more than it is the method of a single experimenter.[18] In fact, whether it can be called a method at all is questionable; and so far as it is the name for a historical group or movement, it bespeaks the heterogeneity of literary history. Nevertheless, Fenollosa's text was seminal for Pound, although it was not for other Imagists, but one cannot speak of its "influence" on his theory, and certainly not on his theory of the Image. Still, one can read Pound's Imagist theory through a text which, after all, was first published as an appendix to a collection of Pound's essays, edited with a few explanatory notes, in a manner that must have concealed its own accidental origin. For the essay itself is a Poundian reconstruction, out of Fenollosa's notes, and the accidents of its own "organic" form await the explanations of a textual editor. In his notes to the text, Pound transcribed Fenollosa's speculations into his own. He chose to emphasize their mutual discovery of "interpretative metaphor" in contrast to "ornamental metaphor," either metaphor as "analogy" or as symbolism—that is, interpretation which translates, carries over, displaces, transcribes; a metaphorics that disturbs the theory of metaphor. Pound's theory of the Image is not simply a postulate of form or style, but a theory of generative and dislocating force—in a sense, a theory of translation, or better, transcription. The Image, by which he means the poem as a condensation (Fenollosa's "shorthand" cipher) defines stylistic precision as an "objectification" which overthrows the *aporia* between two senses

[18]Some of the following section was treated, in a slightly different way, in my essay "Pound and the Decentered Image," *The Georgia Review*, 29 (Fall 1975), 565-591.

of figural language (or rhetoric), between trope as visual representation and trope as displacement, between form and force. In Pound's definitions, the Image (that is the whole Poem) is always a "node" or "cluster" of figures, a constellation of radical differences, and a transformative machine which represents a movement across these points of difference. The radical, the Image, is a "field"—in short, "originally" a text.

The Image, Pound wrote, may be defined as an "intellectual and emotional complex in an instant of time." And Pound confesses that he takes the word "complex" from a London psychiatrist and follower of Freud, Bernard Hart. As a "complex" the Image would suggest something like a Gestalt, according to Herbert Schneidau,[19] and would therefore constitute a kind of mapping (and thus a figural displacement) of its mental object. But the Image has no object as such. It displaces time linearity (and succession) into a figural space (a "moment of time"), producing a formal mirage (a *sens*). The unconscious has no time, nor any object. It is displaced as time, as consciousness, and thus as a movement of images. Time, therefore, does not represent, but is presented as the explicit (and explicatory) movement of language, its presencing/absencing. Time is a play of figure. The poem as Image, then, can translate only by constellating this play of images. Pound's psychological metaphor for the Image as "complex" anticipates the deconstruction of Freud's Unconscious as a term for presence or for nondifference, and the dreamwork as a *mise en scène* of writing. The "complex" is an Image of differences known only in the play of translations. The "complex" is translation and interpretation of symptoms, signs, and not of "experience." The Image is a layering of images or other texts.

The well-publicized tenets of Imagism speak of the Poem as a "direct treatment of the 'thing,' whether subjective or objective" in a way that throws interpreters off the track, since it suggests a return to immediacy as objectivity. But "thing" is already in quotation marks, like Nietzsche's "thing-in-itself," or already a figure of some "object," and what is "direct" in this definition is the

[19]Schneidau, *Ezra Pound: The Image and the Real* (Baton Rouge: Louisiana State University Press, 1969), pp. 99–100.

"treatment" of signs or symptoms. The Image is curative, then, only in the sense of interpreting, of bringing to consciousness (as form, visibility). The force of writing disseminates by radical displacement, by condensation, staging, transcribing. Thus the tenet arguing for strict economy—to use no descriptive, ornamental, or unnecessary word—and the tenet rejecting metronomic repetition (set verse rhythm) for variations governed by the play of the "musical phrase" suspend the notions of both immediacy and mediation, and suggest a poetics that precedes the thinking of the play of presence and absence. Pound's Image recapitulates, by reproducing the primordial event of a writing without origin, a writing at the origin.

Pound's own example of the characteristic Image poem speaks of superpositions, the gliding of one image over the other. But superpositioning, while suggesting a pure spatiality, must include the temporalizing play, the sucession of images which repeat one another in their difference, repeat by weaving together or inscribing that which cannot be reduced to a singularity. That is why Kenner can interpret the little "Metro" poem as a repetition and condensation of Persephone's eternal return, literally of opening or blooming: "The apparition of these faces in the crowd; / Petals on a wet, black bough." "In a poem of this sort," Pound wrote, "one is trying to record the precise instant when a thing outward and objective transforms itself, or darts into a thing inward and subjective."[20] The "instant" is movement itself, caught in a complex of superimposed differences, of crossing lines of force. Superpositioning cannot escape successivity, the act of the second image displacing the first even as it carries forward the memory (trace?) of that sign displaced, negated, repeated, and effaced. There is no perception here, certainly not of nature; the natural image grows in a mythic garden, or text.

In Pound's "Metro," the textural (and textual) contrast of fallen petals on a background that once sustained them carries forward an "apparition," that is, a previous image or a trace that effaces itself. An image of falling or dying nature, which includes a living, blooming nature, recapitulates an image of re-

[20]*Gaudier-Brzeska* (New York: New Directions, 1970), p. 89. First published in 1916.

membered presence or of presencing that includes its own death. The play of images is patternless outside of the textual field, the interpretation. That is, the textual weave, the projection of an "experience," is a remembered "perception" superscripted upon a mythic text of repetition. Pound discovered his modern Image of Persephone/Kore in an appropriate place: the Metro or Underground is a place of transversal, crossing, the translation of appearance/disappearance. The Image is a scene of writing, a figuration of its own condensation. One has only to recall Pound's own anecdote (in *Gaudier-Brzeska*) of the experience which triggered the poem (it was not really an experience in the "Metro" but a reflection on the significance of formalizing or rendering that already re-remembered moment). The poem went through several versions, or textual condensations, until the final Image became a map of the process of displacement and reinscription. If the poem retells the myth of Kore, or of *āletheia,* it renders it as a violence of writing. While the poem may be an Image of Spring, of unconcealment, of blooming, it also is an Image of the "apparition," of the appearance of the sign/Image itself, whose face, like Kore's, is inscribed with marks of its own death. For if the poem has anything at all in common with the Kore archetype—and I am by no means convinced that Kenner's insight is anything more than an arbitrary critical analogy—it is because Pound's text, like the "original" myth, is a graph of "memory," of remembering, and not a representation of nature's becoming.

More than two decades after his radical polemics on behalf of Imagism had produced its stylistic revolution, Pound recognized the problem of earlier Imagist definition to lie in the mimetic prejudice associated with the term "image," and he sought to re-emphasize the temporality (the *praxis*) which Vorticist theory had featured: "The defect of earlier imagist propaganda was not in misstatement but in incomplete statement. The diluters took the handiest and easiest meaning, and thought only of the STATIONARY image. If you can't think of imagism or phanopoeia as including the moving image, you will have to make a really needless division of fixed image and praxis or action."[21] Pound's use of *phanopoeia* refers to a lexicon developed much earlier,

[21] *ABC of Reading* (New York: New Directions, n.d.), p. 52.

which also includes the terms *melopoeia* and *logopoeia*.[22] These three terms, which correspond to the three tenets of Imagism, suggest the movement or play of images (*phanopoeia*), of sounds (*melopoeia*), and meanings or ideas (*logopoeia*). The common property of each of these elements is movement or "play." In *phanopoeia*, the images are "thrown," not intended. The visual is reinscribed as a play of differences (that is, in writing), which decenters any imagistic representation. More significantly, Pound gives *phanopoeia*, the thrownness of images over one another, a priority over *melopoeia* and *logopoeia*. Like Fenollosa, therefore, he gives priority to the image as hieroglyphic writing, and thus to the graphic play opened up.

On the other hand, although Pound repeats Fenollosa in attributing to nature the genesis of this play, he does not assume that nature governs the system of language it presumably sets in play. Like Nietzsche, he views nature as a field of irreducible energies, of conflicting forces. The poetic imagination, as in Nietzsche, is seminal—and Pound, at least in one place, followed Nietzsche in suggesting that the brain consisted of seminal fluid from which images spurted like "ejaculations."[23] Like seeds, these images lead a life independent of the source (the brain) which begets them. Divorced from the naturalism of the description, which Pound only halfway embraces, since he is commenting on Rémy de Gourmont's *Natural Philosophy of Love,* the metaphor subscribes to an origin that is already diacritical, like the two hemispheres of the brain. The origin was irreducibly a play of seminal differences. Thus graphic or image play is the primary language of this productive dynamic, but the images are not natural—they are neither exteriorizations of an interiority, nor representations. They present only their own play of energies. The "image," then, "is not an idea. It is a radiant node or cluster," a "Vortex," a form that resists any collapsing of differences into unity.

This freedom from the commanding origin, this play of

[22]See Pound, *Literary Essays* (New York: New Directions, 1954), pp. 25–26. The terms are repeated elsewhere, esp. in *ABC of Reading.*

[23]"Postscript" to Rémy de Gourmont, *The Natural Philosophy of Love,* trans. Ezra Pound (New York: Liveright, 1922), pp. 295–296.

originating forces, informs the modern long poem. The *praxis* of the moving image puts in question the idea of the unified or autotelic text, or the thought of poetic closure. It also resists the possibility of a text commanded by any one of its elements: a controlling theme, a privileged point of view, authorial intentionality, image cluster, or central symbol. The possibility of the long poem opened up by the decentering of Imagism was, in fact, contrary to any New Critical holism that was derived from it. For example, Kenneth Burke (who is hardly a subscriber to such holisms) has employed the metaphor "qualitative progression" to account for the continuity between elements that were quantitatively or logically irreconcilable, suggesting that the long poem developed by a kind of inner dialectic in which similar residual qualities overcame heterogeneous quantities to move the poem toward totalization and closure.[24] Another Burkean term, "perspective by incongruity," offered a similar psychological and dialectical explanation of the linked analogies between otherwise incoherent or heterogeneous elements. The strategy to domesticate or acculturate *The Waste Land,* to make it "readable" and thus to shore "fragments" against our psychic ruins, becomes a model for interpreting all those long poems like *The Bridge* or *The Cantos.* The model of metaphysical conceit or Symbolist synaesthetics is called up to justify incongruity and fragmentariness as an inaugural movement that signifies the ultimate yoking and reconciliation of opposites, the poem's triumphant closure upon itself, its becoming an object, synecdoche of the unity of which it is only a broken sign.

Formalist criticism tends to isolate a privileged image cluster or a master word (symbol) which assures the poem's totalization of its elements: thus the "autotelic" resolves all incongruities and limits the play of antitheses it opens up, in order to display its telic power. Of course, New Critical formalism presumably derived from a description of these experiments in the overcoming of extreme incoherence, much as classical formalism derived from Aristotelian descriptions of the classical stage. That is, formalism derives from a willed interpretation, an interpretation already inscribed in a larger body of interpretation

---

[24]*Counter-statement* (Chicago: University of Chicago Press, 1957), pp. 124-125.

(metaphysical or theological) which the poems not only mirror but realize, in their sacred (closed) objectivity.

In an essay contemporary with *The Waste Land,* Eliot advocated what he called the "mythical method" as the way by which the modern writer, faced with the chaos of modern history, might find a "model" of order for his work to imitate, to repeat as a structural ground.[25] Lacking a coherent system of belief or a credible idea of order, the modern writer, he suggested, must either appropriate one from a past writing, as Joyce did in *Ulysses,* or fabricate his own system, as Yeats had in *A Vision.* In either case, the appropriated or fabricated system would serve as an a priori source of images, a privileged point of reference. This timeless fiction (that of a circle totalizing its images, themes, and so on) not only lends authority to the signs or images appropriated from it, but signifies the general form of mastery or totalization. Thus allusion, quotation, reference, and the like reenact the gathering or regathering of the many into the One. The essay is a restatement of Eliot's idea, in "Tradition and the Individual Talent," of the "ideal order" of "existing monuments" which composes the "timeless" tradition—the "presence" of history repeatedly manifest in the body of artistic forms. The "mythical method," and its primary strategies—reference, citation, allusion, and quotation—confirm art as "timeless" repetition of the Same, repetition as incorporation. That which governs this repetition is a *logos,* a logocenter or *spiritus mundi,* which realizes itself in language and speaks, in the Gnostic movement of the poem, simultaneously of its presence as an absence. In Eliot's most striking metaphor, the "tradition" or "existing order" of art is always complete, and each new work alters it "if ever so slightly," therefore supplementing its completeness. The same must be claimed for every poem. Its incorporation, literally, of the fragments and archives of a previous art, incorporates the absence of the origin. All texts supplement that which supplements them, displacing that origin which commands their ultimate ef-

---

[25]"'Ulysses,' Order and Myth," *The Dial* (Nov. 1923); reprinted in Mark Schorer et al., eds., *Criticism: The Foundations of Modern Literary Judgment* (New York: Harcourt, Brace, 1948), pp. 269-270.

facement. But Eliot sees no problems with this "incorporation," except the problem of disbelief in a transubstantial moment.

This notion of "reference" or allusion functions within a certain nostalgia for the center, and within a movement of an absent presence (language) that defers the return to center. "Past" signs inscribed within a system of "present" signs mark the time of a history: Eliot's "turning world" that repeats the "still-point." There is no master text but a library of simultaneous texts, the tradition; even the Bible is only another catalogue of the distanced Word. One might argue that allusions or references within individual poems function in the same fashion as new poems function in the "existing totality" of the "tradition." But whereas Eliot saw this within the metaphysical view of history and textuality, as the unity of a becoming and thus a repetition of the Same, Pound's Imagist-Vorticist theory opens up the question of textuality by putting in quotation marks the authority of Being. What his poetics makes necessary is the "repeat of history," but like a musical repetition in a fugue rather than a quartet, a repetition that does not close or return absolutely upon itself.[26] Where allusion might suggest a past and privileged point of reference, Pound's repetition inscribes without reducing the fragment, the sign of the present-past. Hence that past is already textual, or pre-textual. Pound's Vortex literally winds itself upon a previous text, reinscribing it. But by inscribing the past text into the present text, Pound underscores the architectonics of the repetition, the construction of one house upon another, an incorporation that does not dissolve all into one body. The past text is never the present text. And the present text, insofar as it alludes to a past text, is never fully present. The time of the poem is the time of its play, its translation, the time produced in its signature of its own operation. Presence is a formal construction, and a mirage, always already an Image.

In one of those unorthodox examples which characterize the *ABC of Reading*, Pound compares modernist poetic method to that of the contemporary "bookkeeper" who employs a "loose-

---

[26]See *The Letters of Ezra Pound: 1907–1941*, ed. D. D. Paige (New York: Harcourt, Brace, 1950), p. 210.

leaf system."[27] This system separates "archives" from "facts that are in use," and allows the bookkeeper to retrieve either past or present facts and to "use" them in a relation not dictated by chronology or nostalgia. The example characterizes Pound's sense of the modern Image. The facts of a poem are not references, except as they refer to another text. And every fact in use (present fact) may have an intertextual relation to an "archive" (the signs of the past), but only as an indeterminate spatio-temporal relation. A "loose-leaf system," which is more modern than a palimpsest, redistributes the chronological reference but does not violate the force or play of alterity. It does, however, suspend the privilege of the "archive." Detail can be retrieved or left out of play, but no detail commands the system totally. The "loose-leaf" system makes possible a new interpretation of "use," of usage, and therefore reinscribes within the possibility of poetry an anti-usury. A privileged pre-text does not rule the system; nor are "archives" relegated to a place of sacred significance, of archeological fragments from which one can remount the stream of history or memory. What is meaningful is the play of signs, not their reference to a lost or concealed meaning. The present facts repeat the "archives," but with a difference. This kind of system resists the wearing out (effacement) of facts that allows Pound to associate linguistic imprecision with economic usury of language. The irreducible difference of the Image, the play it inscribes and produces endlessly, makes it a writing device that repeats original creation, that is, original coinage. The Image moves because it resists equivalences. When Pound borrowed the archaeological figure of the *paideuma* from Leo Frobenius for the "complex of in-rooted ideas" that governed the structure of every culture, he named a center or origin that was irreducibly complex and inseparable from the "play" (the *paidia*) that Plato saw as the danger of language.

At this point, however, it is time for a textual leap. What Vorticism opens or doubles (the question of textuality as representational or productive), Pound amplifies in *The Cantos*. On the other hand, the degree to which Pound participated in a radical reopening of the idea of literature is repeated and, in-

[27] *ABC of Reading*, p. 38.

deed, pro-jected in the work of Charles Olson. It is there that we began, in Olson's decentering, in his return to Melville to follow Melville's wandering writing. To return to Olson, then, is to return to the disruptive "project" of a "post-Modernism" which has only the privilege of a certain repetition already inaugurated in the "beginning of writing."

Olson's poetry, like his criticism, inscribes itself from its beginning in a field of old texts, the "limits" enclosing every individual subject. "Limits / are what any of us / are inside of . . . " (*MP*, 17). The limited self is only a force in a field of forces, and not a commanding subject of history, the hero. Its "limits" are its language, the field of language in which every subject arises and a field it can never command. The self has no proper beginning. It produces no history or teleology: "[T]here is no 'history.' (I still keep going back to, the notion, this is (we are) merely, the *second time* (that's as much history as I'll permit in, which ain't history at all . . . " (*SW*, 113). (This history, like Olson's parentheses, will not close.)

To go back to come forward, as Olson said of Melville, is to seize the beginning as already begun. The poet is "merely, the *second time*." His originality is already a repetition, a temporalization that disrupts the notion of a "first" time by marking its figural nature. The poet who is the *first* to look *again* at the "start of human motion" (*MP*, 15) repeats the Original Act, the First Murder, in the sense that he fractures the dream of some original, recuperable purpose. Olson's poetics begin as a determined attack on logocentrism, and thus on the Modernist poetry, like Eliot's, that presumes to totalize the great (Western) tradition. In his "Letter to Elaine Feinstein," which has become an official postscript to the essay on "Projective Verse," Olson writes of his own archeological researches into the earliest languages as a decentering of the Image: "I am talking from a new 'double axis': the replacement of the Classical-representational by the primitive-abstract. . . . I mean of course not at all primitive in that stupid use of it as opposed to civilized. One means it now as 'primary'" (*SW*, 28). Thus the image as representation, as "referential to reality," is seen as the nostalgic invention of "history." Olson's leap backward into prehistory destroys the teleological fiction which had displaced the localism of preclassical culture. The ancient "Image, therefore, is vector," centered on a "'content' (multiplicity: originally, and repetitively, chaos—Tiamat: wot the Hindo Europeans knocked out by giving the Old Man (Juice himself) all the lightning" (*SW*, 29). The "primary," the first, is force—already multiple and temporalizing. Like Olson's punctuation, the Image disseminates rather than closes.

"We have lived long in a generalizing time," he writes in "Human Universe," and that means since "450 *B.C.*" (*SW*, 53). Our language is inescapably metaphysical and obscures the history of language's invention in a myth of origins—the fall. "Unselectedness," says Olson, "is man's original condition" and culture emerges by selection, by "act." Man is a force who signifies himself as a mark, as writing. Man begins as the already begun. There is no inaugural selecting act, no Adamic naming, but only babble (Babel) and the beginning as selection.

For Olson's poet, the first act is to displace the fiction of origins, to reintroduce Desire: "intention" as "the old Kosmos—or order imposed on Chaos in the creative beginning from it by Spirit of Desire, and by all three of mud, and then from mud the World Egg—becomes a condition, even if with a more precise vocabulary, of each one of us . . . " (*SVH*, 51). In this *Special View of History,* chance and accident precede and displace the fiction of original unity, generating "history" as a space of play. Life genetically occurs as "autoclytic multiplication": "life is the chance success of a play of creative accidents. It is the principle of randomness seen in its essential application; not in any serial order imposed at random on either change or accident . . . but in the factual observation of how creation does occur: by the success of its own accident" (*SVH*, 48). "Ontogeny creates phylogeny" (*SVH*, 49). In the beginning was a chaos, a freeplay, the cultural space or graph Joyce called "chaosmos." "Selection," as in the act of writing, has no privileged beginning. To recall Williams, there are no ideas before things and no "things" without "relation." Selection begins in seeing the local difference, in "factual observation," or looking. Looking is not perception, however, not the constitutive act of a subject. Nor is it empirical ordering. Looking is situated at the place where selection begins, in the first accidental marking of difference and relation, a grammar governed by neither subject nor *archē*, an an-archy, a multicentered field:

> There are not hierarchies, no infinite, no such many as mass
> > there are only
> eyes in all heads,
> to be looked out of
> > > > > [*MP*, 29]

Language, however, is already informed with hierarchies. The language of poetry appeals to the unity of the Word, and thus to the commanding presence of the "Old Man (Juice himself)" who possesses all the "lightning." To recuperate the cultural origin in "selection" is to seize a beginning already begun, to recover the play of writing. Selection is not *āletheia*, but a productive interpretation, an act of appropriation. Thus when Olson calls this recuperation a return to "speech" and "breath," it is not the speech of logocentrism, but language marked by an irreducible doubleness, hieroglyph or ideogram: "Logos, or discourse, for example, has, in that time [since 450 B.C.], so worked its abstractions into our concept and use of language that language's other function, speech, seems so in need of restoration that several of us go back to hieroglyphs or to ideograms to right the balance. (The distinction here is between language as the act of the instant and language as the act of thought about the instant.)" (*SW*, 53–54).

There is an inaugural disruption here: of the priority of Being to language. "Selection" does not originate in a "subject," but in the accidental encounter. At this point Olson identifies speech with performance, with the "act" that shatters representation.

Despite the evidence which tempts one to locate Olson's poetics in the oral tradition—his preoccupation with "breath," for example—it is graphic selection that precedes *logos*. The return to speech as act or performance, like the return to "glyph" writing, is an attack on "manuscript" and set verse (the text as representation of thought or expression of self) and therefore upon phonetic writing. Speech, as we will see, becomes for Olson the energy of quantified differences, which has a doubling, a projective and a conjectural effect. It is the act which gives the poem "solidity" by breaking up the prescribed grammars, decentering the narrative "line" into the field of "elements," thereby restoring to the textual space the "play of their separate energies" (*SW*, 21).

The irreducible element of verse is "breath," Olson claims, and not the metered foot. Breath is the mark of temporalization, of a broken and breaking movement, of "spacing." It therefore sets off and marks the productive fact of the "smallest particle" of verse, the syllable. The "syllable" is irreducible difference, signifying both the temporal and spatial play of language. It projects, resisting any center or centering tendency. And this allows Olson to make a distinction which for many critics has seemed contradictory. The return to the elements of breath and syllable has been encouraged, he argues, by the typewriter, by a writing instrument which has made possible "space precisions" and therefore the necessary marking and projection of syllabic difference. The machine, as Olson argues, produces the graph for a reading; it produces a text that in its turn can never govern a reading. Olson's graphic (machine) text is not only a play of elements, it projects multiple readings or voicings that play off its play. Thus Olson, whose poetics derives at least indirectly from oral formulaic scholars like Milman Parry and Albert Lord, and from classical scholars like Eric Havelock who have followed Parry and Lord, links himself to an oral poetics by the very instrument which puts that "tradition" in quotation marks. Olson's poetics, that is to say, opens the idea of the text to performance. Every performance transcribes and projects a difference; it tropes the trope, as in de Man's sense of the *aporia* that opens up the play and hence marks the lack of mastery between conative (philosophical or nominative) language and performative (literary or rhetorical) language.

The contribution of the machine, "space precisions," may be seen to take on a significance beyond the practical spacing or scripting for reading performance. Spacing is inseparable from the elementary quantification or temporalization of verse. And as Derrida indicates, a notion of spacing is fundamental to any thinking about writing.[28] Can Olson's literal emphasis on spac-

---

[28]See "La Double Séance," *La Dissémination* (Paris: Seuil, 1972), pp. 198–317; also, *Of Grammatology*, p. 203, and passim.

ing be elided with Derrida's? Spacing for Derrida is an irruptive function of writing, of marks or grammatic indications which signify the displacement of the sign by a following sign; the *blanc* and the *hymen* (which may stand for the doubleness of all graphic or punctual marks) are syntactical indicators which give place to signs, and thus mark their incompleteness, their doubleness. Spacing for Derrida, therefore, becomes a sign (or nonsign) of the impossibility of any sign's holding a fixed significance. Spacing suspends the semantic depth of the sign. It disrupts the place of the sign even as it inscribes the representational mirage. Spacing is projective and productive or disseminating. We may confidently assume that Olson's concern for spacing goes beyond technique; for his project demands nothing less than a clearing away of the illusion of the closed text, and particularly of the Western, Mediterranean, classical notion of representation.

Derrida's thinking of writing as spacing/dissemination, as a "productive, positive, generative force,"[29] can help us understand what has become, especially for Olson's detractors, a nearly nonsensical formula for "projective" verse. If the "syllable" is the simplest element of verse, that element includes its double: it "is only the first child of the incest of verse (always, that Egyptian thing, it produces twins!)" (*SW,* 18). Its twin is not simply a repetition of the same, but a radical doubling—the syllable's twin is the "line." A syllable commands only its displacement, projecting temporally both word and line, producing the unfolding breath unit: two children, two irreducible units, the twins of *différance.* Here, then, is Olson's formula for the pro-ject: "the HEAD, by way of the EAR, to the SYLLABLE / the HEART, by way of the BREATH, to the LINE " (*SW,* 19). The syllable is uttered in a *place* of irreducible difference, and thus signifies a presence that is not present to itself. The syllable contains its own double re-doubled, the temporal movement of the "line." The line, in its turn, is a unit marked by the inevitable

---

[29]In "Positions," *Diacritics,* 3 (Spring 1973), 41n.: "As *dissemination,* as *différance,* it includes a genetic dimension, it is not simply the interval, the space constituted between two . . . , but spacing . . . , the operation or in any case movement of separation. This movement is inseparable from temporization—temporalization . . . —and from the *différance,* the conflicts of force which are at work."

next "breath," it signifies its own disruptive, discontinuous play, like a path cut through space, like a geo-graph or a map.

The syllable is of the "head," then, because it is the elementary constituent of a semantics, or a semantic mirage. It is also of the "ear" because it demands alterity, or temporalization. It is the elemental unit which must be combined to make the word. The word, therefore, is never singular or nominative, never out of play. And the line is of the "heart" (not the sentimental organ of a unified interiority, but the temporal beat) because like all "life" it moves, advances, repeats, or is disseminated through a play of differences. Or as Olson redefines his concept in an interesting combination of metaphors: the "head . . . ear . . . syllable" makes possible the "PLAY of a mind"; the "heart . . . breath . . . line" provides the "threshing floor for the dance" (*SW*, 19). Play is *différance;* the dance is its decentered repetitions. The two are inseparable and irreducible. Unlike the logocentric "line," Olson's poetic line refuses any closure of its circulation.

Its play projects an ever-expanding unit, a "FIELD," which is a name for the poem. This field cannot be "centered," that is, commanded by a single intentionality or privileged object. It is, rather, a space of relations, of forces always already begun: "each of these elements of a poem can be allowed to have the play of their separate energies and can be allowed, once the poem is well composed, to keep . . . their proper confusions" (*SW*, 21). This play dissolves the referential function of the sign, and reinscribes it within a new system of relations, projecting new fields, not recuperating old ones.

Dance and process are other Olson metaphors for this movement. He relates them to a methodology of "limits," to a poetry set against the logocentric dream of totalization (and thus totalitarianism). In seeking a new methodology, he says, it has been necessary to deconstruct the old methods, to "turn the totalitarian" (*LO*, 106). The new methodology will be based on the model of the city, not the modern city but the early cities of Sumerian and Mayan culture, those ancient places of man's gathering which have survived history (a death) in the traces of their indelible invention, writing or hieroglyphs, that is, their invention of history as writing. From 3378 *B.C.* until about 1200 *B.C.*, he conjectures, "civilization had ONE CENTER, Sumer, in all directions"; thus Olson concludes, "a city was a coherence which, for the first time since the ice [age], gave man the chance to join knowledge to culture" (*HU*, 19). Coherence, however, is not a closed system. In contrast, the historical civilizations which followed in Greece and Rome tried to stabilize this coherence, by locating the center in an idea of man, in humanism. They were marked by logocentrism, and by the rise of the "hero"; Man displaced the community of men (or discourse) as center. In *Letters for Origin,* Olson relates his search for a new methodology to a deconstruction of the epoch of the hero:

> To cohere means to stick together! To hold fast, as
> parts of the same mass!
>   And coherence is defined as connection or *congruity*
>   arising from some common *principle* or idea
> Now if I slug in juxtaposition and composition by field,
> METHODOLOGY as a word of more import than technique—
> as a word also as proper to the change of procedure
> demanded of us in the face of TOTALITY—may be more of
> the cluster of force i take it it is.
> But let's go back to root: to *methodos,* and look!
>   with a way,
>   with a via, with a path (weg, that which died,
> and does not die, which it is any man's job—and the more so
> now, when the old way is dead, long live the methodology
>   in other words, the science of
> the path—what could be more exactly what we are involved
> in—it is not the path, but it is the way the path is
> discovered!   [*LO*, 106]

The classical principle of totalization, of ideational centering, has displaced the coherence of the open or multicentered field in Olson's special (and spatial) reading of history. Method as projection or quest has given way to ethnocentrism and thus authoritarianism. *Methodos* disrupts representation, the law that makes us follow the path, and returns us to that act of cutting the path. To reappropriate the elementary twins of verse, syllable and line, recapitulates the reappropriation of Sumer. Coherence is a work of construction, not an imitation of Truth. Like Pound, Olson appeals to the archeological metaphor, but the archeologist does not presume to recuperate presence. Rather, in his re-search of method, he seeks that cutting edge, the "way" to cut a path and not some path to follow. He seeks the disruptive, productive tool of writing.

For some of Olson's acolytes, his theory advocates a present reappropriation of the past, an authentic return to an authentic "time," to the prehistorical purity of an oral tradition. But Olson is not nostalgic. The past, whether an ideal prehistorical culture or an authoritative past text, is neither the object of his desire nor a point of privileged reference. The remote cultures summon him because they are like a mysterious writing; he would decipher their method, not their meaning. Olson's effort, then, is to recapitulate the process of a "first writing" as the generation of coherence, as a desire for and thrust toward the Center. In this regard, the Center is the place of the dance and of the play of the mind, a scene of writing, as it were. The ancient city exemplifies man's selection; it is a labyrinth that was purely and simply made as an open design, not a representation of an idea, a city of God. To go back means to open up again that "play of creative accidents" which precedes all totalitarian cultures. In Olson's view the modern poet thinks he has written the closure of history and therefore of poetry. What stands between the "postmodern poet" and the figural act of first writing is the history of accumulated texts. To cut through these texts demands a repetition of original research, whether this means going to an archeological site to study a culture whose language has not been deciphered (like the Mayan's) or following the method (the way) of the new scientific analysts, the archeologists and geographers, linguists and revisionary historians.[30]

An Olson poem may graph or map an old document or old text in the same way an archeologist might open up a site. Its purpose is not to sanctify old texts or uncover their origin but to decipher the crux that led to their writing. Old texts incorporate

[30]Among Olson's models of objective scholarship, one should mention certainly the geographer Carl O. Sauer, the linguist Edward Sapir, the mathematician Georg Riemann, Werner Heisenberg (for his radical modification of relativity), the anthropologist Leo Frobenius whom Pound found so central to the modern, the Greek scholar Eric Havelock, and several archeologists who had uncovered and decoded the sites of Sumer. These are scholars who have advanced the search and effected a "change of paradigm" (to use Thomas Kuhn's phrase) in their discipline, without presuming to have arrived at or recuperated the Truth. Theirs is the method of "Document."

the doubleness of history. To use a favorite Olson metaphor, history is a Moebius strip, a single surface that always returns upon itself; it is not the exterior of some interior presence, not simply the expression of God or the "unity of a becoming." History is a single surface of successive events, like successive perceptions, that return into themselves, cross through and efface each other, repeat themselves, but always with a difference. Each repetition is an asymptote. Olson therefore calls this a method of "Document" as opposed to the method of "Narration"; for in the latter, the narrator as personal interpreter dominates the movement of the text, and governs its closure. The poem as "document" throws together (thus conjectures) old texts, mapping them, so as to "re-enact" their making (*HU*, 127).

Present poems do not absorb old texts but take movement, a kind of spacing, from them. Documents decenter the lyrical voice, the centering or narrative subject. But the poet's performance (method) also decenters the documents. Affiliation maps and demythologizes the fiction of narrative or filiative order.[31] In the juxtaposition of documents, the author does not determine the field, since there is a multiple of authors. "Curiosity," says Olson, drew man's attention to the things around him, including the detail of other human objects. This motivated his measurings, his cosmic interpretations (*SW*, 58). This interpretive act inscribes or maps the "Spirit of Desire." Like the Dresden codex, Stonehenge, and the ruins of Angkor Wat, the poem will be a projective machine, not some nostalgic sign of a past, a past-present. The poem—that is, the postmodern poem which aspires to be original, a first poem, in that it must repeat what is seen by the "first human eyes ... /at the start of human motion (just last week/300,000,000 years ago" (*MP*, 15)—must be a "glyph," a mark in nature, a mark signifying the intercourse of man and nature, the place of man, his placement toward nature,

[31] See Derrida, *Of Grammatology*, pp. 107–108: "one should meditate upon all of the following: writing as the possibility of the road and of difference, the history of writing and the history of the road, of the rupture, of the *via rupta*, of the path that is broken, beaten, *fracta*, of the space of reversibility and of repetition traced by the opening, the divergence from, and the violent spacing, of nature, of the natural, savage, salvage, forest ... ; it is difficult to imagine that access to the possibility of a road-map is not at the same time access to writing."

the meeting point of an irreducible dance. Thus the poem is not recuperative but productive. Yet, it is a threshold, like the "skin" where man and nature interact, the place of the dance or play, of a *différance* which can never be stilled or closed. Olson, then, can argue, like Vico or Rousseau, that original language was figural, poetic. Yet it is instrumental, though in a strange way. If the "instrumentation of selection" is always located on this "threshold" (*SW*, 60), it precedes the self as subject, just as it precedes nature as object, or any originary being. The "skin" is a "cutting edge," not a thing or a place at all, but the field of language marked in every "glyph." No history can begin from this non-origin, this "skin" which is neither an inside nor an outside. No single "way" can be retrieved from this cut. In the beginning was "*methodos*" the cutting edge, the threshold. To recuperate method, however—to go back to go forward, to recover the thrownness, in both Heidegger's and Olson's sense—is to overcome at last "American" belatedness, or to put its nostalgia in the parentheses of a "literary history." The "project" of an "American" poetics, if one can condense a history that does not exist, has been to invent a machine of its own origins—to invent or re-invent "language," an "Image," where the fiction of Being can be entertained, not as that which has been lost and can be recuperated, but as that which has been invented as a pure fiction so that it can be destroyed, or deconstructed, in the "beginning again." The "project" of "American" poetry has always been anarchic rather than archeo-logical, or as one might say, archeo-clastic, a myth of origins that puts the myth of origins in question, that puts itself in question. It is a poetry of uprootedness, of radical innocence, of the radical origin, of the radical as origin—the "decentered" "Image."

Gérard Genette

Valéry and the
Poetics of Language

In writing of Valéry and the *poetics of language,* I use that
deliberately Bachelardian phrase (quite legitimately, since there
is a poetics of space and a poetics of reverie, as well as, by implication, a poetics of fire, air, earth, and water) to mean the
human imagination applied to language, as it is applied elsewhere to space or the elements, and also to mean the poetic or,
more generally, literary investiture of those images and that reverie. It seems to me that one major—if not *the* major—axis of
the linguistic imagination is the idea of, the desire for, and,
provisionally, the *myth* of a *motivation* of the linguistic sign or
(quite properly in this particular context) the *word.* In an even
more specific sense, what is involved here is the idea of motivation by *analogy*—a relation of resemblance, a mimetic relation—
between "the word" and "the thing."

In our European literary and philosophical tradition, this idea
was first presented and examined in Plato's *Cratylus.* I say "in
Plato's *Cratylus*" instead of "by Cratylus in Plato's dialogue" because Cratylus' affirmation of the so-called "fitness of signs" [*jus-
tesse des noms*] is seconded by Socrates when he argues against
Hermogenes in the first part of the dialogue. Though he does
not really articulate it, Hermogenes argues for what we would
call in Saussurian terms, the *arbitrariness* of language, or more
precisely, its conventional nature. And it is this position which
Socrates, in a sort of palinode, ends up at least partially defend-
ing against Cratylus. As a result, Plato's own position on the
matter remains partly unknown or obscure. But that is of little

importance for my subject here: I have referred to Plato only so
that I could borrow from him the eponymous figures of Cratylus
and Hermogenes to symbolize the two opposing—but not
contradictory—theses of the mimetic motivation and the con-
ventionality of language.

In general, modern linguistics seems to have decided in favor
of Hermogenes: this is one of the principal emphases of Saussure's *Course in General Linguistics;* and, even earlier, it was the
opinion of W. D. Whitney and William James, who picturesquely
expressed it by stating that "the word *dog* does not bite." To go
back still further, the idea can be found in the *Encyclopedia:*
"Words have no necessary relationship with that which they express."

Let me make it clear that, in reviewing these opinions, I do not
pretend to oppose "knowledge" to "ignorance" or "truth" to
"error." That would be all the more improper in view of the fact
that Saussure's affirmation of the *arbitrariness of the sign* has always been a matter of controversy, even among his own followers. Furthermore, linguists such as Otto Jespersen, Edward
Sapir, Roman Jakobson, and Ivan Fónagy have made numerous
attempts to identify as precisely as possible what Jakobson
calls—using a vocabulary borrowed from C. S. Peirce—the
"iconic" elements of language: at the very least, this shows that in
their view such elements are not totally nonexistent.

Still, the fact remains that the so-called scientific position is to
a certain extent and by its very nature a *deceiving* position, a
position which frustrates human desire insofar as this desire is
invested in myths. Linguistics states quite flatly that language is
essentially conventional, though it admits certain traits of mimetic motivation that must be located and analyzed (a task that is
not always easy). In opposition to this flat and purely empirical
position, we will call *Cratylism* (as Roland Barthes proposes) "that
great secular myth which wants language to imitate ideas and,
contrary to the precisions of linguistic science, wants signs to be
motivated."[1]

---

[1]"Proust et les noms," *To Honor Roman Jakobson* (The Hague: Mouton, 1967),
p. 158.

In calling Cratylism a myth, as does Barthes, I do not mean to designate it as an error in opposition to a truth, but rather as a thought oriented, to use Freudian terminology, more by the pleasure principle than by the reality principle. It is a thought, be it true or false (or more-or-less true or more-or-less false), that is first and foremost the expression of a desire. The mimetic interpretation of language, it seems evident to me, corresponds to an almost universal (this does not necessarily mean "natural") desire whose cause remains unknown but whose force and drive each of us can feel within himself. Whether true or false, Cratylism is a myth: it is above all a *seductive* thought.

I shall make no attempt here to sketch the history of Cratylism from Plato's time to our own. My intention is merely to situate Valéry's position in this secular debate. Doing so requires a brief review of the stage in Cratylism's history which immediately preceded Valéry himself. This brings us obviously to Mallarmé.

In order to appreciate the shift brought about by Mallarmé in the history of the "linguistic imaginary," one must establish a distinction between what I shall call, for lack of better terms and without any connotation of value, primary and secondary Cratylism. Primary Cratylism, that of Cratylus himself, consists in simply positing linguistic signification as a mimesis of the object by the noun (here language is almost always reduced to a collection of words, most often nouns, to the exclusion of verbs and tool-words, and it thus becomes what Saussure disdainfully called a "nomenclature"). One can try to explain this mimesis by an elementary symbolism of phonemes and/or graphemes. Such symbolism is most often supported by a simple list of words containing those phonemes or graphemes and expressing the idea supposedly evoked by each. Thus it is said that the sound *T* evokes stopping or stability, and that this capacity for evocation is demonstrated by the number of words, such as *table, top,* or *tomb,* that contain the consonant and express this idea or some similar one. Obviously, it is enough to choose one's examples well, to ignore contrary examples, and to be able to count on the compliance of one's audience (reader or interlocutor). Thus Socrates, after having posited that *R* is the phoneme of movement, is able to devote a digression to the Greek word *kinesis* without Hermogenes' interrupting him to point out the surprising absence of that phoneme in the very word that signifies "movement."

I would also include within primary Cratylism the somewhat more difficult attempts to base the expressive value of phonemes on articulatory physical considerations, as when Socrates explains the symbolism of the sliding of *L* by the sliding of the tongue over the palate, or the size symbolism of *A* and *E* by the fact that both are long vowels. This is still primary Cratylism in the sense that it concerns what certain linguists call "natural" language, a language which is presented as equipped with a mimetic aptitude that is in some way *native*.

Anyone who has read *Les Mots anglais,* published in 1877, can see that Mallarmé practiced this form of Cratylism. The first chapter fits into a long line of previous speculations that runs from the end of the eighteenth century and even includes the idea, which had been dear to President Charles de Brosses, that a word's entire signification—what Mallarmé calls its "radical virtue"[2]—lies in its consonants, and particularly in its initial or "attack" consonant. This leads to lists of words grouped by "families" according to their first letter, as well as to those symbolic values such as: *B* = production, giving birth, fecundity; *C* = prompt and decisive attack; *D* = continuous action without variation, stagnation, heaviness, obscurity; *GL* = joy and light; and so on.

One may object here that *Les Mots anglais* is a marginal work, of which Mallarmé himself wrote to Verlaine that "it would be better not to mention it" (p. 663). Yet just because the work's intention and object were purely pedagogical and/or commercial does not mean that profound dreams were not invested in it, and since my topic of discussion is Mallarmé's influence on Valéry, I need only quote the latter's opinion: "*Les Mots anglais* is perhaps the most revealing document that we possess regarding the private work practices of Mallarmé."[3]

---

[2] *Oeuvres complètes* (Paris: Pléiade, 1945), p. 965. All further quotations from Mallarmé are taken from this edition.

[3] *Oeuvres* (Paris: Pléiade, 1957), I, 686. All further quotations from Valéry are taken from this and the second volume (1960) of this edition.

From the outset one trait distinguishes Mallarmé's Cratylism from that maintained by his predecessors; for perhaps the first time, the "demon" of analogical motivation exerts itself on a *foreign* language. Before Mallarmé, Cratylian tradition involved either treating one's mother tongue as if it were the only one in existence, as Socrates did, or else, like de Brosses and Court de Gébelin, positing in principle that one speaks of the universal originating language, and then, in fact, reasoning on the basis of material furnished by one's native language, which is always treated as "supreme" (to borrow a word from Mallarmé himself).

For Mallarmé, on the contrary, the object of Cratylian reverie is not only a foreign language (English), but, very specifically, the most foreign element in this language of dual origin, what he calls its Gothic or Anglo-Saxon heritage—to the exclusion of all vocabulary imported from France at the time of the Norman invasion. The privilege of foreignness, if not of ethnographic *estrangement,* is clearly marked in the last sentence of the first book: "One seldom sees a word so surely as from the outside, from where we are—in other words, from a foreign land" (p. 975).

Primary Cratylism in *Les Mots anglais* does not therefore function as an analogic motivation of the language (French) that Mallarmé "normally" used as speaker and poet. Quite to the contrary, English appears here, from the exterior and at a distance, as some sort of almost inaccessible linguistic paradise, and therefore as the image of a *lost* linguistic paradise or *linguistic utopia* recognized and assumed as such. It is the image of a hypothetically or mythically original language, ideally and miraculously expressive, such as everyday language *is not.* English, therefore, becomes the locus and object not of enjoyment, but of *regret:* it is the inverted reflection of a lack, or of what Mallarmé calls a "defect," which is the nonexpressive, or nonmimetic character of the (French) language.

This regret, which is both the disavowal of primary Cratylism as a belief in language's motivation and the maintenance of a nostalgic preference with regard to that nonexistent or lost motivation—something like: "I would be delighted if language were mimetic, but I am forced to recognize that it is not"—is clearly and strongly expressed in a famous page from "Crise de vers," which was written at least ten years after *Les Mots anglais*:

> Imperfect languages in that they are several, the supreme one is missing.... But, at once, turned toward the aesthetic, my sense regrets that discourse fails to express objects by strokes that correspond to them in coloring or in aspect, these [strokes] exist in the instrument of the voice, in [various] languages and sometimes within one [alone]. Compared to *ombre* (shadow), [which is] opaque, *ténèbres* (darkness) seems only slightly dark; what disillusionment in the face of a perversity which confers contradictorily a dark timbre on *jour* (day) and a bright one on *nuit* (night). [p. 364]

I discontinue the quotation here in order to close the subject of primary Cratylism: discourse *fails* to coordinate the signifier and the signified, or as Mallarmé and then Valéry called them, the *sound* and the *meaning*. The word *ténèbres* is lighter than the word *ombre,* and the word *nuit* lighter than the word *jour.* The Cratylian coincidence exists "sometimes within one" language (English for example), but not in French. The "perfect" or "supreme" language does not exist, or if it exists, it is elsewhere; perhaps the "good language" is always that of our neighbors. The end of the quotation shows a most unexpected reversal, however, a switch to what I call secondary, poetic Cratylism: "—*Only,* let us know that *verse would not exist:* verse, philosophically, remunerates the defect (*défaut*) of languages [being] the superior complement" (p. 364).

The nonmimetic character of language is thus, in a certain way, the opportunity and the condition for poetry to exist. Poetry exists only to "remunerate," in other words, to repair and compensate for the "defect of languages." If a language were perfect, poetry would have no reason for being, since it would have nothing to repair. Language itself would be a poem and poetry would be everywhere, which obviously means that it would be nowhere. Mallarmé's conversation with Francis Viélé-Griffin in which he lends his interlocutor a thought already his own confirms this even more clearly: "If I follow you correctly, you base the creative privilege of the poet on the imperfection of the instrument that he must use; a language hypothetically adequate [*adéquate*] to translate his thought would suppress the literary man [*littérateur*], who would thereby become Mr. Everybody."[4]

Secondary Cratylism inaugurated here by Mallarmé is therefore no longer a Cratylism of language, but a Cratylism of the poem—or, as Mallarmé said, of *verse*—which finds support in an anti-Cratylism or Hermogenism of language. For the first time in such a clear way, the idea of a *double language*—or, to use Mallarmé's own term, a "double state of the word, raw and immediate on one hand and essential on the other" (p. 368)—is articulated here. The raw and immediate state is that of everyday language, the language of simple communication and conventional, or even commercial, exchange: "it would suffice, in order to exchange human thought, for each person to take, or to put in the hand of another, silently, a bit of change" (p. 368). The "essential" state is obviously that of poetic language:

> Verse which remakes from several vocables one total, new word, foreign to language and seemingly incantatory, completes this isolation of the word, denying, in one sovereign stroke, the element of chance remaining in the terms [the arbitrariness of the sign] despite the artifice of their alternate immersion [*retrempe*] in meaning and sonority, and provokes in one the surprise of hearing [for the first time] such an ordinary fragment of elocution, at the same time that the recollection of the object named basks in a new atmosphere. [p. 368]

In this way appears the familiar and almost obvious notion of *poetic language,* or the *poetic state of language,* which creates a decisive division in the linguistic substance. Henceforth there are two languages in language, one of which (everyday language) is left to arbitrariness and convention, while the other (poetic language) is the refuge of mimetic virtue, the locus of the miraculous survival of the primitive verb in all its "incantatory" power. I will not follow this theory further in Mallarmé, nor deal with the much more difficult question of determining to what extent it works in his poetry. It is now time to return to Valéry.

[4]Viélé-Griffin, "Stéphane Mallarmé, esquisse orale," *Mercure de France,* February 15, 1924, p. 30.

Valéry's thoughts on poetry were, of course, at first a prolongation of Mallarmé's, meditations on the *exemplum* offered by Valéry's one-time mentor. Valéry admired above all in Mallarmé what he called "the identification of 'poetic' meditation with the possession of language, and the careful study in himself [Mallarmé] of their reciprocal relations" (I, 655). Valéry says elsewhere, and the metaphor is revealing, "Mallarmé understood language as if he had invented it" (I, 658). One can say that Valéry's own poetics of language is articulated as a resumption and a new elaboration of Mallarmé's idea of double language.

To begin with, Valéry still shows some fast fading traces of primary Cratylism. In a letter of July 1891 to André Gide, one finds a "word reverie" as Bachelard calls it, or rather, a name reverie—the name of a country—somewhat comparable to those that Proust will give his hero some twenty years later in the last part of *Swann's Way*. Gide writes Valéry that he will travel to Antwerp, and this name inspires in the latter what almost amounts to a short prose poem:

> ANTWERP: A wild and black Baudelaire lies in that word. A word full of spices and pearls, unloaded, under a rainy sky, by a drunken sailor, at the door of a tavern.... The pink lantern draws the blacks to the sad streets where the *enchemisée* stomps in the mud. And songs of a distant tongue, aboard ships sunk in silence, continue in the background. As you see, I let myself stroll on these foreign words until I am near you....[5]

It may be characteristic that this reverie, a kind of derision or caricature of Cratylian reverie, permits one to see without much difficulty that everything which seems to be in a word comes from elsewhere—in this case, from what one already knew, or believed one knew, about the place which the word designates, but which one no longer dares quite say it *resembles*. An important comment on this subject appears in *Tel Quel* (II, p. 637): "The power of verse stems from an *indefinable* harmony between what it *says* and what it *is*. 'Indefinable' enters into the definition. This harmony must not be definable. When it is, it becomes

---

[5] *Correspondance, 1890–1942, André Gide–Paul Valéry* (Paris: Gallimard, 1955), p. 112.

imitative, and that is not good. The impossibility of defining this relationship, together with the impossibility of denying it, constitutes the essence of verse."[6]

It is not an exaggeration to say that Valéry's entire theory of poetic language is contained in this brief passage, as long as it is clarified by other passages. One can now see what I meant by fading traces of primary Cratylism in Valéry's writing: *imitative harmony* is rejected here, not as impossible, following Mallarmé, but as too simple. The author of the line "L'insecte net gratte la sécheresse" from "The Graveyard by the Sea," was in a position to know that imitative harmony is possible. He rejects it not because it is impossible, but because it is too *simple* and especially too univocal. The harmony between what verses *say* and what they *are*, between their signified and their signifier, "must not be definable."

One would be tempted to conclude, from this insistence on the indefinable and this rejection of the traditional resource of imitative harmony, that the harmony at which Valéry aims is *not* imitative, and that consequently his secondary Cratylism, abandoning the value of mimesis, is *no longer* a Cratylism. Such a conclusion would miss the inevitable sense of the word *harmony*, however. To say harmony is to say, necessarily, echo and consonance, affinity in co-presence. The idea of *harmony between sound and meaning* is a more subtle version of Cratylism, but still a version. We must now ask of what this version consists.

As I have said, Valéry takes up and prolongs Mallarmé's idea of the two states of language. The most straightforward formulation of this concept is found in the text entitled "Je disais quelquefois à Stéphane Mallarmé . . . ":

One must choose: either to confine language to the simple transitive function [which is everyday language] of a system of signals; or else to allow some [these are obviously poets] to speculate on its sensory properties by developing its *concrete* effects, its formal and musical combinations. [I, 650]

---

[6]Another version, or echo, is found in *Variété* (I, 685): "Poetry requires that one institute and maintain a certain indefinable harmony between what pleases the ear and what stimulates the mind."

Or perhaps, in this other formulation:

> A poet makes simultaneous use of everyday speech—which satis-
> fies only by being understood and which is therefore purely
> transitive—and of that language which contrasts with it, as a gar-
> den carefully planted with selected species contrasts with the wild
> countryside in which all species grow.... [I, 657]

This opposition figures elsewhere in the famous parallel of
walking and dancing, in which ordinary language is clearly designated by Prose, and the other, of course, by Poetry:

> Walking, like prose, aims at a precise object. It is an act directed
> toward something which we want to reach. Circumstances of the
> moment, such as the need of an object, the impulse of one's desire,
> the state of one's body, one's sight, and the terrain, etc., make
> walking what it *is,* prescribe its direction and its speed, and give it
> an *end.* All the characteristics of walking derive from these instan-
> taneous conditions, which combine *in a different way* each time.
> There are no movements in walking which are not special adapta-
> tions and which are not abolished each time and seemingly ab-
> sorbed by the completion of the act, by the reached goal.
>   Dance is something else altogether. It is doubtless a system of
> acts, but they have their end in themselves. It goes nowhere....
>   Here we rejoin prose and poetry in their contrast. Prose and
> poetry make use of the same words, the same syntax, the same
> forms, and the same sounds or timbres, but they are coordinated
> and stimulated in different ways.... Here is, however, the great
> and decisive difference. When the man who walks has reached his
> goal—as I have said—when he has reached the place, the book, the
> fruit, the object that formed his desire, this possession promptly
> annuls, definitively, his entire act; the effect devours the cause, the
> end has absorbed the means; and whatever the act may have been,
> only its result remains. It is exactly the same with "utilitarian"
> language: the language that just helped me to express my plan, my
> desire, my command, my opinion, this language which has fulfilled
> its duty, collapses and disappears upon arrival. I emitted it so that
> it might perish, so that it might become radically transformed into
> something else within your mind; and I will know that I was *under-
> stood* by the remarkable fact that my discourse no longer exists: it is
> entirely replaced by its *meaning*—that is, by images, impulses, reac-
> tions, or acts which belong to you: in short, by an interior modifica-
> tion of yourself....
>   The poem, on the contrary, does not die for having lived: it is

made expressly to be reborn from its ashes and to become again, indefinitely, that which it just was. Poetry is recognizable by the fact that it tends to reproduce itself within its form: it stimulates us to reconstitute it identically. . . .

As a result, between form and content, between sound and meaning, between the poem and the state of poetry, a symmetry is manifested, an equality of importance, value and power, that is not in prose; it is opposed to the law of prose—which decrees the inequality of language's two constituents. The essential principle of the poetic process—that is, of the conditions of production of the poetic state by the word [*parole*]—is, to my mind, this harmonic exchange between expression and impression. [I, 1330-1332]

As can be seen in this last sentence, the essentially intransitive, or *autotelic*, character of poetic discourse comes from a *harmony* between sound and meaning, which is the central idea of Cratylism. Utilitarian language, that kind which is at work when I ask you for a light and you answer by giving me one (in other words, by converting language into something), disappears upon being comprehended (I, 1324-1326). Poetic discourse, on the other hand, activates itself and is conserved in its form because this form is necessary. Furthermore, this form is necessary because it is in harmony with its own meaning: in a way, poetic discourse somewhat artificially recreates Cratylus' dream of a natural "fitness of signs."

Here, immediately, Valéry's poetic neo-Cratylism clashes with a difficulty that he knew well and always kept in mind: the arbitrariness of the sign, the "defect of languages." How can one create within conventional language a nonconventional state of language? How can one create within "arbitrary" language a harmonic state of language?

That [Valéry says lucidly] is to ask for *a miracle*. We realize that there is hardly an instance in which the connection between our ideas and the groups of sounds that suggest them each in turn is anything more than arbitrary or purely fortuitous. [I, 648]

Or again:

Each word is an instantaneous assemblage of a *sound* and a *meaning* that have no relationship to each other. [I, 1328]

And again:

> It follows from this analysis, that a poem's value resides in the
> indissolubility of sound and meaning. This condition seems to re-
> quire the impossible. There is no relationship whatsoever between
> the sound and the meaning of a word. The same thing is called
> HORSE in English, IPPOS in Greek, EQVVS in Latin, and
> CHEVAL in French; but no operation whatever on any of these
> terms will give me the idea of the animal in question; no operation
> whatever on this idea will give me any of these words—or else we
> would easily know all languages, beginning with our own. [I, 1333]

One must admit that Saussure's principle of the arbitrariness
of the sign has never been so forcefully contrasted to the secular
dream of a harmonic language. This is the strangest, indeed the
hardest part of the contradiction. And yet. . . .

And yet, we are exactly at the edge of what is, for Valéry, the
solution of the enigma. The following sentence seems to contain
the key word: "And yet it is the poet's task to give us the *sensation*
of intimate union between word [*parole*] and mind [*esprit*]" (I,
1333).

The key word is obviously "sensation," which one can safely
interpret, *in this context,* as signifier or, even more radically, as
illusion.[7] The indissolubility of sound and meaning, the harmony
between word and idea is, *language being what it is,* only an *illusory
sensation.* The poet's task is to create this illusion; this task is
magical, but magical in the most devalued, doubtless the most
critical meaning of the term. In performing this task, the magi-
cian is only an illusionist, even if he were to become the first
victim of his own illusion. The following lines from "Poésie et
pensée abstraite" suggest this idea quite well:

> One must consider that this is a totally marvelous result. I say
> *marvelous* although it is not excessively rare. I say *marvelous* in the
> sense that we give to this term when we think about the marvels
> and wonders of ancient magic. One must not forget that poetic
> form was for many centuries enlisted in the service of magic.
> Those who devoted themselves to these strange operations had to
> believe, of necessity, in the power of the spoken word, and even

---

[7]"A poem must create the *illusion* of an indissoluable composition of *sound* and
meaning" (I, 211).

more in the efficacy of this word's sound than in its signification. . . . The *momentary being* who made this verse could not have
made it if he had been in a state where form and content appeared
separately to his mind. On the contrary, he was in a special phase
of his domain of psychic existence, a phase during which the
word's sound and meaning take on or retain an equal
importance—something which is excluded from everyday language, as from the needs of abstract language. [I, 1333–1334]

The verse in which the mimetic necessity of the verbal sign is
realized, in a fleeting and therefore illusory way, is the work of a
momentary being, the poet in a *poetic state.* Once created, however,
the work aims at another, not momentary, being, in whom the
poetic state or Cratylian illusion will be maintained and reproduced each time that he enters and re-enters into contact with
the poetic word. This being is the reader, and of course it is he,
and not the poet, who is, for Valéry, the essential locus of the
poetic happening:

A poet's . . . function is not to feel the poetic state: that is a private
matter. One recognizes the poet—or at least, each person recognizes his own—by the simple fact that he turns the reader into an
"inspired being." Inspiration is, positively speaking, a gracious attribution which the reader makes to his poet: the reader offers us
the transcendent merits of the powers and graces that develop
within him. He searches for and finds in the poet the marvelous
cause of his amazement. [I, 1321]

The amazed reader, the reader in the poetic state is therefore
the reader to whom the "verse," in other words the fragment of
language before him, appears as necessary, definitive, forever
completed and unchangeable, sealed by the indissoluble harmony of sound and meaning. No one is more intimately per-
suaded than Valéry that this amazement is, in a sense, a fortunate illusion; for Valéry, a "completed sonnet" signified only an
"abandoned sonnet" (I, 1375), and the notion of a completed
work—in other words, the notion of the work itself—could have
proceeded only "from fatigue or superstition." Seen from
another angle, this same situation also implies that the poet
abandons the poem, which for him is never completed. The
reader then completes it, and in so doing, turns it into a work.

The completed work is the work (being) read; the Cratylian thaumaturge is the reader.

Such is, in general terms, Valéry's neo-Cratylism or poetics of language, which we have traced both in its development and in its conceptual specificity. Of course, the history of Cratylism does not stop with Valéry, and it might be interesting to follow up the simultaneous and subsequent echoes of the idea of poetic language. There is, for example, Claudel's opposition between ordinary language—which *designates* rather than *signifies* objects, giving us "a sort of practical and rough reduction of this language, its value, which is as banal as change (*monnaie*)"—and the language of the poet, who does not use words "for utilitarian ends, but to constitute from all these sonorous phantoms . . . a picture that is both intelligible and enjoyable."[8] There is also Proust's antithesis between *words* (common nouns), which "give us a clear and banal little picture of things like those hung on school walls" and *names* (proper nouns), which "give . . . a confused image of persons and towns which draws out from their brilliant or somber sonority, the color with which the image is uniformly painted."[9] In addition, there is Sartre's distinction between prosaic, conventional, and exterior *signification,* and poetic *meaning:* "*Signification* is conferred upon an object from the outside by a signifying intention, but [poetic] *meaning* is a natural quality of things."[10]

Finally, there is Jakobson's definition of *poetic function* as an autotelic message centered on itself, and his use, in the essay entitled "Linguistics and Poetics," of Valéry's formula: "the poem is a prolonged hesitation between sound and meaning."[11] (We might mention in passing that Jakobson also quotes another formula, this one by Pope, which is a perfect anticipation of Valéry's theory: "The sound must *seem* an echo of the sense."[12])

[8]*Oeuvres en prose* (Paris: Pléiade, 1965), pp. 47-48.
[9]*A la recherche du temps perdu* (Paris: Pléiade, 1954), I, 378.
[10]*Saint Genet* (Paris: Gallimard, 1952), p. 283.
[11]Roman Jakobson, *Eléments de linguistique générale* (Paris: Minuit, 1963), p. 233. This essay was originally published under the title "Closing Statements: Linguistics and Poetics" in *Style in Language,* ed. T. A. Sebeok (Cambridge, Mass.: M.I.T. Press, 1960).—Ed.
[12]*Eléments de linguistique générale,* p. 240.

All these resonances are sufficient proof that Valéry's (Mallarmé-Valéry's) version of Cratylism—the mimetic virtue of language as a real or illusory privilege of the poem or of poetic language—and therefore the poetic function as a compensation for and a defiance of the arbitrariness of the sign, have become our Vulgate, the implicit fundamental article of our literary aesthetic. It is so familiar, so natural, so transparent to us that, for all intents and purposes, we do not see it any more; we have some difficulty in conceiving that it has not always existed, and perhaps will not always exist. It is not self-evident, however, and in a certain way—which I wanted to show while developing my main thesis—this conception of the poetic function is a historical fact: it already belongs to history—which means, perhaps, to the past.

EUGENE VANCE

Roland and the Poetics of Memory

La différence, c'est ce qui fait que le mouvement de la signification n'est possible que si chaque élément dit "présent," appa-
raissant sur la scène de la présence, se rapporte à autre chose
que lui-même, gardant en lui la marque de l'élément passé et
se laissant déjà creuser par la marque de son rapport à l'élément
futur, la trace ne se rapportant pas moins à ce qu'on appelle
le futur qu'à ce qu'on appelle le passé, et constituant ce qu'on
appelle le présent par rapport même à ce qui n'est pas lui:
absolument pas lui, c'est-à-dire pas même un passé ou un futur
comme présents modifiés. Il faut qu'un intervalle le sépare de
ce qui n'est pas lui pour qu'il soit lui-même mais cet intervalle
qui le constitue en présent doit aussi du même coup diviser
le présent en lui-même, partageant, avec le présent tout ce
qu'on peut penser à partir de lui, c'est-à-dire tout étant,
dans notre langue métaphysique, singulièrement la substance
ou le sujet.

—Jacques Derrida

During a long period of its history, medieval culture granted
special importance to the faculty of memory, and my intention
in this essay is to describe as simply as possible what I believe to be
certain obvious features of this culture that I shall call *commemorative,* and then to show to what extent a commemorative model is
operative in the *Chanson de Roland,* at the level of both deep
narrative configurations and a system of values expressed at the
ethical surface of that poem. I shall also show how, especially in
the second half of the *Roland,* this model is violently disrupted,
and I shall suggest some of the cultural forces that may have
contributed to this disruption.

By "commemoration" I mean any gesture, ritualized or not,
whose end is to recover, in the name of a collectivity, some being
or event either anterior in time or outside of time in order to
fecundate, animate, or make meaningful a moment in the present. Commemoration is the conquest of whatever in society or

in the self is perceived as habitual, factual, static, mechanical, corporeal, inert, worldly, vacant, and so forth.

Even if no theories of memory had been written during the Middle Ages, the strictly pragmatic functions attributed to it in medieval culture would be very much in evidence. It is well known, for example, to what extent the ideal of the *imitatio Christi* impregnated every sphere of the medieval consciousness, and in broader terms one can hardly fail to glimpse the centrality of a commemorative model in the cult of ancestors, in the tradition of precedence in common law, in the ritual of pilgrimages, in the typology of monarchical theory, and in notions as diverse as those of archetype, universal, *exemplum,* authority, *figura,* and miracle, not to mention that of *historia* itself, as a representation of the past: in short, in any pattern of thought that ontologically privileges some moment or principle of origin.

It is easy to show that Christianity—especially that Platonizing strain of Christianity which dominated pre-Scholastic thought for more than seven centuries—is founded upon a commemorative *épistémè* of the purest sort, for its eucharist is centered upon the gestures of a Lord who gathered together with his apostles on the eve of his death to celebrate a final repast (itself a commemoration of the Jewish Passover feast), and who exhorted them thus: "This is my body, which is given for you; do this in remembrance of me"—*in meam commemorationem.*[1]

A commemorative culture will inevitably rationalize its ideologies in the perspective of a metaphysics of signs. If Reality or Truth is conceived of as being anterior to the present—or, more radically, as being anterior to existence itself—this original Truth that is always absent will signify or present itself partially to man in time and space by means of the words and things that constitute his palpable world—*visibilia,* to use a term of St. Paul. At best, these signs can reflect only poorly an ineffable Truth that transcends them; however, one day man will enjoy perfect knowledge, that is, a presence without mediation, without signs: *Videmus nunc per speculum in aenigmate; tunc autem facie ad faciem.*[2]

Like the doctrine of signs, the commemorative impulse is in-

---

[1] Luke 22:19.
[2] I Corinthians 13:12.

separable from a cult of the voice, or what one may call the *phonocentrism* that defines the creative force of the Logos as it was understood in the Middle Ages. According to St. Augustine, God "spoke" the universe through the matter of the abyss during the creation. The syntax of God's discourse is the history of the world.[3] Even though God gave of his substance in an act of material expression that was authentic yet susceptible to corruption, the original *cogito* did not allow itself to be contaminated along with the firmament that is its state-ment:

> It is as when we speak. In order that what we are thinking may reach the mind of the listener through the fleshly ears, that which we have in mind is expressed in words and is called speech. But our thought is not transformed into sounds; it remains entire in itself and assumes the form of words by means of which it may reach the ears without suffering any deterioration in itself. In the same way the Word of God was made flesh without change that He might dwell among us.[4]

In such a cosmogony, any notion of mimesis will ultimately involve regression, and it is the memory that bridges the hiatus between the empirical presence of signifiers and a transcendent signified at the origin of all. This incorporeal otherness can be partially remembered through the traces (*vestigia*) it has left in our souls. One has only to read Book 10 of Augustine's *Confessions,* his *De trinitate,* or his *De magistro* to grasp the radical interchangeability of metaphysics, sign theory, and memory theory in medieval thought.[5]   The importance of memory in the epistemic system of classical culture has been indicated by numerous studies during the last decade and more: the names of Finley, Havelock, Russo, Yates, Vernant, Détienne, and Peabody come immediately to mind.[6] Moreover, in classical antiquity, the commemorative process tends to be allied with operations of the

---

[3]Augustine, *Enarratio in Psalmum XCIX: Confessions,* 12.13.16 and 13.15.16–18.

[4]Augustine, *On Christian Doctrine,* 1.13.12, trans. D. W. Robertson (Indianapolis and New York: Bobbs-Merrill, 1958), p. 14.

[5]See *Confessions,* 1.13.20, and *On Christian Doctrine,* 1.4.4 (Robertson, p. 10). See also E. Vance, "Le Moi comme langage: Saint Augustin et l'autobiographie," *Poétique,* 14 (1973), 164–177; and "Augustine's *Confessions* and the Grammar of Selfhood," *Genre,* 6 (1973), 1–28.

[6]M. I. Finley, "Myth, Memory and History, History and Theory," *Studies in the Philosophy of History,* 4 (1965), 281–302; E. A. Havelock, *Preface to Plato* (Cambridge, Mass.: Harvard University Press, 1963); J. Russo and B. Simon,

organs of speech. We cannot be surprised, then, that in a pre-dominantly oral culture a privileged agent in the ritual of recall should be the speaking poet, in whose performance historical discourse is replenished and vivified with a new inspiration of truth. As Vernant has written:

> Mnemosyne presides, as is well known, over the poetic process. It was obvious for the Greeks that such a process demanded a super-natural intervention. Poetry is one of the typical forms of divine possession and rapture: it is the state of "enthusiasm," in the etymological sense of that word. Possessed by the Muses, the poet is the interpreter of Mnemosyne, just as the god-inspired prophet is the interpreter of Apollo.... The bard and the diviner have in common a single gift of "vision," a privilege that they have paid for with their eyes. Blind to light, they see the invisible. The god who inspires reveals to them those realities that escape the sight of ordinary men. It is a twin vision that bears in particular upon those parts of time inaccessible to mortals: what once was, what has yet to come... in contrast to the diviner who must usually answer for the future, the activity of the poet is oriented almost exclusively toward the past. Not his individual past, nor a past generalized as if it were an empty framework independent of the events that have occurred there, but "ancient times" with its own contents and qualities: a heroic age or, still further, a primordial age, the origin of time.[7]

The proposal that the apotheosis of memory was a determining force in medieval history will no doubt seem an exaggeration to some, yet the vastly suggestive study by Frances Yates has already allowed us to glimpse, however fleetingly, the scope of the problem.[8] The notion of memory, however—like the notion of time, to which it is related—is one of those numerous categories of our daily vocabulary that become massively complex with a moment of scrutiny.

"Homeric Psychology and Oral Epic Tradition," *Journal of the History of Ideas*, 29 (1968), 483–498; F. A. Yates, *The Art of Memory* (London: Routledge & Kegan Paul, 1966); J.-P. Vernant, *Mythe et pensée chez les grecs* (Paris: Maspéro, 1965); Marcel Détienne, *Les Maitres de vérité dans la Grèce archaique* (Paris: Maspéro, 1967); and Berkeley Peabody, *The Winged Word* (Albany: State University of New York Press, 1975). I would like to acknowledge a personal debt to Professors Russo, Vernant, and Détienne, who as colleagues have generously shared their knowledge with me in the past.

[7]Vernant, p. 53; all translations, unless otherwise indicated, are my own.
[8]See Yates, pp. 63–114.

Consider, for instance, the implications of the psychic model one invokes in order to deal with the basic functions of memory. Already in classical antiquity it was clearly understood that acts of recollection or of reminiscence involved a problematic of mediation: how, it was asked, does some absent object of memory relate to the object stimulating its recall in the present? Aristotle claimed that retrieval occurred by three types of mental association: similarity, contiguity, and opposition. Hence, the prelinguistic operations of memory are already essentially rhetorical.[9] Modern theories of memory have regarded such acts of substitution as a kind of primordial violence. Freud held that the passage of an image from the preverbal system of the unconscious into the conscious system of language (or vice versa) involves both radical substitutions and changes of valence: such is the transforming power of repression in our mental activity, hence the potentially pathological ambivalence of the remembering subject to the substance of his own recollections. To recognize that such transformations might indeed occur even in our most familiar rituals of commemoration is to recognize that our daily cultural life is constituted as a balance of the dialectical forces of repression and recollection. In Freud's explanation of Christ's sacrifice, the medieval notion of *imitatio Christi* involves a struggle simultaneously to remember and to repress, a struggle rooted in primal yet unresolved acts of violence:

> If the Son of God was obliged to sacrifice his life to redeem mankind from original sin, then by the law of the talion, the requital of like for like, that sin must have been a killing, a murder. Nothing else could call for the sacrifice of life in expiation. And if the original sin was an offense against God the Father, the primal crime of mankind must have been a parricide, the killing of the primal father of the primitive horde, whose image in memory was later transfigured into a deity.[10]

One need not accept the topical content of the categories that Freud brings to the theater of the mind; however, the complexity that he attributes to their operations of memory is plau-

[9] Aristotle, *De memoria,* 451b18.
[10] Freud, "Thoughts for the Times on War and Death," *The Standard Edition of the Complete Psychological Works of Sigmund Freud,* trans. and ed. James Strachey (London: Hogarth, 1957), XIV, 292–293.

sible enough to suggest that a definition of memory, or a fortiori, a history of its functions, is impossible. If one will grant, however, as Freud himself willingly did, that what we call poetic discourse is a notation that, alongside those of philosophy and psychology, has its own special ways of apprehending a problematic of memory, one will not lack interesting material, especially in the Middle Ages.[11]

With these priorities in mind, I should like to consider certain narrative patterns observable in the *Chanson de Roland,* especially with regard to the mode—rather, the modes—of performance that brought this poem into existence. For if there is any truth in the notion that the basic function of any act of communication is to make experience intelligible, we must be willing to consider that among the things that must be made intelligible is the model that subtends communication itself. In other words, I am suggesting that what we call myth and legend (poetic or not) always tend to be structured no less by their mode of dissemination in culture than by the "events" in the past that such myths are purported to convey, no matter how much these events are accepted as being truly historical. Thus, if memory is the principal means of preserving sacred history, history must serve, reciprocally, to sacralize the faculty of memory. The special interest of the *Chanson de Roland* is that ever since the Romantic age, the *Roland* has always been considered one of the most "historical" of all poems. This reverence notwithstanding, it is not difficult to show that at every level the drama of the *Chanson de Roland* is not only a product but also a drama, and even a tragedy, of memory.

Like so many other poems of the Middle Ages, the *Chanson de Roland* bears all the marks of a long oral prehistory, during which time the primary creative—or rather, conservative—process was that of an oral performance that was also a feat of memory. (I shall explore later the serious consequences of a glaring and important paradox, which is that the *Roland* is accessible to us only as a written text, and that a system of writing has already intervened in the process of transmission.)

To claim that the *Chanson de Roland* is a *drama* of memory is

---

[11]Freud, "The Uncanny," *Standard Edition,* XVII, 219-252.

also to presume that if such a drama originates in a specific legendary corpus, its substance must be compatible enough with modes of oral poetic production to be both conservable and renewable through the ages. We know nothing definite about what we commonly call the historical origins of the poem, but we may be fairly certain that the *Roland* as we possess it is a coagulation of disparate narrative materials that once perpetuated themselves in oral performances during which the poet and his heroes would be simultaneously reborn together, thanks to the memory and voice of the poet. Thus the heroes of the *Roland,* like those of the *Iliad* and the *Odyssey,* speak in the same metrical formulas as the poet; they employ the same epithets, the same lists, and they even share the same foreknowledge of events. The fact that these heroes live only by the memory and the voice of the poet ensures, in other words, a strong cognitive identification between them, and this is evident in the motivation imputed by the poet to the heroes themselves. For if it is the antique glory of the hero that animates the voice of the poet, inversely, it is the commemorative posterity of the singer that inspires the epic blows of the hero. Roland, in short, constitutes himself as the true "author" of his songs, and he is aware that his immortality is to be consummated in the living poetic word:

> "Now let each man take care to deal great blows,
> Lest a bad song be sung of us! . . .
> A bad example shall never be made of me."
>
> [1013–1016][12]

It is not surprising that in such a monologism (Bakhtin) no noun denoting the distinct figure of the poet is available: the twelfth-century poet is known not as an entity, but only through his action, which is that of singing (*chanter*).[13] Moreover, in such action his identity as a poet is not expressed so much as it is possessed by the legendary *gestes* of his heroes. One can imagine, moreover, that the fame of epic singers, like that of certain film

[12]*La Chanson de Roland,* ed. and trans. G. Moignet (Paris: Bordas, 1969). All subsequent references are to this edition; English translations are mine.
[13]I am grateful to Paul Zumthor for sharing this insight with me.

and television actors today, is derived more from their interpretations of certain roles than from their "real" personalities.

The "song," as Roland himself says, is an "example" (*essample*) that revitalizes a moment in time and space—the instance of performance—with a therapeutic truth, a meaning, a *signifié* that re-presents itself each time anew through the phonic substance of speech. Such is the role, Jean Bodel says clearly in the opening lines of another epic, the *Chanson des Saisnes,* of the *matière* of Charlemagne: it must be *voir chacun jour apparent.* Truth is in uttering, not in the utterance. The truth that manifests itself anew "each day" in the oral performance, however, is not something that one grasps objectively, or even, for that matter, subjectively: on the contrary, the commemoration of "truth" abrogates altogether the matrix of self and other. It provokes instead a movement of undifferentiation where the commemorating self is given over to a field of forces that is infinitely (hence fatally) regressive. Its sweep includes the identity of the listener as well, tacitly engaged by the poetic word only to find himself no less dissolved in it. The psychology of the poetic performance is not determined by events of history, but rather by circumstances of language, and the Greeks were eager to analyze it with some precision. As Socrates says to a rhapsode, a man who performs the Homeric poems:

> This gift you have of speaking well on Homer is not an art; it is a power divine, impelling you like the power in the stone . . . which most call "stone of Heraclea." This stone does not simply attract the iron rings, just by themselves: it also imparts to the rings a force enabling them to do the same thing as the stone itself, that is, to attract another ring, so that sometimes a chain is formed, quite a long one, of iron rings, suspended from one another. For all of them, however, their power depends on that lodestone. Just so the Muse. She first makes men inspired, and then through these inspired ones others share in the enthusiasm, and a chain is formed . . . a poet is a light and winged thing, and holy, and never able to compose until he has become inspired, and is beside himself, and reason is no longer in him. So long as he has this reason in his possession, no man is able to make poetry or to chant in prophecy . . . Herein lies the reason why the deity has bereft them [poets] of their senses . . . in order that we listeners may know that it is not they who utter these precious revelations while their mind is not

within them, but that it is the god himself who speaks, and through them becomes articulate to us.[14]

In the oral performance, then, poet, hero, and audience re-create each other in a common, discursive space; yet their presence to each other is consummated only in a regressive series of "magnetic" alignments, through speech, with some originary presence. As in the *Iliad,* this movement is reinforced by the genealogical consciousness of its audience, if we may believe modern scholars who say that the twelve peers and the Christian warriors in the chronicle of the Baligant episode could be identified as distant ancestors by twelfth-century listeners. We have relatively few documents from the Middle Ages which capture the *épistémè* of oral epic discourse, yet the following statement by Jean de Grouchy insists precisely upon the regenerative effect of oral narrative on a crowd of laborers and humble people who have been beaten down by their daily tasks and routines, yet who are revived in a collective regression into the heroic past:

> We call a *chanson de geste* that in which the deeds of heroes and of our ancient fathers are recited, such as the lives and martyrdoms of saints and the adversities that beset men of old for the Faith and for Truth. . . . Moreover, this song must be ministered to the old people, to the laboring folk and to those of humble condition, so that by hearing miseries and calamities of others they may bear more easily their own and so that their own travails may become lighter. And thus this song brings about the conservation [*conservatio*] of the whole community.[15]

Commemoration, however, involves not just an act of retrieval by the mind of the poet but simultaneously the perception of what lies before him in the present as being deficient, as a vice, a lack that the memory will fill; the present may even be seen as an *obstacle* to the possession of some reality or meaning belonging to the past. Such a dialectic is already implicit, as I have said, in the

---

[14]Plato, *Ion,* 533d–534d, trans. L. Cooper (1938), reprinted in *The Collected Dialogues of Plato,* ed. E. Hamilton and H. Cairns (New York: Pantheon, 1961), pp. 219–220.
[15] J. de Grouchy, *De musica,* in "Die Musiklehre des Johannes de Grocheo," ed. J. Wolf, *Sammelbände der internationalen Musikgesellschaft* (1899), I. 90.

duality of the sign as a material *signans* of an immaterial *signatum*. In pragmatic terms, however, such a dialectic could be welcomed and intensified by poets and orators who had mastered the art of memory. For, as Frances Yates has shown, it was customary for orators from classical antiquity to the Renaissance to practice what was called *compositio loci*, that is, to memorize a speech either by linking, however arbitrarily, the elements to be retrieved during performance with physical objects in the orator's immediate presence, or by *imagining* some spatial scene whose details (*imagines*), often made vivid through effects of violence and the grotesque, would swiftly summon up the memory of those elements to be recalled.[16] Thus violence may be understood as being not only the "subject" of oral epic narrative but also as an *aide-mémoire* or as a "generative" force in the production of its discourse. By extension, it is interesting to ask if the semiological prominence given to violence in classical and post-classical culture—the sacrifices, the circumcisions, the tortures, the beheadings, the crucifixions, the quarterings, the burnings—was not primarily mnemonic in function. If the *Odyssey* ends in joyous recollections that reconcile husband to wife and fathers to sons, it also ends with a violent exemplary massacre from which only a bard and a herald are spared, for it is they who will *remember* and *speak*. In a commemorative culture, then, history "stages" itself around events of violence by which the collective judicial memory reinforces itself—*as narrative*.

However one wishes to describe it, the dialectic of presence and absence that arises in the very circumstances of oral performance tends, as we shall now see, to double itself within the *Roland* as basic configurations of narrative that command the relationships of characters both to each other and to the physical world in which they move. Indeed, such a configuration informs the *Chanson de Roland* from the start: the Franks have fought in Spain for seven years, an expanse of time easily understood, in the Middle Ages, as a metaphor—rather, as a synecdoche—for all the travails of earthly existence. Despite the victories of the moment, the Franks are now weary of the war and nostalgic

[16]See Yates, chap. 1.

for "sweet France," the terrestrial seat of God's presence among men (Charlemagne, one will recall, figured as a *vicarius Christi* in medieval iconography). The pagans, who have been his adversaries, imagine how tired Charlemagne must be. As Marsile, their king, puts it:

> "I greatly marvel
> at Charlemagne, who is white-haired and old.
> I would say he's two hundred years old or more.
> Many are the lands where he has wearied his body
> And taken so many blows of lance and spear . . .
> Never will he give up fighting."
>
> [537-543]

The geographical opposition between Spain and France provides to the heroes within the poem and above all to its audience an epistemological framework in which a dialectic between presence and absence is historically significant in both ideological and affective terms. Blancandrin, a Saracen who is Marsile's ambassador to the council of the Franks, concludes the treasonous proposals of the Saracens by eliciting nostalgia in the Franks:

> "You have been in this country long enough.
> You must now return to Aix, in France.
> There my master says that he will follow you."
>
> [134-136]

The topographical location of Roncevaux only makes these feelings more dramatic. Situated in the mountains between Spain and France, Roncevaux serves as a threshold of intense recollections for the war-weary Franks, who now contemplate their tranquil homeland: a place of abundance, security, and appeased desires. The tantalizing proximity of France is all the more poignant in that an imminent and foreknown tragedy separates the Franks from it:

> When they came to the Tere Majur
> They saw Gascoigne, the land of their lords.
> Then they remembered their fiefs and their possessions,
> And their maidens, and their noble wives;
> There's not a one who does not weep for pity.
>
> [818-822]

The passage through Roncevaux stirs up a particularly violent anguish in Charlemagne, who is already grieving for a Roland destined never to return. The future already belongs, as it were, to the past, and such foreknowledge is a condition of that fatalistic cognitive homology of hero, poet, and audience, bound to each other in a single commemorative language. Never does it occur to Charlemagne that he might act to reverse the course of events.

> Above all others, Charles is anguished:
> At the gates of Spain he has left his nephew.
> Pity seizes him, he cannot hold back from weeping.
>
> [823–825]

Moreover, Charlemagne is fated to lose in Roland his "right hand," a privileged agent of his own potency. The experience of Charlemagne is an instance of what seems to be a general tendency of the process of commemoration to be closely associated with—if not to demand—some act of mutilation or immolation. Did not time itself begin with the castration of Kronos—and once again with a crucifixion? Though some in our time might see such acts as manifestations of a castration complex disguised as instances of what Freud calls "organ speech," I suggest that such violence, especially when it occurs in medieval narrative, is a manifestation less of some trauma in the authorial unconscious than of the conflicting nature of words (or things) as signs. For, as medieval thinkers knew so well, any signifier is a corporeal *trace* that must at once subsist and yet efface itself in order to convey a signified that is absent and different from it: that difference may be called "time."

As an epic hero, Roland no doubt appealed to medieval audiences on more than one political or ideological score, but it is easy to show that Roland is also a hero of memory. The force of his memorial "logic" is evident from the very moment he appears in the poem. Blancandrin, one will recall, has just delivered Marsile's treacherous proposals to Charlemagne, who submits the question, as a good feudal lord must, to the counsel of his barons. Roland is the first to speak out; and he initiates his speech not with a rational opinion but with an aggressive outcry and a formulaic recital of his previous conquests. Roland's aggressions in the past, in other words, entirely determine the weight of his argument in the present. Then Roland reinforces his opinion with the *exempla*, likewise remembered from the past, of Basan and Basile, two Christian knights who had been sent as emissaries to the Saracens—at the price of their heads. Thus, counsels Roland, "Pursue the war as you began it." Whether Roland is motivated by an excess of zeal or by outright pride, we the audience know by our privileged perspective that Roland, the champion of the *idée reçue,* is right.

Ganelon's memory, however, is less acute. Eloquent, a good rhetorician, this future traitor persuades the Frankish barons that the present appearance of things suffices as proof that it would be a "sin," as he says, to continue the war. Seduced by Ganelon's speech, the Duke of Naimes, who is ordinarily a paragon of good sense among the Franks, corroborates Ganelon's counsel. "Ben ad parlet li dux," cry the barons; but the irony of this judgment is obvious; the rhetoric of appeasement is subversive not only in ethical terms but in artistic terms as well. Without war, there could be no hero, no history, no song, no *jongleur,* and no audience.[17]

Once Roland and the twelve peers have been named to command the rear guard, a new dilemma arises: faced with the vast numbers of the pagan forces, should the Franks summon the aid of Charles? Perhaps because Oliver seems to have entered the Roland legend late in time and is, accordingly, somehow detached from the heroic (and commemorative) ethic that commands its principal figure, he accepts the empirical evidence of the pagan masses as justification for sounding the alarm. It would seem that Oliver is a champion not primarily of memory but of knowledge that derives from what is present, knowledge that has objective truth and can be treated rationally and even communicated. Even so, Oliver is not to be dismissed as a relativist, as his future conduct in the poem will clearly show. For Roland, by contrast, knowledge is always a priori, and language is never an

[17]Apart from his courage, Ganelon represents an interesting coincidence of ethical principles, both good and bad: he is courageous but also a rhetorician; he is also a liar, a traitor, and a negotiator of peace and monetary exchange. As a creature of evil, Ganelon, like his coconspirators, always turns the signifier against its proper signified.

instrument of true dialogue or exchange but rather of invocation or commemoration or of aggression, and it expresses his bond to a truth that is always both universal and anterior to the present and immutable. We are faced here with an epistemological difference that is finally smothered by events in the *Roland*, yet one that will have great ramifications in the intellectual environment of the century to follow.[18] Roland invokes against Oliver's empiricism the formulaic obligation to respect at any cost the earlier orders of his lord, Charlemagne. Not only does Roland live by the oath of fidelity between vassal and lord (his contractual link to the past); he also evokes, as I mentioned earlier, the importance of his present performance on the battlefield as an *exemplum* for audiences of the future—thanks to the good offices of the *jongleurs*.

But Roland, as we know, is not beyond reproach. And if his idealism is founded upon a rectitude of memory, his pride, like Ganelon's, consists of a willful forgetting; Roland will simply not tolerate Oliver's recalling the earlier threats and the prominent gesture—the dropped glove—that had portended Ganelon's treason:

> "Quiet, Oliver!" Count Roland replies.
> "He is my stepfather: I want no further word about him."
> [1026–1027]

The battle now begins, and at several points the poet makes it clear that a victory on the battlefield is also a victory of memory over oblivion. Moreover, no less for the soldier than for the poet, a triumph of memory culminates in an outcry of the human voice. As the poet says of Oliver,

> Whoever could see him dismember the Saracens
> And throw one dead man upon another
> Could remember a good vassal.
> He does not want to forget Charles' ensign:
> He cries "Munjoy" loud and clear.
> [1970–1974]

[18]For an interesting study of this epistemological change, see Brian Stock, *Myth and Science in the Twelfth Century* (Princeton: Princeton University Press, 1972).

Even the characters themselves give tongue to the commemorative impulse that motivates any true hero, demonstrating, once again, virtues that are perhaps only arbitrarily related
to superlative martial conduct but which are *necessarily* related to
the continuation of oral epic. Oliver's exhortations to fight and
remember are echoed by the praise of the poet:

> "Lords, Barons, hold your ground!
> In God's name I pray you, be careful
> To strike good blows, to take and to give them!
> We must not forget Charlemagne's ensign."
> Upon this word the French cried out.
> Whoever could hear them cry "Munjoy,"
> Such a man would remember the deeds of a good vassal.
> [1176-1182]

The nearer Roland approaches the moment of his death, the
more the action of the poem tends toward that of pure commemoration. Almost surreptitiously a strange substitution of
priorities takes place as a heroics of memory displaces a heroics
of the sword. In other words, the commemorative performance
must ultimately rise to the dramatic surface of its own narrative
vehicle. We may observe here the manifestation of a desire that
outweighs all others in an oral culture, the need to commemorate. In short, during the final moments of Roland's life we
witness a kind of reversal in the process of mimesis: if the oral
poet first imitates the voice and gestures of his heroes, in the end
it is the hero who imitates the poet.

Once all of the twelve peers but Roland have been killed, he
interrupts his heroic struggles and begins to gather up the dead
bodies of his companions in order to have them blessed by Arch-
bishop Turpin and to commemorate their heroism with his
own voice. *Planctus* and prayer, poet and priest, answer to the
single burden of past and future. The spectacle of the bodies
arranged before him, like a dead audience, provokes from Roland a *planctus* and a series of mimetic gestures that are also
those of the poet: indeed, the hero at this point is merely imitating the poet, though with this difference, slight in the eyes of a
good Christian: the audience within the poem is dead and will
not revive, except, one hopes, in heaven.

Roland's final moments provide insight into what we might call the psychology of commemoration, at least to the degree that an isolated hero appears to be addressing only himself. But it is hardly an individualized psychology, because Roland's formulas of conquests belong to a repertory of deeds that are not his alone, and his voice becomes more and more that of history itself speaking to us. After his attempt to break his sword, Durendal, on a stone, Roland discovers in its imperishability a reminder of the numerous conquests that he himself has made in the past as Charlemagne's vassal. The intrinsic virtue of Roland's sword, which has now become his silent interlocutor, encourages, moreover, a sequence of psychic reflexes that are regressive, both chronologically and in an ontological sense. The sword Durendal, we are told, had been given to Charlemagne by God (through the mediation of an obedient angel) with the instructions that Charlemagne should in turn bestow it on one of his best captains. Thus Roland's sword shines with the light of good works that originate, ultimately, with the Father in heaven. Furthermore, the list of conquests that Roland recalls undoubtedly corresponds to the boundaries of Charlemagne's empire as they would have been imagined by an epic poet at the beginning of the twelfth century. Each name in Roland's list of conquests must have coincided with a whole epic cycle, and in its entirety, this list is a capsule expressing the totality of a history that for the eleventh and twelfth centuries was sacred. Though Roland would hardly pass for an intellectual giant in ages to come, at the time he had only to recite the list of his conquests to show that he knew (and had performed) "everything."

If it is true that in a commemorative culture the power to recall is a conquest, then Roland's reminiscences—and the violence that instigates them—mark a victory not only over the world but also over himself. Likewise, with regard to the poetic performance, if the poet succeeds, through memory, in making his voice resonate with a certain heroic timbre that is also his own, we may state that the reminiscences of the victorious Roland are consubstantial with a victory of poetic discourse over obstacles in the mind of the temporal speaker: by the blows of one and the phonemes of the other a culture endures.

To the degree that Roland's personal glory opens, through

speech, into a less and less differentiated field of forces that includes first the presence of a Charlemagne absent and last the Great Magnet hidden behind everything, Roland's commemorations are infinitely regressive. But such regression cannot occur without a certain destruction of the self: the more the self languishes for communion with the infinite, the more it must confront the corruption of its own finitude. If the self is to liberate its own spirit, then the body (whose ontological status is equal to that of a mere signifier) must give way. The self, in other words, must come home from its exile among those multiple and disparate traces that constitute the palpable world yet point beyond themselves to an original, redeeming presence whose eternal, uncreated, indivisible substance is different—absolutely different—from them. Such is the dilemma facing the Christian hero who carries the logic of commemoration to its limits—that is, to the limits of his mortality.

But this is a dilemma for which the Christian religion has remedies, and those remedies also stem from the faculty of memory. Thus, having commemorated the glory of Charlemagne and finally that of God, Roland engages in another type of reminiscence (whose discourse is no less formulaic), in which he becomes momentarily present to himself. The transition (which I have italicized) is clearly signaled in the text:

> He began to remember many different things,
> So many lands that he conquered as a good baron.
> And sweet France, and the men of his clan,
> And Charlemagne, his lord, who nourished him;
> He could not restrain himself from weeping and sighing for them
> *But he does not want to forget himself.*
> He confesses his sins and prays to God for mercy.
>
> [2377-2383]

By means of his memory, Roland now confesses and succeeds in purging himself of the evil that has held him captive of the world: here, the ritual of commemoration gives rise to an act not of recovery but of expulsion. The self willingly discovers within its own substance a *pharmakos* whose expulsion cures the difference between body and spirit, or, more generally (but not more abstractly), between signifier and signified, in a universe of speech. Purifying himself, then, of evil through a labor of memory, Roland recalls the beneficial *exempla* of Lazarus and Daniel, of two mortals in the past who were revived by their faith in God. Thanks again to his memory, Roland is now prepared to quit the vassalage of Charlemagne, his spiritual father and his terrestrial lord, in order to rejoice in an unmediated relationship, *facie ad faciem*, with God the True Father (*Veire Patene*), "who never lies." The first half of the *Chanson de Roland* is nothing other than an exalted Christian "comedy" of memory—and of signs.

Roland dies in the middle of the poem, however, and it is Charlemagne who inherits the bitter consequences of Roland's heroic splendor and brings to them sharp tragic relief. The *Chanson de Roland* is populated by characters who are perhaps static, yet *our* perspective is not so: on the contrary, with the change from a young hero to an old—Charlemagne is a Roland grown old—many of the values and triumphs that seemed so absolute in the first half are thrown radically into question.[19] If it is true that the legend of Roland himself is the most archaic "nucleus" of the epic and that with succeeding eras other characters and episodes (Oliver, Baligant) were added in order to restore symmetries and to revive interest, then we may consider the *Roland* as a poem in which problems of history are not represented *by* language, but rather inscribed *into* language in all of its materiality. Similarly, it seems obvious to me that displacement of Roland by Charlemagne as the central protagonist of this epic also carries with it a disruption of the fundamental epistemic models immanent in the Roland legend, and it is with this shift in mind that I shall now focus on the story of Charlemagne.

From his initial appearance in the *Roland,* Charlemagne is strangely remote from the events that develop around him. Even though Christians and Saracens agree that Charles is the most powerful man in the world, Charlemagne broods in painful silence over the fatal cleavage in his heroic world. Charlemagne's detachment from that world is expressed most obviously in his two centuries of age, a distance from the glory of

[19]In the discussion that follows, I draw freely on points made previously in my book *Reading the Song of Roland* (Englewood Cliffs, N.J.: Prentice-Hall, 1970).

youth which no doubt coincided with a twelfth-century audience's sense of its own remoteness from a "heroic" age—the age
when oral epic discourse was constituting itself, two or more
centuries before. Charlemagne is also strangely undetermined—
indecisive, even—with regard to Ganelon's dispute with Roland,
even though he knows that Ganelon is a "living devil" and that
the division of his army into vanguard and rear guard will result
in the destruction of its best heroes. Charlemagne is also uncertain about the sinister prognostications in his dreams: *videmus
nunc per speculum in aenigmate.* Charlemagne seems especially
remote from the discursive arena around him, in which younger
heroes are so quick to argue, threaten, and boast:

> He bows his head and begins to ponder.
> The emperor holds down his head.
> In his words he was never hasty;
> His custom is to speak with deliberation [*a leisir*].
>
> [138–141]

Charlemagne's silence inspires mostly awe in the first half of
the poem, yet this same detachment from the motivations of the
heroic world will ultimately give rise to a perspective so tragic as
to call into question the adequacy of epic language, if not of all
language itself. By contrast, Roland is a warrior whose motives
and gestures remain profoundly compatible with the ethical values that underlie the traditional formulaic language of his poem,
and both the hero and the poet of the first half of the *Roland*
seem to feel that "meaning" is not something that we need to
discover, but rather something that we assume and perform as
our own: we declare it, we give it off; this is the original but
long-forgotten sense of the word *hermeneuein,* so badly served by
its translation as *interpretatio.*[20] In Roland's actions, then, both
the language and the values of a commemorative culture find
adequate realization, and Roland has every assurance that he

---

[20]Jean Pépin, "L'Herméneutique ancienne," *Poétique,* 23 (1975), 291–300. It is
interesting to note that in v. 2454 of the *Roland,* an angel promises Charlemagne *clartet,* by which he will achieve vengeance. This use of the word *clartet*
shows the semantic overlapping of the notions of "light," "force," and "understanding" (as illumination). Darkness, by contrast, seems to be associated with
impotence and confusion.

will live again, after his death, in the performance of poetic song. The more violent and bloody are his deeds, the more easily they may be remembered and uttered: his victory over the pagans will also be a victory of memory over oblivion. Inversely, he who is most brilliant in battle is also, in the end, he who is the most commemorative: the *planctus* that generally follows episodes of violence is nothing other than a formulaic type of verbal action which doubles, within the universe of the poem, the commemorative function attributed to the poem by the community of audience and poet attempting to recover, through song, their own heroic origins: oral epic usually tends toward the elegiac, and the elegiac presupposes the epic.

As he becomes the protagonist, Charlemagne initiates profound disruptions in the coherence of the epic imagination. Not only is Charlemagne unable to grasp, except dimly, the prophecies of the future revealed to him in his dreams (much less to alter that future by *producing* alternative "interpretations" by his actions); he is equally incapable of reuniting himself with Roland—his nephew, his "son" and link with his own heroic past—and of triumphing in the future: "Against me will rebel the Saxons,/the Hungarians, the Bulgarians" (2921-2922). During the entire second half of the poem, the memory of an absent Roland eclipses (even literally, at one point) all apprehension of the present. Not even the vengeance of Charlemagne on the Saracens ("an eye for an eye" is an especially futile type of "commemoration" because it is also a new beginning)[21] can recover a splendor of young blood irrecoverably lost: at best, the joy of new victories can be only a forgetting of the pain of Roland's loss, rather than a remembrance. Revenge no longer works; hence for Charlemagne there can be no triumph in revenge. To the degree that the heroes of this poem are emanations of a poet's voice, apart from which they have no separate existence, it should not surprise us that, along with its new hero, the very language of the *Chanson de Roland* should inscribe into itself—into its very formulas—a kind of subtle nostalgia, during which a present moment *in* speech is experienced as a falling

[21] "Venge your sons, your brothers and your heirs
Who died the other evening at Roncevaux!" [3411-3412]

off, as a decomposition of a more splendid heroic discourse that was once possible in the universe of the poem. Such is the case, I propose, in the narration of Charlemagne's exhaustion in his grief for Roland; for, if we look closely at the passages evoking the emperor's grief, we see that they are comprised of a sequence of formulas—or of antiformulas—which systematically reverse the content of those earlier formulaic passages where heroes joyfully took up arms in brilliant sunlight in preparation for the fatal glee of combat. Consider, first, this passage, in which the pagan and Frankish forces poise themselves for the attack:

> The pagans arm themselves with Saracen hauberks,
> Most of which have three layers of chain.
> They lace their helmets, the best of Saragossa.
> They gird up their swords of Viennese steel.
> They bear nobel shields, and spears from Valence,
> And flags that are white, blue, and crimson.
> They leave their mules and palfreys;
> They mount their steeds and ride in closed ranks.
> Clear was the day and beautiful the sun.
> There was no armor that did not flame in the light.
> A thousand trumpets sound, to make it more beautiful.
> The noise is great, and the Franks hear it.
> Oliver says, "My comrade, I believe
> That we shall do battle with the Saracens."
> Roland answers, "Ah, may God grant it to us!"
>
> [994–1008]

Consider next how, along with the now exhausted hero Charlemagne, heroic language itself is generated as antiformulas that acquire special poignancy because of their counterpoint with a more glorious heroic discourse, now part of an irretrievable narrative past. A world of warriors once teeming with potency, movement, and exuberance, buoyant with sunlight, color, and fine weapons, has given way to a wasteland (*terre déserte*) of darkness and the dim pallor of moonlight; here men and horses are too fatigued even to stand up under the weight of armor or saddle, much less to rejoice in their recent revenge. This dark night of the heroic soul threatens to become a dark night of poetic language. Even the name "Joyous" given to Charlemagne's sword is invested with a torturesome paradox of a joy born in suffering and death, since Charlemagne's imperial sword contains the tip of the very spear that killed Christ, the man-god nailed to a cross:

> The French dismount on the barren land.
> They have taken the saddles from their horses.
> They remove from their heads the reins of gold.
> They put them afield, where there is much fresh grass.
> They can give them no further care.
> Whoever is that tired sleeps on the ground.
> On that night they do not set up guard.
>
> The emperor has lain down in a field.
> His great spear is by the baron's head.
> That night he does not wish to disarm himself.
> He wears his great saffron-colored hauberk,
> His helmet laced, which is of gemmed gold.
> His sword Joyous is girded at his side,
> A sword without peer, which gleams thirty times a day.
> We know all about the lance
> With which our Lord was killed on the cross.
> Charles has the point, thanks be to God,
> And has had it encased in the golden handle.
> Because of that honor and its great goodness
> The name Joyous is given to the sword.
> The Frankish barons must never forget it.
> And for that they cry out "Munjoy"
> So that nothing can resist them.
>
> Clear is the night and the moon is shining.
> Charles lies down, but he grieves for Roland,
> And for Oliver he is greatly weighed down
> And for the twelve peers and the Frankish people.
> He left them bloodied in death at Ronceval.
> He cannot hold back from weeping and lamenting.
> And he prays that God protect their souls.
> The king is tired, for his pain is very great.
> He falls asleep, for he can endure no more.
> Now the French are sleeping all about the fields.
> Not a horse can stand.
> If he wants grass, he grazes lying down.
> He who has suffered much has learned much.

[2489-2524]

In short, a tragic flourish of counterpoint between joy and grief operates in this passage, not just thematically, but also at the more material level of poetic language as a medium. Though it is true that other formulaic descriptions of the heroic taking up of arms occur in the second half of the *Roland,* their promise is never fulfilled by unequivocally glorious deeds. Epic language is becoming differentiated and alienated from itself—or, to use the terms of Bakhtin, is passing from the *monologic* (which is the precondition of "truth" in language) to the *dialogic,* where "truth" is at best equivocal and relative. This dissipation is the inscription of a hero's death into the poetic Word.

The amazing and poignant gestures of Charlemagne that follow in the *Roland* dramatize, among other things, a very real anxiety of the medieval world before the dilemma of signs: the spirit, it would seem, does *not* always vivify. Unable for the moment to regenerate either the world or the word by a brassy new sequence of heroic deeds of his own, Charlemagne withdraws and devotes himself to the task of commemorating as meticulously as possible the final gestures of his nephew. No longer a theater of blind, unreflective action, the "present" world reduces itself to the status of a mere *trace,* a text inscribed with the past glory of Roland; thus, as Charlemagne walks reverently about the spot where Roland died, he becomes less an epic soldier than an epic *déchiffreur* who interprets Roland's sublime hieroglyphs of blood on grass, his calligraphy of sword blows incised in stone:

> When the emperor goes seeking his nephew
> He finds the flowers of so many plants in the field
> That are crimson with the blood of our barons!
> Pity takes him; he cannot hold back from weeping.
> He came beneath two trees,
> He recognized the blows of Roland on three stones;
> It is no wonder if Charles feels grief.
> He goes now by foot, and goes forth at a full run.
> Between both his hands . . .
> He faints over him, so great is his anguish.
>
> [2870-2880]

Charlemagne vainly attempts to restore the "presence" of Roland by embracing his nephew's dead body—that is to say, a thing whose pure thingness is both an irreducible presence and a conspicuous absence. Despite his efforts to commemorate, regression beyond the inertness of the signifier is impossible for

Charlemagne. Imprisoned in a totally corporeal presence that is a total absence, Charlemagne and the Franks now faint, as if life could symptomatically possess death, its opposite; or, as if by miming the dead, life could somehow "represent" what has been denied to it. But Charlemagne's struggles are as vain as they are extravagant, and he is condemned to survive in a world that will neither signify nor vanish altogether: a "desert," as Charlemagne calls it, a barrenness of futile redundancies. Indeed, the poem's "end" will be merely another unhappy beginning. Thus the devastation of the Frankish empire has left Charlemagne empty of all desire, except the desire to conclude his "exile" in history in order to rejoin the fellowship of his barons, spiritually present to each other in the timeless kingdom of the dead:

> "My nephew is dead, who conquered so much for me. . . .
> Who will lead my army with such force
> When he is dead, who each day led us forth?
> Ah, France, how deserted now you are.
> So great is my grief that I no longer want to live! . . .
> May God grant it, St. Mary's son,
> That before I come to the great gates of Size
> My soul may be severed from my body,
> And be placed among theirs,
> And my flesh be buried beside theirs."
>
> [2920-2942]

Broadly speaking, the vision of death imparted to Roland's passion at Roncevaux is ultimately one of compensation, reintegration, and even fruition as martyrs blossom into the "holy flowers" of the saved. Roland and his companions had been absolved and blessed well in advance of their dying, and after their death Roland's last gesture as a good feudal lord was to gather together the bodies of his peers and to commemorate their glory in song; shortly Roland would incant his own salvation as well and be borne aloft to heaven by Gabriel and Michael, God's most chivalrous angels. Thus all Christian warriors could be certain, it seemed, of being reunited in heaven's sublime peerage and of being remembered on earth in song.

But the experience of death that prevails in the wasteland that Charles inherits is quite opposite. Here death is not a reward but a punishment that degrades even the punishers. We witness first the tenuous triumph of a skinny Thierry over a magnificent Pinabel; then we are told that thirty of Ganelon's relatives are hanged for having pledged their loyalty to his person and his cause; finally we witness the drawing and quartering of Ganelon himself, a knight who quite properly defended his honor under the old dispensation only to find himself defined as a traitor under the new. In contrast with the ultimately integrative vision of death that was manifested earlier in the martyrdom of Charlemagne's troops, death becomes a centrifugal force, a violent dispersion of things both material and spiritual as Ganelon's limbs are torn from his body in "splendid torment" by four wild, thirsty horses.[22] One last time chivalric blood spews formulaically onto the green grass, but now it is the unredeemable blood of a traitor. Not only the heroic world but heroic language itself has lost its center:

> Each of his nerves is tightly stretched
> And all his body's members split apart:
> The bright blood spills onto the green grass.
> Ganelon has died like a hateful traitor.

[3970–3973]

Such as it is, the conclusion of the *Song of Roland* points more to unending violence than to forgiveness or consolation. True, there is the baptism of Bramimonde, a pagan woman who abandons the pagan law for that of the true God, yet this is hardly material for a new epic; if anything, it marks the obsolescence of the old. The past hangs over the present only as memories that are painfully in conflict. The hardships of Charlemagne, who must set forth once more, this time for the city of Imphe in the perhaps infinitely distant land of Bire, are the hardships of a man who has come to hate the heroic role with which history has burdened him; and it is no less clear that this desolate, two-hundred-year-old man is radically at odds with a poetic language that will neither serve him nor let him die:

[22]I owe this insight in part to a sentence in a seminar research paper by Lucie Brind'Amour, University of Montreal, 1975.

The emperor does not want to set forth.
"O God," says the king, "how painful is my life."
He weeps from his eyes and pulls on his white beard.

[3999–4001]

It seems to me that the tragedy of the *Roland* is not primarily that of a poet who has "used" language to express the purgative anguish of nobel souls: the *Roland* is less a tragedy *in* language than a tragedy *of* language itself, the loss of force in the heroes of this poem being a way of dramatizing a more pervasive loss of signification in the world. It is a poem that transcribes into its very substance a loss of transparency—of *apparence,* to borrow Jean Bodel's term—and a fatal discovery of the opacity of signifiers and, by extension, of all things. A cleavage is produced in the *Roland* between thought and action, between the knower and the known, and between the world and language. The seemingly permanent semantic universe of formulaic discourse is disrupted by discontinuities that are those of time itself, which an ethics of memory cannot finally remedy. If true temporal perspective is lacking in the verb system of the *Roland,* its semantic and cognitive shifts express this perspective in a perhaps more profound and tragic way. Meaninglessness in language is the soul's death. As John of Salisbury wrote, near the time when the *Roland* was written down, "A word's force [*vis*] consists in its meaning [*sensus*]. Without the latter, it is useless, and (so to speak) dead. Just as the soul animates the body, so, in a way, meaning breathes life into a word."[23]

The ending of the *Roland* may be admired and explained in many ways, and ever since the poem's discovery a century and a half ago, each generation of readers has discovered in it their own provocations and rewards. By way of conclusion, I should like to return briefly to a problem that I deferred earlier, one that stems, frankly, from concerns of our own time: that the *Roland,* for all the marks of its oral tradition, is available to us not as an oral performance, but only as a written text. If it is true,

[23]John of Salisbury, *Metalogicon,* II.4, trans. Daniel McGarry (Berkeley: University of California Press, 1962), p. 8.

as scholars claim (correctly, I believe), that the most archaic legends of the *Roland* endured three centuries and more as oral narrative, what new cultural constraints, we may ask, were brought to these legends by the intervention of the *technè* of writing? If it is true that any narrative is shaped at least in part by the process of its dissemination, is it not possible that the dyptich structure of the *Roland* documents, in some painful way, a historical transition from an oral *épistémè* to one of writing—a passage necessarily seen, however, from the experience of a culture of scriptors contemplating its *pre*-history as some kind of paradise of the oral word?

Admittedly, we know very little about the way a culture of scriptors selects the legends (or their variants) it will preserve from the infinitely variable repertory available in an oral tradition, but I would say that it is safe to assume that as a rule writers tend to choose material—and to organize it—in accordance with their own mode of experiencing the world. Hence it is perhaps not unreasonable to speculate that at least part of the fascination that the legends of Roland and Charlemagne held (and still hold) for a culture of scriptors was precisely that they delineated, in the successes and failures of their principal heroes, a problematic of memory that had special poignancy for the mind of the scriptor laboring in the language of interpersonal communication (as opposed to Latin) to create, with his text, a material object that would "forget" him and his "truth" as it became closed upon itself and assumed the alien existence of an economically negotiable commodity. I would suggest that the story of Charlemagne, which is one of progressive alienation and isolation from a world of people, things, and language, is also a story in which the scriptor found a reflection of his own potential destiny. Given the importance in the Middle Ages of the notion of the world-as-text, Charlemagne's tragedy in the world is one in which the scriptor could no doubt easily find analogies with his own potential fate in the labor of letters, which were seen as arbitrary signs of arbitrary signs, hence doubly remote from the reality they would represent.

Of course, such conjectures can hardly be "scientifically" proved—but neither can it ever be proved that "our" Roland died historically in Roncevaux or, on the contrary, that the *Ro-*

land sprang during some "sacred minute" into the mind of an inspired "Franc de France." Though it would be silly to suggest that the *Song of Roland* is first and foremost a song of writing, we have every reason to examine its implicit models of communication for indications of disruption and change that might correspond to an epistemological crisis rooted in the competing cultural functions of speech and writing.

Though I believe that there are many such indications, I shall mention only one. It involves a fundamental shift in the conceptions that Roland and Charlemagne express, respectively, about the mode in which the memory of Roncevaux will be conserved and communicated to the future. Roland, one will recall, hurls himself into the fray with the conviction that his legend will live on in song: his epic blows will animate the performance of both bard and hero in generations to come, and his blood will flow forever in words. Charlemagne, by contrast, though he quite properly deciphers Roland's last moments and delivers the most moving and elaborate *planctus* in the whole poem, immediately thereafter undertakes to monumentalize the glory of Roland and Oliver not in song but in the more viable medium of stone:

> The emperor had Roland's body prepared,
> And Oliver's and the Archbishop Turpin's.
> He had all three opened right before him,
> And had all of their hearts wrapped in silk,
> And placed inside a coffin of white marble. . . .
> He brought his nephew back to Blaye,
> And Oliver, his noble companion,
> And the Archbishop, who was wise and bold.
> He places the lords in white coffins:
> The barons are buried at St. Roman.
>
> [2962–2966, 3689–3693]

If we assume (as did John of Salisbury) that there is a close affinity between stone monuments and texts—each conserves the memory of something important that is absent—and that the epitaph is an instance of textuality in one of its most awesome and enduring forms, then we may see in Charlemagne's instincts a fundamental change in the notion of monumentality. This change coincides, moreover, with a general tendency of twelfth-century vernacular culture, as its languages assumed the status of writing, or of *grammatica*, to confer upon these languages a function of "monumentality" (Paul Zumthor) previously reserved for Latin. (Such concepts would of course be elaborated more specifically later by Dante.) Since we discover suspiciously late in the *Roland* (v. 2955) that Charlemagne's army is fairly swarming with "bishops, abbots, monks, canons, and tonsured priests," we may safely deduce that at the end of the eleventh century these clerical custodians of the letter became suddenly quite eager to identify themselves as proper heirs to Roland's legend. Moreover, with later written versions of the story of Roncevaux, the story of the burial of the twelve peers tended to become more elaborate (and contradictory), reflecting, once again, the desire of literate clerical poets to appropriate the prestige of Roland's legend by attaching it to their parish or monastery.[24] Such details may, of course, be interpreted in ways that have no necessary bearing on the historical function of texts, but there is no question but that even in the twelfth century such leading churchmen as John of Salisbury and Thomas Aquinas argued very clearly for the text as the privileged device by which society conserved its memories of the past and by which men distant in time and space remained "present" to each other.[25]

Such claims for the text as society's best *aide-mémoire* are disturbingly complacent, however, and one may easily imagine that for poets and their audiences the transition from an oral or preliterate culture to that of inscriptions and texts involved some kind of violence. Yet if a radical anxiety about the difference between uttering and writing was felt at such a time, it was surely not easily expressed (in writing). Perhaps in this light we should look more carefully at Charlemagne's personal tragedy to see what analogies it might have with the scriptor's experience of detachment from the world about which he writes. To formulate an admittedly mannered question: If Roland is Charlemagne's "right hand" cut off, is this not also the writer's right hand writing itself off?

[24]Ramon Menendez Pidal, *La Chanson de Roland et la tradition épique des Francs,* rev. ed., ed. René Louis, trans. I. Cluzel (Paris: Picard, 1960), pp. 112–126.

[25]John of Salisbury, *Policraticus,* II.12–13; Aristotle, *On Interpretation, Commentary by St. Thomas and Cajetan,* trans. J. Oesterle (Milwaukee: Marquette University Press, 1962), II.2., p. 24.

No culture could have been more obsessed with the problems and dangers of textuality than the Christian Middle Ages; and lest writing become, as Socrates had earlier called it, "the language of the dead," Christian culture maintained potent weapons. Not the least of them may be found in the Bible, the archtext *par excellence,* which perpetrated its hermeneutic dream (one of an ultimate presence, a voice spoken and heard in the duration of all time)[26] precisely by anathematizing those who lived by the law of the opaque letter, those who took the text of the Bible "literally": in particular, the scriptor as mere scribe, to be associated with the despised Pharisees. For the scribe is one who lives by externals: he favors the signifier at the expense of the signified; he neglects what is "inside" the otherwise killing letter. Here we may recall Christ's magnificent curse of the scribes who have defiled the temple and who have dared to sit blindly on the throne of Moses, the inspired author of the Pentateuch. Surely the curse helped prevail upon the early witnesses of this living Word to mind their alphas and omegas. It is an expansive, *vocal* curse, of which I need cite only this passage in which Christ compares the subversive text of the scribe to the empty cup and the tomb:

> Woe to you, scribes and Pharisees, hypocrites! because you clean the outside of the cup and the dish, but within they are full of robbery and uncleanness. Thou blind Pharisee! clean first the inside of the cup and the dish, that the outside too may be clean. Woe to you, scribes and Pharisees, hypocrites! because you are like whited sepulchres, which outwardly appear to men beautiful, but within are full of dead men's bones and of all uncleanness. So you outwardly appear just to men, but within you are full of hypocrisy and iniquity.[27]

[26]Psalms 18:2: "The heavens declare the glory of God, and the firmament proclaims his handiwork. Day pours out the word to day, and night to night imparts knowledge; not a word nor a discourse whose voice is not heard; through all the earth their voice resounds, and to the ends of the world their message."

[27]Matthew 23:25–28.

MICHAEL RIFFATERRE

Generating Lautréamont's Text

Les Chants de Maldoror has been dismissed as a hoax or the work of a madman; admired as black humor; extolled as a masterpiece of the literature of evil in the tradition that flourished in the second half of the nineteenth century in France, from late Romanticism to Decadent Symbolism. Nowadays critics are inclined to regard the *Chants* as negative rhetoric aimed at destroying the rhetorical tradition, debunking the aesthetics of originality through plagiarism, and exposing literary conventions by parodying them or exploiting them *ad absurdum*.[1]

However divergent, all these interpretations agree that what characterizes Lautréamont's verbal behavior is exaggeration: in everything he writes he goes too far, seeking either to parody or to shock.[2]

Since the reader's reactions are just as important a part of the literary phenomenon as the text itself,[3] and since lay readers and critics alike sense this exaggeration—variously ascribed to psychological imbalance or lack of aesthetic instinct, to bad taste,

---

[1]On the evolution of Lautréamont criticism (to 1968), see the convenient *Images de Lautréamont* by Frans De Haes (Gembloux, Belgium: 1969). The pioneering study on the cantos as literary form remains P. W. Nesselroth's *Lautréamont's Imagery* (Geneva: Droz, 1969). From the viewpoint presented here, among the more pertinent studies are Michel Charles, *Rhétorique de la lecture* (Paris: Seuil, 1977); J. M. Agasse, "Notes pour une rhétorique des *Chants*," *Entretiens*, 30 (1971), 175–185; and Lucienne Rochon, in Ph. Fédy, A. Paris, J. M. Poiron, L. Rochon, *Quatre Lectures de Lautréamont* (Paris: Nizet, 1973).

[2]On Lautréamont's exaggeration, see Michel Deguy's illuminating essay in his *Figurations* (Paris: Gallimard, 1969), pp. 233–268.

[3]On the role of the reader, see Deguy, especially p. 237; also my "Explication des faits littéraires" in my *Production du texte* (Paris: Seuil, 1979).

to willful defiance of moral conventions or calculated distortion of literary ones—my purpose is to use this consistent reaction as a point of departure for analyzing the mechanisms of Lautréamont's poetic language.

It will not do to assume the existence of perennial aesthetic or moral standards to which the text does not adhere. Taste, morals, and even such concepts as balance, symmetry, formal order, and the like are elusive variables, always shifting; and even if we could reconstitute the exact rules Lautréamont was rebelling against, they would not necessarily explain the persistence of reader reaction down to our own time. We must therefore start with a nonvariable, that is, the text, and try to find out how the rules generating literary texts apply to Lautréamont's.

I propose that any text can be shown to be generated from a minimal sentence or *matrix* (sometimes from a kernel word whose semes may be actualized into words, these words then forming a matrix)[4] in accordance with two rules of expansion and conversion. *Expansion* means that *every component of the matrix generates a form more complex than itself.* I shall call each such component a *generator,* and the segment of the resulting text derived from it I shall call a *transform.* The generator and the transform are semantic and functional homologues. From a generator composed of one word, expansion generates a group of words, a phrase or a sentence.

Conversion means that the text is generated by the *simultaneous modification of the same factor in every semantically relevant component of the matrix.*

This passage about disillusionment, for instance: "[He] drags along [*promène*] the bitter delights of disenchantment to the banquet tables and into the satin beds wherein slumbers the pale priestess of love, paid with the glitter of gold"[5] can be analyzed

---

[4] From the following analyses, it will be clear that if the matrix sentence is to be capable of generating a text, it must actualize a semantic or narrative structure. Only the polarizations made possible by binary oppositions or their transformations (by inversion, or transformation into equivalences) supply the power for generating the text.

[5] *Maldoror*, canto 3, stanza 1, *Oeuvres complètes*, ed. Pierre-Olivier Walzer (Paris: Pléiade, 1970), p. 134; henceforth references will be to the canto and stanza and, in brackets, to the page of the original French text in the Pléiade edition. The translations are mine, although I have followed where possible Alexis Lykiard's impressive English version of *Maldoror* (New York: Apollo Editions, 1973).

as an expansion in several stages on a matrix *He drags along his disillusionment into orgies.* I derive this matrix from the character the lines concern, a subtype of the Romantic hero. Wherever he goes in search of fulfillment, he finds only justification for what the French sometimes called *désespérance,* more often *spleen.* Because matrices cannot be found in the text itself, I have tried to use established stereotypes for phrasing the matrices: that is why I chose *to drag along* here with a predicate expressing a state of mind, a cliché translating into a metonymy the aimless and fruitless wanderings of the hero himself. The negative result *disillusionment* expands into *bitter delights,* an oxymoron made necessary by the hero's masochistic personality. Orgies, the stereotypical example of disappointing pleasure from Balzac to Baudelaire and Flaubert, generates the two standard complementary appetites (here again a cliché might be used: *the pleasures of bed and board*). Erotic lust generates a further explanatory and descriptive expansion: *the bed in which the prostitute sleeps.* At this point, however, conversion intervenes: pleasure leads nowhere, but still it has to be something better than lewd revelry; it has to have the magic of temptation, it must resemble an initiation into (false) mysteries—here again all we need is a Romantic stereotype: *the religion of pleasure.* Consequently every word of the expansion must be modified with positive markers, raising the lexicon to a loftier level: *satin beds* is thus derived from *bed,* the *slumbers* of elevated style from *sleeps,* and *priestess of love,* an accepted euphemism, from *prostitute.* The priestess of love derivation may be misleading, however, for the term extenuates the seme *venality* which *whore* would keep explicit. Yet venality must be retained to express the seme *deceitfulness in pleasure.* Hence a compensatory expansion: *a paid prostitute.* This last crude phrase is in turn converted into nobler language. But again, all this actualizes the seme *deceit* and the word for gold is therefore grammatically subordinated to the word for glitter (significantly, the conversion borrows from a preexistent, well-tested phrase, the proverb *all that glitters is not gold*). I have insisted on the clichés in the matrix and in the various stages of the textual derivation because they form a highly visible, if implicit, background or context against which the reader cannot help setting the explicit text.

This is why the concept of matrix and derivation therefrom may be the explanation for the consistency of reader reaction to Lautréamont: the reader has the opportunity to compare pre- and post-transformation versions because the text is so built as to facilitate reconstruction of the matrix. Then reading is comparing.

Such is the case in *Maldoror*. Its matrices are either easily inferred or made inescapable assumptions because the text points toward another text that preexists: this model is latent, but comes readily to the mind of anyone who speaks the language naturally, it is a *cliché* or a *descriptive system*—a network of actual words (not just meanings, as would be the case with a semantic field) associated with a kernel word. A descriptive system is easily identified because it has a grammar defining the reciprocal rela- tionships of its components, and together they form stereotyped phrases.

Now if the matrix *is* obvious, the derivation from it is by defini- tion more complex. It is thus impossible to read *the fields where battle roars* (3.1 [132]) without thinking of the compound *battlefield,* and sensing that it generated the phrase. Supposing that these obvious transformations recur frequently, and they do, complexity is bound to be interpreted as excess.

If the matrix is not obvious, the *transformation* must be. The more obvious it is that all the words of the text bear similar markers despite the variations demanded by the progress of the verbal sequence, the more that sequence seems to have been tampered with, the more it looks like a word game, and the easier is the translation back into the matrix. This is what hap- pens when there is conversion without expansion, and when as a result matrix and derivation are coextensive. Some of *Maldoror's* most outrageous shockers result from such derivations. Like the episode where two angels decide to abandon our sin-ridden planet—one version of a familiar theme, and thus a metatext whose components are also texts derived from texts. The angels, winging their way back to their celestial abode, "left far behind them the rocky [*rocailleux*] chamber pot where the constipated anus of the human cockatoo [*kakatoès*] jerks itself about [*se dé- mène*], until they could no longer descry the suspended silhouette of the filthy planet" (3.1 [133]). If we consider these

obscene images separately, we shall not be able to find many
passages to match their gratuitousness or their bad taste, typical
of the Romantic Young Turks. But the point is that we cannot
pick out these images one by one: their total sequence is an
obvious transform from *this insignificant planet where humanity
makes its futile fuss.* The motif is very familiar, the traditional
debunking of cosmic anthropomorphism. Instead of the proud
city reduced to an anthill (a similar theme), here the whole
round earth shrinks—the usual image is a small ball of mud with
a fungoid little mankind growing on it. Earth may be represented as a narrow stage upon which men struggle, hemmed in
humiliatingly, where all their labors and their aspirations come
to naught, where all is what the cliché calls a *futile fuss.*
Baudelaire used this model for a version milder than Lautréamont's but structurally identical: his earth is compared with a
soup pot, mankind's pointless activities with the boiling soup:

> The sky! the black lid of the great cooking pot,
> In which boils mankind, imperceptible and huge![6]

Lautréamont's text differs only in that it is bolder, disturbingly
so. His obnoxious choice of code is simply the climax of a sequence describing the stench of sin on earth, a puritanic cliché
that generates the following expansion a few lines before my
quotation: *dense exhalations of greed, pride . . . rising like pestilential
vapors from its [the earth's] hideous surface* (3.1 [133]). It is easy
enough to infer reeking feces from these evil smells, the easier
because we already have the literary cliché that inferior beings
are *the earth's excrements.*[7] From which the jump to the repellent
equation of *man* and *ass* is facilitated by the fact that *cul* is a
synecdoche common in vulgar French (albeit not quite so common as *con*) for opprobrious reference to a stupid person. The
epithet is doubly tautological, since *constipated* further negati-
vizes *ass* in its literal meaning, and as a lowbrow colloquial
metaphor for narrow-minded, stiff-necked characters it also fits
the figurative meaning. As for *rocailleux* (rocky), its function as

[6]Baudelaire, *Fleurs du Mal,* "Le Couvercle," ll. 13–14.
[7]It is also a familiar image in La Fontaine, whose fables French schoolboys still
learn by heart.

an adjective is to warn us that *chamber pot* is only a metaphor. But even so, it participates in the conversion process, because *rocailleux* as opposed to its synonym, *rocheux*, seems to have inherited the pejorative connotation of *rocaille* (rubble) as opposed to *roc* (rock). *Rocaille* has uses, it is true, which are not negative at all, although the *-aille* suffix normally is so. But in such a context its negative properties are (re)activated by contiguity.[8] *Jerks itself about* does look alien to the excremental context and would seem to be wrong for a seated posterior. But precisely this is one more proof that the text is not generated by a term-for-term, one-thing–one-word reference to reality. Indeed, the verb does not fit a referential construct. But it does fit a conversive complex, since the complex is the pejoration of the matrix and *to jerk about* is the ridiculous synonym we wanted for *to make a fuss*. Thus the negative transformation at one and the same time abides by the cardinal rule of the conversion, and absorbs into the verb the connotations divided between epithet and noun in the *futile fuss* cliché. Another departure from the conversion would seem to be the "human cockatoo," since there is the much-used metaphor: people with nothing of their own to say are parrots, but this has no relevance here. In fact, however, the parrot metaphor was picked from among metaphors pejorative in a general way because it could be particularized into *kakatoès*; not that these particular parrots are apter for mimesis, but their first two syllables are isolated by a strange ending found nowhere else in French. This points to the fact that these syllables seem to make sense by themselves, and their meaning (*caca*) is of course wholly appropriate in context: men are described in anal code.

Passages more gratuitous than this would be hard to find, yet the tasteless phantasms issue from a vigorous concatenation. So

[8]Reading is indeed a rigorously controlled decipherment, even where appearances are so blatantly gratuitous: such an epithet as *planetary* or *terrestrial* would have let the cat out of the sentence bag. *Mountainous*, a common metonym for our planet, would have denied the pot its belly. Suppose we had *muddy:* very tempting, since muddy has both referential accuracy and a moral symbolism conformant to the conversion's constants. But that would have looked like a euphemism for the vessel's more specific contents. Whereas *rocailleux* (rocky), pointing a sharp finger at earth's bones, is perfectly appropriate (in another passage Lautréamont sets in opposition *rocky continents* [4.7; 180] and *this fluid element,* the surrounding seas).

that we may well wonder, first, how so multiple an overdetermination can still look so free-wheeling, and second, whether what makes it typical of Lautréamont is just that his chosen images are more shocking than Baudelaire's derivation from the same matrix. Certainly Baudelaire eschewed an extreme defiance of verbal taboos, but then the impact of Lautréamont's relatively more ruthless audacities must depend partly on the evolution of taste, and even today's readers are somewhat shockproof in comparison with his earlier public.[9] The answer is that Lautréamont's verbal scandals look gratuitous and are thus more shocking; they will remain so, even as the reader becomes inured to the obscenities, for they result from formal textual factors whose objective existence cannot be altered by any subjective vagaries of a reader's aesthetics or moral sensitivities or social standards.

These factors are two. First, the selection of words at the top or bottom of the paradigmatic scale is not dictated by the referential function of language, but follows a rule of *lexical particularization*. Second, these transforms are not direct substitutes for their generators, but are indirect or second-degree substitutes, so to say, since they never appear in isolation but are always surrounded by more or less extensive fragments of the descriptive systems to which they belong.

What I mean by lexical particularization should become clear if a comparison is made among the three levels of derivation from a kernel word, *calamity*, in this story of two angels whose appearances on earth are portents of disaster: "[They] used to appear on earth, surrounded by clouds, during grand epochs of calamity, when a dreadful war threatened to plant its harpoon on the breasts of two enemy nations, or when cholera was getting its slingshot ready to hurl putrefaction and death into entire cities" (3.1 [132]). The first expansion makes explicit only what is presupposed by the kernel, since war and epidemic are dreadful examples of heaven-sent scourges. True, there seems to be

---

[9]Baudelaire, too, could be pretty daring: for instance, his images of intestinal worms (*Fleurs du Mal,* "Au Lecteur," l. 21). On the other hand, he was prosecuted for less heinous obscenities than Ducasse's.

more to it than a plain expansion, since *war* is given a melodramatic adjective, while *cholera* is substituted for the more general
but less lurid term. Both, however, simply actualize and ex-
teriorize the *destructiveness* seme that is part of *calamity*'s semantic
makeup.[10] The second level of expansion is the two sets of verbs:
both actualize a presupposition of the two angels' appearance.
Because they are represented as harbingers of calamity,
threatened and *ready to hurl* are variations on the future implicit in
the imminent disaster. More precisely, they transfer the markers
of the future tense from the morphological to the lexical level,
translating them literally into phrases descriptive of impending
doom. The transformation is akin to the fleshing out of an
algebraic formula with actual numbers, or better yet, it is like
shifting from an abstract picture to a representational painting.
The third stage or outer limit reached by the progress of the
derivation depicts the allegorical weapons and their targets (its
own matrix, itself the outcome of the two preceding stages of
expansion, is *war threatened two enemy nations, and cholera entire
cities*). In the context both weapons are unexpected, for they
have hardly any literary status as words. They are also very
specific. They therefore differ from those common in allegories,
whose names are likely to be either nondescript—spear, for instance, indicating merely that the character holding it is noble
and powerful—or only specific enough to enable the reader to
identify the allegorical character by his attributes (e.g., the scythe
is held by Father Time). But instead of the spear of Mars, we
have here the whaler's harpoon, and a child's slingshot, or at
most David's, in either case disconcerting in connection with
cholera (rather than something like Baudelaire's urn from which
a wintry allegory pours *mortality upon the fog-enshrouded sub-*

---

[10]The morphological differences between the two derivations prove that both
are simultaneous and equivalent: because the shape of the word *cholera* is foreign
enough to catch the eye, it functions as a stylistic superlative of *epidemic* without
need for an epithet, whereas such a plain everyday word as *war* needs one to
keep the balance. *Cholera* may impress the modern reader less than would
plague, but I am sure *cholera* played well enough upon nineteenth-century fears;
these people were still shaken by the horrors of the 1832, 1849, and 1853–54
epidemics, as well as the more recent cholera of 1865–67.

urbs).[11] This precision, however, does not help the reader to any real visualization: *harpoon* simply sounds crueler than spear, even though their blades may in reality be shaped the same, just as *scimitar* (aside from its possible role in a mimesis of exoticism—and even that requires no visualization, since the exotic spelling sufficiently conjures up exoticism, even for the reader who has never seen the thing) suggests a weapon sharper and more lethal than a mere sword. Quite simply, then, any word with conspicuous formal features, such as a technical term or an archaism, a foreign borrowing, a new coinage, any such word, regardless of its own specific meaning, serves as the hyperbole for its more frequent or less peculiar or less specialized synonym, partial or total. This is the phenomenon I should now like to rephrase as my rule of lexical particularization: *In any lexical paradigm of synonyms (or antonyms), the word with the least collocability or the most morphological peculiarity confers maximal emphasis upon its metaphorical or metonymic meaning in a given context.*

Obviously, the more such particularization, the more outlandish the appearance of the text, and as a consequence expansion produces a lexical overloading that is interpreted, according to context, as expressing paroxysm, or as mimetic of a kind of hysterical reality perception, or as mere mannerism. I am thinking of such typical passages as the following, where it is difficult to distinguish between these three possibilities: "the murmurings [*murmures*] and conspiracies that rise in unison from the surface of the spheres, and with fierce wing graze the papillose edges of your perishable eardrum" (5.4 [200]).[12] It is derived from a matrix *murmurings graze your ears,* In this challenge of Maldoror to the

---

[11] *Fleurs du Mal,* "Spleen (I), " l. 4. It is perfectly possible that Lautréamont is alluding to Flaubert's depiction of a catapult used by mercenaries besieging Carthage (*Salammbô,* chap. xiii, Dumesnil ed., II, 91), where carrion, garbage, and corpses shot into the streets cause an outbreak of the plague. Published six years before *Maldoror, Salammbô* was greeted as a shocking "compendium de la férocité." See the remarks of a critic quoted by Dumesnil, I, cxii ff: you would swear he is writing about *Maldoror.* In fact, it looks as if he were plagiarizing it before its birth. Ducasse must have been attracted by the reaction *Salammbô* elicited. But the argument is irrelevant, since there is no reason to believe that a reader should connect *Salammbô* and *Maldoror* the way he connects an intratextual matrix and its derivation (except by chance, as I did).

[12] The allusion to the music of the spheres is made, of course, because this is a cosmic conflict between God and the Archfiend.

Creator, the new Lucifer plays upon the dual meaning of French *murmures,* "whispers" or "rebellious mutterings," which accounts for the splitting of *murmures* into whispers and conspiracies and the epithets for the allegorical wing and the eardrum.[13] But *murmurings* as "whispers" generates the expansion on *to graze the ear.*[14] Since a whisper is barely audible, its metaphorical transformation into another sensory lexicon amounts to a lexical implementation of a seme of *near imperceptibility* or perhaps *lightness of touch.* Thus the derivation, all along the sentence, repeats this same seme in various words: *surface, graze* (with the subexpansion *to graze with a wing,* which is also a literary stereotype),[15] *edges,* and above all *papillose* and *eardrum.* Obviously these technical words replacing *ear* focus on the ear's sensory apparatus proper. But as words conspicuous by their scientific connotations and their peculiar spelling harking back to the Latin and Greek, they merely function as hyperbole of the anxious, straining ear of the scared listener, and this provides the drama required in the context.

As I said before, the rule of particularization provides only one of two explanations why *Maldoror*'s impact remains impervious to linguistic attrition and cultural change, that is, to changes in the reader's perception of the text. The other reason is that the *basic unit of derivation from matrix to text is not the word but groups of words:* for a given generator, the transform is an expansion embedded within the overall expansion and/or conversion. There are three types of such derivations. The three have in common the fact that the representations they give rise to are at most appearances. They use descriptive devices, they have all the trappings of realistic style, and still they can never yield a believable mimesis of reality. In the first type, the conversion of a given word activates one more component of the descriptive

---

[13]The epithet for eardrum is hyperbolic at the level of style, since it modifies a metonym for the whole poem, and *that* person is God: so that *perishable* is oxymoric.

[14]Which phrase, let me point out, is not my own contrivance but a well-established cliché, in itself a tautological expansion of the noun *murmure* in the form of a predicate (noun, verb, object = sound, contact, organ of perception).

[15]This French stereotype usually being a metaphor for a narrow escape, a brush with death, and the like. A common variant, which pursues the particularizing lexical variation on the semic motif, is *to feel the wing fan your skin.*

system than is needed. In the second type, the descriptive system is actualized as far as necessary to develop the full meaning or even separate semes of a word in the text generated by conversion. In the third, the descriptive system merely saturates that text with a paradigm of synonyms.

The first type of derivation arises from the irrelevant use of a descriptive detail that is precise, even technical. The conversion of a generator produces two transforms instead of one: the word actually substituted for the generator and a word describing some characteristic feature of that direct substitute. But this detail performs—or rather usurps—the functions that should be exercised by the direct or primary substitute. The latter's role is reduced to identifying the detail, to spelling out what representation it belongs to and what word it stands for. Nothing in the chamber pot stanza prevented Lautréamont from representing men directly as excrement, since there was already a stereotyped precedent for that. Instead, he derives *kakatoès* from the *men* of the matrix (since generator and transform share *caca*), and then displaces the pun, transferring its grammatical function to the name of the pertinent area of the human cockatoo's anatomy—pertinent in that it actualizes the implied meaning of the pun. This body part, in turn, is not designated in toto but through a synecdoche referring to its functional area (this process, by the way, is no different from the escalation of expletives observed in vulgar speech). Finally, the unfortunate synecdoche is further particularized in the shape of its Latin, or technical, equivalent. Nor is this procedure limited to obscenities. In the *priestess of love* stanza we saw the glitter annex the function of the gold. Elsewhere glory is said to have *begotten the astonished admiration of the indefinite cable of generations* (3.1 [132]),[16] where *indefinite cable* represents only an expansion of the *-s* denoting the plural of *generation;* whereas *generations* converts the real semantic core of the matrix, *an always admired glory,* that is, its adverb. Describing a mother as she rushes toward her

---

[16]Note here the extreme of particularization, which goes beyond the limits of usage: in the guise of malapropism, *indefinite* goes *infinite* one better; and the lowbrow *cable* replaces *chain,* the accepted metaphor.

son, who has just fainted on a couch, Lautréamont says that *she stepped toward the fringe of the sofa, the sole object of her loving solicitude* (6.4 [228])—so that a mere ornament is made to stand for the whole piece of furniture, as if the sofa were mentioned only to identify the fringe, whereas actually the sofa is the comical substitute for the recumbent figure. In short, the derivation resembles a sketchy periphrasis, but one that has retained its key, that is, its kernel word. It contains only the components belonging to the outer reaches of the descriptive system that supplies the periphrasis with its lexicon; or the components of little functional use within that descriptive system; or, again, the components normally censured, and censored, by social convention. But while language denies them any importance, textual relevance is bestowed upon them by the matrix. The detail or synecdoche multiplies by two the transformation of the generator: thus stress is laid upon the seme common to the primary transform and the secondary or synecdochic transform, that is, a seme corresponding to the conversion markers. The true function of this pseudorealism is to give visible shape, as it were, to that seme: *anus* emphasizes the relationship between man and his planet, their common paltriness, whereas Baudelaire's text does not show the affinity between *cooking pot* and *mankind; fringe* replaces the son's humanness with the furniture's inanimateness, a simple humorous exchange; *glitter* replaces gold with its deceptiveness; and so on.

In the second type of derivation, the text unfolds the whole (or most) of a relevant word's descriptive system (i.e., a word whose generator actualizes the basic structure of the matrix). Take the following passage, which looks to be a takeoff on conventional lyrical literature—the umpteenth variant of a theme found everywhere: "He leans on the windowsill. He contemplates the moon, pouring down upon his breast a cone of ecstatic rays wherein silvery atoms of ineffable softness flutter like moths" (5.7 [217]).

Here, as nearly always, contemplation of the moon calls for reciprocal attention: the moon showers its contemplator with light, or just gazes back at him—as in a poem of Victor Hugo's that precedes *Maldoror* by a mere dozen years:

> She rises, she casts a long sleepy ray
> Into space, into the mystery, the abyss,
> And we gaze steadily at each other,
> She shining and I suffering.[17]

Like the verse, our prose fragment expands upon *he contemplates the moon shining down upon him*. The expansion proper[18] is closer than Hugo's to traditional allegorical humanization, except for the disrupting addition *cone of rays* or *beams*—disrupting because the technicalism *cone*, borrowed from optics or simple geometry, jars with the allegorical style and the emotional lyricism of *ecstatic*. The technicism is not irrelevant the way *fringe* is in the sofa example,[19] but still the scientific precision of shape is out of keeping with lyrical poetic style. What is wholly unreal, however, is the general picture of atoms fluttering in the light, not just the pseudorealistic detail. Moonbeams do not look like that; only sunbeams do. What we have here, in fact, is simply a nocturnal version of the familiar motes-dancing-in-a-sunbeam motif, a standard feature of the literary summer light filtering through closed shutters. This is a conversion that employs as material for its transforms words taken from the commonplace representation of night: the *golden atoms*,[20] motes in a ray of sunlight, exchange their gold for the silver of moonlight; daytime *butterflies* become nighttime moths (*phalènes*). All these changes have the same significance: they create a positive aesthetic and "moral" orientation in harmony with *flutter*, suggesting sweet feelings, and with the cliché *ineffable softness*, derived from *soft light*, implicit in moonlight. The orientation is part and parcel of the moonlight theme used in literature to symbolize soothing

[17] *Les Contemplations* (1856) V, xiii ("Paroles sur la dune"), ll. 25–28.
[18] That is, *down upon him*, generating the synecdoche *upon his breast*, *shines* generating the metaphor *pours down rays of light*.
[19] It is nonetheless one more instance of the first type of pseudorealistic derivation. Accordingly, the detail is not even descriptively accurate, since light rays form a cone only when they emanate from a narrow source, such as an aperture at close range.
[20] The transformation of motes into atoms is not technical, as *cone* is. Atom has been a metaphor (or hyperbole) for any tiny particle ever since Lucretius used this motif of dust dancing in a ray of sunlight as a reverse metaphor to explain his concept of literal atoms (*De rerum natura*, 2.114–141).

contemplativeness. Madame de Staël classified it as one of *the known methods of lulling the soul to sweet repose.*[21]

Here again, as in the derivation of the first type, the text, conform as it may to the literary tradition, is generated at the expense of mimesis. Compounding the jolt of *cone,* the disruption in the reference to reality shows up again in *ecstatic,* an adjective that hardly makes sense as modifying *rays,* but has patently been displaced from a cliché that associates it with the theme of contemplation: *ecstatic contemplation* or *contemplative ecstasy.*[22] The strangeness of *ecstatic* as a modifier of *rays* either is perceived as merely a stylistic twist for the sake of artificiality or tips the reader off that the moon gazer's contemplative mood is being transferred to the moon itself (a transfer that may not be without precedent; witness the Endymion myth). This transposition of roles is the same mechanical shift that produces the antiphrastic rewriting of famous philosophical maxims in Lautréamont's *Poésies.* The absurdity of antiphrasis in *Poésies* and here the slight humor of the adjectival shift force the reader to decode the text as an allusion, whether or not it is interpreted as parody, to the traditional text they alter (here the theme, rescued from its linguistic limbo by the recognition of the passage as its transform). The derivation is thus perceived as a metalanguage about a convention, and therefore as a conscious artifact twice over.

Derivation of the third type is the most strikingly conspicuous because the sequences it generates are made up of words semantically compatible but grammatically incompatible. That is, a conversion, giving all the pertinent components of a text the same marker, is achieved by borrowing that text's words from a single descriptive system (which is common practice in literary language) but without any regard for the system's grammar (which is not).

A familiar philosophical or religious theme, for instance, is the

---

[21]Staël, *De l'Allemagne* (1810), Part II, chap. xxviii.

[22]*To contemplate* is a component of the matrix as I have hypothesized it. The fact that the verb as such is not transformed by expansion or conversion does not make it an exception to my rule: the transformation occurs in the form of the explicit displacement of *ecstasy* or *ecstatic,* an implicit corollary of *to contemplate.*

soul as prisoner within the body. Quite a few French Baroque poems transcode the description of the body into a *prison* descriptive system: the flesh is chains, life is bondage, death is the key, and so on. The transcoding uses the grammar that goes with the lexicon, that is, it respects the natural relationship among these words that makes for verisimilitude. Indeed, the aim of the extended metaphor is to prove its aptness by pursuing the analogy, step by step, between a likely body and a believable jail. Whereas Lautréamont writes: *I feel my soul is padlocked into my body's bolt* (3.1 [136]). Certainly *padlock* and *bolt* belong to the jail's mimesis,[23] but the second cannot contain the first, *into* is the wrong grammar, and *bolt* replaces the cell it is supposed to lock.

Grammar may be too narrow a term, and elsewhere conversion involves plain contradiction, as when this snake is squashed: "flattening on the reddened grass, with a blow of my heel, the receding curves of your triangular head" (5.4 [199]). The triangular head is a cliché of snake descriptions, and so is *receding curves,* but body and head, coils and triangle are mutually exclusive. In both passages, then, the lexical slots of the descriptive syntax are filled with misplaced words. But all these words refer to the matter of the text. The effect is that of a color print in which the colors have run over their proper boundaries. The destroyed syntax, the encroaching lexicon annul the mimesis but leave intact the repetitive insistence upon essential characteristics of prison and of snake. The words are not permitted their normal hierarchy and mutual collocability, hence they are deprived of the power to organize a picture, but they retain the power of repetition, that is, they all refer to one kernel word that remains unuttered yet is the more effectively evoked through repeated allusions concentrically pointing to the latent prison and the unmentioned snake. But if the descriptive system is thus reduced to a paradigm of metonyms of the same kernel, this amounts to its being a paradigm of synonyms. The text this paradigm generates is attention-getting because as a mimesis it is

[23]Not quite. If *bolt* really is part of the mimesis of jail, the padlock belongs rather to the inglorious locks of flimsier doors, such as a toolshed's, and has no prison pathos. This lowbrow technicism illustrates once more the role of lexical particularization.

all wrong. But since the syntactic variations appear incapable of distributing the words in a reasonable way, they have to be read as a kind of musical variation on a single motif, a sequence saturated with variants of an unsung key word. Or else— perhaps I have been carried away by the temptation of "poetic" simile—the sequence resembles a doughnut, for the function of the words is to point to the hole, to a lexical void that generates a whole text to compensate for the invisibility of that central word and to compel the reader to solve its riddle.[24]

This lexical void need not be filled with the word the descriptive system has for a kernel. Such a sentence as *to have fastened to the flank of mankind such a crown of wounds* (5.5 [202]) cannot be regarded simply as a paradigm circling around a verb for "wound," or for the moral sin the wound obviously signifies. For the semantic incompatibilities (you do not crown a flank, or fasten a crown, for that matter; a crown of wounds makes no sense, except perhaps as an allusion to the Stigmata) are not just logical incompatibilities whose distortions are perceived by reference to a preestablished standard of body description. The abnormalities here distort the very body of Christ, for every illogical or unacceptable collocation bears upon some cliché of the Passion: the wound in the side, the crown of thorns, the identification of mankind with the Redeemer. The semantic void thus pointed to by the sequence of malapropisms (the sentence is something like a prolonged spoonerism) is Christ as the sacrificial lamb and as man, Christ not as a person or a symbol of himself but as a metonym of the ever gaping wound that is the metaphor of sin.[25]

If generalities can be drawn from so sketchy an analysis, a first conclusion would be that however "mad" Lautréamont's text may look, its madness is never that of irrational lucubration.

[24]See my *Semiotics of Poetry* (Bloomington: Indiana University Press, 1978), pp. 13ff. and 138–150. Cf. J. Peytard, "La Rature de Dazet ou la métamorphose du sens," *Littérature*, 4 (December 1971), 68–78; M. Charles (see note 1).
[25]This compound displacement is perfectly in accord with Christian mythology, where sin is still "to cause the wounds of Our Lord to bleed anew" (for example, Rimbaud's letter to Delahaye, March 5, 1875, in his *Oeuvres complètes*, ed. A. Adam [Paris: Pléiade, 1972], p. 296).

Every component in the text is linked to its matrix by so rigorous a concatenation that, indeed, *everything is explained, the important and the most minute details alike* (4.5 [175]). There is nothing even obscure, and deviance from language or from context serves only to call attention to inescapable presuppositions, the way gravitational anomalies in a planetary orbit reveal the presence of an invisible celestial body.

A second point is that the rules I have proposed only formalize in terms of discourse analysis phenomena that seem, to critics and readers alike, to extend beyond language. Yet all of them, especially parody and plagiarism, but also the very deduction of a philosophy of evil from a descriptive system of good, all of them are susceptible of matrix analysis. The very name the author chose for himself is symbolic: from Eugène Sue's text *Latréaumont*, Lautréamont is generated by conversion. What must be emphasized here is that beyond specific texts and sundry literary allusions, *Maldoror* parodies language itself, using clichés and its descriptive systems—that is, its verbal myths—as basic units for its reconstruction, or perhaps for a replay. Since parody, or even a replay, presupposes a differentiation from the matrix, we must conclude that Lautréamont's text is a case of generalized catachresis.

In this respect it differs from the rest of literature only in that the catachresis is always visible and calls attention to itself, evidently because Lautréamont systematically maintains the totally mechanical character of his textual derivation. Thus all traces of reference to reality are eliminated and all possibility of interpreting the text as reality's representation is canceled. Expansion does not represent exaggeration: it is the icon of exaggeration. Similarly, conversion, by subjecting every word to one principle of transformation, functions as an icon of maniacal obsessiveness. It may not be an oversimplification to suggest that *Maldoror* is a *texte de rupture* in that it replaces the literature of mimesis by the literature cf iconicity.

Directions for Further Research

To make the entries on the contributors as useful as possible, I have provided brief sketches of their interests as well as descriptions of the nature of their published work. I have, however, restricted the contributors' bibliographies to their books and most representative articles. Likewise, the listing of "criticism" on each contributor is not exhaustive. Its only purpose is to help orient the reader who is not familiar with Continental criticism but who wishes to continue his reading on a given critic.

The Bibliography proper is also limited to significant and representative works of the sixties and seventies. Its aim is to provide the reader with a choice of critical—theoretical as well as methodological—options. Thus it stresses theoretical and methodologically innovative works, and focuses on French critics and American critics influenced by French theories. That Booth, Frye, and Hirsch are not included is neither an oversight nor an indication of lack of interest in their work, but rather because they represent a strain of criticism already familiar to most American readers.

The Bibliography is divided into sections, to help the reader find his coordinates. A section on structuralism provides a first step in explaining the general directions out of which post-structuralism has evolved. The concluding section is devoted to periodicals that have participated in shaping Franco-American intellectual activity in the last fifteen years. The other five sections (Literary Criticism, Philosophy, Psychoanalysis, Anthropology, and Linguistics) list works of criticism relevant to structuralist and post-structuralist thinking according either to methodology or to subject matter. The criterion used—not always successfully, as the distinctions are often far from being clear-cut—is the following: where methodology is predominant over subject matter, a work is listed under the appropriate methodological rubric, and the reverse in the opposite instance. If Octave Mannoni's *Clefs pour l'imaginaire* appears under "Psychoanalysis" although he deals with literary material, it is because in his case the methodology rather than the literature in question is primary. John Irwin's *Doubling and Incest,* which makes use of extensive psychoanalytical material, appears nevertheless under "Literary Criticism" for precisely the opposite reasons. These are just two examples that illustrate the difficulties and potential distortions involved in this process of classification. Nevertheless, I hope that these divisions will be useful in giving the reader a general sense of direction within the broad framework of contemporary criticism.

A few technical remarks to conclude. I have tried not to duplicate entries: the works of the contributors are not listed in the Bibliography, and works that appear under one rubric do not appear under another; for example, Derrida's reading of Lacan appears under Derrida only and not under Lacan. Finally, when available, titles in translation are listed in brackets.

Contributors

Roland Barthes

Undoubtedly the most prolific and influential French writer-critic of his generation. For the fifteen years before 1975, Barthes's seminar in the VIe section of the Ecole Pratique des Hautes Etudes was the place where the best and most advanced developments in criticism were systematically tested. Since 1975, Barthes has taught literature and semiology at the prestigious Collège de France.

A man for all seasons, Barthes has produced significant intellectual and critical work since the early fifties. His writings range from Bachelardian phenomenology to sociocriticism, from Hjelmslevian to Saussurian linguistics, from Freudian to Lacanian influences, from strict semiotic practice to more recent post-structuralist conceptions of textual productivity, from theories of writing to theories of reading, from commentaries on the most diverse authors from Racine and Brecht to Sade, Fourier, Loyola, and . . . Barthes himself. Barthes can be read as a theorist, a critic, or a writer; his work can be cut up along methodological lines or according to function or subject matter. Barthes's writing simply cannot be reduced to one line of thought, one system, or one point of view. Its power and freshness reside precisely in the divergent—even contradictory—elements and needs that it brings into play and attempts to satisfy. His publications include:

Le Degré zéro de l'écriture. Paris: Seuil, 1953; Gonthier, 1964. [*Writing Degree Zero.* London: Cape, 1967.]

Michelet par lui-même. Paris: Seuil, 1954.

Mythologies. Paris: Seuil, 1957; Points, 1970. [*Mythologies.* London: Cape, 1972.] Essays on modern myths followed by a lengthy study of the linguistic nature of myth.

Sur Racine. Paris: Seuil, 1963. [*On Racine.* New York: Hill and Wang, 1964.]

La Bruyère: Du mythe à l'écriture. Paris: Union Générale d'Editions, 1963.

Essais critiques. Paris: Seuil, 1964. [*Critical Essays.* Evanston: Northwestern University Press, 1972.] Essays on criticism, literature, structuralism, writing, and various authors: Foucault, Robbe-Grillet, Voltaire, Kafka, Brecht, Michelet, La Bruyère, and others.

La Tour Eiffel. Lausanne: Delpire, 1964.

La Voyageuse de nuit. Paris: Union Générale d'Editions, 1965.

Critique et Vérité. Paris: Seuil, 1966.

Le Système de la mode. Paris: Seuil, 1967. [A part of this, "The Diseases of Costume," is in *Partisan Review,* 34 (1967).]

S/Z. Paris: Seuil, 1970. [*S/Z.* New York: Hill and Wang, 1974.] On Balzac's *Sarrazine.*

L'Empire des signes. Paris: Skira, 1970. On Japanese culture.

Sade, Fourier, Loyola. Paris: Seuil, 1971. [*Sade, Fourier, Loyola.* New York: Hill and Wang, 1976.]

Le Plaisir du texte. Paris: Seuil, 1973. [*The Pleasure of the Text.* New York: Hill and Wang, 1975.]

Roland Barthes par Roland Barthes. Paris: Seuil, 1975. [*Roland Barthes.* New York: Hill and Wang, 1977.]

Fragments d'un discours amoureux. Paris: Seuil, 1977. [*A Lover's Discourse: Fragments.* New York: Hill and Wang, 1978.]

Image-Music-Text. New York: Hill and Wang, 1977. Essays from the 1968–1972 period.

Leçon. Paris: Seuil, 1978.

Sollers écrivain. Paris: Seuil, 1979.

"Eléments de sémiologie." *Communications,* 4 (1964). Reprinted in *Le Degré zéro de l'écriture.* Paris: Gonthier, 1964. [*Elements of Semiology.* London: Cape, 1967.]

"Introduction à l'analyse structurale des récits." *Communications,* 8 (1966). ["An Introduction to the Structural Analysis of Narrative," *New Literary History,* 6:2 (1974).]

"L'Ancienne Rhétorique: Aide-mémoire." *Communications,* 16 (1970).

The body of criticism devoted to Roland Barthes is extensive. As an introduction to his work, the reader will find especially useful Barthes's two interviews with Raymond Bellour in his *Le Livre des autres* (Paris: L'Herne, 1971). Aside from sections devoted to Barthes in all of the major books on structuralism (such as Culler's *Structuralist Poetics,* Scholes's *Structuralism in Literature,* and Jameson's *The Prison-House of Language*), the two best books on Barthes are Stephen Heath's *Vertige du déplacement: Lecture de Barthes* (Paris: Fayard, 1974) and Louis-Jean Calvet's *Roland Barthes: Un Regard politique sur le signe* (Paris: Payot, 1973). An introductory study of his work up to *S/Z* is also available in the *Barthes* by Guy de Mallac and Margaret Eberbach (Paris: Editions Universitaires, 1971).

There have also been numerous special issues of various reviews on Barthes's work: chief among them are *Tel Quel*, 47:1 (1971), which includes a number of insightful articles, a complete bibliography, and an important interview with Barthes; *Critique*, 302 (1972); and *L'Arc*, 56 (1974). Among the earlier articles on Barthes that have not lost their interest: Genette's "L'Envers des signes" in his *Figures;* Kristeva's "Le Sens et la mode" in *Critique*, 247 (1967), (also reprinted in her *Semiotikē*, pp. 60–89); Michel Butor's "La Fascinatrice" in his *Répertoire IV* (Paris: Minuit, 1974), and Leo Bersani's "Is There a Science of Literature?" in *Partisan Review*, 39 (1972). Recent and more controversial discussions pro or con Barthes are: Michael Riffaterre's "Sade, or Text as Fantasy," *Diacritics*, 2:2 (1972); Frank Kermode's "The Uses of Codes," in Seymour Chatman, ed., *Approaches to Poetics* (New York: Columbia University Press, 1973), pp. 51–79; Jacques Ehrmann's "L'Emprise des signes" in *Semiotica*, 1 (1973); and Fredric Jameson's "The Ideology of the Text" in *Salmagundi*, 31–32 (1976). See also the collection of essays *Prétexte: Roland Barthes* (Paris: Union Générale d'Editions, 1978).

Gilles Deleuze

A philosopher by training, Deleuze teaches at the University of Paris, Vincennes. He has been actively involved in all aspects of the literary, philosophical, and political developments that have been associated with the contemporary French critical scene. His work cuts across the domains of philosophy (Hume, Nietzsche, Kant, Bergson, Spinoza), literature (Proust, Carroll, Artaud, Klossowski, Kafka), and psychoanalysis (he has written several books in collaboration with the psychoanalyst Félix Guattari). His publications include:

Empirisme et subjectivité: Essai sur la nature humaine selon Hume. Paris: Presses Universitaires de France, 1953.

Nietzsche et la philosophie. Paris: Presses Universitaires de France, 1962.

La Philosophie critique de Kant. Paris: Presses Universitaires de France, 1963.

Proust et les signes. Paris: Presses Universitaires de France, 1964. Revised and supplemented edition, 1970. [*Proust and Signs.* New York: G. Braziller, 1972.]

Nietzsche. Paris: Presses Universitaires de France, 1965.
Le Bergsonisme. Paris: Presses Universitaires de France, 1966.
Présentation de Sacher-Masoch. Paris: Minuit, 1967; 10/18, 1971. [*Masochism: An Interpretation of Coldness and Cruelty. Together with the Entire Text of* Venus in Furs, *by L. von Sacher-Masoch.* New York: G. Braziller, 1971.]
Spinoza et le problème de l'expression. Paris: Minuit, 1968.
Différence et répétition. Paris: Presses Universitaires de France, 1969.
Logique du sens. Paris: Minuit, 1969. On the structure of fantasy and simulacrum in Lewis Carroll, Artaud, Klossowski, Plato, and others.
Capitalisme et schizophrénie: L'Anti-Oedipe (in collaboration with F. Guattari). Paris: Minuit, 1972. [*Capitalism and Schizophrenia: Anti-Oedipus.* New York: Viking, 1977.]
Kafka: Pour une littérature mineure (in collaboration with F. Guattari). Paris: Minuit, 1975.
Rhizôme (in collaboration with F. Guattari). Paris: Minuit, 1976.
Dialogues (in collaboration with C. Parnet). Paris: Flammarion, 1977.
"La Méthode de dramatisation." *Bulletin de la Société Française de Philosophie,* 61:3 (1967).
"Schizologie." Preface to Louis Wolfson, *Le Schizo et les langues.* Paris: Gallimard, 1970.

Michel Cressole's *Deleuze* (Paris: Editions Universitaires, 1973) is an overall introduction to Deleuze's work. A forthcoming book by Jacques Aumêtre, *Deleuze,* to be published by Grasset, should be of greater interest. Among the many essays on Deleuze's earlier works, Michel Foucault's "Theatrum Philosophicum," *Critique,* 282 (1970), on *Logique du sens* and *Différence et répétition,* stands out. A translation of this article exists in Foucault's *Language, Counter-Memory, Practice,* pp. 165–196. Other articles of interest: André Glucksmann's "Préméditations Nietzschéennes," *Critique,* 213 (1965); Robert Mauzi's "Les Complexes et les signes," *Critique,* 225 (1966), on Deleuze's *Proust;* Claude Rabant's "Sacher-Masoch ou l'échange fou," *Critique,* 273 (1970); Angèle Kremer-Marietti's "Différence et qualité," *Revue de Métaphysique et de Morale,* 3 (1970), on *Différence et répétition;* and Jeffrey Mehlman's "Portnoy in Paris," *Diacritics,* 2:4 (1972), on Deleuze's Wolfson. *L'Anti-Oedipe* is the subject of two brilliant articles by René Girard ("Système du délire") and Jean-François Lyotard ("Capitalisme énergumène"), both in *Critique,* 306 (1972). A collective volume, *Les Chemins de l'Anti-Oedipe* (Toulouse: Privat, 1974), and two special issues, one of the review *Esprit,* 12 (1972), and the other of *Sémiotexte,* 2:3 (1977), are likewise devoted to the *Anti-Oedipus.* Shorter essays on Deleuze and a complete bibliography appear in the special issue devoted to him by *L'Arc,* 49 (1972).

Paul de Man

Born in Belgium, Paul de Man has taught at Cornell, Zurich, Johns Hopkins, and is presently professor of French and Comparative Literature at Yale. He has written extensively on the rhetoric of contemporary criticism—New Criticism, structuralism, post-structuralism—as well as on avant-garde European critics: Binswanger, Lukács, Blanchot, Poulet, and most recently, Derrida.

De Man's own brand of deconstructive criticism has been extremely influential in American intellectual circles. It consists in bringing forth the paradoxical discrepancies that characterize and are constitutive of literary language in general. The most systematic formulation of the "blindness and insight" that constitute literary modernity is made in his "The Rhetoric of Blindness: Jacques Derrida's Reading of Rousseau," an essay that appears in *Blindness and Insight.* De Man's extensive work on Nietzsche, Proust, and Rousseau is to culminate in a forthcoming book which offers a theory of figural language centered on these authors. His publications to date include critical editions of Flaubert's *Madame Bovary* (New York: Norton, 1965) and *The Poetry of John Keats* (New York: New American Library, 1966), and *Blindness and Insight: Essays in the Rhetoric of Contemporary Criticism* (New York: Oxford University Press, 1971). The book contains in addition to essays on Lukács, Binswanger, Blanchot, and Poulet, two crucial essays: the one mentioned above on Derrida's Rousseau and "Literary History and Literary Modernity." He is author also of many other essays, among them "The Rhetoric of Temporality" in *Interpretation: Theory and Practice,* ed. Charles Singleton (Baltimore: Johns Hopkins University Press, 1969); "Genesis and Genealogy in Nietzsche's *The Birth of Tragedy,*" *Diacritics,* 2:4 (1972); "Theory of Metaphor in Rousseau's *Second Discourse,*" *Studies in Romanticism,* 12:2 (1973), reprinted in *Romanticism: Vistas, Instances, Continuities,* ed. D. Thorburn and G. Hartman (Ithaca: Cornell University Press, 1973); "Nietzsche's Theory of Rhetoric," *Symposium,* 28:1 (1974); "Action and Identity in Nietzsche," *Yale French Studies,* 52 (1975); "The Timid God," *Georgia Review,* 29:3 (1975); "Political Allegory in Rousseau," *Critical Inquiry,* 2:4 (1976); "The Purloined Ribbon," *Glyph,* 1 (1977); and "The Epistemology of Metaphor," *Critical Inquiry,* 5:1 (1978).

De Man's method of investigation has been discussed in insightful and perceptive essays: Angus Fletcher's "The Perpetual Error," *Dia-*

critics, 2:4 (1972); Richard Klein's "The Blindness of Hyperboles: The Ellipses of Insight," *Diacritics*, 3:2 (1973); Eric Gans's "Anamorphose du cercle," *Critique*, 329 (1974); and Frances Ferguson's "Reading Heidegger: Jacques Derrida and Paul de Man," *Boundary 2*, 4:2 (1976).

Jacques Derrida

The founder of deconstructive criticism, Derrida is *maître-assistant* in philosophy at the Ecole Normale Supérieure in Paris. He has written remarkably influential essays in almost every field of the human sciences: philosophy (Husserl, Kant, Nietzsche, Heidegger, Lévinas, Foucault), literature (Artaud, Rousseau, Bataille, Jabès, Mallarmé), anthropology (Lévi-Strauss), psychoanalysis (Freud, Lacan, Abraham), and linguistics (Saussure, Benveniste, Searle).

To say that Derrida has had a powerful influence on the importation of Continental criticism to America is to understate the case. And yet the difficulty of his writing has kept his work from reaching a broad American audience. Translating him has been no easy task, and the result even in the best of cases has not matched the language of the original; hence reading Derrida in translation poses its own problems. Another question is where to start in his corpus of writings. There is no easy answer, although his interviews provide a first access to understanding his way of thinking and his method. See especially the interview with Kristeva entitled "Sémiologie et grammatologie" in *Positions* and the two more recent ones in *Digraphe*, 8 (1976) and 11 (1977). Among his scholarly works, *Of Grammatology* and the essay "La Pharmacie de Platon" (in *La Dissémination*) are more accessible than his other publications, a list of which follows:

L'Origine de la géométrie de Husserl. Translation and introduction by Jacques Derrida. Paris: Presses Universitaires de France, 1962.
La Voix et le phénomène. Introduction au problème du signe dans la phénoménologie de Husserl. Paris: Presses Universitaires de France, 1967. [*Speech and Phenomena, and Other Essays on Husserl's Theory of Signs.* Evanston: Northwestern University Press, 1973.]
L'Ecriture et la différence. Paris: Seuil, 1967. [*Writing and Difference.* Chicago: University of Chicago Press, 1978.] Essays on Foucault, Jabès, Artaud, Lévi-Strauss, Lévinas, Freud, Bataille, Rousset, and Husserl.
De la grammatologie. Paris: Minuit, 1967. [*Of Grammatology.* Baltimore: Johns Hopkins University Press, 1976.]
Positions: Entretiens avec Henri Ronse, Julia Kristeva, Jean-Louis Houdebine, Guy Scarpetta. Paris: Minuit, 1972.

La Dissémination. Paris: Seuil, 1972. Includes "La Pharmacie de Platon"; "La Dissémination" (on Sollers); and "La Double Séance" (on Mallarmé).

Marges de la philosophie. Paris: Minuit, 1972. A collection of essays related to the languages of philosophy. Includes "Le Supplément de copule" which appears in translation in this volume, and "La Mythologie blanche," another important essay which has been translated in *New Literary History,* 6:1 (1974) as "The White Mythology: Metaphor in the Text of Philosophy." Harvard University Press is preparing a translation of the whole volume.

Glas. Paris: Galilée, 1974.

(et al.), *Mimésis desarticulations.* Paris: Galilée, 1975.

Eperons: Les Styles de Nietzsche. Venice: Corbo & Fiore, 1976. Parallel translations of a text by Derrida in four languages: French, English, Italian, and German. With an introduction by Stefano Agosti.

Limited Inc. (Baltimore: Johns Hopkins University Press, 1977). An English translation of this monograph on Searle appears in *Glyph,* 2 (1977).

La Vérité en peinture. Paris: Flammarion, 1978.

"L'Archéologie du frivole." Preface to Condillac, *Essai sur l'origine des connaissances humaines.* Paris: Galilée, 1973.

"Le Facteur de la vérité." *Poétique,* 21 (1975). ["The Purveyor of Truth." *Yale French Studies,* 52 (1975).]

"Fors." Preface to N. Abraham and M. Torok, *Cryptonymie: Le Verbier de L'Homme aux loups.* Paris: Aubier-Flammarion, 1976. ["Fors: The Anglish Words of Nicolas Abraham and Maria Torok." *Georgia Review,* 31:1 (1977).]

"L'Age de Hegel." In GREPH, ed., *Qui a peur de la philosophie?* Paris: Flammarion, 1977.

"Scribble." Preface to Warburton, *Essai sur les hiéroglyphes.* Paris: Aubier-Flammarion, 1978.

Quite a few French critics have written about Derrida. Roger Laporte's essay "Une Double Stratégie" in the collective volume *Ecarts: Quatre Essais à propos de Jacques Derrida* edited by Lucette Finas (Paris: Fayard, 1973), is a perceptive and unpretentious study of Derrida's critical trajectory; Henri Meschonnic's "L'Ecriture de Derrida" in his *Le Signe et le poème* (Paris: Gallimard, 1975) is useful; and François Laruelle's *Machines textuelles: Déconstruction et libido d'écriture* (Paris: Seuil, 1976), which claims to analyze Derrida's deconstructive techniques within a Nietzschean problematic, addresses itself strictly to the specialist. The American side is just as rich, if not richer, than the French criticism on Derrida. To mention a few essays that espouse different perspectives: M. H. Abrams's "The Deconstructive Angel," *Critical Inquiry*, 3:3 (1977); Murray Krieger's "Poetics Reconstructed: The Presence of the Poem," *New Literary History*, 7:2 (1976); and a powerful essay by Edward Said, "The Problem of Textuality: Two Exemplary Positions," *Critical Inquiry*, 4:4 (1978). Gayatri Spivak has written a long and useful preface to her translation of *De la grammatologie*, and she explains in it in great detail many of Derrida's concepts and critical moves. For a more playful and more elaborate "Derridean" reading of Derrida's more recent writings, see Spivak's "*Glas*-Piece: A Compte-Rendu," *Diacritics*, 7:3 (1977), and Geoffrey Hartman's "Monsieur Texte: On Jacques Derrida, His *Glas*" and "Monsieur Texte II: Epiphany in Echoland," *Georgia Review*, 29:4 (1975) and 30:1 (1976). See also Joseph Riddel's "From Heidegger to Derrida to Chance: Doubling and (Poetic) Language," *Boundary 2*, 4:2 (1976), and Charles Altieri's "Wittgenstein on Consciousness and Language: A Challenge to Derridean Literary Theory," *MLN*, 91:6 (1976). A special issue of *L'Arc*, 54 (1973), containing a number of interesting articles by Catherine Clément, Emmanuel Lévinas, Hélène Cixous, Edmond Jabès, Roger Laporte, and Sylvère Lotringer is available, and the *Oxford Literary Review* has published (July 1978) an issue devoted to Derrida, with articles by, notably, Derrida, Vincent Descombes, Jean-Luc Nancy, and others.

Eugenio Donato

Eugenio Donato has taught at Cornell, Johns Hopkins, Montreal, and the State University of New York at Buffalo, and he is now chairman of the department of French and Italian at the University of California, Irvine. In the past ten years, Donato has been instrumental in introducing the best of Continental criticism to an American readership. He is currently completing a book entitled *The Script of Decadence: Essays on the Fictions of Flaubert*. His publications include *The Structuralist Controversy: The Languages of Criticism and the Sciences of Man*, co-edited with Richard Macksey (Baltimore: Johns Hopkins University Press, 1970 and 1972), and numerous articles: among them, "*Tristes Tropiques*: The Endless Journey," *MLN*, 81:3 (1966); "Of Structuralism and Literature," *MLN*, 82:5 (1967); "The Two Languages of Criticism," in *The Structuralist Controversy*, 1970; "Language, Vision and Phenomenology: Merleau-Ponty as a Test Case," *MLN*, 85:6 (1970); "The Shape of Fiction: Notes Towards a Possible Classification of Narrative Discourses," *MLN*, 86:6 (1971); "'Per selve e boscherecci Labirinti': Problems of Narrative in Ariosto's *Orlando Furioso*," *Barroco*, 4 (1973);

"Structuralism: The Aftermath," *Substance,* 7 (1973); "'A Mere Labyrinth of Letters'/Flaubert and the Quest for Fiction/A Montage," *MLN,* 89:6 (1974); "Lévi-Strauss and the Protocols of Distance," *Diacritics,* 5:3 (1975); "'Here, Now'/'Always, Already': Incidental Remarks on Some Recent Characterizations of the Text," *Diacritics,* 6:3 (1976); "Flaubert and the Question of History: Notes for a Critical Anthology," *MLN,* 91:5 (1976); "The Idioms of the *Text:* Notes on the Language of Philosophy and the Fictions of Literature," *Glyph,* 2 (1977); "The Ruins of Memory: Archeological Fragments and Textual Artifacts," *MLN,* 93:4 (1978); "Divine Agonies: Of Representation and Narrative in Romantic Poetics," *Glyph,* 6 (1979).

Michel Foucault

Foucault, who holds the chair of philosophy at the Collège de France, is perhaps the most powerful figure in French intellectual circles today. Since 1961 when the first of his highly provocative books (*Folie et déraison*) appeared, he has published a steady stream of philosophico-historical and more recently of politico-historical works. Foucault's work cannot be neatly classified; it is interdisciplinary at all levels. His writings touch upon literature, philosophy, history, and politics, tracing themes across these domains, borrowing their techniques, and translating them into a highly original Foucaultian system: a taxonomy of discourses. Foucault's early style is somewhat opaque, although his more recent work is highly readable; thus for the American reader unaccustomed to French intellectual discourse, it might be beneficial to approach his work in reverse chronological order, starting with his two most recent books, *Discipline and Punish* and *The History of Sexuality.*

Foucault has often accused his critics and commentators of missing the point of his work—and often they have. This is a strong reason for approaching him through the interview route. His interviews are numerous, self-explanatory, and the best introduction to his ideas and methodology. On his earlier work, see his two interviews with Raymond Bellour (in his *Le Livre des autres.* Paris: L'Herne, 1971); on the work of his mid-period, see his important position-paper "Réponses au cercle d'épistémologie" (in *Cahiers pour l'Analyse,* 9, [1968]). On his more recent work, two excellent interviews appear in *Hérodote,* 1 (1976) and in *Politiques de la philosophie,* ed. Dominique Grisoni (Paris: Grasset, 1976); the latter is entitled "Les Jeux du pouvoir." Foucault's publications include:

Maladie mentale et psychologie. Paris: Presses Universitaires de France, 1961.

Folie et déraison: Histoire de la folie à l'âge classique. Paris: Plon, 1961. [Partially translated as *Madness and Civilization: A History of Insanity in the Age of Reason.* New York: Pantheon, 1965.] *Histoire de la folie,* followed by two essays, "Mon Corps, ce papier, ce feu," and "La Folie, l'absence de l'oeuvre," (an answer to Derrida's critique of Foucault's book) was republished by Gallimard in 1972.

Raymond Roussel. Paris: Gallimard, 1963.

Naissance de la clinique: Une Archéologie du regard médical. Paris: Presses Universitaires de France, 1963. [*The Birth of the Clinic.* New York: Pantheon, 1973.]

Les Mots et les choses: Une Archéologie des sciences humaines. Paris: Gallimard, 1966. [*The Order of Things: An Archeology of the Human Sciences.* New York: Pantheon, 1972.]

L'Ordre du discours. Paris: Gallimard, 1971. ["The Discourse on Language." Appendix to *The Archeology of Knowledge,* 1972.]

Ceci n'est pas une pipe: Deux lettres et quatre dessins de René Magritte. Montpellier: Fata Morgana, 1973.

Surveiller et punir: Naissance de la prison. Paris: Gallimard, 1975. [*Discipline and Punish: The Birth of the Prison.* New York: Pantheon, 1978.]

Histoire de la sexualité. Vol. I: *La Volonté de savoir.* Paris: Gallimard, 1976. [*The History of Sexuality.* Vol. I: *An Introduction.* New York: Pantheon, 1978.] Five more volumes are announced to complete this history of sexuality.

Language, Counter-Memory, Practice. Selected Essays and Interviews by Michel Foucault. Ithaca: Cornell University Press, 1977. Essays on literature and philosophy, among which are two important ones: "What Is an Author?" and "Nietzsche, Genealogy, History," and an interesting discussion with Deleuze entitled "Intellectuals and Power."

Microphysique du pouvoir. Turin: Einaudi, 1978.

(Ed.) *"Moi, Pierre Rivière, ayant égorgé ma mère, ma soeur, et mon frère ...": Un Cas de parricide au XIXe siècle.* Paris: Gallimard, 1973. [*"I, Pierre Rivière, having slaughtered my mother, my sister, and my brother ...": a case of parricide in the 19th century.* New York: Pantheon, 1975.]

The criticism on Foucault is extensive, both in French and in English. Among French publications, see Jean Baudrillard's controversial *Oublier Foucault* (Paris: Gallimard, 1977); Gilles Deleuze's analysis, *Un Nouvel Archiviste* (Montpellier: Fata Morgana, 1972); Annie Guedez's *Foucault* (Paris: Editions Universitaires, 1972); Angèle Kremer-Marietti's *Michel Foucault* (Paris: Seghers, 1974); an excellent recent article by Bernard-Henri Lévy, "Le Système Foucault" (in *Politiques de la philosophie,* 1976); and a forthcoming book by Christian Jambert, *Michel*

Foucault, éducateur (to be published by Grasset). Among American critics of Foucault, Edward Said, "Michel Foucault as an Intellectual Imagination," *Boundary 2*, 1:1 (1972), and "An Ethics of Language," *Diacritics*, 4:2 (1974), and Hayden White, "Foucault Decoded: Notes from the Underground," *History and Theory*, 12:1 (1973), have been the most perceptive and sympathetic critics of Foucault's enterprise. Three recent essays of interest are Leo Bersani's "The Subject of Power," *Diacritics*, 7:3 (1977); David Carroll's "The Subject of Archeology or the Sovereignty of the *Epistémè*," *MLN*, 93:4 (1978); and Shoshana Felman's "Madness and Philosophy or Literature's Reason," *Yale French Studies*, 52 (1975). See also the special issues on Foucault of *Critique*, 343 (1975), "A propos d'un livre [*Discipline and Punish*] de Michel Foucault," and *L'Arc*, 70 (1977), "La Crise dans la tête."

Gérard Genette

Along with Barthes and Todorov, Genette is one of the best known of the French literary critics associated with the Ecole Pratique des Hautes Etudes and the journal *Poétique*. The range of Genette's interests is extremely broad, both in relation to the number of authors he covers and in regard to the different approaches to literary language he discusses. His first two volumes of essays are concerned with a linguistic-semiotic type of structuralism. The unifying element of these earlier essays comes from his interest in the theoretical and technical problems of narrative, which culminates in his major study of the nature of narrative in *Figures III:* "Discours du récit: Essai de méthode," undoubtedly destined to become one of the standard texts for the study of the poetics of fiction.

Genette's search for a semiological definition of the literary phenomenon is continued in *Mimologiques,* in which he explores various theories about the mimetic nature of language. His latest book, *Introduction à l'architexte,* studies variations in narrative modes and types of textuality. His publications include:

Figures. Paris: Seuil, 1966. Essays on Proust, Robbe-Grillet, Borges, Flaubert, Valéry, Barthes ("L'Envers des signes"), structuralism ("Structuralisme et critique littéraire"), poetry, and other subjects.

Figures II. Paris: Seuil, 1969. Essays on Balzac, Stendhal, Proust, Mme. de Lafayette, criticism and literature, and an important essay, "Frontières du récit," which discusses the distinction between fictional narrative and the essay. It appears in translation in *New Literary History*, 8:1 (1976) under the title "Boundaries of Narrative."

Figures III. Paris: Seuil, 1972. Recent trends in criticism, the new poetics, metaphor, metonymy, and his major essay on Proust, "Discours
du récit: Essai de méthode," translated as *Narrative Discourse* (Ithaca:
Cornell University Press, 1979). Genette's Proust material is summarized in his essay "Time and Narrative in *A la recherche du temps
perdu*" in *Aspects of Narrative,* ed. J. Hillis Miller (New York: Columbia
University Press, 1970), pp. 93–118.
Mimologiques. Paris: Seuil, 1976.
Introduction à l'architexte. Paris: Seuil, 1979.

Among American critics, Scholes and Culler discuss Genette's work in
their books; Seymour Chatman has an excellent essay on *Figures III,*
"Genette's Analysis of Narrative Time Relations," *Esprit Créateur,* 14:4
(1974). Also on this topic, see Shlomith Rimmon's "A Comprehensive
Theory of Narrative: Genette's *Figures III* and the Structuralist Study of
Fiction," *Poetics and Theory of Literature,* 1 (1976). Among French critics
dealing with Genette's work, see Jean Moreau's "Figures inversibles,"
Critique, 309 (1973); Jean-Louis Bachelier's "La Poétique lézardée: *Figures III* de G. Genette," *Littérature,* 12 (1973); Michel Pierssens's "L'In-
discipline," *Critique,* 353 (1976) (on *Mimologiques*); and an important
essay that enters into dialogue with Genette's figurative schema: Samuel
Weber's "Le Madrépore," *MLN,* 87:7 (1972), a shorter version of which
appears in *Poétique,* 13 (1973). For a summary bibliography of Genette's
publications, see *Style,* 8:1 (1974).

René Girard

René Girard, who teaches at The Johns Hopkins University, is without a doubt one of the most important figures both in French and
American intellectual circles. His early work *Deceit, Desire, and the Novel*
is widely acclaimed as one of the classics of literary criticism. In recent
years, Girard's interests have shifted from theoretical studies of fiction
and criticism to a more interdisciplinary type of research. His present
work cuts across the comparative study of literature, Classical studies,
and religious studies, and embraces the fields of anthropology, philosophy, and psychoanalysis. Girard's broad and almost unparalleled interdisciplinary interests converge in his project of explaining the genesis of
culture in the light of his theory of the "scapegoating mechanism."

Girard had a collection of essays published by the Johns Hopkins
University Press in 1978. He is currently working on a book on Shakespeare in the context of his problematic of mimesis. Two long interviews
with him, in *Esprit,* 11 (1975), and in *Diacritics,* 8:1 (1978), will provide

the reader with the best introduction to the complexity and range of the Girardian system of thought. Girard's publications include:

Mensonge romantique et vérité romanesque. Paris: Grasset, 1961. [*Deceit, Desire, and the Novel: Self and Other in Literary Structure.* Baltimore: Johns Hopkins University Press, 1965.] A reading of Cervantes, Proust, Stendhal, Dostoevsky, and others in the light of the problematic of desire and mediation.

Proust: Twentieth Century Views, ed. René Girard. Englewood Cliffs, N.J.: Prentice-Hall, 1962.

Dostoievski: Du double à l'unité. Paris: Plon, 1963.

La Violence et le sacré. Paris: Grasset, 1972. [*Violence and the Sacred.* Baltimore: Johns Hopkins University Press, 1977.] A theory of the origins of culture via a reading of the great literary and philosophical authors in addition to contemporary ethnological and psychoanalytical material: Sophocles, Shakespeare, Plato, Lévi-Strauss, and Freud.

Critique dans un souterrain. Lausanne: L'Age d'Homme, 1976. A critique of psychoanalytical theory of desire from the point of view of literature. Elaborates a theory of mimetic desire, shows its metamorphoses and evolution through the works of Dostoevsky, Hugo, Dante, and Camus's *La Chute.* Includes an excellent critical analysis of Gilles Deleuze's *Anti-Oedipe.*

Des choses cachées depuis la fondation du monde. Paris: Grasset, 1978. A theory of culture, a new psychology, and a discussion of Judeo-Christian writing in the context of Girard's theory of mimesis.

"To Double Business Bound": Essays on Literature, Mimesis, and Anthropology. Baltimore: Johns Hopkins University Press, 1978.

On Girard's early work, see Michel Deguy's "Destin du désir et roman," *Critique,* 176 (1962); on *La Violence et le sacré,* see Pierre Pachet, "Violence dans la bibliothèque," *Critique,* 303–304 (1972); Carl Rubino's review essay in *MLN,* 87:7 (1972); and Eric Gans's "Pour une esthétique triangulaire," *Esprit,* 11 (1973). A special issue of *Diacritics,* 8:1 (1978), "The Work of René Girard," includes essays by Hayden White, Michel Serres, Sandor Goodhart, and a long text by Philippe Lacoue-Labarthe, "Mimesis and Truth" (the original version of this essay, "Typographie," appears in *Mimesis desarticulations,* 1975), which discusses the Derridean differences from the Girardian model.

Neil Hertz

Neil Hertz teaches eighteenth- and nineteenth-century English literature and critical theory at Cornell University. He has written on Lon-

ginus, Flaubert, Wordsworth, George Eliot, and Freud. Among his publications: "Wordsworth and the Tears of Adam," *Studies in Romanticism,*
7:1 (1967); "Flaubert's Conversion," *Diacritics,* 2:2 (1972), "Lecture
de Longin," *Poétique,* 15 (1973); "The Notion of Blockage in the
Literature of the Sublime" in *Psychoanalysis and the Question of the Text,*
ed. Geoffrey Hartman (Baltimore: Johns Hopkins University Press,
1978); and "Recognizing Casaubon," *Glyph,* 6 (1979).

Louis Marin

Semiology, philosophy of language, literary and art criticism: Louis
Marin writes with equal ease in all of these domains. His publications
range from studies in biblical narrative to studies on ethnology, from
the semiotics of painting to the semiotics of fairy tales. His writings have
evolved from a strict semiotic-structuralist practice to one that analyzes
the production of meaning in literary texts and paintings. Marin has
taught at the University of California, San Diego, and at The Johns
Hopkins University; he is presently Directeur d'Etudes in the VIe section at the Ecole Pratique des Hautes Etudes and is completing a book
on the problem of enunciation in autobiography. His publications include:

A. R. Radcliffe-Brown. *Structure et fonction dans la société primitive.* Paris:
    Minuit, 1968. Translation and a long introduction, "Présentation de
    Radcliffe-Brown et Lévi-Strauss," by Louis Marin.
Etudes sémiologiques. Paris: Klincksieck, 1971. A collection of articles
    dealing with the possible applications of a linguistic semiology to the
    study of paintings—subject matters, still lifes, patterns of colors, rela-
    tionships of forms to color—as well as drawings, coins, a study of
    Pascal's *Pensées* and some biblical narratives.
Sémiotique de la Passion: Topiques et figures. Paris: Bibliothèque de Sci-
    ences Religieuses, 1971. A rigorous semiotic treatment of the Gos-
    pels.
Utopiques: Jeux d'espace. Paris: Minuit, 1973. A study of utopian texts
    (More's *Utopia,* nineteenth-century utopias, Xenakis' cosmic vertical
    city, Disneyland) to show that they perform a point-by-point neutrali-
    zation of historical reality.
*La Critique du discours: Sur la "Logique de Port-Royal" et les "Pensées" de
    Pascal.* Paris: Minuit, 1975. A semiological approach—including a
    critique of the ideological foundation of the sign—to Classical
    theories of language and representation which are proven to be the
    models for the production of ideology.

Détruire la peinture. Paris: Galilée, 1977.
Le Récit est un piège. Paris: Minuit, 1978. Narrative strategies in La Fontaine, Cardinal de Retz, Perrault, and Racine.

On Marin's *La Critique du discours,* see Jean-François Lyotard's excellent study "Que le signe est hostie et l'inverse, et comment s'en débarrasser" in *Critique,* 342 (1975); on Marin's other works, see the special issue devoted to him by *Diacritics,* 7:2 (1977), which includes two particularly interesting studies: one by Fredric Jameson ("On Islands and Trenches: Neutralization and the Production of Utopian Discourse") and one by Jean-Marc Blanchard ("The Pleasures of Description").

Joseph Riddel

Joseph Riddel teaches modern American and English poetry and poetic theory at the University of California, Los Angeles. He has written extensively about the nature of the language of "modernist" and "post-modernist" American poets, especially Williams, Eliot, Pound, Stevens, and Olson. Among American critics, Riddel has probably been the most successful at transplanting Derridean analytical concepts into a radically different medium and at establishing new grounds and new figures for a modern American poetic theory. He is presently completing a book on this subject in the context of the philosophical texts of Nietzsche and Heidegger and of deconstructive criticism. His publications include *The Clairvoyant Eye: The Poetry and Poetics of Wallace Stevens* (Baton Rouge: Louisiana State University Press, 1965); *C. Day Lewis* (New York: Twayne, 1971); *The Inverted Bell: Modernism and the Counter Poetics of William Carlos Williams* (Baton Rouge: Louisiana State University Press, 1974); and various essays. Among the more recent are: "Interpreting Stevens: An Essay on Poetry and Thinking," *Boundary 2,* 1:1 (1972); "Pound and the Decentered Image," *Georgia Review,* 29:3 (1975); and "From Heidegger to Derrida to Chance: Doubling and (Poetic) Language," *Boundary 2,* 4:2 (1976). See also the interesting exchange between J. Hillis Miller ("Deconstructing the Deconstructors" in *Diacritics,* 5:2 [1975]) and Riddel ("A Miller's Tale," *Diacritics,* 5:3 [1975]) regarding the nature of deconstructive criticism.

Michael Riffaterre

Michael Riffaterre is Chairman of the Department of Romance Languages at Columbia University. He has been unquestionably the most instrumental critic in the development of stylistic studies in America, and has written over a hundred articles in the domain of literary theory and criticism, systematically calling for an objective and scientific approach to the analysis of literary forms. Riffaterre's method is having a considerable impact on the study of poetry and literary language in general, partly because of the broad range of his writings, which spans the French and English literatures of the nineteenth and twentieth centuries (Hugo, Maeterlinck, Baudelaire, Blake, Wordsworth, Ponge, Breton, Surrealism) and the work of modern critics such as Barthes, Lévi-Strauss, and Jakobson. Riffaterre's two most recent books on the semiotic properties of poetic language promises to open new and exciting possibilities for poetic as well as stylistic studies. Among his earlier publications are *Le Style des Pléiades de Gobineau* (New York: Columbia University Press, 1957) and *Essais de stylistique structurale* (Paris: Flammarion, 1971), a collection of articles advancing guidelines for stylistic analyses and setting the basis, through applications to selected works and problems, for structural stylistics. *Semiotics of Poetry* (Bloomington: Indiana University Press, 1978) is concerned with the roles of intertextuality and overdetermination in poetic discourse. His latest book, *La Production du texte* (Paris: Seuil, 1979), is an attempt to integrate literary theory and semiotics in order to develop a typology of intertextuality and to transform textual analysis into a theory of reading. His many articles include: "Le Poème comme représentation," *Poétique*, 4 (1970); "The Stylistic Approach to Literary History," *New Literary History*, 2:1 (1970); "Système d'un genre descriptif," *Poétique*, 9 (1972); "Interpretation and Descriptive Poetry: A Reading of Wordsworth's 'Yew-Trees,'" *New Literary History*, 4:2 (1973); "The Self-sufficient Text," *Diacritics*, 3:3 (1973); "The Poetic Functions of Intertextual Humor," *Romanic Review*, 65:3 (1974); "Le Tissu du texte," *Poétique*, 34 (1978); "La Syllepse intertextuelle," *Poétique*, 39 (1979).

To follow Riffaterre's theoretical trajectory the reader is referred, for his early works, to his essay on Baudelaire's "Les Chats" (in *Essais de stylistique structurale*); for his "mid-period" work, there is an excellent presentation of his methodology and aims in his "L'Explication des faits littéraires" [in Doubrovsky and Todorov, ed., *L'Enseignement de la littérature* (Paris: Plon, 1971)]. This essay is followed by an important discussion between Riffaterre and his "critics" (pp. 366–397) that the reader will find quite useful. The essay included in this volume represents the latest refinements in Riffaterre's system. For further discussions of his work, see Scholes's *Structuralism in Literature* and

Geoffrey Hartman's "The Use and Abuse of Structural Analysis: Riffaterre's Interpretation of Wordsworth's 'Yew-Trees'" in *New Literary History*, 7:1 (1975).

Edward Said

Edward Said teaches theory and philosophy of criticism and modern comparative literature at Columbia University. After writing a relatively traditional study of Joseph Conrad, he has published over twenty essays dealing specifically with contemporary criticism. Said's range of reference and analysis is impressively wide: it extends from literary figures such as Conrad, Hardy, T. E. Lawrence, Hopkins, Flaubert, Mallarmé, Valéry, Mann, and Dostoevsky, to nonliterary writers such as Vico, Renan, Marx, Freud, and Merleau-Ponty, and to the most important structuralist and post-structuralist critics: Barthes, Lacan, Ricoeur, Lévi-Strauss, Foucault, and Derrida. Said is also active in the fields of politics and culture, applying the concepts at work in his literary production to political structures and cultural processes. His most recent book, for instance, is a polemical study of the intellectual and political history of Orientalism. Said discusses his relationship to literature and politics in a long and comprehensive interview in *Diacritics*, 6:3 (1976). This is an excellent starting point for the reader who wishes to become familiar with the work and thought of a complex and powerful critic. His publications include:

Joseph Conrad and the Fiction of Autobiography. Cambridge: Harvard University Press, 1966.

Beginnings: Intentions and Method. New York: Basic Books, 1975; Baltimore: Johns Hopkins University Press, 1978. A methodological and philosophical speculation on what it means to "begin" a work. In the process of his investigation, Said reappraises the masterworks of Western literature in the light of modern methodological innovations.

Orientalism. New York: Pantheon, 1978. A political and intellectual history of Orientalism analyzing the process by which Orientalist discourse has transformed the Orient from a historical and cultural entity into a textual phenomenon.

The Question of Palestine. New York: Times Books, 1979.

Criticism between Culture and System. Cambridge: Harvard University

Press, 1980. An analysis and an appraisal of "cultural" versus "textual" criticism.

Said's work has been the object of a special issue of *Diacritics*, 6:3 (1976), which includes four excellent contributions by Eugenio Donato, J. Hillis Miller, Joseph Riddel, and Hayden White. See also the comprehensive and perceptive review of *Beginnings* by Homer Obed Brown in *MLN*, 91:5 (1976).

Michel Serres

"Sailor, philosopher, and mathematician," reads a description of Serres on the jacket of one of his books. And indeed, Serres, who is primarily a philosopher of science, does not hesitate to cut across the traditional divisions between science, philosophy, and literature. A text is a system of laws, and criticism describes the *states* of the text. Thus, claims Serres, "criticism is a generalized physics." Science, philosophy, and literature are not isolated phenomena; they belong to the same (hi)story, that of knowledge. Whether knowledge is written in philosophical, literary, or mathematical language, it nevertheless articulates a common set of problems that transcend academic disciplines and artificial boundaries. What needs to be discovered is how to decode it correctly and to translate it from one language to the other. This global enterprise of deciphering the writing of the world and its strategies of knowledge is the ultimate goal of Michel Serres, whose erudition, dexterity at handling a wide range of subjects, and originality are without match. Serres teaches his many skills at the University of Paris I (Sorbonne) and at The Johns Hopkins University. His publications include:

Le Système de Leibniz et ses modèles mathématiques. 2 vols. Paris: Presses Universitaires de France, 1968.
Hermes. Paris: Minuit, 1968—.
  Vol. I: *La Communication,* 1968 and 1972. On the emergence of a theory of communication through the relationship between science, philosophy, and literature: Plato, Descartes, Leibniz, Michelet, Foucault, Molière, and others are discussed.
  Vol. II: *L'Interférence,* 1972. A new epistemology based on the concept of interference (from information theory) as the operator of a theoretical network that applies to various domains, from science to literature: Bachelard, Brillouin, Xenakis, pop literature, and other topics.
  Vol. III: *La Traduction,* 1974. Strategies of translation in the fields of

science, philosophy, and painting: François Jacob, Jacques Monod, Leibniz, Carnot, Auguste Comte, Descartes, Pascal, La Tour, and Turner.

    Vol. IV: *La Distribution,* 1977. Scientific discourse in its relation to power and knowledge: Michelet, Nietzsche, La Fontaine, Boltzmann, Bergson, and others.

Jouvences: Sur Jules Verne. Paris: Minuit, 1974.

Auguste Comte: Cours de philosophie positive. Vol. I. Paris: Hermann, 1975.

Esthétiques sur Carpaccio. Paris: Hermann, 1975.

Feux et signaux de brume: Zola. Paris: Grasset, 1975. A brilliant investigation of Zola's work in the light of nineteenth-century thermodynamic theories.

La Naissance de la physique dans le texte de Lucrèce: Fleuves et turbulences. Paris: Minuit, 1978. Modern science reassessed in the context of the mechanics of fluids, the writings of Archimedes, and Lucretius' *De rerum natura.*

Le Parasite. Paris: Grasset, 1980.

Serres's work is the object of a special issue of *Critique,* 380 (1979) entitled "Interférences et turbulences," which includes contributions by Shoshana Felman, René Girard, Ilya Prigogine and Isabelle Stengers, Pierre Pachet, Claude Mouchard, and Michel Pierssens, in addition to a complete bibliography of his publications.

Eugene Vance

    Vance is a specialist in medieval poetics and in critical theory. He has taught at Yale and Toronto, and created the Program of Comparative Literature at the University of Montreal. He has written on various writers and genres from Augustine to Chaucer, with special emphasis on literary reflections of the medieval debate about the nature of language as a system of signs. Vance was the organizer of the 1977 Cerisy-la-Salle colloquium, *L'Archéologie du signe,* on medieval sign-theory and poetics, a transcription of which he is in the process of editing. His works include *Reading the Song of Roland* (Englewood Cliffs, N.J.: Prentice-Hall, 1970 and 1972); "Language as Action," ed. Eugene Vance: special issue of *Yale French Studies,* 45 (1970); a forthcoming book *Mervelous Signals: Poetics and Sign Theory in the Middle Ages;* and numerous articles, among them: "Spatial Structure in the *Chanson de Roland,*" *MLN,* 82:4 (1967); "The Word at Heart: *Aucassin et Nicolette* as a Medieval Comedy of Language," *Yale French Studies,* 45 (1970); "Le Combat érotique chez Chrétien de Troyes: De la figure à la forme," *Poétique,* 12

(1972); "Signs of the City: Medieval Poetry as Detour," *New Literary History*, 4:1 (1973); "Le Moi comme langage: Saint Augustin et l'autobiographie," *Poétique*, 14 (1973); "The Poetics of Desire and the Joy of the Text," *Diacritics*, 4:1 (1974) and "Mervelous Signals: Poetics, Sign Theory, and Politics in Chaucer's *Troilus*," *New Literary History*, 10:2 (1979).

Bibliography

STRUCTURALISM

Periodicals

Aletheia, "Le Structuralisme," 4 (1966). Articles by Barthes, Thion, Lévi-Strauss, Godelier, and Axelos.

Cahiers Internationaux de Symbolisme, "Le Structuralisme," 17–18 (1969). Articles by Durand, Piaget, Gonseth, and Rudhardt.

Communications, "L'Analyse structurale du récit," 8 (1966). The classic issue for the study of narrative, with articles by Barthes, Genette, Todorov, Greimas, Bremond, and others.

Esprit, "Structuralismes: Idéologie et méthode," 5 (1967). Articles by Bertherat, Burgelin, Conilh, Cuisenier, Domenach, Dufrenne, Ladrière, and Ricoeur.

Esprit Créateur, "New Critical Practices I and II," 14:3 and 14:4 (1974). From Bachelardian and thematic criticism to discussions of structuralism, narratology, and the groups *Tel Quel* and *Change.*

La Pensée, "Structuralisme et marxisme," 135 (1967). Articles by Mouloud, Dubois, Cohen, Deschamps, and others.

Revue Internationale de Philosophie, "La Notion de structure," 74–75 (1965). Articles by Granger, Martinet, Mouloud, Francastel, Paci, and others.

Les Temps Modernes, "Problèmes de structuralisme," 246 (1966). Articles by Pouillon, Barbut, Greimas, Godelier, Bourdieu, Macherey, and Ehrmann.

Twentieth Century Studies, "Structuralism," 3 (1970). Todorov and Kristeva are among the contributors.

Yale French Studies, "Structuralism," 36–37 (1966). Essays by Martinet, Lévi-Strauss, Scheffler, Lacan, Ehrmann, Riffaterre.

Anthologies

Ehrmann, Jacques, ed. *Structuralism.* Garden City, N.Y.: Anchor, 1971. Reprint of *Yale French Studies,* 36–37 (1966). The controversy Riffaterre–Jakobson/Lévi-Strauss highlights this issue, which includes in addition good selections from Lacan's and Lévi-Strauss's works.

De George, Richard, and Fernande De George, eds. *The Structuralists.* New York: Doubleday, 1972.

Krieger, Murray, ed. *Directions for Criticism: Structuralism and its Alternatives.* Madison: Wisconsin University Press, 1976 and 1977. Scholars affiliated with the School of Criticism and Theory at the University of California, Irvine, discuss the pre- and post-structuralist critical climate. Essays by Girard, Said, White, Adams, Freedman, and Krieger.

Lane, Michael, ed. *Structuralism: A Reader.* London: Cape, 1970. Good, readable, selection of the most characteristic early structuralist writings: Saussure, Barthes, Jakobson, Lévi-Strauss, Godelier, and others.

Macksey, Richard, and Eugenio Donato, eds. *The Structuralist Controversy: The Languages of Criticism and the Sciences of Man.* Baltimore: The Johns Hopkins University Press, 1970. The most important and theoretically most advanced collection of essays on structuralism. Girard, Barthes, Lacan, Derrida, Goldmann, Hyppolite, Rosolato, among many others.

Macksey, Richard, ed. *Velocities of Change: Critical Essays from* MLN. Baltimore: The Johns Hopkins University Press, 1974. Excellent overview of contemporary European and American criticism. Articles by Barthes, Goldmann, Kermode, Girard, de Man, Miller, and others trace in exemplary fashion the evolution of critical theory from the early fifties to the mid-seventies. In addition to reviewing major theories and issues in criticism, this collection of essays offers ten critical profiles of influential theorists, including Lukács, Auerbach, Bachelard, Sartre, Merleau-Ponty, Poulet, Derrida.

Robey, David, ed. *Structuralism: An Introduction.* London: Oxford University Press, 1973. Culler, Eco, Leach, Lyons, and Todorov discuss the implications of structuralism each in his respective discipline.

Simon, John K., ed. *Modern French Criticism: From Proust and Valéry to Structuralism.* Chicago: University of Chicago Press, 1972. Valuable essays by de Man, Said, Beaujour, and Velan, among others.

Structuralisme et marxisme. Paris: Union Générale d'Editions, 1970. Essays by Bottigelli, d'Allonnes, Deprun, and Culioli.

Théorie d'ensemble. Paris: Seuil, 1968. Essays by Foucault, Barthes, Derrida, Kristeva, Sollers, Ricardou, Pleynet, Thibaudeau, Goux, and others. Although this volume cannot, strictly speaking, be labeled structuralist, it nevertheless includes some of the best essays discussing the ramifications of structuralism around the *Tel Quel* group in the mid-sixties.

Books and Articles

Auzias, Jean-Marie. *Clefs pour le structuralisme.* Paris: Seghers, 1968.

Bastide, Roger, ed. *Sens et usage du terme structure dans les sciences humaines et sociales.* The Hague: Mouton, 1962. Essays by Lévi-Strauss, Benveniste, Morazé, Lefebvre, Barthes, Pouillon, and others.

Benoist, Jean-Marie. *La Révolution structurale.* Paris: Grasset, 1975.

Boudon, Raymond A. *A quoi sert la notion de "structure"?* Paris: Gallimard, 1968. [*Uses of Structuralism.* London: Heinemann, 1971.]

Corvez, Maurice. *Les Structuralistes.* Paris: Aubier-Montaigne, 1969.

Culler, Jonathan. *Structuralist Poetics: Structuralism, Linguistics, and the Study of Literature.* Ithaca: Cornell University Press, 1975.

Doubrovsky, Serge. *Pourquoi la nouvelle critique: Critique et objectivité.* Paris: Mercure de France, 1966.

Fages, J.-B. *Comprendre le structuralisme.* Toulouse: Privat, 1967.

———. *Le Structuralisme en procès.* Toulouse: Privat, 1968.

Funt, David. "The Structuralist Controversy." *Hudson Review,* 22:4 (1969).

Floyd, Merrell. "Structuralism and Beyond: A Critique of Presuppositions." *Diogenes,* 92 (1976).

Gandillac, M., et al. *Entretiens sur les notions de genèse et de structure.* The Hague: Mouton, 1965.

Goldmann, Lucien. "Entretien sur le structuralisme." *L'Homme et la société,* 1 (1967).

Glucksman, Miriam. *Structuralist Analysis in Contemporary Social Thought: A Comparison of the Theories of Claude Lévi-Strauss and Louis Althusser.* London: Routledge & K. Paul, 1974.

Hawkes, Terence. *Structuralism and Semiotics.* Berkeley: University of California Press, 1977.

Jameson, Fredric. *The Prison House of Language: A Critical Account of Structuralism and Russian Formalism.* Princeton: Princeton University Press, 1972.

Lefebvre, Henri. *Au-delà du structuralisme.* Paris: Anthropos, 1971.

Millet, Louise, and M. D'Ainvelle. *Le Structuralisme.* Paris: Editions Universitaires, 1970.

Parain-Vial, Jeanne. *Analyses structurales et idéologies structuralistes.* Toulouse: Privat, 1969.

Pettit, Philip. *The Concept of Structuralism: A Critical Analysis.* Berkeley: University of California Press, 1975.

Piaget, Jean. *Le Structuralisme.* Paris: Presses Universitaires de France, 1968. [*Structuralism.* London: Routledge & K. Paul; New York: Basic Books, 1970.]

Scholes, Robert. *Structuralism in Literature.* New Haven: Yale University Press, 1974.

Sebag, Lucien. *Marxisme et structuralisme.* Paris: Payot, 1964.

Viet, Jean. *Les Méthodes structuralistes dans les sciences sociales.* The Hague: Mouton, 1965.

Wahl, François, ed. *Qu'est-ce que le structuralisme?* Paris: Seuil, 1968. Essays by Todorov, Safouan, Sperber, Ducrot, and Wahl.

Weimann, Robert. "French Structuralism and Literary History: Some Critiques and Reconsiderations." *New Literary History,* 4:3 (1973).

POST-STRUCTURALISM

One could argue that many of the volumes under the heading of structuralism touch already on post-structuralist issues. This is inevitably true to a certain extent. Since post-structuralism as a movement cannot be clearly bracketed, it is just as hard to find anthologies or critical works that deal solely with post-structuralist problematics. The volume that comes closest to concretizing these tendencies is the special issue of *Yale French Studies*, 52 (1975), "Graphesis: Perspectives in Literature and Philosophy." It includes, among other contributions, essays by Derrida, de Man, Lyotard, Marin, and Serres, each addressing in his own way the problems raised in post-structuralism.

LITERARY CRITICISM
(Including Literary History, Poetics, and Narratology)

Althusser, Louis. *Montesquieu, la politique et l'histoire*. Paris: Presses Universitaires de France, 1959.

Bal, Mieke. *Narratologie: Les Instances du récit*. Paris: Klincksieck, 1977.

Bataille, Georges. *La Littérature et le mal*. Paris: Gallimard, 1957.

———. *L'Erotisme*. Paris: Gallimard, 1957. [*Death and Sensuality: A Study of Eroticism and the Taboo*. New York: Ballantine Books, 1969.]

Bellemin-Noël, Jean. *Vers l'inconscient du texte*. Paris: Presses Universitaires de France, 1979.

Bersani, Leo. *A Future for Astyanax: Character and Desire in Literature*. Boston: Little, Brown, 1976. Studies the correlations in literature between ways of conceiving desire and ways of conceiving character, from Racine to the realistic novel and modernist literature.

———. *Baudelaire and Freud*. Berkeley: University of California Press, 1977.

Blanchot, Maurice. *L'Espace littéraire*. Paris: Gallimard, 1955.

———. *Le Livre à venir*. Paris: Gallimard, 1959.

———. *L'Entretien infini*. Paris: Gallimard, 1969. Extensive essays on the essence of writing and literature, the concept of the Book and various studies on Nietzsche, Heidegger, Char, Sade, Marthe Robert, and others.

(On Blanchot): Collin, Françoise. *Maurice Blanchot et la question de l'écriture*. Paris: Gallimard, 1971.

Laporte, Roger, and Bernard Noël. *Deux Lectures de Maurice Blanchot*. Montpellier: Fata Morgana, 1973.

Wilhem, Daniel. *Maurice Blanchot: La Voix narrative*. Paris: Union Générale d'Editions, 1974.

Bloom, Harold. *The Anxiety of Influence: A Theory of Poetry*. New York: Oxford University Press, 1973.

———. *A Map of Misreading*. New York: Oxford University Press, 1975.

———. *Poetry and Repression*. New Haven: Yale University Press, 1976.

Bouazis, Charles, ed. *Essais de la théorie du texte*. Paris: Galilée, 1973.

Bremond, Claude. *Logique du récit*. Paris: Seuil, 1973.

Charles, Michel. *Rhétorique de la lecture*. Paris: Seuil, 1977. Rabelais, Plato, Lautréamont, Montaigne, and Constant in the light of a rhetorical approach to reading.

Chatman, Seymour, ed. *Approaches to Poetics.* New York: Columbia University Press, 1973.

——. *Story and Discourse: Narrative Structure in Fiction and Film.* Ithaca: Cornell University Press, 1978. Very useful and comprehensive presentation of problems associated with the narrative.

Cohen, Jean. "Théorie de la figure." *Communications,* 16 (1970).

——. "Poésie et motivation." *Poétique,* 11 (1972).

Cohen, Ralph, ed. *New Directions in Literary History.* Baltimore: The Johns Hopkins University Press, 1974.

Culler, Jonathan. See the rubric "Structuralism."

——. "Literary History, Allegory, and Semiology." *New Literary History,* 7:2 (1976).

——. "Presupposition and Intertextuality." *MLN,* 91:6 (1976).

Dällenbach, Lucien. *Le Récit spéculaire: Essai sur la mise en abyme.* Paris: Seuil, 1977.

Damisch, Hubert. *Ruptures, cultures.* Paris: Minuit, 1976.

de Diéguez, Manuel. *L'Ecrivain et son langage.* Paris: Gallimard, 1960. Essays on literary criticism, Valéry, Paulhan, Barthes, Blanchot, Bachelard, Sartre.

Doubrovsky, Serge, and Tzvetan Todorov, eds. *L'Enseignement de la littérature.* Paris: Plon, 1971. Contributions by Bernard Pingaud, Doubrovsky, Zumthor, Greimas, Barthes, Jacques Leenhardt, Genette, Riffaterre, Michel Deguy, Michel Beaujour, and Todorov. Both essays and discussions included in this volume are valuable—although dated, at times.

Ferrara, Fernando. "Theory and Model for the Structural Analysis of Fiction." *New Literary History,* 5:2 (1973).

Fish, Stanley. *Self-Consuming Artifacts: The Experience of Seventeenth-Century Literature.* Berkeley: University of California Press, 1972.

Galay, Jean-Louis. "Esquisses pour une théorie figurale du discours." *Poétique,* 20 (1974).

Gasché, Rodolphe. "The Scene of Writing: A Deferred Outset." *Glyph,* 1 (1977). Melville in the light of deconstruction.

Grivel, Charles. *Production de l'intérêt romanesque: Un Etat du texte (1870–1880), un essai de constitution de sa théorie.* The Hague: Mouton, 1973.

Hamon, Philippe. "Qu'est-ce qu'une description?" *Poétique,* 12 (1972).

Hartman, Geoffrey. *The Fate of Reading and Other Essays.* Chicago: University of Chicago Press, 1975.

——. "Literary Criticism and Its Discontents." *Critical Inquiry,* 3:2 (1976).

——, ed. *Psychoanalysis and the Question of the Text.* Baltimore: The Johns Hopkins University Press, 1978. Essays by Derrida, Hartman, Neil Hertz, Cary Nelson, Murray Schwartz, Norman Holland, and Barbara Johnson.

Hassan, Ihab. "POSTmodernISM." *New Literary History,* 3:1 (1971).

Irwin, John. *Doubling and Incest, Repetition and Revenge: A Speculative Reading of Faulkner.* Baltimore: The Johns Hopkins University Press, 1975.

Iser, Wolfgang. *The Act of Reading: A Theory of Aesthetic Response*. Baltimore: The Johns Hopkins University Press, 1978.

Jacobs, Carol. *The Dissimulating Harmony: The Image of Interpretation in Nietzsche, Rilke, Artaud, and Benjamin*. Baltimore: The Johns Hopkins University Press, 1978.

Jameson, Fredric. See the rubric "Structuralism."

———. *Marxism and Form*. Princeton: Princeton University Press, 1971.

———. "Demystifying Literary History." *New Literary History*, 5:3 (1974).

———. *Fables of Aggression: Wyndham Lewis, the Modernist as Fascist*. Berkeley: University of California Press, 1979.

Kibedi-Varga, A. *Rhétorique et littérature*. Paris: Didier, 1971.

Krieger, Murray. *Theory of Criticism: A Tradition and Its System*. Baltimore: The Johns Hopkins University Press, 1976.

Kristeva, Julia. *Semiotikē: Recherches pour une sémanalyse*. Paris: Seuil, 1969. Essays on the elaboration of meaning in the texts of Roussel, Barthes, Rabelais, Lautréamont, Mallarmé, and others.

———. *Le Texte du roman: Approche sémiologique d'une structure discursive transformationnelle*. The Hague: Mouton, 1970.

———. *La Révolution du langage poétique: L'Avant-garde à la fin du dix-neuvième siècle; Lautréamont et Mallarmé*. Paris: Seuil, 1974.

———. *Polylogue*. Paris: Seuil, 1977. Practices of symbolization in language, painting (Giotto, Bellini), literature (Artaud, Joyce, Céline, Beckett, Bataille, Sollers), and the human sciences.

———, Jean-Michel Ribettes, et al. *Folle Vérité: Vérité et vraisemblance du texte psychotique*. Paris: Seuil, 1979.

(On Kristeva): Caws, Mary Ann. "*Tel Quel:* Text and Revolution." *Diacritics*, 3:1 (1973).

Coquet, J. C. "Sémiotique et linguistique." In his *Sémiotique littéraire*. Paris: Mame, 1973.

Heath, Stephen. "Théâtre du langage." *Critique*, 331 (1974).

Lewis, Philip. "Revolutionary Semiotics." *Diacritics*, 4:3 (1974).

Lacoue-Labarthe, Philippe, and J.-L. Nancy. *L'Absolu littéraire: Théorie de la littérature du romantisme allemand*. Paris: Seuil, 1978.

Lejeune, Philippe. *Le Pacte autobiographique*. Paris: Seuil, 1975.

Macherey, Pierre. *Pour une théorie de la production littéraire*. Paris: Maspero, 1966. [*A Theory of Literary Production*. London: Routledge & Kegan Paul, 1978.]

Mehlman, Jeffrey. *A Structural Study of Autobiography: Proust, Leiris, Sartre, Lévi-Strauss*. Ithaca: Cornell University Press, 1974.

———. *Revolution and Repetition: Marx/Hugo/Balzac*. Berkeley: University of California Press, 1977.

Meschonnic, Henri. *Pour la poétique*. Paris: Gallimard, 1971—.

Vol. I: *Essais*, 1971.

Vol. II: *Epistémologie de l'écriture: Poétique de la traduction*, 1973.

Vol. III: *Une Parole d'écriture*, 1973.

Miller, J. Hillis, ed. *Aspects of Narrative: English Institute Essays.* New York: Columbia University Press, 1971. Contains essays on reader-response criticism by Wolfgang Iser and on time and narrative in Proust by Gérard Genette.

_____. "Stevens' Rock and Criticism as Cure." *Georgia Review,* 30:1 and 2 (1976).

_____. "Ariadne's Thread: Repetition and the Narrative Line." *Critical Inquiry,* 3:1 (1976).

_____. "The Critic as Host." *Critical Inquiry,* 3:3 (1977). See also M. H. Abrams's response in the same issue, "The Deconstructive Angel."

Norris, Margot. *The Decentered Universe of* Finnegan's Wake. Baltimore: The Johns Hopkins University Press, 1977.

Pierssens, Michel. *La Tour de Babil: Essai sur la fiction du signe.* Paris: Minuit, 1976.

Pleynet, Marcelin. *Art et littérature.* Paris: Seuil, 1977.

Prince, Gerald. *A Grammar of Stories.* The Hague: Mouton, 1973.

_____. "Introduction à l'étude du narrataire." *Poétique,* 14 (1973).

Que peut la littérature? Paris: Union Générale d'Editions, 1965. Essays by Faye, Ricardou, Sartre, Semprun, and others.

Ricardou, Jean. *Pour une théorie du nouveau roman.* Paris: Seuil, 1971.

Robert, Marthe. *Roman des origines et origines du roman.* Paris: Grasset, 1972.

_____. *Livre de lectures.* Paris: Grasset, 1976.

Searle, John R. "The Logical Status of Fictional Discourse." *New Literary History,* 7:2 (1976).

Singleton, Charles, ed. *Interpretation: Theory and Practice.* Baltimore: The Johns Hopkins University Press, 1969.

Sollers, Philippe. *Logiques.* Paris: Seuil, 1968. Essays on Sade, Dante, Lautréamont, Artaud, Roussel, Bataille, Mallarmé, Kafka.

_____, ed. *Bataille.* Paris: Union Générale d'Editions, 1973.

Starobinski, Jean. *L'Oeil vivant II: La Relation critique.* Paris: Gallimard, 1970. Essays on criticism, literature, psychoanalysis, Rousseau, Hamlet.

_____. "Considerations of the Present State of Literary Criticism." *Diogenes,* 74 (1971).

_____. "On the Fundamental Gestures of Criticism." *New Literary History,* 5:3 (1974).

_____. "The Meaning of Literary History." *New Literary History,* 7:1 (1975).

Todorov, Tzvetan. *Littérature et signification.* Paris: Larousse, 1967. A structuralist reading of Laclos's *Les Liaisons dangereuses.*

_____. "Poétique." in *Qu'est-ce que le structuralisme?,* ed. F. Wahl. Paris: Seuil, 1968. Reprinted under the same title as a monograph in the Points series (1973).

_____. *Grammaire du Décaméron.* The Hague: Mouton, 1969.

_____. *Introduction à la littérature fantastique.* Paris: Seuil, 1970. [*The Fan-*

tastic: A Structural Approach to a Literary Genre. Ithaca: Cornell University Press, 1975.] On E. A. Poe, Hoffmann, Gogol, Nerval, and others.

———. *Poétique de la prose.* Paris: Seuil, 1971. [*The Poetics of Prose.* Ithaca: Cornell University Press, 1977.] Essays on Constant, Artaud, James, Khlebnikov, *The Decameron, The Odyssey.*

———. *Théories du symbole.* Paris: Seuil, 1977. A history of the "symbol," the "symbolic" imagination, and "symbolic" acts, through the works of Augustine, the German Romantics, Lévy-Bruhl, Freud, Saussure, and Jakobson.

———. *Symbolisme et interprétation.* Paris: Seuil, 1978. Symbolic language analyzed via the models of patristic exegesis and classical philology.

———. *Les Genres du discours.* Paris: Seuil, 1978. Collection of essays on Stendhal, Constant, Baudelaire, Rimbaud, Dostoevsky, Novalis, Poe, James, Conrad, the nature of literary language, jokes, magical discourse, and so forth.

———, ed. *Théorie de la littérature.* Paris: Seuil, 1965. On the literary theories of the Russian formalists: Chklovski, Propp, Tomachevski, Jakobson, and others.

(On Todorov): Bellemin-Noël, Jean. "Des formes fantastiques aux thèmes fantastiques." *Littérature,* 2 (1971).

    Bremond, Claude. "Observations sur la *Grammaire du Décaméron.*" *Poétique,* 6 (1971).

    Lotringer, Sylvère. "Vice de forme." *Critique,* 286 (1971).

An annotated bibliography of Todorov's published writings appears in *Style,* 8:1 (1974).

White, Hayden. *Metahistory: The Historical Imagination in Nineteenth-Century Europe.* Baltimore: The Johns Hopkins University Press, 1973.

———. *Tropics of Discourse: Essays in Cultural Criticism.* Baltimore: The Johns Hopkins University Press, 1978.

Zéraffa, Michel. "La Poétique de l'écriture." *Revue d'Esthétique,* 24 (1971).

PHILOSOPHY

Agacinski, Sylviane, Jacques Derrida, et al. *Mimesis desarticulations.* Paris: Flammarion, 1976.

Althusser, Louis. *Lire le Capital* (in collaboration with E. Balibar). 2 vols. Paris: Maspéro, 1965. [*Reading* Capital. New York: Pantheon, 1970.]

———. *Pour Marx.* Paris: Maspéro, 1965. [*For Marx.* New York: Pantheon, 1969.]

———. *Lénine et la philosophie.* Paris: Maspéro, 1968. [*Lenin and Philosophy and Other Essays.* New York and London: Monthly Review Press, 1971.]

_____. *Réponse à John Lewis*. Paris: Maspéro, 1972. ["Reply to John Lewis (Self-Criticism)." *Marxism Today*, October-November, 1972.]

_____. *Eléments d'autocritique*. Paris: Hachette, 1973.

_____. *Philosophie et philosophie spontanée des savants*. Paris: Maspéro, 1973.

_____. *Positions*. Paris: Editions Sociales, 1976.

(On Althusser): Rancière, Jacques. "Mode d'emploi pour une réédition de *Lire le Capital*." *Les Temps Modernes*, 328 (1973).

Benoist, Jean-Marie. *Tyrannie du Logos*. Paris: Minuit, 1975.

Bourdieu, Pierre. *Esquisse d'une théorie de la pratique*. Paris: Droz, 1972.

Bouveresse, Jean. *La Parole malheureuse: De l'alchimie linguistique à la grammaire philosophique*. Paris: Minuit, 1971. Wittgenstein and the philosophy of language.

Corngold, Stanley. "*Sein und Zeit:* Implications for Poetics." *Boundary 2*, 4:2 (1976).

Descombes, Vincent. *Le Même et l'autre: Quarante-cinq ans de philosophie française (1933–1978)*. Paris: Minuit, 1979.

de Diéguez, Manuel. *Science et nescience*. Paris: Gallimard, 1970.

Gil, Fernando. *La Logique du nom*. Paris: L'Herne, 1971. Frege, Russell, Wittgenstein, and the problem of representation.

Glucksmann, André. *Les Maîtres penseurs*. Paris: Grasset, 1977. Fichte, Hegel, Marx, and Nietzsche.

Goldmann, Lucien. *Sciences humaines et philosophie*. Paris: Gonthier, 1966. [*The Human Sciences and Philosophy*. London: Cape, 1969.]

Grisoni, Dominique, ed. *Politiques de la philosophie*. Paris: Grasset, 1976. Important collection with essays by Châtelet, Derrida, Foucault, Lyotard, and Serres.

Klossowski, Pierre. *Nietzsche et le cercle vicieux*. Paris: Mercure de France, 1969.

Kofman, Sarah. *Nietzsche et la métaphore*. Paris: Payot, 1974.

Lacoue-Labarthe, Philippe. "La Fable." *Poétique*, 1 (1970).

_____. "Le Détour." *Poétique*, 5 (1971).

_____. "L'Oblitération." *Critique*, 313 (1973).

_____. "L'Imprésentable." *Poétique*, 21 (1975).

_____. "Typographie." In Agacinski et al. *Mimesis desarticulations*. Paris: Flammarion, 1976. All five of these essays question the relationship literature entertains with philosophy.

Lévesque, Claude. *L'Etrangeté du texte: Essai sur Nietzsche, Freud, Blanchot et Derrida*. Paris: Union Générale d'Editions, 1978.

Lyotard, Jean-François. *Discours, figure*. Paris: Klincksieck, 1971.

_____. *Rudiments païens*. Paris: 10/18, 1977.

Marshall, Donald G. "The Ontology of the Literary Sign: Notes toward a Heideggerian Revision of Semiology." *Boundary 2*, 4:2 (1976).

Mouloud, Noël. *L'Analyse et le sens*. Paris: Payot, 1976.

Nancy, Jean-Luc. *Le Discours de la syncope*. Vol. I: *Logodaedalus*. Paris: Aubier-Flammarion, 1976. On Kant.

Parain, Brice. *Petite Métaphysique de la parole*. Paris: Gallimard, 1969.

Pautrat, Bernard. *Versions du soleil: Figures et système de Nietzsche*. Paris: Seuil, 1971.

Ramnoux, Clémence. *Héraclite, ou l'homme entre les mots et les choses*. Paris: Les Belles Lettres, 1968.

————. *Etudes présocratiques*. Paris: Klincksieck, 1970.

Rey, Jean Michel. *L'Enjeu des signes: Lecture de Nietzsche*. Paris: Seuil, 1971.

Ricoeur, Paul. *De l'interprétation: Essai sur Freud*. Paris: Seuil, 1965. [*Freud and Philosophy: An Essay on Interpretation*. New Haven: Yale University Press, 1970.]

————. *Le Conflit des interprétations*. Paris: Seuil, 1969. Philosophy and psychoanalysis reappraised.

————. "The Model of the Text: Meaningful Action Considered as a Text." *New Literary History*, 5:1 (1973).

————. "Metaphor and the Main Problem of Hermeneutics." *New Literary History*, 6:1 (1974).

————. *La Métaphore vive*. Paris: Seuil, 1975. Rhetoric, from Aristotle and Fontanier to Benveniste.

La Situation actuelle sur le front de la philosophie. Cahiers Yenan No. 4. Paris: Maspéro, 1977. Five studies from a Marxist perspective on Deleuze, Lacan, and Althusser.

Tort, Michel. "De l'interprétation ou la machine herméneutique." *Les Temps Modernes*, 237–238 (1966).

————. "Le Concept freudien de 'représentant.'" *Cahiers pour l'Analyse*, 5 (1966).

————. "Freud et la philosophie." *L'Arc*, 34 (1968).

————. "La Psychanalyse dans le matérialisme historique." *Nouvelle Revue de Psychanalyse*, 1 (1970).

Veyne, Paul. *L'Inventaire des différences*. Paris: Seuil, 1976.

Wahl, François. "La Philosophie entre l'avant et l'après du structuralisme." In his *Qu'est-ce que le structuralisme?* Paris: Seuil, 1968. Reprinted as *Philosophie*. Paris: Points, 1973.

PSYCHOANALYSIS

Anzieu, Didier. "Freud et la mythologie." *Nouvelle Revue de Psychanalyse*, 1 (1970).

Balmary, Marie. *L'Homme aux statues: Freud et la faute cachée du père*. Paris: Grasset, 1979.

Baudry, Jean-Louis. "Freud et la 'création littéraire.'" *Tel Quel*, 32 (1968). Reprinted in *Théorie d'ensemble*. Paris: Seuil, 1968.

Benveniste, Emile. "Remarques sur la fonction du langage dans la découverte freudienne." In his *Problèmes de linguistique générale*. Paris: Gallimard, 1966. ["Remarks on the Function of Language in Freudian Theory." In *Problems in General Linguistics*. Vol. I. Coral Gables: University of Miami Press, 1971.]

Binswanger, Ludwig. *Discours, parcours et Freud.* Paris: Gallimard, 1970. Translation from the German.

Carroll, David. "Freud and the Myth of the Origin." *New Literary History,* 6:3 (1975).

Clavreul, Jean. *L'Ordre médical.* Paris: Seuil, 1977.

Clément, Catherine, et al. *Pour une critique marxiste de la théorie psychanalytique.* Paris: Editions Sociales, 1973.

_____. *Le Pouvoir des mots: Symbolique et idéologique.* Paris: Mame, 1974.

_____. *Miroirs du sujet.* Paris: Plon, 1975.

Descombes, Vincent. *L'Inconscient malgré lui.* Paris: Minuit, 1977.

Le Désir et la perversion. Paris: Seuil, 1967. Interesting collection of essays by Guy Rosolato, J. P. Valabrega, Pierra Aulagnier-Spairani, Jean Clavreul, and others.

Ey, Henri, ed. *L'Inconscient.* Paris: Desclée de Brouwer, 1966. Essays by Serge Leclaire, Jean Laplanche, Lacan, Conrad Stein, Alphonse de Waelhens, and others.

Green, André. *Un Oeil en trop: Le Complexe d'Oedipe dans la tragédie.* Paris: Minuit, 1969. French psychoanalytical readings on Greek and Shakespearean tragedy.

Guattari, Félix. *Psychanalyse et transversalité.* Paris: Maspéro, 1972.

Hesnard, André. *De Freud à Lacan.* Paris: E.S.F., 1970.

Lacan, Jacques. *Ecrits.* Paris: Seuil, 1966. [*The Language of the Self.* Baltimore: The Johns Hopkins University Press, 1968. Includes extensive and valuable commentary by Anthony Wilden on Lacan's "Fonction et champ de la parole et du langage en psychanalyse." See also *Ecrits. A Selection.* London: Tavistock, 1977.]

_____. *Télévision.* Paris: Seuil, 1973.

_____. *De la psychose paranoiaque dans ses rapports avec la personnalité,* followed by *Premiers Ecrits sur la paranoia.* Paris: Seuil, 1975.

_____. *Ecrits inspirés.* Besançon: Editions Arep, 1977.

_____. *Le Séminaire.* Paris: Seuil, 1973—. (Lacan's lectures, to be published in a series of twenty volumes.)

Livre I: Les Ecrits techniques de Freud, 1975.

Livre II: Le Moi dans la théorie de Freud et dans la technique de la psychanalyse, 1977.

Livre XI: Les Quatre Concepts fondamentaux de la psychanalyse, 1973.

Livre XX: Encore, 1975.

On Lacan): Fages, J.-B. *Comprendre Jacques Lacan.* Toulouse: Privat, 1971.

Kremer-Marietti, Angèle. *Lacan et la rhétorique de l'inconscient.* Paris: Aubier-Montaigne, 1978.

Lacoue-Labarthe, P., and J.-L. Nancy. *Le Titre de la lettre.* Paris: Galilée, 1973.

Palmier, Jean-Michel. *Lacan.* Paris: Editions Universitaires, 1970.

Rifflet-Lemaire, Anita. *Jacques Lacan.* Brussels: Dessart, 1970.

Laplanche, Jean. *Hölderlin et la question du père*. Paris: Presses Universitaires de France, 1961.

——, and Serge Leclaire. "L'Inconscient, une étude psychanalytique." *Les Temps Modernes*, 183 (1961). ["The Unconscious: A Psychoanalytic Study." *Yale French Studies*, 48 (1972).]

——, and Jean-Baptiste Pontalis. "Fantasme originaire, fantasme des origines, origine du fantasme." *Les Temps Modernes*, 215 (1965). ["Fantasy and the Origins of Sexuality," *International Journal of Psychoanalysis*, 49 (1968).]

——, and Serge Leclaire. *Vocabulaire de la psychanalyse*. Paris: Presses Universitaires de France, 1967. [*The Language of Psychoanalysis*. New York: Norton, 1973.] A must for anyone interested in Lacanian psychoanalytical concepts.

——. *Vie et mort en psychanalyse*. Paris: Flammarion, 1970. [*Life and Death in Psychoanalysis*. Baltimore: The Johns Hopkins University Press, 1976.]

——. "Dérivation des entités psychanalytiques." In *Hommage à Jean Hyppolite*. Paris: Presses Universitaires de France, 1971. A translation of this text on the meaning of metaphor and metonymy in psychoanalytic theory appears in *Life and Death in Psychoanalysis*.

Leclaire, Serge. *Psychanalyser: Essai sur l'ordre de l'inconscient et la pratique de la lettre*. Paris: Seuil, 1968.

——. *Démasquer le réel*. Paris: Seuil, 1971.

Lyotard, Jean-François. *Dérive à partir de Marx et Freud*. Paris: Union Générale d'Editions, 1973.

——. *Des dispositifs pulsionnels*. Paris: Union Générale d'Editions, 1973. [A section has been translated as "Adorno as the Devil." *Telos*, 19 (1974).]

——. *Economie libidinale*. Paris: Minuit, 1974.

——. *Les Transformateurs Duchamp*. Paris: Galilée, 1977.

(On Lyotard): See the special issue of *L'Arc*, 64 (1976) which includes articles by Lyotard, Dufrenne, Marin, Damisch, Charles, and others; see also Lacoue-Labarthe's "Note sur Freud et la représentation." *Digraphe*, 3 (1974).

Mannoni, Octave. *Clefs pour l'imaginaire ou l'autre scène*. Paris: Seuil, 1970. Essays on Freudian texts, Mallarmé, Rimbaud, James, Proust, theatrical illusion, and other subjects.

——. *Freud: The Theory of the Unconscious*. London: New Left Books; New York: Random House, 1971.

Ortigues, Edmond. *L'Oedipe africain*. Paris: Plon, 1966.

Pasche, Francis. *A partir de Freud*. Paris: Payot, 1969.

Pontalis, Jean-Baptiste. *Après Freud*. Paris: Gallimard, 1968. Contains three psychoanalytical readings of Flaubert, James, and Leiris.

——. *Entre le rêve et la douleur*. Paris: Gallimard, 1977.

Rey, Jean-Michel. *Parcours de Freud: Economie et discours*. Paris: Galilée, 1974.

Roland, Alan, ed. *Psychoanalysis, Creativity, and Literature: A French-American Inquiry.* New York: Columbia University Press, 1978.

Rosolato, Guy. *Essais sur le symbolique.* Paris: Gallimard, 1969.

Roustang, François. *Un Destin si funeste.* Paris: Minuit, 1976. The master-student relationship in the context of contemporary psychoanalytic theory and Freud's own life.

Safouan, Moustafa. "De la structure en psychanalyse, contribution à une théorie du manque." In *Qu'est-ce que le structuralisme?* ed. F. Wahl. Paris: Seuil, 1968. Reprinted as *Psychanalyse.* Paris: Points, 1973.

――――. *Etudes sur l'Oedipe: Introduction à une théorie du sujet.* Paris: Seuil, 1974.

Todorov, Tzvetan. "Freud sur l'énonciation." *Langages,* 17 (1970).

Turkle, Sherry. *Psychoanalytic Politics: Freud's French Revolution.* New York: Basic Books, 1978.

Viderman, Serge. *Le Céleste et le sublunaire.* Paris: Presses Universitaires de France, 1977.

Wilden, Anthony. *System and Structure: Essays on Communication and Exchange.* London: Tavistock, 1972.

Wolfson, Louis. *Le Schizo et les langues ou la phonétique chez le psychotique.* Paris: Gallimard, 1970.

ANTHROPOLOGY

Baudrillard, Jean. *L'Echange symbolique et la mort.* Paris: Gallimard, 1976.

Dumézil, Georges. *Mythe et épopée.* Paris: Gallimard.

Vol. I: *L'Idéologie des trois fonctions dans les épopées des peuples indo-européens,* 1968.

Vol. II: *Trois Types épiques indo-européens: Le Héros, le sorcier et le roi,* 1971.

Geertz, Clifford. *The Interpretation of Cultures.* New York: Basic Books, 1974.

De Heusch, Luc. *Pourquoi l'épouser? et autres essais.* Paris: Gallimard, 1971.

Leach, Edmund. *Genesis as Myth.* London: Cape, 1969.

Lévi-Strauss, Claude. *La Vie familiale et sociale des indiens Nambikwara.* Paris: Société des Américanistes, 1948.

――――. *Les Structures élémentaires de la parenté.* Paris: Presses Universitaires de France, 1949. Revised edition with a new preface, Paris, The Hague: Mouton, 1967. [*The Elementary Structures of Kinship.* Boston: Beacon, 1969.]

――――. *Race et histoire.* Paris: UNESCO, 1952. [*Race and History.* Paris: UNESCO, 1952.]

――――. *Tristes Tropiques.* Paris: Plon, 1955. Revised edition, 1968. [*Tristes Tropiques.* New York: Atheneum, 1963.]

――――. *Anthropologie structurale.* Vols. I and II. Paris: Plon, 1958 and 1973.

[*Structural Anthropology*. I and II. New York: Basic Books, 1963 and 1976.]

———. *Leçon inaugurale au Collège de France*. Paris: Publications du Collège de France, 1960. [*The Scope of Anthropology*. London: Cape, 1969.]

———. *Entretiens avec Claude Lévi-Strauss* (in collaboration with G. Charbonnier). Paris: Plon, 1961. [*Conversations with Claude Lévi-Strauss*. London: Cape, 1969.]

———. *Le Totémisme aujourd'hui*. Paris: Presses Universitaires de France, 1962. [*Totemism*. Boston: Beacon, 1963; London: Merlin Press, 1964.]

———. *La Pensée sauvage*. Paris: Plon, 1962. [*The Savage Mind*. Chicago: University of Chicago Press, 1966; London: Weidenfeld and Nicolson, 1967.]

———. *Mythologiques*. Paris: Plon.
   Vol. I: *Le Cru et le cuit*, 1964. [*The Raw and the Cooked*. New York: Harper & Row, 1969.]
   Vol. II: *Du Miel aux cendres*, 1966. [*From Honey to Ashes*. New York: Harper & Row, 1973.]
   Vol. III: *L'Origine des manières de table*, 1968. [*The Origin of Table Manners*. New York: Harper & Row, 1978.]
   Vol. IV: *L'Homme nu*, 1971.

———. *La Voie des masques*. Geneva: Skira, 1975.

———, ed. *L'Identité*. Paris: Grasset, 1977.

(On Lévi-Strauss): Special issues of *L'Arc*, "Claude Lévi-Strauss," 26 (1965), and of *Esprit*, "La Pensée sauvage" et le structuralisme," 11 (1963).

Bellour, Raymond, and Catherine Clément, eds. *Claude Lévi-Strauss*. Paris: Gallimard, 1979.

Boon, James A. *From Symbolism to Structuralism: Lévi-Strauss in a Literary Tradition*. Oxford: Blackwell, 1972.

Clément, Catherine. *Lévi-Strauss, ou la structure et le malheur*. Paris: Seghers, 1974.

Courtés, Joseph. *Lévi-Strauss et les contraintes de la pensée mythique*. Paris: Mame, 1973.

Cressant, Pierre. *Lévi-Strauss*. Paris: Editions Universitaires, 1970.

Gardner, Howard. *The Quest for Mind: Piaget, Lévi-Strauss, and the Structuralist Movement*. New York: Random House, 1972; Vintage, 1974.

Leach, Edmund. *Claude Lévi-Strauss*. New York: Viking Press, 1974.

Marc-Lipiansky, Mireille. *Le Structuralisme de Lévi-Strauss*. Paris: Payot, 1973.

Paz, Octavio. *Claude Lévi-Strauss: An Introduction*. Ithaca: Cornell University Press, 1970.

Rossi, Ino, ed. *The Unconscious in Culture: The Structuralism of Claude Lévi-Strauss in Perspective.* New York: Dutton, 1974.

Loundsbury, Floyd. "L'Analyse structurale des termes de parenté." *Langages,* 1 (1966).

Makarius, Raoul. *Structuralisme ou ethnologie: Pour une critique radicale de l'anthropologie de Lévi-Strauss.* Paris: Anthropos, 1973.

Mauss, Marcel. *Sociologie et anthropologie.* Paris: Presses Universitaires de France, 1950. [The chapter entitled "Essai sur le don" is translated as *The Gift: Forms and Functions of Exchange in Archaic Societies.* New York: Free Press, 1954.]

———. *Oeuvres I. Fonction du sacré.* Paris: Minuit, 1968. [The chapter entitled "Essais sur la nature et la fonction du sacrifice" is translated as *Sacrifice.* Chicago: University of Chicago Press, 1964.]

Pouillon, Jean. "Malade et médecin: le même et/ou l'autre." *Nouvelle Revue de Psychanalyse,* 1 (1970).

———, and P. Maranda, eds. *Échanges et communications: Mélanges offerts à Claude Lévi-Strauss.* The Hague: Mouton, 1970.

Roheim, Geza. *Psychoanalysis and Anthropology.* New York: International University Press, 1950.

Sperber, Dan. "Le Structuralisme en anthropologie." In *Qu'est-ce que le structuralisme?* ed. F. Wahl. Paris: Seuil, 1968. Reprinted as *Anthropologie.* Paris: Points, 1973.

———, and Pierre Boudon. "A propos de la notion d'échange et de la grammaire générative." *L'Homme,* 8:2 (1968).

Turner, Terence. "Oedipus: Time and Structure in Narrative Form." In *Forms of Symbolic Action,* ed. R. Spencer. Seattle: University of Washington Press, 1969.

LINGUISTICS, SEMIOTICS AND RELATED SUBJECTS

Baudry, Jean-Louis. "Linguistique et production textuelle." In *Linguistique et littérature.* Paris: La Nouvelle Critique, 1968.

Benveniste, Emile. *Problèmes de linguistique générale.* 2 vols. Paris: Gallimard, 1966 and 1974. [*Problems in General Linguistics.* Vol. I. Coral Gables: University of Miami Press, 1971.]

———. *Le Vocabulaire des institutions indo-européennes.* Paris: Minuit, 1970.
Vol. I: *Economie, parenté, société.*
Vol. II: *Pouvoir, droit, religion.*
[*Indo-European Language and Society.* Coral Gables: University of Miami Press, 1973.]

Blanchard, Jean-Marc. "Sémiostyles: Le Rituel de la littérature." *Semiotica,* 14:4 (1975).

Bloomfield, Morton W. "Stylistics and the Theory of Literature." *New Literary History,* 7:2 (1976).

Carontini, E., and D. Peraya. *Le Projet sémiotique*. Paris: Editions Universitaires, 1975.

Chabrol, Claude. *Sémiotique narrative et textuelle*. Paris: Larousse, 1973.

Chatman, Seymour, ed. *Literary Style: A Symposium*. New York: Oxford University Press, 1971.

Chomsky, Noam. *Cartesian Linguistics*. New York: Harper & Row, 1966. [*La Linguistique cartésienne* complemented by *La Nature formelle du langage*. Paris: Seuil, 1969.]

Coquet, Jean-Claude. *Sémiotique littéraire: Contribution à l'analyse sémantique du discours*. Paris: Mame, 1973.

Delas, Daniel, and Jacques Filiolet. *Linguistique et poétique*. Paris: Larousse, 1973.

Dubois, Jacques, et al. *Rhétorique générale*. Paris: Larousse, 1970.

Ducrot, Oswald. "Le Structuralisme en linguistique." In *Qu'est-ce que le structuralisme?* ed. F. Wahl. Paris: Seuil, 1968. Reprinted under the title *Linguistique*. Paris: Points, 1973.

––––. *Dire et ne pas dire: Principes de sémantique linguistique*. Paris: Hermann, 1972.

––––, and Tzvetan Todorov. *Dictionnaire encyclopédique des sciences du langage*. Paris: Seuil, 1972. [*Encyclopedic Dictionary of the Sciences of Language*. Baltimore: The Johns Hopkins University Press, 1979.] This book is a must for semioticians and literary critics.

Eco, Umberto. *L'Opera aperta*. Milan: Bompiani, 1962, 1971. [*L'Oeuvre ouverte*. Paris: Seuil, 1965.] A semiological approach to literature, language, and the theory of communication, followed by a study of Joyce.

––––. *La Struttura assente: Introduzione alla ricerca semiologica*. Milan: Bompiani, 1968.

––––. *A Theory of Semiotics*. Bloomington: Indiana University Press, 1976.

(On Eco): Deely, John. "The Doctrine of Signs: Taking Form at Last." *Semiotica*, 18:2 (1976).

Fish, Stanley. "What is Stylistics and Why are They Saying Such Terrible Things About It?" In *Approaches to Poetics*, ed. Seymour Chatman. New York: Columbia University Press, 1972.

––––. "How Ordinary is Ordinary Language?" *New Literary History*, 5:1 (1973).

––––. "How to do Things with Austin and Searle: Speech Act Theory and Literary Criticism." *MLN*, 91:5 (1976).

––––. "Structuralist Homiletics." *MLN*, 91:6 (1976).

Fowler, Roger, ed. *Style and Structure in Literature: Essays in the New Stylistics*. London: Oxford University Press, 1975.

Greimas, A. J. *Sémantique structurale: Recherche de méthode*. Paris: Larousse, 1966.

––––. *Du sens: Essais sémiotiques*. Paris: Seuil, 1970.

––––. *Maupassant, la sémiotique du texte: Exercices pratiques*. Paris: Seuil, 1976.

_____. *Sémiotique et sciences sociales.* Paris: Seuil, 1976.

_____, ed. *Sign, Language, Culture.* The Hague: Mouton, 1970.

_____, ed. *Essais de sémiotique poétique.* Paris: Larousse, 1971.

(On Greimas): Bremond, Claude. "Le Modèle constitutionnel de A. J. Greimas." *Semiotica,* 5:4 (1972).

    Courtés, Joseph. *Introduction à la sémiotique narrative et discursive.* Paris: Hachette, 1976.

    Wing, Nathaniel. "Semiotics of Poetry: The Meaning of Form." *Diacritics,* 4:3 (1974).

Guiraud, Pierre. *La Sémiologie.* Paris: Presses Universitaires de France, 1971.

Hamon, Philippe. "Pour un statut sémiologique du personnage." *Littérature,* 6 (1972).

Jakobson, Roman. *Selected Writings.* 5 vols. The Hague: Mouton, 1962, 1964, 1971, 1978, and 1979.

_____. *Essais de linguistique générale.* 2 vols. Paris: Minuit, 1963 and 1973.

_____. *Questions de poétique.* Paris: Seuil, 1973.

_____. *Main Trends in the Science of Language.* New York: Harper & Row, 1974.

_____. *Six Leçons sur le son et le sens.* Paris: Minuit, 1976. Preface by Claude Lévi-Strauss.

_____, and M. Halle. *Fundamentals of Language.* The Hague: Mouton, 1956.

_____. For a bibliography, see *Janua Linguarum,* series minor, No. 134. The Hague: Mouton, 1971.

Kristeva, Julia, et al. *Essays in Semiotics/Essais de sémiotique.* The Hague: Mouton, 1971.

_____, et al. *La Traversée des signes.* Paris: Seuil, 1975.

_____ (in collaboration with J. C. Milner and N. Ruwet). *Langue, discours, société: Pour Emile Benveniste.* Paris: Seuil, 1975.

Le Guern, Michel. *Sémantique de la métaphore et de la métonymie.* Paris: Larousse, 1973.

Léon, Pierre R., et al. *Problèmes de l'analyse textuelle/Problems of Textual Analysis.* Montreal, Paris, Brussels, Philadelphia: Didier, 1971. Contributions by Pierre Guiraud, Paul Bouissac, Henri Mitterand, Jean-Claude Chevalier, Michael Riffaterre, Serge Doubrovsky, Gérard Genette, and others.

Leroy, Maurice. *Les Grands Courants de la linguistique moderne.* Brussels: Presses Universitaires de Bruxelles, 1967.

Linguistique et littérature: Texte intégral du colloque de Cluny. Paris: La Nouvelle Critique, 1968. Essays by Baudry, Kristeva, Sollers, Pleynet, and others.

Martinet, André. *Eléments de linguistique générale.* Paris: Armand Colin, 1960. [*Elements of General Linguistics.* London: Faber, 1964.]

_____. *La Linguistique synchronique.* Paris: Presses Universitaires de France, 1966.

_____. *La Linguistique: Guide alphabétique.* Paris: Denoël, 1969.

Martinet, Jeanne. *Clefs pour la sémiologie.* Paris: Seghers, 1973.

de Mauro, Tullio. *Une Introduction à la sémantique.* Paris: Payot, 1969. Translation from the Italian.

Metz, Christian. *Essais sur la signification au cinéma.* 2 vols. Paris: Klincksieck, 1968 and 1972. [*Film Language.* Vol. I: *A Semiotics of the Cinema.* New York: Oxford University Press, 1974.]

——. *Langage et cinéma.* Paris: Larousse, 1971. [*Language and Cinema.* The Hague: Mouton, 1974.]

Mounin, Georges. *Problèmes théoriques de la traduction.* Paris: Gallimard, 1963.

——. *Introduction à la sémiologie.* Paris: Minuit, 1970.

Ortigues, Edmond. *Le Discours et le symbole.* Paris: Aubier, 1962.

Pariente, Jacques, ed. *Essais sur le langage.* Paris: Minuit, 1969. Essays by Cassirer, Chomsky, Jakobson among many others.

Rastier, François. *Essais de sémiotique discursive.* Paris: Mame, 1974.

Rey, Alain. *Théories du signe et du sens.* Paris: Klincksieck, 1973.

Robin, Régine. *Histoire et linguistique.* Paris: Armand Colin, 1973.

Ruwet, Nicolas. *Introduction à la grammaire générative.* Paris: Plon, 1968.

——. *Langage, musique, poésie.* Paris: Seuil, 1969.

Saussure, Ferdinand de. *Cours de linguistique générale.* Paris: Payot, 1972; critical edition by Tullio de Mauro. [*Course in General Linguistics.* New York: McGraw-Hill, 1966.]

——. *Les Anagrammes de Ferdinand de Saussure.* Paris: Republications Paulet, 1968.

(On Saussure): Culler, Jonathan. *Saussure.* London: Fontana Modern Masters, 1976.

                Mounin, Georges. *Saussure ou le structuraliste sans le savoir.* Paris: Seghers, 1968.

                Starobinski, Jean. *Les Mots sous les mots: Les Anagrammes de Ferdinand de Saussure.* Paris: Gallimard, 1971.

Schefer, Jean-Louis. *Scénographie d'un tableau.* Paris: Seuil, 1969.

Scholes, Robert. "Towards a Semiotics of Literature." *Critical Inquiry,* 4:1 (1977).

Searle, John. *Speech Acts: An Essay in the Philosophy of Language.* Cambridge: Cambridge University Press, 1969.

Sebeok, Thomas. "Is a Comparative Semiotics Possible?" In *Echanges et communications,* ed. Pouillon and Maranda. The Hague: Mouton, 1970.

——. *Semiotics: A Survey of the State of Art.* The Hague: Mouton, 1971.

——. *The Sign and Its Masters.* Austin: University of Texas Press, 1979.

——, ed. *Approaches to Semiotics.* The Hague: Mouton, 1964.

Segre, Cesare. *I Segni e la critica.* Turin: Einaudi, 1969. [*Semiotics and Literary Criticism.* The Hague: Mouton, 1975.]

Weinrich, Harald. *Tempus: Besprochene und erzählte Welt.* Stuttgart: Verlag W. Kohlhammer, 1964. [*Le Temps: Le Récit et le commentaire.* Paris: Seuil, 1973.]

(On Weinrich): O'Meara, Maureen. "From Linguistics to Literature: The Un-Timeliness of Tense." *Diacritics*, 6:2 (1976).

PERIODICALS

L'Arc. A quarterly that devotes itself to special issues. Contributions in *L'Arc* are short but often of high quality. See especially the numbers on Bachelard, Bataille, Freud, Hegel, Lacan, Barthes, Derrida, Lyotard, Merleau-Ponty, Mauss, Lévi-Strauss, and Deleuze.

Bulletin de la Société Française de Philosophie. Publishes the proceedings of the lectures and discussions that take place at the Société de Philosophie. Derrida, Foucault, Serres, and others have published some of their more important essays in the *Bulletin*.

Cahiers du Cinéma. The "avant-garde" film review—Barthes, Bellour, Metz, and the best literary semiologists are regular contributors. Of special interest is No. 185 (1966), "Film et roman, problèmes du récit."

Cahiers pour l'Analyse. Published (between 1966 and 1969) essays in epistemology by members of the Ecole Normale Supérieure. The *Cahiers* had a strong influence on the philosophical and psychoanalytical wings of the structuralist movement. Among its important issues are: Nos. 1/2 (1966), "La Vérité. Qu'est-ce que la psychologie?"; No. 3 (1966), "Sur l'Objet de la psychanalyse"; No. 5 (1966), "Ponctuation de Freud"; and No. 9 (1968), "Généalogie des sciences."

Change. Published by Seuil in Paris. Specializes in linguistic and semiotic approaches to literature. See for instance No. 1 (1969), "Le Montage"; No. 3 (1969), "Le Cercle de Prague"; and No. 5 (1970), "Le Dessin du récit."

Communications. Published by the Ecole Pratique des Hautes Etudes. It has been at the heart of the structuralist movement. Nos. 4 (1964), 8 (1966), and 16 (1970), respectively on "Recherches sémiologiques," "L'Analyse structurale du récit," and "Recherches rhétoriques," are a must for anyone interested in the questions raised and alternatives offered by structuralism. See also more recently an unusual issue, No. 23 (1975), "Psychanalyse et cinéma."

Critical Inquiry. Review published by the University of Chicago Press. It favors a pluralistic approach to literature and has been publishing excellent essays by both American- and French-oriented critics. See especially the "Special Issue on Metaphor," 5:1 (1978).

Critique. Published by Minuit, it specializes in review articles and from time to time devotes a special issue to an author or a topic. See for instance the recent special issues on psychoanalysis, "La Psychanalyse vue du dehors I & II," No. 333 (1974) and No. 346 (1976), and the issue "Lectures de Nietzsche," No. 313 (1973). Overall, *Critique* is considered, as is *Poétique*, a bellwether of criticism in France.

Diacritics. Published by the Johns Hopkins University Press, *Diacritics* originates from the Department of Romance Studies at Cornell University. Together with *New Literary History*, it has been instrumental in promoting Continental criticism in the United States. It publishes mostly review articles and sometimes special issues.

L'Homme. The French ethnological review.

Langages. Published by Larousse, it is the leader in the field of linguistic-oriented criticism. Among its central aims is to bring outside problematics to the linguistic domain. Contributions are generally excellent. Numbers of special interest are: No. 12 (1968), "Linquistique et littérature"; No. 13 (1969), "L'analyse du discours"; No. 17 (1970), "L'Enonciation"; No. 18 (1970), "L'Ethnolinguistique"; No. 21 (1971), "Philosophie du langage."

Littérature. Important review published by Larousse and the Department of French Literature of the University of Paris (Vincennes). Among numbers dealing specifically with problems of criticism: No. 3 (1971), "Littérature et psychanalyse"; No. 10 (1973), "Fonctionnements textuels"; No. 13 (1974), "Histoire/Sujet"; No. 17 (1975), "Les Jeux de la métaphore"; No. 18 (1975), "Frontières de la rhétorique"; and No. 26 (1977), "Imaginaire et idéologique: Questions de lecture."

New Literary History. Published by the Johns Hopkins University Press and edited by the Department of English at the University of Virginia. *NLH* has played an important role in bringing together successfully the best in American and European criticism. Contributions are always informed and interesting. Among numbers of direct relevance to contemporary criticism: 3:1 (1972), "Modernism and Postmodernism"; 7:1 (1975), "Critical Challenges"; 7:2 (1976), "Poetics: Some Methodological Problems"; and 9:2 (1978), "Soviet Semiotics and Criticism: An Anthology."

Nouvelle Revue de Psychanalyse. Founded in 1970 and published by Gallimard. Each issue focuses on a psychoanalytic topic that it develops in an interdisciplinary context. The quality of the contributions to date has been excellent in all respects. This review has not yet received the attention it deserves among English-speaking readers.

Poétique. Published by Seuil, and edited by Genette, Todorov, and Cixous, this review has maintained itself in the vanguard of critical thought. *Poétique* is probably the most influential review of literary criticism in France today. Among numbers of particular interest, two important ones discuss the relationship between literature and philosophy: No. 5 (1971), "Rhétorique et philosophie," and No. 21 (1975), "Littérature et philosophie mêlées." In the more specifically literary domain, see No. 24 (1975), "Narratologie"; No. 26 (1976) "*Finnegan's Wake*"; No. 27 (1976), "Intertextualité"; and No. 32 (1977), "Genres."

Revue d'Esthétique. Published by Christian Bourgois, it combines a literary, a linguistic, and an aesthetic problematic. Nos. 2-3-4 (1973), collectively entitled "Cinéma: Théorie, lectures," provide an all-encompassing overview of film theory in the past ten years.

Sémiotexte. Published by members of the Department of French at Columbia University; specializes in post-modern French criticism.

Semiotica. Published by Mouton in collaboration with the Association Internationale de Sémiotique and Indiana University. The leader in semiotic studies.

Silicet. Published by Seuil since 1968, it is the official review of the Freudian School of Paris founded by Lacan.

Sub-stance. Published by the Department of French and Italian at the University of Wisconsin—Madison. This review has been very hospitable to modern schools of criticism.

Tel Quel. Published by Seuil, this journal was at the center of structuralist exchanges in the late sixties and very early seventies. It has lost ground dramatically in the past several years, as it has espoused a much narrower Maoist ideological point of view.

Topique. "Revue freudienne" and competitor of Lacan's *Silicet.*

Yale French Studies. Published by the Department of French at Yale, it has focused more and more, in the last ten years, on problems of criticism. Four issues deserve particular attention. Nos. 36-37 (1966), "Structuralism"; No. 48 (1973), "French Freud"; No. 52 (1975), "Graphesis: Perspectives in Literature and Philosophy"; and Nos. 55-56 (1977), "Literature and Psychoanalysis."

Name Index

Subject Index

absence: of being, 112-115; in epic, 383-384; and presence, 396-397; semantic value of, 115. *See also* presence

American literature, 322-358; crisis of, 323; problem of beginnings in, 322, 328, 333

anthropology, structural analysis in, 21-22. *See also* structural anthropology

Arabian narratives, 142, 144

Arabic linguistic speculation, 166-170

Aristotelian categories, 86, 88-106; and being, 105; confusion between thought and language categories, 102; empiricism of, 95; as figures, 91; and grammar, 94; homology between thought and language categories, 99; logical status of, 93; organization of, 104-105n. *See also* category; categoriality; Kantian categories

author: Barthes's view of, 78-79; as censorship, 44; and Christian tradition, 150-151; and criticism, 23, 69, 151; disappearance of, 143-145; Foucault's view of, 41-44, 141-160; ideological status of, 158-160; irreducible individuality, 163; Melville's concept of, 330-331; name of, 145-147; vs. reader, 138; realistic status of, 150; as regulator of fiction, 159; role with regard to discourse, 147, 421; transdiscursive, 153-154; valorization system of, 141; and writing, 144-145

author-function, 148-153, 159-160; characteristics of, 148-151, 153; in fields other than literature, 153. *See also* author

beginnings: in Melville, 326-327; in Olson, 328, 349-351. *See also* American literature

being: absence of, 112-115; and Aristotelian categories, 105-107; grammar and etymology, 114-115, 118; and Greek language, 107-109; in history of metaphysics, 117-118; in Indo-European languages, 111; and language in Olson, 351; as linguistic category, 91, 113-114, 116, 119; in ontology, 111, 116-117, 120, 248; philosophical vocation of, 110; as presence, 35; and representation, 248-250; in stoic philosophy, 53, 281-282; supplementary feature of, 115; and thinking, 109; transcategoriality of, 110; transcendental character of, 107; and truth, 120

body: and language, 282-284, 287; schizophrenic, 286-288

castration complex, 385. *See also* Oedipal model

categoriality, 89-90, 92. *See also* Aristotelian categories

category: history of the word, 90-91. *See also* Aristotelian categories; categoriality; Kantian categories

center: Eliot's nostalgia for, 346-347; Olson's desire for, 355-356

characterization, 203-204

Christian: epic, 384-403; exegesis, 150-151; hero, 390

Textual Strategies

Designed by Richard Rosenbaum.
Composed by The Composing Room of Michigan, Inc.
in 10 point Baskerville, 2 points leaded,
with display lines in Baskerville.
Printed offset by Vail-Ballou Press, Inc. on
Antique Cream stock, 50 pounds basis.
Bound by Vail-Ballou Press.